Cambridge studies in medieval life and thought

Edited by WALTER ULLMANN, LITT.D., F.B.A.
Professor of Medieval History in the
University of Cambridge

Third series vol. 14

ROBERT WINCHELSEY AND THE CROWN

1294–1313

CAMBRIDGE STUDIES IN
MEDIEVAL LIFE AND THOUGHT

THIRD SERIES

ROBERT WINCHELSEY AND THE CROWN
1294–1313

A study in the defence of ecclesiastical liberty

JEFFREY H. DENTON

*Senior Lecturer, Department of History
University of Manchester*

CAMBRIDGE UNIVERSITY PRESS

CAMBRIDGE

LONDON   NEW YORK   NEW ROCHELLE

MELBOURNE   SYDNEY

Published by the Press Syndicate of the University of Cambridge
The Pitt Building, Trumpington Street, Cambridge CB2 1RP
32 East 57th Street, New York, NY 10022, USA
296 Beaconsfield Parade, Middle Park, Melbourne 3206, Australia

First published 1980

Printed in Great Britain by
Western Printing Services Ltd, Bristol

British Library Cataloguing in Publication Data
Denton, Jeffrey Howard
Robert Winchelsey and the Crown 1294–1313.
(Cambridge Studies in medieval life and thought: 3rd
series; 14).
1. Church and state in England
2. Church and state – Roman Catholic Church
3. Winchelsey, Robert
I. Title II. Series
322′.1′0924   BR750   79-41807

ISBN 0 521 22963 4

TO ERIKA AND ANDREA

CONTENTS

PREFACE

I have accumulated a large debt of gratitude to many friends, colleagues, librarians and archivists, too numerous to mention by name, for the book has been long in the making. Successions of Manchester Special Subject students have made important contributions, not least in their own probing of the sources. I am grateful to them all. Through every stage, from initial research onwards, I have been privileged to enjoy the constructive and painstaking criticisms of Professor C. R. Cheney. No debt could be greater. My thanks go, too, to Dr R. G. Davies and to Mr Philip Gaskell for their assistance and helpful comments, to the Rev. A. J. Cuthbert Smith and the Rev. Dr J. R. Wright for permission to read their theses, and to Dr P. C. Saunders who, in addition, shared with me, most generously, his expert knowledge of the *coram rege* rolls, to Dr Michael Prestwich who very kindly made available transcripts from the memoranda rolls of 1297 and answered many queries, and to Professor E. L. G. Stones, Mrs J. M. B. Stones and Professor Walter Ullmann for frequent help and advice. A grant from the British Academy assisted me in the collection of unprinted letters of Robert Winchelsey for a projected edition, an undertaking which has aided directly the preparation of this book.

Without the support of close relatives and friends, and others who chose to give encouragement, the work would not have been completed. My hope that I have not betrayed their trust is signalled by the dedication to my daughters Erika and Andrea. A book carries memories of place; for me especially of Cambridge, Greenwich, Great Corby and Babbacombe.

January 1979

ABBREVIATIONS

*(For all the printed works abbreviated in the footnotes
see the Bibliography)*

BIHR	*Bulletin of the Institute of Historical Research*
BL	British Library
Cant. D. & C.	Canterbury, Dean and Chapter Muniments
CUL	Cambridge University Library
CYS	Canterbury and York Society
DNB	*Dictionary of National Biography*
EHR	*English Historical Review*
HMSO	Her/His Majesty's Stationery Office
JEH	*Journal of Ecclesiastical History*
LRO	Lincoln Record Office
PRO	Public Record Office
RS	Rolls Series
TRHS	*Transactions of the Royal Historical Society*
VCH	*Victoria County History*

INTRODUCTION

In the often-told drama of the challenge to universal papal claims
by the emerging 'nation–states' of the west it is Philip the Fair
and his agents who hold the centre-stage, first with Boniface VIII,
and later, by contrast, with Clement V. The king of England and
the archbishop of Canterbury play relatively minor rôles in this
story of bitter confrontation and papal submission. But it would be
misleading to see the events and issues which embroiled Archbishop Winchelsey with Edward I and Edward II as a sub-plot to
the main, Franco-papal, struggle. The conflict is a separate and
largely independent drama, changed, certainly, by relations with
France and by new papal decrees and new papal policies, but
developing, in essentials, from the primary concern of all parties
with local traditions and rights, whether of the English Crown or
of the English clergy. Fundamental questions about the ultimate
control of Church property and the allegiance of churchmen lie at
the heart of the Franco-papal dispute, and they undoubtedly form,
too, the backdrop to the story to be told here; but our eyes must be
fixed not so much upon the Roman Church, with its legislative
autonomy and its claims of overriding authority, as upon English
conditions and English customs.[1] This is, as we shall see, in no
way to deny the outstanding importance of the papacy for
England, or of England for the papacy. It is simply to insist that
the study of the defence of the English Church's liberty and the
study of the political career of Robert Winchelsey must begin and
end in England. If we comprehend the aims and actions of
Winchelsey vis-à-vis the Crown, we may also comprehend some
of the main political, and legal, elements in the pope's binding
relations with both the king and the *Ecclesia Anglicana*.

This is not a book about political or legal theory, though the

[1] See Gray, 'Canon law in England'.

I

powerful influence of political and legal principles is an underlying assumption throughout.[2] Much has been written – and will
be written – about the ecclesiastical views of the later thirteenth
and fourteenth centuries.[3] As we well know, the conflicts between
sacerdotium and *regnum* were certainly not only, even if essentially, ideological, and they were certainly not limited to learned
circles. Any attempt to understand the complex interplay between
developing theories and changing practices presents the historian
with the most challenging of problems. One approach is to begin
with the outstanding issues of the day – as, for example, taxation –
and to see the political claims and counter-claims in the context of
current realities. In England the stated ecclesiastical beliefs of
this period, however clear their connections with broad patterns
of thought, stemmed very largely from, and are often best seen in
relation to, considerations of immediate practical questions.
A study of Winchelsey's political career can be seen as a possible
starting-point for a deeper comprehension of the whole issue of the
co-existence of *spiritualia* and *temporalia*.

The sacerdotalist beliefs of the archbishop emerge as consistent
and coherent. This is not the case with the beliefs of those who did
not support his point of view. For their attitude the evidence is
piecemeal and often indirect. An analysis is needed, more detailed
than has been possible here, of the ecclesiastical standpoint, not
only, if it can be brought into focus, of Edward I and Edward II
in propriis personis, but more especially of their governments,
consisting largely as they did of churchmen, of all ranks. It is a
study which must be undertaken outside the limits of the political
life of one prelate – though a full investigation of the career of the
royal servant Bishop Walter Langton, for example, would surely
prove illuminating. The king's supporters must certainly have
believed that the interests of the realm required the clergy to
abandon some elements of their liberty, some aspects of their claim

[2] For three major studies see Kantorowicz, *King's Two Bodies*, Ullmann,
Principles of Government and Politics and Post, *Studies in Medieval Legal
Thought*.
[3] See two recent important contributions: G. Leff, 'The apostolic ideal in later
medieval ecclesiology', *Journal of Theological Studies*, xviii (1967), 58–82 and
W. Ullmann, 'Boniface VIII and his contemporary scholarship', *Journ. of
Theol. Studies*, xxvii (1976), 58–87.

to separate status. Winchelsey's fight was against *all* lay encroachments upon ecclesiastical rights. Even so, and despite the increasing influence of Roman law and civil lawyers, we should be
cautious in our use of the labels 'lay' or 'secular' to describe the
views of the supporters of the Crown. The strength of Winchelsey's voice and the extent of his influence, for example among
the regulars and the lower clergy, must not in themselves persuade
us that he and his like alone had ecclesiastical interests at heart.

While this book is often concerned with relations between
ecclesiastical and royal jurisdictions, it has not been possible to deal
in any comprehensive way with all the questions arising from the
existence of two systems of law, not even with all the grievances
which the clergy under Winchelsey's leadership presented to the
Crown. While there are important studies relating, for instance,
to regalian rights, caption following excommunication, writs of
prohibition and criminous clerks,[4] much more work remains to be
done. In political terms some issues were naturally more important than others. A thorough investigation of the working together of the two laws in the late thirteenth and early fourteenth
centuries would have important questions to consider, for there
was, in some respects at least, a distinct increase in the aggression
of royal government towards ecclesiastical jurisdiction early in the
1290s, at about the time that Winchelsey – and Boniface VIII –
came to office. In writings concerned with the operations of royal
and ecclesiastical courts and with the king's relationship with his
Church there is frequently talk, not without some justification, of
co-operation and *contenementum*.[5] But one thing must be stressed
without equivocation: Robert Winchelsey's attempts to prevent
further erosion, as he saw it, of ecclesiastical rights can in the final
analysis only be seen in terms of struggle and conflict. The dispute
was not a narrow one concerned merely with legal procedures.
It was a political, and ideological, dispute about the cure of souls
and the social and constitutional standing of the Church and the

[4] E.g. Howell, *Regalian Right*, Logan, *Excommunication*, Flahiff, 'Use of pro-
hibitions by clerics', and idem, 'Writ of prohibition to court christian' and
Cheney, 'Punishment of felonous clerks'. For a broad and useful survey see
Jones, 'Relations of two jurisdictions'.
[5] See Jones, 'Relations of two jurisdictions', pp. 80-2 and Powicke, *Henry and
Lord Edward*, pp. 713-18.

priesthood. This is demonstrated not simply by the events of 1297, the year of crisis, but by an examination of the whole relationship of the archbishop with the Crown. Fundamental principles were in question.

Chapter 1

THE MAN: HIS LEARNING AND SANCTITY

CHARACTER

Robert Winchelsey was a man of stern and determined character. 'He was equitable in all things, severe in his censures and no respecter of persons, nor could many gifts ever turn him from justice.'[1] So commented a Cistercian chronicler. The attacks upon the archbishop by another chronicler, William Thorne of St Augustine's Canterbury, are hardly to be trusted considering the acrimonious conflict between the abbey and the archbishop especially between 1300 and 1303.[2] But Thorne's bitterness reflects the resolution with which Winchelsey had fought the abbey's attempts to gain bulls granting exemption to their churches. This is how Thorne described Winchelsey when the archbishop was suspended from office in 1306: a man 'hateful to God and proud, who throughout the whole realm of England had by the pride of his lips, like a harlot, brought disgrace on the priesthood and the clergy, and exercised unheard of tyranny over the people... this unhappy man, who often, proudly boasting, used to say "No man beneath the sky do I fear", was now proved a liar, for he feared both pope and king, and was afraid of losing what he had or of suffering worse afflictions because of his imperfections'.[3] On at least one occasion there was conflict between the vigilant archbishop and another exempt Benedictine abbey, St Albans. Winchelsey wished to stay at the abbey of St Albans on his way to Scotland in 1300, but, refusing to set his seal to a declaration presented to him by the abbot that this would not prejudice the rights of the abbey in future, he lodged in the town

---

[1] *Chronica de Melsa*, II. 328. See II Chronicles 19:7.
[2] Thorne wrote late in the fourteenth century but probably used earlier accounts: see below, p. 180 n. 13.
[3] *Scriptores Decem*, pp. 2004–5 (see Thorne, pp. 387–8).

instead. There was hard feeling against the archbishop, who put the church of St Stephen under interdict because the sacrist had not rung the bells. And when Winchelsey left the town there was a scuffle in which a representative of the abbey was thrown from his horse.[4] These squabbles were the order of the day.

There are other small, but more telling, indications of Winchelsey's harshness. We are informed by his chancellor that he held Simon of Ghent, bishop of Salisbury, in deep affection in his own rough way ('suo modo rudo').[5] Walter Stapledon, as bishop-elect of Exeter, sent his brother to Winchelsey to negotiate for him in the unsuccessful attempt to gain permission for his consecration to take place away from Canterbury; in the bishop-elect's account of what transpired we learn that Winchelsey, annoyed that Stapledon had not come himself to arrange the day of his own consecration, rudely interrupted his brother and declared with his customary ferocity ('ferocitate solita') that he would not agree to such a request for as long as he lived.[6] The chronicle of Lanercost tells the story of the archbishop rebuking the abbot of Osney at the March council of 1297 for submitting to the Crown; as a result the abbot died of a heart attack in his lodgings in London.[7] In the dispute concerning St Oswald's Gloucester, claimed as a royal free chapel, the story was apparently invented of the archbishop receiving a crucial royal writ, which Winchelsey denied obtaining; it is an indication of the archbishop's reputation that his supposed reaction on obtaining the writ was one of fury and obstinacy: 'acting as though he had the poisoned brain of a madman, he at length declared that he had no wish to make any reply'.[8] He had the reputation, as we shall see, of great generosity to the poor, the sick and the contrite, but in matters of Church policy he put principles before people. This sternness of character did not mean that Winchelsey was without friends.[9] He gained widespread respect for his leadership of the English Church and for his constant efforts to unite the English clergy. Yet the overall impression is of a rather lonely figure. There was no outcry from the clergy when he was suspended and exiled.

[4] *Gesta Abb. Mon. St Albani*, ed. H. T. Riley (RS, 1867–9), II. 47–8.
[5] *Reg. Gandavo*, p. 320. [6] *Reg. Stapeldon*, p. 10. [7] Below, p. 126.
[8] *Select Cases King's Bench*, III. 138–9, 143–4, and *Reg. Corbridge*, II. 87–8.
[9] See below, pp. 42–4.

Winchelsey's anonymous biographer from Christ Church Canterbury tells us that as a boy he was physically handsome, amiable and gracious to everyone, of natural gooodness, easy to teach and clever. In older age he was corpulent and of good complexion, and at table he was affable and good-humoured. The biographer was especially impressed by his deeds of charity, and his life of chastity, of penance and of religious devotion.[10] This is a eulogy which, we might suspect, will fail to bring us very near to the nature of the man. But there is little need to regret, in Winchelsey's case at least, the scantiness of the evidence for a study of the inner man and of personal characteristics, for there can be no separation of his life of personal devotion and determination from his life of public devotion and determination. We shall learn much of what we need to know about the man as we trace his early career, understand his reputation and examine his policies and political outlook.

EARLY CAREER

It is probable that Robert was brought up in Old Winchelsea in Kent, as suggested by the inclusion in his will of 100 marks for the fabric of the church of St Giles Winchelsea.[11] Although 'Winchelsey' has become accepted as his surname, 'of Winchelsea' would more accurately reflect the original form of his name.[12] His family background is obscure, but we know that he had a brother Henry Winchelsey[13] and a nephew John Winchelsey. John, to whom the archbishop bequeathed his bible containing his own glosses,[14] pursued a career which, if much less distinguished than that of his uncle, followed similar lines. He studied at Oxford and obtained canonries at Salisbury, Lincoln, Hereford and Wells; in 1326 he became a Franciscan at Salisbury and died soon after.[15]

Although there is no precise evidence, it could well be right,

[10] *Anglia Sacra*, I. 11, 13.
[11] *Reg.*, p. 1342. For his early career see esp. Cuthbert Smith, 'Scholastic career' (and idem, 'Robert Winchelsey and his Place in the Intellectual Movement') and Emden, *Oxford*, p. 2057.
[12] The name is without doubt a toponymic. At one point the Hagnaby chronicle refers to him in error as 'of Pevensey': BL Cotton Vespasian B xi, fo. 38v.
[13] *CPR 1272–81*, p. 252.   [14] *Reg.*, pp. 1341–2.
[15] Le Neve, *Fasti 1300–1541*, s.v. Winchelsea, and Emden, *Oxford*, p. 2056;

as asserted in Matthew Parker's *De Antiquitate*,[16] that Winchelsey attended school at Canterbury. According to his anonymous fourteenth-century biographer Robert excelled at his early studies in grammar. We are told that as a youth he went to Paris to study in the faculty of arts; soon he was a master in arts and shortly afterwards he was made rector of the four nations, that is, head of the faculty of arts.[17] We know that he was rector in July 1267.[18] A candidate for the mastership must have passed his twentieth birthday and had to take an oath to teach for two years at Paris; he was probably elected rector during these two years. Thus Winchelsey cannot have been born later than 1247, and most probably, having in mind his biographer's belief that academic achievements came early in his life, not before the early 1240s.[19]

It is not clear how soon after 1267 Winchelsey returned to England; nor is it clear in which year he began his theological studies at Oxford. His first ecclesiastical appointment, in April 1272, was as rector of Wood Eaton, Oxfordshire, a church which he held, at least initially, *in commendam*.[20] We can only guess at Winchelsey's activities during the mid-1270s, but if he occupied the rectory of Wood Eaton, it was convenient for the schools of Oxford, only two miles distant. By June 1276 he was canon of Lincoln, holding the prebend of Marston St Lawrence, which by October 1277 he had transferred for the prebend of Leighton Manor.[21] Amauri de Montfort, son of Simon de Montfort, claimed possession of the prebend against Winchelsey, but Amauri's claim was almost certainly untenable.[22] In January 1278 royal protection for three years was granted to Winchelsey because of a journey overseas.[23] His purpose is unknown: possibly he returned

and see Cuthbert Smith, 'Robert Winchelsey and his Place in the Intellectual Movement', I. 239–40.
[16] Parker, *De Antiquitate*, pt ii. 208, and, thence, Godwin, *Bishops*, p. 79.
[17] *Anglia Sacra*, II, 11–12.
[18] *Chartularium Univ. Paris.*, I. 418.
[19] Cuthbert Smith, 'Scholastic career', p. 103.
[20] The advowson was in the hands of the abbot and convent of Eynsham, whose patron was the bishop of Lincoln: *Rotuli Hugonis de Welles*, ed. F. N. Davis, H. E. Salter and W. P. W. Phillimore (CYS, 1907–9), II. 47, and Wood, *Monasteries and Patrons*, pp. 29–30.
[21] Le Neve, *Fasti 1066–1300*, III. 82, 85, and *CPR 1272–81*, p. 232.
[22] *Reg. Epistolarum Peckham*, I. 90 and Powicke, *Henry and Lord Edward*, pp. 610n, 647 and n.
[23] *CPR 1272–81*, p. 252.

8

to Paris for a spell, this time to undertake, or to continue, his studies in theology.

At all events, it was at Oxford that he obtained his doctorate of theology. Surviving *quaestiones* of Winchelsey's in Assisi MS 158 are undoubtedly derived from disputations at Oxford. The last two stages in the granting of the degree were the disputations known as the vesperies and the inception. A *responsio* of Winchelsey's in a disputation of a certain Master Luke of Ely survives, as does a *quaestio* at his vesperies, and a *quaestio* at his inception when Simon of Ghent, future bishop of Salisbury, was the respondent.[24] By August 1288 Winchelsey had incepted and was a regent-master in theology.[25] And he was also by the same date chancellor of the university.[26] He could well have incepted and become chancellor before 1288, for his successor William of Kingscote was possibly already elected chancellor late in 1288.[27] The only firm date that we have for Winchelsey's predecessor as chancellor, Hervey de Saham, is 30 April 1286.[28] Winchelsey was still at Oxford c. 1289–90 for he presided at the vesperies of John of Monmouth, later bishop of Llandaff.[29] His biographer tells us that after he had been chancellor of the university he took up residence in St Paul's London as archdeacon of Essex and was responsible for the teaching of theology there. We know that he was arch-deacon of Essex by August 1288, before he incepted as doctor of theology, and it is possible that he had already held the arch-deaconry for a number of years, for the man who apparently preceded him, Roger de la Legh, had become dean of St Paul's in October 1283.[30] Also, by Michaelmas 1288, he had links with the cathedral priory of Canterbury and was described as the protector of the prior's papal privileges.[31] With the archdeaconry Winchelsey

---

[24] Little and Pelster, *Oxford Theologians*, esp. pp. 42–52, 103.
[25] *Reg. Swinfield*, p. 190.
[26] Ibid., and *Munimenta Academica*, ed. H. Anstey (RS, 1868), I. 44.
[27] *Annales Monastici*, IV. 316–18 and *Oxford Formularies*, II. 356.
[28] *Reg. Epistolarum Peckham*, III. 921.
[29] Little and Pelster, *Oxford Theologians*, p. 97.
[30] Ibid., pp. 115–16.
[31] PRO KB27/114 m. 46. This case was between the king and the prior of Christ Church Canterbury concerning St Martin's Dover, continued from Michaelmas 1286: see KB27/101 m. 33d, and Denton, *Royal Chapels*, pp. 62–3. The prior had excommunicated the subprior, and certain monks, of Dover, 'per magistrem Robertum de Wenchelse archidiaconum Essexie conservatorem

held the prebend of Oxgate.[32] Possibly he undertook the teaching of theology at St Paul's as a result of Bishop Gravesend's ordinance for the establishment of a resident lecturer in theology there.[33] Oxford Magdalen College MS 217 contains *quaestiones* described in the table of contents as Robert Winchelsey's *quaestiones* disputed at London when he taught there.

Quaestiones disputatae of Winchelsey's are to be found in four manuscripts: Assisi MSS 158 (twelve *quaestiones*) and 196 (two *quaestiones*),[34] Oxford Magdalen College MS 217 (eight *quaestiones*) and Oxford Balliol College MS 63 (six *quaestiones* and two *quodlibeta*).[35] In addition, the flyleaf of Prague Metropolitan Chapter Library A. 17. 2 contains the beginning of a *quaestio* which appears in the first of the Assisi MSS and also in the Magdalen MS.[36] Whether this represents the whole of Winchelsey's works, we cannot be certain.[37] The two Assisi MSS are very similar in content, but a whole sequence of *quaestiones* by Winchelsey appears only in MS 158 and an important *quaestio* on the unity of form appears only in MS 196. The eight *quaestiones* in the Magdalen MS are distinct from the rest, for these are the lectures which Winchelsey delivered at St Paul's; while they are basically the same *quaestiones* which Winchelsey disputed at Oxford, they appear in a revised form.[38] The Balliol MS contains four *quaestiones* which are also in Assisi MS 158 and two which appear in the revised form in the Magdalen MS; in addition to these six *quaestiones* (fos. 112r–131v), there are two *quodlibeta* (fos. 132r–161v) which Cuthbert Smith has shown convincingly to be the work of Winchelsey.[39]

privilegiorum ipsius prioris Cantuariensis a curia Romana successoribus suis et sibi concessorum'. And see J. C. Russell, *Dictionary of Writers* (*BIHR*, Spec. supplement III, 1936), p. 142.

[32] Le Neve, *Fasti 1066–1300*, I. 14, 68.

[33] A. G. Little, 'Theological schools in medieval England', *EHR*, LV (1940), 624–5.

[34] For these two MSS see P. Glorieux in *Recherches de Théologie Ancienne et Médiévale*, VIII (1936), 282–95 and D. H. Pouillon, ibid., XII (1940), 329–58.

[35] See Cuthbert Smith, 'Scholastic career', pp. 107–17. Only two of the *quaestiones* are in print: Little and Pelster, *Oxford Theologians*, pp. 137–45.

[36] This is the *quaestio*, ibid., pp. 142–5.   [37] See Emden, *Oxford*, III. xlvi–xlvii.

[38] For an edition of these *quaestiones* (Oxford Magdalen Coll. MS 217, fos. 341r–367r) see Cuthbert Smith, 'Robert Winchelsey and his Place in the Intellectual Movement', II. 1–365.

[39] Cuthbert Smith, 'Scholastic career', pp. 111–15.

Winchelsey gained praise as chancellor of the university for his support of the rights of students and as a prudent man with a sense of justice.[40] He also achieved some fame as a teacher. The usefulness of his *quaestiones* and *quodlibeta* is illustrated by their inclusion in manuscripts which were the working collections of texts prepared by individual students. The *quodlibeta* in particular show Winchelsey at the peak of his academic career, for the *disputatio de quolibet* was in effect an open forum, during which questions could be freely asked of the master. Winchelsey was primarily concerned with an examination of the philosophical basis for an understanding of the Trinity. He followed closely the reasoning of Aquinas. One of the first controversies arising out of the teaching of Aquinas was related to his doctrine on the Trinity, and the Magdalen MS is a collection of texts concerned very largely with this debate.[41] Both sides of the argument are represented: the teaching of Henry of Ghent, which runs counter to the teaching of Aquinas, is followed by Winchelsey's *quaestiones*, treating the Trinity from Aquinas's standpoint, and by the anonymous *Egidius contra Thomam* which examines the attacks of Giles of Rome upon Aquinas. This last work contains specific references to Winchelsey's *quaestiones*, and Winchelsey may even have been the author of it.

There is no evidence to link Winchelsey with the controversies surrounding the work of Aquinas at Paris, but he must have been to some extent involved in the controversies at Oxford. That he was a secular master no doubt shielded him from the heat of the debate between the Franciscans and the Dominicans, which turned especially upon the belief of Aquinas and his supporters in the unity of substantial form in man, that is, the unity of body and soul. To some Franciscans this belief seemed to exclude the possibility of a 'form of corporeity' and posed the problem, for example, of the identity of Christ's body after his death. In England the debate culminated in Archbishop Pecham's condemnation in 1286 of the Dominican Richard Knapwell, one of the leading Oxford theologians.[42] Although Winchelsey seems to have

---

[40] *Anglia Sacra*, I. 12 and *Oxford Formularies*, I. 59.
[41] Cuthbert Smith, 'Scholastic career', pp. 121–6.
[42] See Douie, *Pecham*, pp. 280–301 and the refs. at p. 286 n. 3.

avoided being publicly implicated in this dispute, there can be little doubt where he stood. His dependence upon and acceptance of the views of Aquinas, first noted by Pelster,[43] have been confirmed in the detailed study by Cuthbert Smith. Following Aquinas he maintained, for example, that the three persons of the Trinity can be distinguished by relations and not by origin. He aimed to clarify and to extend the arguments of Aquinas. Yet it is interesting that in the one surviving *quaestio* which touched upon the most pressing problem of the day he defended the doctrine of the plurality of forms and never faced directly the crucial issue of whether there was in man only one substantial form as Aquinas had maintained.[44] Archbishops Kilwardby and Pecham had condemned Aquinas's doctrine. Can it be that Winchelsey deliberately proscribed his teaching because of their condemnations? It is hard to believe that he was pusillanimous, especially at a time when more and more scholars were accommodating themselves to the outlook of Aquinas, but he may well have disliked the bitterness of the controversy which so engaged the friars. While he played an important rôle on the academic stage, he chose not to have the spotlights focussed upon him. In the estimation of Cuthbert Smith his work is 'abstract to a degree, closely reasoned, coldly impersonal, with none of the religious intensity which marks the more personal approach of the mystic...nevertheless, a model example of scholastic thought at its best'.[45]

It is important to take account of Winchelsey's early career and academic background to understand the man and his allegiances. We need not look far for confirmation of the emphasis which he placed upon learning.[46] His refusal to confirm the election of Robert Orford to the bishopric of Ely on the grounds of insufficient learning;[47] his important collection of books, biblical and patristic,

---

[43] Little and Pelster, *Oxford Theologians*, p. 71, and see D. A. Callus, 'The problem of the unity of form and Richard Knapwell', p. 132, in *Mélanges Offerts à Étienne Gilson* (Toronto and Paris, 1959).

[44] Little and Pelster, *Oxford Theologians*, p. 158 and Cuthbert Smith, 'Robert Winchelsey and his Place in the Intellectual Movement', I. 185–8.

[45] Cuthbert Smith, 'Robert Winchelsey and his Place in the Intellectual Movement', I. 16–17.

[46] K. Edwards, 'Bishops and learning', pp. 70–1, 74–8, 85.

[47] Graham, 'Administration of Ely during vacancies', pp. 67–70.

along with almost all the works of Aquinas;[48] his suggestion that the learned monks of Christ Church Canterbury should enjoy certain privileges; his generosity towards the poor students of both Oxford and Cambridge; and his practice of appointing graduates to vacant benefices, a policy which can be illustrated by his support of William du Boys, William of Thetford and Simon of Faversham and which in the eyes of some was to strengthen the case for his canonisation.[49] It is tempting to argue for some relationship between his philosophical and theological training and his political opinions. Perhaps his concern for the community of the realm should be viewed in the context of the views of Aquinas and his school, as in the justification of war when waged in defence of the interests of the common good,[50] and as in the emphasis upon communal interests in the *De Regno*.[51] But, having in mind the extreme difficulty of establishing links between schools of speculative thought and pragmatic political beliefs,[52] as well as the lack of political or social ideas in Winchelsey's works, it is quite impossible to make ideological connections between Winchelsey's theological beliefs and his policies as archbishop. The circle of scholars to which Winchelsey belonged at Oxford has left few traces of an interest in political theory. Nonetheless, there is every indication that he was one of a group of theologians and secular masters who had a special devotion to the traditions of the English Church. Many of them became bishops of note.[53] One was an older man, Richard Swinfield, as also was Oliver Sutton, another episcopal colleague, who, though not a doctor of theology, had spent many

---

[48] M. R. James, *Ancient Libraries of Canterbury and Dover* (Cambridge, 1903), pp. 135–7, *Reg.*, pp. xxxiii, 1344 and N. R. Ker, *Medieval Libraries of Gt Britain* (2nd edn, London, 1964), p. 243. To the list in the latter should be added Cambridge Trinity Coll. MS 383, the *Sentences* of Peter Lombard with annotations ('Sententie Manducatoris R. de Wynch' Archiepiscopi'); most probably Trinity MSS 382, 384 and 385 were Winchelsey's too.

[49] Little and Pelster, *Oxford Theologians*, pp. 80, 254, 263 and *Reg.*, p. 716.

[50] See F. H. Russell, *The Just War in the Middle Ages* (Cambridge, 1975), pp. 258–91.

[51] See J. Catto, 'Ideas and experience in the political thought of Aquinas', *Past & Present*, LXXI (1976), 11–19.

[52] See A. Gewirth, 'Philosophy and political thought in the fourteenth century', pp. 125–64, in *The Forward Movement of the Fourteenth Century*, ed. F. L. Utley (Columbus, 1961).

[53] Little and Pelster, *Oxford Theologians*, pp. 73, 78–81, 97–8, 260 and *Snappe's Formulary*, pp. 323–4; and see below, p. 34.

years at Oxford. But others had certainly been fellow students and contemporary teachers: Ralph Walpole, John of Monmouth, Simon of Ghent, John Dalderby, Thomas Cobham and Roger Martival, the last two gaining promotion to the episcopal bench after Winchelsey's death. Monmouth, Ghent and Martival had also been chancellors of the university, in 1290, 1291 and 1293 respectively. These were men whose interests lay in the pastoral work of the Church; they were conservative and sacerdotalist in outlook; their concern in politics was with the liberties of the clergy.[54] Their theological studies were closely linked with their devotion to the cure of souls. Not one of them had been openly involved in the bitter academic controversy that stirred Kilwardby and Pecham; the outspoken Thomists at Oxford were all Dominicans.[55] The secular masters, whose interests were largely insular,[56] stood aloof from the Franciscans and Dominicans.

From theology to the work of the diocese was a natural step. When Winchelsey, at the age of about fifty, became archbishop, he put aside the work of the scholar, but there was no break in his career. There can be no doubt that learning was, in the eyes of the electing monks of Canterbury, a major qualification for the office of archbishop; and it could well be that Winchelsey had achieved renown for his discretion and his powers of leadership both as rector at Paris, for he held office there immediately after disturbances between the nations in the university,[57] and also as regent-master and chancellor at Oxford, carefully avoiding conflict with the mendicants. His election as archbishop, on 13 February 1293, was a peaceful affair. But he had to seek papal confirmation. He left England for Italy on 1 April 1293 and, delayed by a long papal vacancy, returned as archbishop on 1 January 1295.[58]

---

54 See B. Smalley, 'Oxford University Sermons 1290–93', pp. 310–13, in *Medieval Learning and Literature: Essays Presented to R. W. Hunt*, ed. J. J. G. Alexander and M. T. Gibson (Oxford, 1976).
55 Roensch, *Early Thomist School*, pp. 28–83.
56 See D. Knowles, 'Some aspects of the career of Archbishop Pecham', *EHR*, LVII (1942), 199–200 (Winchelsey 'had his centre of gravity, so to say, fixed in England').
57 *Anglia Sacra*, I. 12 and *Chartularium Univ. Paris.*, I. nos. 409, 416.
58 See Graham, 'Winchelsey: from election to enthronement'.

POSTHUMOUS REPUTE

Winchelsey died on 11 May 1313[59] in his manor at Otford, Kent, where he had been ill from the beginning of the year. His body was brought to his cathedral priory on 21 May.[60] At the gate of the priory the monks who had carried the body from the hospital of St James, just outside the city, were met by Henry Woodlock (bishop of Winchester), John Droxford (bishop of Bath and Wells), John Ketton (bishop of Ely), and John of Monmouth (bishop of Llandaff). The latter, as the senior bishop of the group, led the prayers. After vespers on 22 May, the whole convent chanted the dirge, after which nine lessons were read by the prior (Henry of Eastry), the abbot of Langdon, the abbot of St Radegund's, the abbot of Lesnes, the abbot of Battle, the abbot of Faversham, the bishop of Ely, the bishop of Winchester, and the bishop of Llandaff, and the precentor and five monks chanted Timor Magnus, Dies Illa, and Nunc Christe. On the following day, 23 May, the bishop of Llandaff, after preaching on the text 'Know ye not that there is a great prince called Abner fallen this day in Israel',[61] officiated at mass and at the funeral rites. The body was laid to rest in a tomb 'towards the south before the altar of St Gregory'.[62] The tomb survived until the sixteenth century, for it was seen by John Leland around the year 1540: 'In the crosse isle on the South side of the quire: Bisshop Winchelsey in a right goodly tumbe of marble at the very but ende yn the waulle side.'[63] Probably very soon afterwards,[64] and certainly before 1572, it was demolished. Its desecration was noted in Matthew Parker's *De Antiquitate* as a mark of the popular veneration of Winchelsey as a saint.[65]

[59] He had drawn up his will four days earlier: see *Reg.*, pp. xxxii–xxxiv, 1340–8.
[60] For the following account see BL Harleian 636, fo. 233v.
[61] II Samuel 3:38.
[62] 'mist en sepulture en meme cele eglise devers le suth devaunt lauter Seynt Gregoire le pape': Bl Harl. 636, fo. 233v. See also *Flores Hist.*, III. 155: 'in australi parte dicte ecclesie'.
[63] *The Itinerary of John Leland*, ed. L. T. Smith (London, 1909), pt VIII. 39.
[64] C. E. Woodruff and W. Danks, *Memorials of Canterbury Cathedral* (London, 1912), pp. 296–7.
[65] Parker, *De Antiquitate*, pt ii. 223: 'Sepulchrum eius, quia populus eum mortuum tanquam sanctum fraequens adoravit, demolitum atque deiectum est.' In his *Survey of London*, first published in 1598, John Stow testified to the continued reputation of the archbishop for almsgiving: edn of 1720, pt i. 275.

He had been a forceful and courageous archbishop, and also a man who, although belonging to no religious order, had lived a simple and devout life. He had shown a single-minded concern for the welfare of the English Church. But no archbishop, however much he may avoid the snares of involvement in secular government, could fail to be a political leader. And the death and funeral of Winchelsey were events of great political significance.[66] Although a notarial instrument[67] shows that Walter Reynolds, bishop of Worcester, and Walter Stapledon, bishop of Exeter, were also present at the exequies, and the earl of Gloucester too, along with the four bishops noted by the chronicler, the archbishop's funeral was nonetheless a relatively quiet affair, much quieter than the ceremony of his enthronement had been on 2 October 1295.[68] Edward II had been in Canterbury on 20 and 21 May 1313, but departed before the funeral took place. On the very day of the funeral Edward, at Dover, corresponded secretly with Clement V, notifying the pope of his plan to approach him concerning his own nominee for the now vacant see of Canterbury.[69] The king's nominee was Bishop Reynolds, who was the king's confidant and chancellor of the realm. When Clement in his reply wrote of Winchelsey's 'vicious policies and perverse acts' he was supporting the king's party among the clergy in England. The archbishop had been throughout his term of office deeply involved in a political wrangle concerning the relationship of the English clergy with the Crown, and his saintly way of life, along with his learning, was seen by many churchmen, including chroniclers, as a facet of that political wrangle. His opponents were now determined to reverse his policies. When the archbishop's old friend and ally, John of Monmouth, preached on the text concerning the murder of the 'great prince called Abner' he must have recalled that Abner, having agreed to assist David in bringing the Israelites to peaceful acceptance of his rule, had been suspected of being a spy and a traitor. The words of the bishop's text had been

---

[66] Denton, 'Canterbury appointments: the case of Reynolds', pp. 317–25.
[67] Cant. D. & C., Reg. Q, fos. 73r, 81r.
[68] Ibid., fos. 38v–39r, and see Graham, 'Winchelsey: from election to enthronement', p. 175.
[69] Denton, 'Canterbury appointments: the case of Reynolds', pp. 319–20, 322.

spoken by the lamenting King David. But in May 1313 King
Edward II was not in mourning.

Winchelsey's reputation for sanctity lived on for over two and
a half centuries, but it was at its height, naturally, in the years
immediately following his death. The first appraisals of the archbishop come from two contemporary chroniclers, both of whom
sang Winchelsey's praises in the context of passionate support for
his political rôle in defending the liberties of the English Church.
Their assessments of the archbishop are similar and there can be
no doubt that they represent the prevailing opinion of the English
clergy. For the author of the *Vita Edwardi Secundi*[70] Winchelsey
had 'strengthened the temple of the Lord' and 'protected the
Church'. Unlike the false prophets of Israel, he had gone into
battle and had stood as a defence for the clergy.[71] This chronicler
gave a brief account of the crisis of 1297, conveying the impression
that the events were fresh in his memory: Edward I's orders for
the 'tallaging' of the clergy; the archbishop's refusal to allow the
king's orders to take effect and his assertion of the clergy's freedom from royal exactions in accordance with canon law; the
king's wrathful attack upon the possessions of the clergy and
Winchelsey's consequent sentence of excommunication; the seizure
of the goods of the archbishop, who was compelled to travel on
foot; and the final repentance of the king and his orders for the
Church to remain free. It is a highlighted account of the archbishop's most critical year. Yet in detail, and also very largely in
emphasis, it will be substantiated below. The chronicler's appraisal
closed with a brief mention of Winchelsey's suspension for two
years, during which time the revenues of the see were confiscated.
The crisis of 1297 and the archbishop's suspension certainly provide the central events of Winchelsey's conflict with the Crown.
The author of the *Vita*, later in his narrative,[72] attacked Winchelsey's successor, Reynolds, as an unlettered royal favourite, and in
this way he illumined the wise prophet by contrast with the false
prophet. This contrast was not simply, or primarily, one of

---

[70] *Vita Edwardi II*, pp. 40–2.
[71] 'Ascendit namque ex adverso et opposuit se murum pro clero.' See Ezek. 13:5.
[72] *Vita Edwardi II*, pp. 45–6.

personalities. It was a contrast of beliefs about the position of the Church and the clergy in society.[73]

A monastic chronicler of Westminster, Robert of Reading, made the same point even more forcefully, though with few references to details of the archbishop's career.[74] He wrote that while the king's eyes were moist as the archbishop lay dying there were more tears in the eyes of churchmen. Winchelsey, the chronicler stressed, had not been shaken by fear or seduced by blandishments, nor had his resolve been broken by injuries, exile, the loss of his temporal goods, and the roars and threats of the great. Among the latter the writer must have included both Edward I and Edward II, and very probably Clement V too. The archbishop, we are told, had defended the rights and the honour of his church of Canterbury. 'He was a man whose qualities of mind were so outstanding', the chronicler continued, 'that he cannot be assessed here in writing, but happy is the church of Canterbury, which God through the merits of so great a protector has in his mercy blessed each day with many miracles, for this church will, through these manifestations, bring faith to all those coming and wishing to see the mighty works of the Lord.' We cannot doubt that the miracles were understood as public revelations ('publico visu') in acknowledgement of supreme leadership in defence of the English Church. As for Winchelsey's successor: the devil, we are told, entered into the heart of Walter Reynolds, a malicious and deceitful man, who ruled unworthily the see of Worcester and was so unlettered that he was quite unable to decline his own name; he was wickedly ambitious for the office of archbishop, and to secure unlawful promotion he bribed the pope, who was insatiably greedy, with large quantities of gold and silver, in contempt of Christ and to the manifest prejudice of the church of Canterbury. The chronicler's attack was upon the wicked personal qualities of Reynolds, as well as upon the pope, and, of course, indirectly, the king. But the issues that lie beneath the personal onslaught are public and political. Reynolds had been a member of Winchelsey's episcopal bench since 1308, but he was caricatured by Robert of Reading as a layman: 'vir laicus'. To contem-

[73] Denton, 'Reynolds and ecclesiastical politics', esp. pp. 248–9.
[74] *Flores Hist.*, III. 154–5.

porary chroniclers[75] Winchelsey was on the side of the angels, Reynolds on the side of the devil. It is important to understand why.

The first hint of an answer can be seen in the St Albans chronicle of John de Trokelowe, who is a lone voice supporting the promotion of Reynolds.[76] Here we are informed that Clement V made every effort to appoint a man who would bring an end to the constant tribulations which vexed the English Church, and Reynolds was chosen because of the special favour in which he was held by the king and because he behaved circumspectly in his dealings with everyone, tempering the prevalent bitterness between the king and the magnates. This account is entirely royalist in tone. Like the others it has its own distinct bias, for we know full well that Clement V was, in fact, completely submissive to the wishes of Edward II.[77] Trokelowe wrote that Winchelsey had ruled over the church of Canterbury in a praiseworthy way for the whole of his term of office. But there is no mention of the king's attacks upon the archbishop. Rather, we are told quite simply that Winchelsey had favoured the magnates of the land in seeking intrepidly their liberties against the king.[78] This point, which it is difficult not to see as criticism of Winchelsey by Trokelowe, had not been raised at all by the other chroniclers. Yet it is Trokelowe's sole reference to Winchelsey's policies as archbishop. Among the clerical chroniclers there thus appears to have been a clear division of opinion about the essential features of Winchelsey's career. The men who were the first to assess his career present us with a problem. Should the archbishop be commended for his staunch protection of the English Church against the aggressions and usur-

---

[75] See the similar assessment in *Chronica de Melsa*, II. 328–9; and see the chronicle of 'Peter of Ickham' (Cambridge Corpus Christi Coll. MS 339 (ii), fo. 38v: 'toto tempore suo ecclesiam sibi commissam rexit viriliter et protexit et pro sua fideli constantia in ecclesie sue tuitionem multimodas creberrime adversitates sustinuit. Ad cuius sepulcrum operatur altissimus miracula gloriosa.' We read, too, of Winchelsey in a list of obits in BL Arundel 68, fo. 27r: 'Iste profecto pastor egregius, insigne speculum prelatorum, moribus et virtutibus alios antecellens, sic cordis munditie pudicitiam sociavit, sic carnis stimulos subreptantes cautius mortificavit ut a multis putaretur in carne vivere preter carnem, cuius solida constantia molestius eventibus non tepuit nec nimis terreri nec muneribus flecti potuit viam deserere veritatis.'
[76] Trokelowe, pp. 81–2.
[77] Denton, 'Canterbury appointments: the case of Reynolds', pp. 322–3.
[78] 'magnates terrae in suis libertatibus petendis intrepide contra regem fovisset'.

pations of the Crown? Or should we lay at his door the weakening of the authority of Edward I and Edward II because of a
policy of alliance with the lay lords? We may wish to avoid
deciding between two opinions that are not, in fact, mutually
exclusive, but since the questions are posed for us by contemporaries we cannot avoid a close interest in them. They force upon us
another question, of crucial importance: does the veneration of
Winchelsey and the hatred of Reynolds suggest a political split,
a radical division of opinion, within the English Church?

Concerning the bitterness directed against Reynolds there is a
good deal to be learned from the reaction of the clergy to his
policies during the first years of his pontificate.[79] The bishops were
remarkably silent, but from the lower clergy, secular and regular,
there was very strong opposition to the new archbishop's efforts to
persuade the clergy to grant taxes on their income more freely to
the king for the war in Scotland. Reynolds's aim was to give
greater control over the clergy to the Crown by trying to bring
ecclesiastical councils into parliament. These aims contrasted
starkly with the principles accepted by Winchelsey, and the clergy
were well aware of the contrast. For most of them, though
clearly not all, Reynolds, the royal clerk, was overturning the just
policies of Winchelsey, the defender of clerical liberties.

Winchelsey has rightly been seen as one in a line of political
leaders in England who, in large measure because of their oppo-
sition to the Crown, attained popular veneration for sanctity.
For only a few men (and not all of them leading opponents of the
Crown) did this veneration result in canonisation: Archbishops
Becket and Edmund Rich, and Bishops Hugh of Lincoln, Richard
Wich of Chichester and Thomas Cantilupe of Hereford. A similar
cult surrounded many more than these canonised saints: Stephen
Langton, Robert Grosseteste and Robert Winchelsey, and also the
baronial leaders Simon de Montfort and Thomas of Lancaster.
Russell produced evidence of a 'consciousness that this group
represented justice and that in their veneration justice was
honored.'[80] Two of Winchelsey's episcopal colleagues, William of
March (Bath and Wells) and John of Dalderby (Lincoln), should

---

[79] Denton, 'Reynolds and ecclesiastical politics', *passim*.
[80] Russell, 'Canonization of opposition to the king', p. 286.

perhaps be included in the group.[81] Opposition to the crown and
defence of ecclesiastical rights were clearly important factors often
leading to popular sanctity; and sanctity in England was associated
especially with the episcopate.[82] The outstanding saint-bishops
were not, of course, the bishops who often behaved like temporal
lords (as Anthony Bek, bishop of Durham), nor the bishops who
took up arms, of which there are only few examples in England,[83]
nor yet the curialists (as Robert Burnell of Bath and Wells, Walter
Langton of Coventry and Lichfield, or Walter Reynolds of
Worcester and Canterbury); the saint-bishops were those who
combined orderly episcopal government with notable learning,
and devotion to pastoral care with the combating of secular
encroachments upon ecclesiastical prerogatives.

The offerings made at Winchelsey's tomb amounted to £50 in
the course of the first year following his death. In 1319 they were
almost double that sum.[84] It is from letters dated from the spring
of 1319 that we first learn of the petition for Winchelsey's canonisation. Thomas, earl of Lancaster, had apparently approached
Pope John XXII concerning the procedure for such a petition, and
had been informed that the testimony of the prelates, clergy, and
people of England concerning the 'life, merits and miracles' of
the archbishop would be required at the papal curia.[85] The pope
had given little hope of a successful outcome for the petition, since
it was not customary for the Roman Church to act with any
precipitation in such a case. Yet Lancaster was undeterred. On
13 March 1319 Prior Henry of Eastry wrote to Thomas thanking

[81] See Kemp, *Canonization*, pp. 118, 120–1, Tout, *Chapters*, II. 17 and n, and
below, pp. 72–3, though as Tout pointed out, March, the clerk trained in
the king's wardrobe, was a most unusual candidate for canonisation.
[82] See Brentano, *Two Churches*, esp. pp. 174–80, 221–2, 236–7.
[83] Anthony Bek fought in Flanders and Scotland: Fraser, *Bek*, pp. 71, 75–6, 211.
For the one disastrous occasion on which William Melton (archbishop of York
1317–40) took to the field against the Scots (the battle of Myton-on-Swale
1319) see R. M. T. Hill, 'An English archbishop and the Scottish war of
independence', *The Innes Review: Scottish Catholic Historical Studies*, XXII
(1971), 59–71. Concerning knight-bishops see Highfield, 'The English
hierarchy', pp. 135–6 and Brentano, *Two Churches*, pp. 203–4.
[84] Woodruff, 'The miracles of Winchelsey', p. 111, citing 'the accounts of the
monastic treasurers', that is Cant. D. & C., Miscellaneous Accounts Book II.
[85] For copies of the bull, apparently of 27 Dec. 1318, see *Literae Cantuar.*, III.
400–1, *Reg. Martival*, II. 319–20, Somner, *Antiquities*, pt I. app. 56 and *CPL*,
II. 422.

him for his letters, which had asked for written evidence of the miracles God was working and had worked through Archbishop Robert, and assuring him that this evidence would be sent as soon as possible.[86] But the earl seems to have been dissatisfied with this reply, for on 7 April he wrote again to the prior and convent of Canterbury asking for a written testimony of the archbishop's miracles, including the report of miracles which hung in front of the tomb. This time Thomas sent his clerk, Ralph of Houghton, who immediately set about the task of collecting the evidence required.

An inquest held by Ralph of Houghton in the presence of eight assessors in the priory of Christ Church lasted from Monday 31 April until Thursday 3 May, and all the evidence received and corroborated was set down in a notarial act. Two supplementary inquests were held by a notary public, Thomas Besiles, on 1 May at Bonnington, in the parish of Goodnestone, and at Sandwich. The inquiries produced stories of the sort commonly found in medieval processes of canonisation. Evidence was brought for the performance of sixteen miracles, most of which were concerned with cures of mental and physical ailments; for example a certain Catherine, a nun of Bungay, was cured of madness at the archbishop's tomb. All except one of the miracles, the exorcism of an evil spirit, had taken place after the archbishop's death. The miracles, recorded as part of the necessary evidence of the archbishop's sanctity, provide the historian with an indication of his popular fame. But the testimonies of men who had been closely associated with the archbishop are of greater interest. Two monk-chaplains, another monk of Christ Church Canterbury, and three others of Winchelsey's *familia* gave statements about the archbishop's life: John Spicer, who had been one of the archbishop's chaplains for about two years; Alan of Twitham, the archbishop's private chamberlain, who had been with Winchelsey during his

---

[86] *Concilia*, II. 486, from CUL Ee. v. 31, fo. 199r. The whole inquisition, ibid., fos. 202r–205v, is printed in *Concilia*, II. 486–90, and much less accurately in Woodruff, 'The miracles of Winchelsey', pp. 117–23. Woodruff was unaware that this material relating to the process was already in print. Oxford Bodleian Hatton 99, fos. 178–9, is part of a schedule of miracles and has details of the cases of William, son of Bartholomew le Kyng, Amabilia, daughter of Thomas of Bonnington, and Richard Wybert of Sandwich (compare *Concilia*, II. 490).

suspension;[87] James of Bourne, who had been in the archbishop's service as his 'special valet'[88] for twenty-two years and had known Winchelsey for forty-two years, and had also been with him during his suspension; Robert of Malling, who had served primarily as an auditor in the archbishop's court of audience; Gilbert of Bishopstone, who had been one of the archbishop's chaplains for four years, corroborated Spicer's statement; and Twitham's statement was corroborated by Brother Bertramus.

All testified to the extent of the archbishop's almsgiving and generosity. Spicer believed that in this respect Winchelsey had no equal in England, and Twitham noted not only that he doubled, or even trebled, his almsgiving on feast-days, but also that he distributed food three times a week to all who came to his gate and gave money if there was not enough food to go round. Both Twitham and Bourne stated that he sought out the sick and those unable to come to his gate so that they could also receive his gifts, and that he often gave away his clothes, especially to poor priests. Robert of Malling, before telling the story of how, during the visitation of the diocese of London, an evil spirit departed from a woman whom the archbishop had absolved from the sin of perjury in his court, also emphasised the archbishop's generosity, claiming that in addition to his usual almsgiving he sent food every day to those living nearby who were bed-ridden. According to Bourne it was on Winchelsey's orders that all the profits of the church of Mayfield, which was appropriated to the archbishopric, were given to the poor with only the expenses for upkeep deducted. But it was not simply for generosity that the archbishop was venerated. Spicer told of how the altar cloths were often moistened by his tears when he was celebrating mass, for it was as though he could actually see Christ crucified; and at confessions, said Twitham, the archbishop shared the grief of those who came to him. At the end of his statement Bourne claimed that evidence could be brought to prove many miracles concerning animals and birds. Spicer believed that the archbishop had lived his life from beginning to end 'without any fault', and he was struck by the physical suffering which Winchelsey must have endured. He had been

[87] *Reg.*, p. 1341.   [88] *Reg.*, p. 1343.

present at the archbishop's death[89] and claimed that it had been discovered that the archbishop's thighs were without skin and flesh. This was explained as the result of his secret mortifications of the flesh and by the fact that he rarely slept in a made-up bed ('raro in lectis stratis cubabat'). If perhaps overdrawn, these testimonies to the sanctity of the archbishop's life are nonetheless worthy of close attention, for they are the direct statements, witnessed and corroborated, of men who had known the archbishop well. While on the one hand there must have been pressure upon them to produce evidence of weight for the canonisation process, on the other hand these attestations represent the knowledge and beliefs of Winchelsey's own household clerks.

The list of miracles and the testimonies were drawn up as a notarial act by the notary public Thomas Nichole of Canterbury, sealed by Prior Eastry, and sent to Thomas of Lancaster with a letter commending the earl's efforts to secure Winchelsey's canonisation. But the matter did not long remain the sole concern of Thomas of Lancaster and the monks of Canterbury, for the former had also addressed Archbishop Reynolds on the subject. On 14 November 1319 Reynolds commissioned the bishops of London and Chichester to inquire into the reputed miracles of the late archbishop in their own dioceses and in the diocese of Canterbury.[90] This commission was perhaps extended to include the bishop of Rochester, for three weeks later Prior Eastry, writing to Lancaster to acknowledge further letters from him, informed the earl that the bishops of London, Chichester and Rochester had been ordered 'to inquire in the dioceses of Canterbury, Rochester, London and Chichester concerning the life and the reputation and other matters, including the miracles, relating to Archbishop Robert'.[91] In May 1320 the prior of Canterbury testified to the authenticity of the miracles revealed by the investigations of the bishop of Rochester in the diocese of Canterbury; but this is apparently the only outcome of the inquiries which had been commissioned for the dioceses of south-east England.

Other bishops, perhaps all the other bishops, of the province

[89] Cant. D. & C., Reg. Q, fos. 73r, 81r.
[90] *Literae Cantuar.*, III. 398–400.
[91] *Concilia*, II. 491, from CUL Ee. v. 31, fos. 211v, 213v–214r.

were instructed by Reynolds to inquire into the miracles and
reputation of Winchelsey in their own dioceses. The letter to
Roger Martival, bishop of Salisbury, is dated 28 May 1320,[92] and
it seems possible that the archbishop had waited for the results of
the inquiries in the dioceses in which Winchelsey's fame was likely
to be at its greatest before ordering more widespread investigations.
Reports from at least three dioceses have survived (Salisbury, Bath
and Wells, and Worcester), but they tend only to indicate either
that the prelates lacked enthusiasm for the matter or that the
archbishop's reputation was not very marked outside the south-
east corner of England, for the three reports from Roger Martival,
John Droxford and Thomas Cobham are almost identical.[93] The
Martival letter is slightly longer, but apart from a few minor differ-
ences the three texts follow each other word for word. All these
claimed, in brief, that Winchelsey was a man of outstanding merit,
well known for his learning, diligent in his priestly office, and
lavish in almsgiving, a man who promoted to dignities and benefices teachers of the Holy Scriptures, scholars and others of proved
merit, who gave generous help to poor scholars of Oxford and
Cambridge, and who suffered patiently many persecutions for the
laws and liberties of the Church. But none of these reports was
written from the local diocese: they were all compiled, 'copied'
would perhaps be more accurate, at London, and the ones from
Droxford and Martival are dated 27 and 29 October 1320. The
prelates were attending a parliament at this time, and had, it
seems, been called upon to present their evidence in support of the
process for canonisation. The result was a letter to the pope, dated
9 November, from all the bishops of the province of Canterbury
describing in general terms the saintly qualities of their late archbishop.[94] At about the same time the university of Oxford also
wrote to the pope giving details of Winchelsey's outstanding life
and pleading for his canonisation, as also did Thomas of Lancaster
on 2 January 1321 and Edmund, earl of Arundel, on 6 January
1321. In March a letter from the prior and convent of Canterbury
added further weight to the earlier testimonies and claimed that

[92] *Reg. Martival*, II. 300-1.
[93] Ibid., II. 301-2, *Concilia*, II. 499 (calendared in *Reg. Drokensford*, p. 183)
and *Reg. Cobham*, p. 98.
[94] *Reg. Martival*, II. 318-19 and BL Add. 6159, fos. 101v-102r.

Winchelsey's canonisation would excite a more willing devotion in the English people and hasten the reformation of the whole kingdom.[95]

In 1322 Thomas of Lancaster rose in active rebellion and was executed on 22 March. In July of that year Prior Eastry pleaded with the earl's brother, Henry, that he should support the proceedings which Thomas had initiated.[96] But only after the recognition of the 'good earl Henry' in 1326 were the monks able to resume their attempt successfully. At the parliament which had reassembled after the coronation of Edward III, early in 1327, a petition was received and accepted that letters be sent to the pope recommending the canonisation of both Robert Winchelsey and Thomas of Lancaster. Perhaps under the guidance of Henry of Lancaster – official guardian to Edward III – the king himself wrote to the pope first in a petition for the canonisation of Thomas of Lancaster, and later, on 8 March, extolling the saintly qualities of the late archbishop of Canterbury. At about the same time Reynolds and the suffragans of Canterbury sent a further plea to the pope, including a list of miracles wrought by Winchelsey.[97] This may well have been a new list, for the results of the earlier inquiries made in and near Canterbury in May 1319 had been forwarded to Thomas of Lancaster who had sent them to the pope in January 1321. And the prior and convent re-dated their petition of March 1321 and sent it again to the pope on 12 March 1327.[98]

The appeals to have Winchelsey enrolled as a saint had been supported with evidence of miracles and letters testimonial such as had accompanied the petitions for Archbishop Edmund Rich and others. But there is scarcely a hint of the papal attitude towards it. Perhaps John XXII's initial warning to Thomas of Lancaster to the effect that canonisation was not an honour bestowed lightly is an indication that the archbishop was not considered a likely nominee. Indeed, it would have been something of a *volte face* if

---

95 *Oxford Formularies*, I. 58–60, BL Add. 6159, fos. 102r–103v, and *Concilia*, II. 500–1, from CUL Ee. v. 31, fo. 220r–v.
96 *Literae Cantuar.*, I. 70–1.
97 *Rot. Parl.*, II. 7, 11, *Rot. Parl. Hactenus Inediti*, pp. 116–17, *Foedera*, II. ii. 695–6, *Literae Cantuar.*, III. 401–2, *Anglia Sacra*, I. 173–4 and *Concilia*, II. 536.
98 BL Add. 6159, fos. 102v–103v, and CUL Ee, v. 31, fo. 258v.

the papacy had decided to champion Winchelsey at this stage. Like Stephen Langton and Robert Grosseteste before him, his career had drawn him into conflict with the papacy. The patience with which the archbishop had suffered suspension is cited in many of the petitions as a prime reason for his canonisation; but that suspension had been, as we shall see, at papal command. He had been summoned to the pope's presence because he had failed, in Clement V's words, to 'walk in the paths of pontifical modesty'.[99] The appeal from the prelates in 1327 claimed that the archbishop had all the qualities of a true martyr, and only the prudence, good faith and wisdom of Edward I prevented his martyrdom. There is some truth in this, but the martyrdom of Winchelsey had also been prevented by his own prudence, good faith and wisdom. His defence of the English Church had been calm and considered. His was not the temperament of a martyr. Limitations had been placed on his fame by his own unobtrusive qualities. But it is abundantly clear that the strength of his case depended upon the degree to which he could be regarded as having justly opposed the Crown. Clement V had certainly not regarded his opposition as just. It is difficult to believe that there was ever much chance of Winchelsey becoming a saint.

The archbishop's fame was naturally strong at Canterbury. His first biographer was probably a monk of Christ Church Canterbury, writing in the third quarter of the fourteenth century. This biographer, in his *Lives of the Archbishops of Canterbury*, which ends with the promotion of William Whittlesey in 1369, was able to trace the history of Winchelsey's career in considerable detail.[100] None of the archbishop's predecessors was given such detailed treatment, and even the careers of his two successors, Walter Reynolds and Simon Mepham, occupy together only a sixth of the space devoted to Winchelsey. The ascription by Wharton of these *Lives* to Stephen Birchington, who became a monk at Christ Church Canterbury in 1382, was rash,[101] and the

[99] *Annales London.*, p. 145. See below, p. 232.
[100] *Anglia Sacra*, I. 11–17, from Lambeth Palace Lib., MS 99, fos. 132v–135v.
[101] See J. Tait, *Chronica Johannis de Reading et Anonymi Cantuariensis* (Manchester, 1914), pp. 63–8. Wharton was apparently unaware that it was a second MS, not extant, though very similar to the extant *Vitae*, that was cited as a source in Parker, *De Antiquitate*, and ascribed to Stephen

man who first set himself the task of writing a lengthy assessment of Winchelsey's career remains anonymous.

There are aspects of this first 'life' of the archbishop which render it suspect as a faithful and balanced account, for the author could see no fault in the archbishop. It follows in the tradition of the chroniclers' brief encomiums. Yet it is tersely, if rather crudely, written, and much of the detailed information which it provides can be substantiated from other sources. Indeed, the biographer clearly used documentary evidence which survived at Canterbury. The account of the seizure of the priory in 1297 was almost certainly derived from public instruments still at Canterbury,[102] and the long description of the archbishop's devout life was based, at least to some extent, upon the report which was drawn up after the investigations at Canterbury in 1319 into the sanctity of the archbishop. The documentary basis of the 'life' makes it a prime source for understanding Winchelsey's career. We can use with some confidence information that it supplies. Fifty years after the archbishop's death the offerings at his tomb had dwindled to nothing,[103] but the tradition at Canterbury concerning his life was still both strong and accurate.

How much we must allow for the biographer's bias in presenting the evidence is another question. His account of Winchelsey's early life is highly coloured: as a boy Robert was so excellent a student of grammar that no one before had been his equal, and he so excelled all others in his life, conduct, character and learning that it was generally predicted that he would become archbishop; while he was at the papal curia awaiting consecration it was held that no one of equal merit had been seen from the kingdom of England and he was believed to be worthy of the papal office; after Celestine V's election it was divulged that the pope intended to make Winchelsey a cardinal, but the archbishop, considering the great expense of this promotion for his cathedral church, persuaded the pope to change his mind and to grant him per-

Birchington. The lost Birchington MS appears to have been a continuation of the extant and anonymous *Vitae*, for the biographies had been extended to at least 1381. BL Cotton Julius B iii, fos. 31v–42r, is an abbreviated version of the *Vitae*.
102 *Anglia Sacra*, I. 14–15, and see below, pp. 111–12.
103 Woodruff, 'The miracles of Winchelsey', p. 116.

mission to return to his see.[104] It would be unwise to regard such details as these as unfounded, but equally unwise to set great store by them. In the context of this account they form, along with much other evidence of Winchelsey's excellence, a preamble to the events of his period of office as archbishop. After the emphasis upon his learning, his pastoral work, his preaching and his saintly character, we pass to a long description of the outlawry of the clergy and the seizure of the archbishop's goods in 1297, followed by an account of his suspension from office from 1306 to 1308. The theme of the biography becomes clear: it is the persecution of Winchelsey by the Crown.

'The enemies of human kind, seeing this man of God succeed so notably in the office committed to him, inflamed the mind of the king against the archbishop...so that he was put outside the grace, peace and protection of the king and deprived of all his possessions and goods...and when some men of great standing, councillors of the king, feigning to be his friends and zealous for the peace and honour of the Church, tried to persuade him to seek the good will of the king, he refused to go against his conscience...The king's ministers planned an act of exceptional cruelty, and evil men, famed for their malefactions, seized and barred the priory of Christ Church Canterbury...so that, in complete innocence and for no reasonable cause, the highest church of the land was reduced to a state of poverty and of scandalous desolation greater than that of any other church.' At length, the biographer tells us, king and archbishop were reconciled (July 1297), but, after a short time, through the work of the devil, the king's mind was again inflamed with great hatred and hostility against the archbishop, whom he considered to be his manifest enemy and whose suspension from office he achieved by petitioning the pope. The archbishop, protesting his innocence, suffered the suspension and citation to the pope's presence with reverence, but at the papal curia he suffered a grave illness and for a long time lost the use of his limbs. When he returned to England he was strong in spirit, though weak in body, and he continued his work of reprimanding the king (now Edward II) in his parliaments and councils, for the abuses of his power, and urged the king to desist

104 *Anglia Sacra*, I. 12.

from wrongdoing and from the oppression of the people. Such, in brief, is the tenor of the first biography of the archbishop. This view of the archbishop's life no doubt commanded very wide respect among churchmen. How far it was a justifiable assessment can only be determined after the evidence has been surveyed afresh. But the first biographer certainly mapped out a route which all must follow: we cannot avoid concentration upon the learning and devotion to the Church of Robert Winchelsey, and the events of 1297 and the suspension of 1306–8 are without question the focal points of interest in the story of his relations with the Crown.

To judge from the multitude of manuscript copies of constitutions ascribed to Winchelsey concerning stipendiary priests, church ornaments and tithes,[105] it was upon these that Winchelsey's fame during the later middle ages rested. The inference would be wrong. The constitutions were copied and re-copied with others on the same topics irrespective of author because they provided practical rules for administrators. They do indeed reflect the archbishop's concern for the organisation of the English Church and its financial structure at the parochial level. But his work in this field did not fire the interest of contemporary chroniclers, nor of the fourteenth-century biographer. The next biographer was John Joscelyn, secretary to Archbishop Parker, in the sixteenth century.[106] Compiling the *De Antiquitate* Joscelyn put together material concerning Winchelsey from a number of chronicles, including *Flores Historiarum*, and the histories of Walter of Guisborough, Adam Murimuth and William Thorne, and also the fourteenth-century 'life' in a copy apparently bearing the name of Stephen Birchington.[107] Joscelyn followed his sources closely, adding some documentary evidence, as, for example, the bull of Clement V of 22 January 1308 revoking any papal commission already made for the crowning of Edward II,[108] and on the whole he avoided major errors of chronology or detail. Although he

105 See Cheney, 'So-called statutes of Pecham and Winchelsey' and *Councils*, pp. 1382–93.
106 Parker, *De Antiquitate*, pt ii. 207–23. For authorship see M. McKisack, *Medieval History in the Tudor Age* (Oxford, 1971), pp. 47–8.
107 Above, p. 27 n. 101.
108 Parker, *De Antiquitate*, pt ii. 219 and below, p. 246 n. 276.

brought together a good deal of miscellaneous material, Joscelyn was interested, above all, in the political allegiances of the archbishop. To the fourteenth-century Canterbury monk, still reflecting views that were current in Winchelsey's own age, there had been little difficulty in interpreting the evidence: the archbishop's devotion could be readily understood as both to the Church and to the kingdom. But for the post-Reformation author it was impossible to ignore the supposedly erroneous obedience of pre-Reformation churchmen to the pope and the corresponding failure to obey kings 'to whom they were subject by divine and human law'. Contumacy, Joscelyn wrote, was at that earlier time called constancy and the liberty of the Church. His bias is thus of interest only for the study of the sixteenth century.

The less detailed account of Winchelsey's archiepiscopate in Godwin's *De Praesulibus*, first published in 1601 in English,[109] avoided the temptation of making broad political judgments, but here the story of the archbishop's career has become a little more garbled. Godwin noted that Winchelsey was charged with treason by Edward I for plotting to deprive the king of his kingdom in favour of his son. This unsubstantiated statement is derived directly from Thorne's chronicle[110] and had been repeated too in Parker's *De Antiquitate*. Godwin has added his own comment: the archbishop pleaded for mercy more passionately than became a guiltless man. The whole passage in *De Praesulibus* was embellished more than three centuries later in the remarkably trivial and absurdly unhistorical biography by Dean Hook published in 1865.[111] The 'lives' of the archbishop had certainly not improved over the centuries. Indeed, the best was still the earliest. Yet there was soon a sudden change. Stubbs's *Constitutional History*, first published in 1866, revealed the political and constitutional importance of Winchelsey's opposition to the Crown; and in 1882, in his introduction to the first volume of *Chronicles of Edward I and Edward II*, Stubbs provided a perceptive summary of the archbishop's relations with Edward I.[112] However brief, this has

[109] Godwin, *Bishops*, pp. 79–83.
[110] Thorne, p. 387.
[111] W. F. Hook, *Lives of the Archbishops of Canterbury*, III (London, 1865), 368–454.
[112] *Chronicles Edward I & II*, I. ci–cxii.

remained the best account of Winchelsey's political career. The biography by Tout, printed in 1900 in the *Dictionary of National Biography*, is more detailed but less interpretative; at the other extreme, the interpretation of the evidence by Capes in 1903,[113] although interesting, is a somewhat wild defence of Edward I. Naturally there is much to debate, and much to correct, in Stubbs, Tout and Capes, but the foundations were being laid for all further work on the archbishop's career. The present study is, of course, greatly indebted to the many and varied endeavours of historians since that time, but only one historian, Rose Graham, has shown a concentrated interest in Winchelsey, an interest which stemmed from the long and painstaking task of editing his register. Even so, and despite the new account of Winchelsey's life in her introduction to the register,[114] Rose Graham attempted not so much a 'life' of the archbishop as the elucidation of specific subjects suggested by the letters in the register.

Capes questioned the statesmanship and patriotism of Winchelsey, regarding him as a misguided 'partisan of papal policy' and a man of 'resolute and uncompromising self-assertion'. It is a view that has been echoed in a recent study of Edward I's reign.[115] But the scholarship of the twentieth century has for the most part moved in a contrary direction. Intensive work on the organisation and administration of the English Church has placed on a high pedestal the aims and aspirations of thirteenth-century churchmen.[116] Rose Graham's account of Winchelsey's career follows this trend. We are rarely allowed to doubt that the protection of clerical rights was intrinsically noble and just. Naturally this was the predominant opinion of the clergy of the age, including the men of learning and the chroniclers, and their point of view has deserved careful examination. But the clergy's defence of their rights often meant opposition to the Crown. Are we to be drawn into giving approval to that opposition? As the histories of Henry

---

113 W. W. Capes, *The English Church in the Fourteenth and Fifteenth Centuries* (London, 1903), pp. 26–44.
114 *Reg.*, I. v–xxxiv.
115 Prestwich, *War, Politics and Finance*, pp. 258–9.
116 See, for example, Hill, *Oliver Sutton*; and for Winchelsey's work as administrator of the diocese and province of Canterbury see esp. Churchill, *Canterbury Admin.*, passim.

II's conflict with Becket have so often shown, the habit of taking sides tends to decrease rather than to enhance our understanding of the contemporary issues and problems. A cool and balanced assessment was not at all the aim of the committed fourteenth-century biographer. Given his assumptions and beliefs concerning the English Church he was on firm ground in providing an appraisal of the archbishop. The present biographer, with his dispassionate intentions, cannot fail to falter.

Chapter 2

EPISCOPAL COLLEAGUES

It was very largely Winchelsey's achievements as a man of learning that led to his appointment to high office in the Church. At Oxford he had been one of a group of eminent secular masters which included three future bishops: John of Monmouth (bishop of Llandaff 1297–1323), Simon of Ghent (bishop of Salisbury 1297–1315) and John Dalderby (bishop of Lincoln 1300–20); and another scholar, probably known to the group, was a secular master at Cambridge: Ralph Walpole (bishop of Norwich 1289–99, and bishop of Ely 1299–1302).[1] There is no evidence of a close relationship at any stage in their careers between Dalderby and Winchelsey, though more would be known of Dalderby's episcopate if his registers were in print. Walpole gave moderate support to the archbishop during the critical year of 1297. But both Monmouth and Ghent were strong supporters of Winchelsey during that year, and with both these bishops Winchelsey formed lasting friendships. Simon had acted as responding bachelor at Winchelsey's inception as a regent-master; and Winchelsey had presided at the vesperies of John of Monmouth. Both Simon and John succeeded Winchelsey as chancellors of the university of Oxford. The appointment of John to the see of Llandaff, which

[1] Little and Pelster, *Oxford Theologians*, pp. 4, 69, 115–16, 131, 138–42, 179, *Snappe's Formulary*, pp. 46–9, 323–4, and Emden, *Cambridge*, s.v. Walpole. For the careers of bishops see esp. *DNB* and Emden, *Oxford*. The bishops of Henry III's reign are assessed in Gibbs and Lang, *Bishops and Reform*, and of Edward II's reign in W. E. L. Smith, *Episcopal Appointments*. For many bishops whose careers overlap the reigns of Edward I and Edward II see K. Edwards, 'Social origins and provenance of bishops', 'Bishops and learning' and 'Political importance of bishops'. There is a brief account of royal and papal influence in elections during the thirteenth century in A. H. Sweet, 'The control of English episcopal elections in the thirteenth century', *Catholic Historical Review*, new ser. VI (1926–7), 573–82. I have benefited also from the use of A. P. Champley, 'The Appointment of Bishops in England during the Reign of Edward I' (Manchester B.A. thesis, 1972).

had been vacant since 1287, was, unusually, the sole responsibility of the archbishop. Immediately after his consecration in 1294 Winchelsey sought to remedy the difficult situation concerning the see of Llandaff, and Celestine V granted him the authority to collate the bishopric.[2] We can hardly be surprised at Winchelsey's choice of a secular clerk and a doctor of theology; and John of Monmouth appears to have been a wise choice, for, although born in England, he had lived for a long time in Wales, could speak the Welsh language and was known and loved by the people.[3] In 1295 Simon of Ghent obtained an important position on the road towards his election, two years later, to the bishopric of Salisbury: Winchelsey appointed him to a prebend in the cathedral church of Salisbury in accordance with a papal grant authorising the archbishop to collate a prebend in each of the cathedral churches and secular colleges of his province.[4] There is no mistaking the kind of training that Winchelsey preferred for those in high office in the Church.

As a man of learning Winchelsey followed in the tradition of his predecessors, Archbishop Kilwardby, Dominican, and Archbishop Pecham, Franciscan. But Winchelsey was a secular clerk, as were the great majority of his contemporary bishops (28 out of 34 bishops of the Canterbury province between 1295 and 1313). During his term of office only one English bishop was a friar: William Gainsborough, bishop of Worcester, 1302–7, Franciscan, appointed, like Kilwardby and Pecham, by the pope.[5] Four monastic cathedrals had monk-bishops: Robert Orford and John Ketton, bishops of Ely 1302–10 and 1310–16; John Salmon,

[2] Douie, *Pecham*, pp. 269–70, *Reg.*, pp. 5–11, 513–14, *Councils and Eccles. Documents*, ed. Haddan and Stubbs, i. 610–12, and M. Altschul, *A Baronial Family in Medieval England: the Clares 1217–1314* (Baltimore, 1965), pp. 274–5. Also see W. Greenway, 'The election of John of Monmouth, bishop of Llandaff, 1287–97', *Morgannwg: Transactions of the Glamorgan Local History Society*, v (1961), 3–22.
[3] *Reg.*, p. 514. Delay before the restoration of temporalities and the ceremony of consecration was caused by further conflict with Gilbert of Clare, earl of Gloucester and Hertford, and by Boniface VIII's revocation of all the acts of his predecessor.
[4] *Reg.*, pp. 31–2 and see pp. 22, 38. In 1295 Ghent acted as Winchelsey's representative in the dispute with the earl of Gloucester concerning the temporalities of the bishopric of Llandaff: *CPR 1292–1301*, p. 152.
[5] For the disputed election at Worcester in 1302 see esp. *Worcester Sede Vacante Register*, pt i, intro. pp. v–vii.

bishop of Norwich 1299–1325; Thomas Wouldham, bishop of Rochester 1292–1317; and Henry Woodlock, bishop of Winchester 1305–16.

Very few bishops in England at this time came from a high aristocratic background. Two of Winchelsey's early colleagues were sons of successive earls of Salisbury: Nicholas Longespee, bishop of Salisbury, who died in 1297 and Roger Longespee, bishop of Coventry and Lichfield, who died late in 1295.[6] Although some bishops were of very humble origin, most were from the middle ranks of society, either from the families of knights and lesser magnates or, as probably was Winchelsey, from the families of town-dwellers. The archbishop thus found among his episcopal colleagues many men of a similar background and a similar training in the schools and in the working of the dioceses. The fact that he had much in common with many of his colleagues was probably one of the reasons for the success of this strong-willed archbishop in establishing a unity of direction over the southern province of the English Church, though this success certainly does not imply a unanimity of political outlook among the bishops.

A majority of Winchelsey's episcopal colleagues were university-trained, that is, at least 22 out of 34. Since a background of learning was a distinctive feature of the English episcopate, and had been a characteristic of so many archbishops of Canterbury throughout the thirteenth century,[7] those of Winchelsey's colleagues who were not university-trained stand out from the rest. They are divided into two separate groups. The first comprises the five monk-bishops, for, rather surprisingly, there appears to be no evidence that any one of them studied at a university. Although these Benedictines were in no way isolated from politics, as can be seen from the careers of John Salmon and Henry Woodlock,[8] yet they were all local men and they involved themselves relatively little in affairs outside their dioceses. In these two respects they were certainly distinct from the royal clerks who form the second

---

[6] A. R. Malden, 'The will of Nicholas Longespee, bishop of Salisbury', *EHR*, xv (1900), 524 and Gibbs and Lang, *Bishops and Reform*, p. 190.

[7] See T. H. Aston, 'Oxford's medieval alumni', *Past & Present*, LXXIV (1977), 27–8. For a comparison with Italian bishops see Brentano, *Two Churches*, pp. 210–13.

[8] K. Edwards, 'Political importance of bishops', pp. 313, 317, 320, 322–3.

group of bishops with no scholastic training. A large number of bishops served the Crown in one capacity or another at some time during their careers, but four of Winchelsey's colleagues were pre-eminently curialist bishops, following in the footsteps of Edward I's great chancellor, the bishop of Bath and Wells, Robert Burnell. They were men who owed their promotion to service in the king's government, in which they held the highest offices: Walter Langton, keeper of the king's wardrobe 1290–95, royal treasurer 1295–1307 and 1312, bishop of Coventry and Lichfield 1296–1321;[9] John Langton, royal chancellor 1292–1302 and 1307–10, bishop of Chichester 1305–37;[10] John Droxford, acting treasurer in 1295, keeper of the king's wardrobe 1295–1309, bishop of Bath and Wells 1309–29; and Walter Reynolds, keeper of the wardrobe of Prince Edward 1301–7, royal treasurer 1307–10, chancellor 1310–14, bishop of Worcester 1308–13 and archbishop of Canterbury 1313–27. The promotion of Reynolds in 1313 as Winchelsey's successor was a major turning-point: it marked the triumph of the *curiales* over the men of learning who believed, above all, in the defence of ecclesiastical rights.[11]

But are we right to assume that, as for the episcopate during the reign of Henry III, there was an almost unbridgeable gulf concerning relations with the Crown between the 'courtier' bishops and the learned bishops? Marion Gibbs drew the distinction very clearly. Of the *curialis* she wrote: 'A prelate who had attained his position through being privy to the abuses of pluralities, non-residence, and royal intrusion into benefices . . . would consider the advantages and certainly not the iniquity and evil effects of the system; for, untrained in theology, his only criteria in judging ecclesiastical problems would be expediency and custom.' But in the *magistri* appointed to bishoprics after Henry III's minority she saw an opposite political outlook: they 'never held secular offices after their appointment, but on the contrary were, when there

---

[9] The papal nuncios, the bishops of Albano and Palestrina, referred to Walter Langton as *magister* in error: see *Literae Cantuar.*, I. 22 and Cant. D. & C., Eastry Correspondence v, no. 21 .

[10] Despite indications of links with Oxford and Cambridge (see ref. in Little and Pelster, *Oxford Theologians*, p. 280), there appears to be no conclusive evidence that he studied at either university: cf. Emden, *Oxford*.

[11] Denton, 'Canterbury appointments: the case of Reynolds'.

is evidence, in opposition to the Crown: perhaps supporting Grosseteste in protesting against secular encroachments on the *privilegium fori*, or methods of lay taxation of spiritualities, or insisting that the king should abide by the articles of *Magna Carta* and act by the advice of "natural counsellors"....'. She did, however, admit qualifications to her argument: 'both by reflecting that some *magistri*, as bishops, were little noteworthy in their day, and by a consideration of the valuable work done by a minority of the *curiales*'.[12]

The need to make qualifications has in some ways increased by the end of the century. Partly because of the generally firm control over the English Church by Edward I and the effects of the continuing failure of the 'reforming' party among the clergy to secure redress of grievances, it is clear that many bishops were men of compromise. Between *magister* and *curialis* the lines are certainly very often blurred. As later during the reigns of Edward II and Edward III[13] there were many graduates who served in royal government, among the most important being Master William of Louth (keeper of the king's wardrobe 1280–90, dean of St Martin-le-Grand 1283–90, bishop of Ely 1290–8), Master William of March (royal treasurer 1290–5, dean of St Martin-le-Grand 1290–c.1294, bishop of Bath and Wells 1293–1302), Master Ralph Baldock (briefly royal chancellor in 1307, bishop of London 1306–8), and Walter Stapledon (master of arts and doctor of canon and civil law, royal treasurer 1320–5, bishop of Exeter 1308–26). It would be unwise to assume that the fact that these men held high office as servants of the Crown set them apart from other bishops in most matters of ecclesiastical government and administration, and the group includes men of resourcefulness and independence, like William of March, and notably Walter Stapledon. It is interesting that where episcopal registers of the *curiales* survive (as for Stapledon, Droxford and Reynolds), they provide evidence of the granting of quite large numbers of licences to rectors for study, in accordance with Boniface VIII's constitution 'Cum ex eo' (1298).[14] Undoubtedly we must take care not to create

---

[12] Gibbs and Lang, *Bishops and Reform*, pp. 23–4, 48–9, 50.
[13] Highfield, 'The English hierarchy', p. 117.
[14] Boyle, 'The constitution "Cum ex eo"', p. 297, and see Lichfield Joint

the impression of a firm division between the royal and the non-royal bishops, the unlettered and the lettered, with each side supposedly holding different views upon most issues of concern to the English clergy.[15] There was no 'party' system, and the curialist bishops rarely seem to form a distinct group in themselves.

Yet, the matter of the legal and constitutional relationship of the clergy to the Crown continued to be of central political importance for the English bishops, and on this critical question we can discern an unmistakable and deep-seated division of opinion and of policy within the episcopate. It is a striking fact that it was those bishops (Walter Langton, Droxford and Reynolds) whose careers were linked most closely to royal government, even if they were not always in royal favour, who were the men with no university training. They were open to the damaging, if distorted, charge of being *illiterati* in an age when literacy and clerical status were bound inextricably together. At the other extreme, those bishops (Ghent, Monmouth, Walpole, Dalderby and Winchelsey) who avoided all service of the Crown, except very occasionally, for example as diplomatic envoys, were not simply masters of arts but theologians of known distinction. Another doctor of theology, Richard Swinfield, bishop of Hereford 1283–1317, must be included in this group, though he was a less prominent figure, perhaps because of ill-health. The devout and learned diocesan Oliver Sutton, bishop of Lincoln 1280–99, must be included too, for he had spent many years at Oxford as a regent-master in arts, had studied canon and civil law and, when he left Oxford to become dean of Lincoln in 1275 (at about the same time that Winchelsey became a canon of Lincoln), he was preparing to become a master in theology.[16] The political division within the

Record Office, Reg. W. Langton, which, Mr P. Gaskell informs me, contains over 160 licences for study. R. M. Haines argues for a distinction of viewpoint between the secular clerks and the monk-bishops, rather than between the academic and the non-academic bishops, concerning the use of benefice income for non-resident students: 'The education of the English clergy', pp. 8–9. The number of licences in Henry Woodlock's register (see Boyle, p. 297) in fact suggests otherwise, but with the exception of John Salmon's register of institutions, Woodcock's is the only extant register of Winchelsey's monk-bishops.

[15] See Highfield, 'The English hierarchy', esp. pp. 115–16.
[16] Hill, *Oliver Sutton*, pp. 3–4, and see Brentano, *Two Churches*, pp. 177–80.

episcopate is especially apparent during the crisis with the Crown in 1297, when Ghent, Monmouth and Sutton were the bishops who gave firmest support to Winchelsey and those who gave no support at all were the curialist bishops. It is probably no co-incidence that Simon of Ghent's register shows him to have been unusually concerned to grant licences of study to rectors and particularly careful in the appointment of 'curates' to serve churches during the absence of rectors.[17] The most learned bishops, and the bishops most concerned about learning, stood in the tradition of Robert Grosseteste and, through a devotion to cure of souls, believed in fighting for the privileged status of the clergy and in eschewing involvement in secular government.[18]

The number of royal servants who obtained bishoprics increased significantly after 1313.[19] This is not to imply that Edward I and Edward II had been notably unsuccessful during Winchelsey's archiepiscopate in securing the appointment of men of their own choosing. In addition to the important curialists in southern sees noted above, two royal servants became archbishops of York: Henry Newark (1296–9) and William Greenfield (1306–15). But we must not assume that a deep political, even less, anti-clerical, significance lies behind every example of support given by the Crown to a particular candidate,[20] and it is clear that there were in any case severe limits to the capacity of the Crown to control appointments. There are few signs, for example, of deliberate with-holding of temporalities from bishops-elect,[21] notwithstanding the importance to the king of the revenues of vacant bishoprics.[22] The accepted procedure for episcopal elections rarely admitted of

17 C. J. Godfrey, 'Non-residence of parochial clergy in the fourteenth century', *Church Quarterly Review*, CLXII (1961), 434–5, 440, 444 and Boyle, 'The constitution "Cum ex eo"', pp. 284–5, 298; and see Pantin, *English Church in Fourteenth Century*, pp. 111–13.
18 See Pantin, 'Grosseteste's relations with papacy and crown', pp. 178–208 and Gibbs and Lang, *Bishops and Reform*, pp. 164–7.
19 W. E. L. Smith, *Episcopal Appointments*, pp. 20–49 and Pantin, *English Church in Fourteenth Century*, pp. 9–18.
20 See, for example, W. Greenway, 'The election of David Martin, bishop of St David's 1293–6', *Journal of the Hist. Soc. of the Church of Wales*, x (1960), 9–16.
21 But see Graham, 'Administration of Ely during vacancies', pp. 52–60 and *Councils*, pp. 1206–7; for instances in 1323 and 1326 see W. E. L. Smith, *Episcopal Appointments*, pp. 27, 45.
22 Howell, *Regalian Right*, pp. 159–64, 240–3.

anything more decisively and openly coercive than advice and persuasion. Of course, for various reasons it might well be difficult to resist royal persuasion. Yet there was resistance. The king's clerk Boniface of Saluzzo, for instance, failed to gain election at Ely in 1310.[23] The most notable instances in Edward I's reign of the king's failure to gain the appointment of his candidate concerned the king's chancellor, Robert Burnell, for he was successfully opposed at Canterbury in 1270, and, following appeals to the pope, at Canterbury again in 1278 and also at Winchester in 1280.[24] The efforts to secure the promotion of Burnell from the bishopric of Bath and Wells illustrate how important it was to the king, not simply to have key supporters on the episcopal bench, but also, if possible, to be able to promote them to noteworthy and wealthy sees. Winchester and Canterbury were very much more wealthy than Bath and Wells.[25] In his relations with the English Church the king's hand was greatly strengthened if his chancellor, of all his ministers, held high episcopal office.

After Burnell's death in 1292 John Langton became chancellor of the realm and remained in office until 1302. During Winchelsey's first years as archbishop the only prominent royal servant to obtain a bishopric was the king's treasurer, Walter Langton. But when Ely became vacant in 1298 every effort was made by the king to secure the election of John Langton to this see. Ely was an extremely wealthy bishopric, according to the 1291 assessment inferior only to Winchester, and it had been held in recent years by two very prominent royal clerks: John of Kirkby (1286–90) and William of Louth (1290–8). The disputed election at Ely in 1298–9 was a *cause célèbre*, and there can be no doubt whatever that the king adopted all possible means to obtain his chancellor's appointment and very little doubt that Winchelsey was strongly opposed to it. There was to be another vacancy at Ely in 1302 and on this occasion Winchelsey opposed the monk elected as

[23] W. E. L. Smith, *Episcopal Appointments*, p. 15.
[24] Denton, 'Canterbury appointments: the case of Reynolds', p. 319, Douie, *Pecham*, pp. 47–8, 106 and A. J. Cosgrove, 'The elections to the bishopric of Winchester, 1280–2' in *Studies in Church History*, III, ed. G. J. Cuming (Leiden, 1966), 169–78.
[25] Stubbs, *Constitutional Hist.*, II, last column of table facing p. 580, and see *English Historical Documents: IV 1327–1485*, ed. A. R. Myers (London, 1969), p. 725.

bishop, Robert Orford, on grounds of insufficient learning. The two disputed Ely elections illustrate forcibly the different, and at times divergent, aims of Crown and archbishop, the one supporting royal clerks and the other eager for a learned episcopate. Boniface VIII overrode the king on the one occasion and the archbishop on the other;[26] and John Langton obtained his bishopric (Chichester 1305–37) when he was no longer Edward I's chancellor.

The extant sources are generally inadequate for an analysis of Winchelsey's personal relations with individual bishops; but it comes as no surprise that the evidence points towards close ties of friendship between Winchelsey and the two scholar-bishops Simon of Ghent and John of Monmouth. Ghent did not model himself entirely upon Winchelsey: he acted as a royal envoy in the negotiations with France in 1299, and in 1309 it was clearly with difficulty that he was persuaded not to oppose the archbishop's renewed claim to prerogative jurisdiction for the probate of wills of those with possessions in more than one diocese.[27] But the bishop of Salisbury was, nonetheless, a firm adherent of his archbishop. In his diocese he appears to have been particularly eager to take action against non-resident and pluralist clergy, and against incumbents who had not been ordained within a year of presentation to their benefices, and this resulted in conflict with at least one royal clerk.[28] When the archbishop consulted him in 1309 concerning the pope's revocation of Gaveston's excommunication he replied that he would give his support to whatever the archbishop decided on the matter.[29] He was commissioned to act for the archbishop in 1307. In 1311 he deputised for Winchelsey on three occasions: first, as one of the ordainer-bishops, to obtain the consent to the Ordinances of those members of the clergy who were present in London for a session of parliament; secondly, to publish the Ordinances, for the first time, on 27 September in St Paul's churchyard; and thirdly, to act as one of the archbishop's

---

26 For details see Graham, 'Administration of Ely during vacancies'; and for the first dispute see also PRO E159/72 mm. 16–17d, 21d, 32d, 59, 69d.

27 *Reg. Gandavo*, pp. x, 294–6, 318–20 and Lambeth Palace Lib., MS 244, fo. 100.

28 *Reg. Gandavo*, pp. 44–5, 60–2, 84–6 and *Cal. Chanc. Warr.*, I. 161.

29 *Reg. Gandavo*, pp. 316–17.

commissaries in the December parliament.[30] There can be no doubt that there was a bond of friendship and trust between the two prelates. Michael de Berham, Winchelsey's chancellor, assured Ghent that the archbishop held him above all others in deep and sincere affection; and Ghent himself wrote at Winchelsey's death that he grieved the more because he had enjoyed the privilege of the archbishop's close affection.[31]

Winchelsey's relations with John of Monmouth are not quite so well documented. But the bishop of Llandaff supported the archbishop in 1297, and Winchelsey did not lose confidence in him, for during the last four months of his life Monmouth acted as his vicar-general, even to the extent of undertaking a short but extensive visitation of the diocese of Canterbury. It was Monmouth who officiated at Winchelsey's funeral, and, alone among the bishops, perhaps because of his services as vicar-general, he was remembered in Winchelsey's will and received a hundred marks and a precious ring.[32]

But Winchelsey may have had a closer friend among the English prelates than either Ghent or Monmouth. Anthony Bek, bishop of Durham, had a long and very active career as a royal clerk and was not at all the kind of bishop with whom Winchelsey might have been expected to form a lasting friendship. Yet there can be no doubt about the bond that existed between the two men. Although Bek had only a short and undistinguished career at Oxford it was possibly there that he first made the acquaintance of Winchelsey.[33] Winchelsey's letters to the bishop, addressing him as 'amico precordialissimo', 'amico confidentissimo', or 'amico pre ceteris confidenti', strike a more personal note than any other letters from the archbishop.[34] In January 1298, for example, he describes his state of health to Bek.[35] Their high

---

[30] *Reg. Stapeldon*, pp. 18–19, *Reg. Gandavo*, pp. 391, 417–18, K. Edwards, 'Political importance of bishops', p. 321 n. 6 and Davies, *Baronial Opposition*, pp. 366–7.

[31] *Reg. Gandavo*, pp. 320, 451.

[32] Above, p. 15 and *Reg.*, pp. 1338–40, 1342.

[33] Emden, *Oxford*, pp. 151–2.

[34] Before his consecration Winchelsey on at least one occasion (*Reg.*, p. 1285) referred to Henry of Eastry, prior of Christ Church Canterbury, as 'amico suo precordiali', but never repeated this style after he became archbishop.

[35] *Reg.*, p. 218.

regard for each other is illustrated by Bek's offer of an escort for the archbishop through the diocese of Durham in 1300, and by Winchelsey's concern that there should be no bitterness between Bek and the archbishop's proctor at Rome, Reginald of St Albans.[36] The relationship was of political importance. The bishop of Durham acted for both king and archbishop as arbiter and mediator. In October 1295 he was appointed to arbitrate for the king in the dispute between Winchelsey and the earl of Gloucester concerning the temporalities of the diocese of Llandaff.[37] On many occasions Winchelsey required Bek to use his influence with the king and with the king's council: in 1296 to prevent the council from recommending that the archbishop be sent to France to take part in the negotiations for peace: in 1298 to secure justice for the barons of the Cinque Ports; and in 1299 both to assist the bishop of Chichester in his business with the king and to achieve a just restoration of the Meinill lands to the custody of the archbishop.[38] In return Winchelsey showed particular concern for the interests of Bek, pleading for him when it was rumoured that he had oppressed his clergy by urging them to buy royal protection in 1297, and at his request granting a year's absence to the rector of Hothfield and forestalling the sequestration of the fruits of Foulden belonging to John of Sheffield.[39] Bek clearly gave some support to Winchelsey during his clash with the king in 1297 and after.[40] There can be little question that the archbishop's position during the closing years of Edward I's reign was much the weaker because of Bek's disfavour with the king at this time. It seems significant that Winchelsey had chosen as perhaps his closest associate and adviser a prelate from outside the province of Canterbury and a prelate who, although he held no high office of state, was frequently to be found at the centre of political affairs.

It is greatly to Winchelsey's credit that it is impossible to find any direct evidence that the important political division between himself and the curialist bishops was at the heart of any of the jurisdictional disputes with his suffragans, even though, as we

[36] Fraser, *Bek*, pp. 146–7 and *Reg.*, pp. 284–5.
[37] *CPR 1292–1301*, p. 152 and *Reg.*, p. 741.
[38] *Reg.*, pp. 126, 290, 693–4.
[39] *Councils*, p. 1108 and *Reg.*, pp. 76, 256, 537, 806.
[40] Below, pp. 161, 235.

shall see, these disputes were for the most part with bishops who were closely associated with royal government. He did not deliberately promote factionalism and he believed firmly in the need, whenever possible, of a united clergy. But this belief was combined with a determination to defend his metropolitical rights, which led him into a number of disputes with individual bishops. His authority over his bishops is seen at its most effective when he was on visitation. Over a third of the articles of inquiry which he designed for his use on visitation concerned the work of the bishop whose diocese was under examination, and his visitation articles provide an impressive indication of the extreme care with which he fulfilled his metropolitical duties.[41] As an example of his thoroughness, thirty-six charges were made against Godfrey Giffard, bishop of Worcester, after Winchelsey had visited the Worcester diocese in 1301.[42] Following the completion of his first visitation of his own diocese, he began the visitation of the diocese of Rochester on 2 March 1299, and out of the next seven years Winchelsey spent a total of two and a half years visiting six dioceses, an average of five months for each.[43] They were long and painstaking perambulations, with every part of each diocese covered. The pioneering Boniface of Savoy had visited four dioceses in one year, 1253, and Pecham had visited nine in the course of 1283 and 1284.[44] Winchelsey's failure to visit more than a total of six dioceses must be seen in relation to the extremely elaborate nature of his visitation procedures. Also, after his suspension (1306–8) he was too ill to travel extensively. His close scrutiny of six dioceses illustrates the firmness of purpose that governed every aspect of Winchelsey's administration of his Church.

---

[41] *Reg.*, pp. 1290–6, and for a study of Winchelsey's visitations, diocesan and metropolitical, see J. H. Denton, 'The Career of Robert Winchelsey' (Cambridge Ph.D. Thesis, 1966), pp. 275–98. Churchill (*Canterbury Admin.*, I. 156–8) found no evidence that Winchelsey ever claimed the authority of a 'legatus natus': but see *Reg. Gandavo*, pp. 262–3 and *Reg. Boniface VIII*, II. 627.

[42] Thomas, *Survey of Worcester*, app. pp. 63–73. See Graham, 'Metropolitical visitation of Worcester'.

[43] Rochester (2 Mar.–c. 29 June 1299); Chichester (12 Dec. 1299–c. 23 May 1300); Worcester (14 Mar.–28 July 1301); London (19 Feb.–2 Aug. 1303); Norwich (26 Feb.–31 July 1304); Winchester, *sede vacante* (7 Jan.–8 Feb. 1305), *sede plena* (8 Nov. 1305–26 Feb. 1306).

[44] Churchill, *Canterbury Admin.*, II. 148.

The archbishop's disputes with individual bishops on juris-dictional issues deserve attention. It is important to note from the first that only one of these disputes was with a bishop from the learned group with whom he had a special affinity. There were no open disputes with Ghent, Monmouth, Swinfield, Sutton or Walpole. Nor did the archbishop visit the dioceses of these bishops. When he visited Norwich Walpole was no longer bishop. The one exception is the dispute between Winchelsey and John Dalderby, who succeeded Sutton as bishop of Lincoln, concerning the diffi-cult problem of the administration of the wills of those with churches or with property in several dioceses. The case principally concerned the will of Hugh Bardolf, a tenant-in-chief who had died in 1304 and whose estates had been spread throughout thirteen counties;[45] but at the same time another case was in dispute concerning the will of Thomas of Adderbury.[46] Pecham had asserted as an established right the prerogative of the arch-bishop to administer such wills and had been involved in disputes on this matter with Oliver Sutton and Thomas Cantilupe (bishop of Hereford 1275–82).[47] Although it seems clear that Pecham had asserted the right with considerable success, it must not be thought that either he or Winchelsey established the practice of supervising the execution of all the wills of those with goods in several dioceses; but both claimed the right to exercise the privilege at their own discretion. It was this claim which Dalderby opposed, not in order to protect the rights of all the suffragan bishops but rather to defend his specific claims as bishop of Lincoln. The dispute, which involved the bishop in appeals to the pope, began in 1308–9 and continued after Winchelsey's death.[48] Eventually, in 1319, Arch-bishop Reynolds and Dalderby came to an amicable settlement,

---

[45] See *Cal. Inq. P.M.*, IV, no. 236, *CFR*, I. 497 and *CCR 1302–7*, pp. 329, 440–1.
[46] Lambeth Palace Lib., MS 244, fos. 92, 98v, 99r, *Cal. Inq. P.M.*, IV. no. 432, *CFR*, I. 558 and *Reg.*, pp. 1141–4, 1153.
[47] For the early history of the archbishop's prerogative in testamentary matters see Coote, *Practice of Eccles. Courts*, pp. 64–71, Churchill, *Canterbury Admin.*, I. esp. 380–5, Douie, *Pecham*, esp. 210–11, 223–5, Jacob, 'Archbishop's testa-mentary jurisdiction', pp. 35–41, M. M. Sheehan, *The Will in Medieval England* (Toronto, 1963), pp. 200–5 and *Councils*, pp. 765, 824, 1080–1.
[48] *Reg.*, pp. 1131–41, 1144–53, LRO Reg. Dalderby (III), fos. 163, 167r, 179r, 181r, 191v, 194, Lambeth Palace Lib., MS 244, fo. 106v, *Reg. Gandavo*, pp. 334–5, 433–5 and *Reg. Reynolds*, p. 11.

which, although in the form of a compromise, favoured the archbishop's prerogative.[49]

All the other disputes were with episcopal colleagues who spent long periods of their careers in royal service. This is a significant fact, even though the documentary evidence of the wrangles gives us no hint of personal animosities or of factional interests. Although John Salmon, monk-bishop of Norwich, was never in royal service under Edward I, he became an active supporter of Edward II and was royal chancellor from 1320 to 1323.[50] From the time of his visitation of the diocese of Norwich, in 1304, the archbishop firmly opposed Bishop Salmon's claim that he had the right to the annates or first-fruits of churches within his diocese. Following perhaps the lead of a canon of Ottobono's legatine council of 1268 or a constitution in the Sext of 1298, Winchelsey inquired of a bishop whose diocese he was visiting 'whether the bishop received the fruits or part of the proceeds of vacant churches of his diocese and for how long and for what reason and by whose authority'.[51] It was no doubt this particular question that led to the long proceedings against Salmon. Papal grants of first-fruits to bishops and archbishops were a common feature of the thirteenth century,[52] but Salmon had no papal privilege and, as Ottobono's canon and Boniface VIII in the Sext allowed, he claimed the right by ancient custom. Confusion appears to have been caused by the difficulty of distinguishing between intercalary fruits, collected during the actual period of a benefice's vacancy,[53] and first-fruits, essentially the fruits collected after the collation of a benefice. Salmon could not convince Winchelsey that he had a right to first-fruits. He appeared before the archbishop's court of audience repeatedly in

---

[49] See Coote, *Practice of Eccles. Courts*, p. 72n (but the agreement is not in *Reg.*) and H. Bradshaw and C. Wordsworth, *Statutes of Lincoln Cathedral* (Cambridge, 1892), I. 324–5.

[50] See *DNB*, L. 205 and K. Edwards, 'Political importance of bishops', pp. 317, 320; Salmon was in royal service very shortly after Edward II's accession.

[51] *Councils*, p. 765, Sext, I. 16. 9 and *Reg.*, p. 1291. For the early history of annates see esp. Lunt, 'First levy of papal annates', pp. 48–64 and idem, *Financial Relations*, pp. 486–502.

[52] See *Regesta Honorii III*, ed. P. Pressutti (Rome, 1888–95), nos. 2257, 2456 (*CPL*, I. 68–71), *Registres de Nicholas IV*, ed. E. Langlois (1905), no. 1856, *Councils*, p. 445, Powicke, *Henry and Lord Edward*, pp. 361–2, Douie, *Pecham*, pp. 68–9 and *CPL*, I. 484. [53] See *Councils*, pp. 342, 500.

1304 and 1305,[54] and in 1306 left London for the papal curia.[55]

It was a propitious time for Salmon to seek papal support, for Clement V suspended Winchelsey from office a month later. The pope declared in Salmon's favour in August, instructing papal executors, the abbots of Westminster, Bardney and St Augustine's Canterbury, to protect the bishop's 'special custom' if they were satisfied as to its legality.[56] They initiated proceedings to establish the nature of the custom, and in a case heard at Osney in 1307 the archbishop's interests were defended by William Boni, the forceful and persistent proctor of William Testa and Peter Amauvin, administrators of the spiritualities of Canterbury during Winchelsey's suspension. But Boni's detailed and unrestrained attacks upon the practices of Salmon were overruled, and judgment was given in favour of the bishop's case, which was supported by only the slenderest of evidence. Boni appealed to the pope against the judgment, and so did Winchelsey in 1310. There are many indications that the archbishop had by far the stronger case. For example, he gave a full account of the promise which Ralph Walpole (bishop of Norwich 1289–99) had made, at the time of his confirmation, to Archbishop Pecham that he would discontinue the 'evil abuse' of collecting first-fruits. But Salmon's claims prevailed.[57] What political forces were at work, we may wonder, preventing Winchelsey from being able successfully to prosecute his obstructive suffragan bishop?

The problems posed for Winchelsey by another bishop, the eminent royal clerk John of Pontoise (bishop of Winchester 1282–1304), arose not from a legal dispute but from a complete break in relations occasioned by Boniface VIII's grant to the bishop on 26 February 1297 of exemption from the jurisdiction of Canterbury.[58] The exemption applied to the whole of Pontoise's diocese, to all his subjects and to all his possessions and the possessions of his church not only in the diocese of Winchester but throughout the province of Canterbury. In spiritual matters he

[54] Lambeth Palace Lib., MS 244, fo. 63v.
[55] *Reg.*, pp. 678–9, *Annales London.*, p. 144, *CCR 1301–7*, pp. 386, 410, 483, 486, 498.
[56] *Reg.*, pp. 1155–6, as *Reg. Clement V*, no. 1288 (*CPL*, ii. 18).
[57] *Reg.*, pp. 1153–84; and see *Reg. Clement V*, no. 8738 (*CPL*, ii. 104).
[58] For refs. see Denton, *Royal Chapels*, p. 18n, and see *Reg.*, pp. xiv–xv.

was subject directly to the jurisdiction of the pope or his legate *a latere*. This probably meant that the bishop was exempt from attending provincial councils, and exempt from the taxes to which the councils gave their consent; at least there is no record of his summons to, or of his attendance at, any of Winchelsey's councils, and no record of his contribution, or the contribution of his diocese, to the tenth of 1297-8. As for the charitable subsidy granted to the archbishop in 1300, William Thorne, the chronicler of St Augustine's abbey, noted that the bishop 'did not consent to the doings and wishes of those who contributed...to the archbishop Robert'. It is interesting to discover in Thorne's work that Pontoise lent his support to St Augustine's in its struggle with the archbishop.[59]

There can be no doubt that Pontoise had obtained this exemption because of his work for both king and pope. After Winchelsey's first meeting with the bishop early in 1295, there was contention about the patronage of the hospital of St Thomas of Southwark and about a provision to the rectory of Middleton;[60] but whether these cases caused an open rift between Pontoise and Winchelsey it is not clear. Pontoise had often been engaged on missions to the pope, and early in 1296 he left England both to represent Edward in negotiations for peace in France and, as principal collector in England of the 1291 papal tenths, to present the final account to the pope.[61] The bishop was a highly trusted royal diplomat, and direct royal influence may have secured the privilege of exemption; possibly it was intended as a conciliatory gesture by Boniface VIII, granted as it was at the time of Edward's crisis with the English clergy. At all events, it gave some protection to Pontoise and to his diocese during frequent absences from England; until 1303 he was Edward's chief representative in the negotiations for peace with France.[62]

[59] Thorne, pp. 385-6.
[60] Below, p. 81, *Reg. Pontissara*, pp. 196-7, 200-1, 812-17, *CPR 1292-1301*, pp. 135, 146, 148 and PRO E159/68 mm. 40, 43d.
[61] Emden, *Oxford*, pp. 1498-9 and below, p. 89.
[62] He was on royal service in 1297-8 (at Rome), 1299, 1300-1 (at Rome), and 1303: see *CPR 1292-1301*, pp. 312, 329, 415, 508-9, 511, 543, *CPR 1301-7*, pp. 127-8, *CCR 1296-1302*, p. 349, *CCR 1302-7*, p. 81, *Foedera*, I, ii. 887, 903-6, 911-12, 920, 922, 950, 952, 957 and Black, 'Edward and Gascony', pp. 518-27.

After Boniface VIII's death Winchelsey petitioned his successor, Benedict XI, not to confirm the privilege.[63] Benedict apparently came to no decision before his death in July 1304, and the exemption terminated when Pontoise himself died six months later. Winchelsey took immediate action to exercise his metropolitical rights: in January and February 1305 he visited the diocese of Winchester *sede vacante* and only six months after the new bishop, Henry Woodlock, had been consecrated he visited it again *sede plena*. For Winchelsey, a vexatious aspect of the exemption had been the desire of some to follow suit. In July 1298 the archbishop asked William Hothum, archbishop of Dublin, to use his influence at Rome to prevent Walter Langton from gaining the exemption that he was trying to obtain with large gifts of money; and in the following year Winchelsey addressed the pope in very strong terms on this question.[64] Winchelsey pleaded for papal support against the hostile attacks of his adversaries. Langton's failure to gain exemption did not prevent the monks of Ely from planning to obtain the same privilege in 1302, after Winchelsey had refused to confirm their bishop-elect.[65]

Finally, it is scarcely surprising to find evidence of dissension between Winchelsey and Walter Langton, bishop of Coventry and Lichfield, Edward I's treasurer and principal minister from 1295 to the end of the reign.[66] Langton had been a clerk of Robert Burnell and from his early life had been known to Edward I. He became a skilful and extremely successful administrator, a worldly bishop who was ambitious for his family and unscrupulous in his exercise of power. In this bishop, more than in any other, we see the antithesis of what Winchelsey stood for. Langton was a product of the king's wardrobe, a notable pluralist,[67] whose active, indeed tumultuous, career was marked by his outstanding loyalty to the Crown. After his long trial, during the early years of Edward II's reign, for malpractices, he was restored to royal favour and reappointed treasurer in 1312, but this angered the ordainers, in-

[63] *Reg.*, pp. 661–5. [64] *Reg.*, pp. 537, 560–1. [65] *Reg.*, p. 636.
[66] For Langton's career see esp. Beardwood, 'The trial of Langton', pp. 5–10 (and *Records of the Trial of Walter Langton 1307–12*, ed. A. Beardwood (Camden 4th ser. VI, 1969)).
[67] Beardwood, 'The trial of Langton', pp. 8–9 and Thompson, 'Pluralism', pp. 57–9.

cluding Winchelsey, who excommunicated Langton because he would give no assurances in a provincial council concerning his oath to observe the Ordinances of 1311.[68] Winchelsey and Walter Langton were in opposing political camps.

There had been a dispute with Winchelsey very soon after Langton was elected bishop in February 1296. In the course of the thirteenth century the prior and chapter of Canterbury had established the right to decide whether suffragan bishops should be given permission to be consecrated elsewhere than at Canterbury.[69] This privilege had its origin in a spurious charter of St Thomas and a suspect bull of 1228, but it had been confirmed by genuine bulls of 1235 and 1238. Pecham had not shown full respect for this privilege of the chapter of Canterbury, but Winchelsey sought with determination to prevent the consecration of his suffragans at any other place than at Canterbury and by any other person than himself. Langton, whose actions certainly amounted to deliberate defiance of the archbishop, gained the support of the papal nuncios, the bishops of Albano and Palestrina, who were negotiating for peace between France and England, and, although Winchelsey used all his powers to require and persuade Langton, he was overruled by a papal concession to the bishop of Albano to consecrate Langton in France.[70] The archbishop had been, in this instance, adamant to no avail. Langton was consecrated at Cambrai on 23 December 1296.

But the new bishop of Coventry and Lichfield could not avoid the profession of obedience to the see of Canterbury; and, according to the continuator of Gervase of Canterbury,[71] this took place after the bishop's return from France in March and was arranged

---

[68] *Councils*, pp. 1371-2, Denton, 'Canterbury appointments: the case of Reynolds', p. 323 and below, p. 266.

[69] See Churchill, *Canterbury Admin.*, I. 273-5, C. R. Cheney, 'Magna Carta Beati Thome: another Canterbury forgery', *BIHR*, xxxvi (1963), 1-26, and Douie, *Pecham*, pp. 184-5.

[70] See *Literae Cantuar.*, I, 22-4, Cant. D. & C., Eastry Correspondence v, no. 21 (calendared in *Historical MSS Commission: Various Collections* (8 vols., 1901-14), I. 262), CUL Ee. v. 31, fo. 68, *Reg.*, pp. 127-9, 143-4, 522-4 and *Reg. Boniface VIII*, nos. 1186, 1380.

[71] Cont. Gervase, p. 314. 11 June 1297 is an error in *Canterbury Professions*, ed. Richter, pp. 87-8: Langton had been confirmed on 11 June 1296 and had taken an oath of fealty to the king (John of Mettingham acting *vice regis*) immediately afterwards (PRO SCI/27/100).

on a particularly lavish scale, involving a profession, with due ceremony, in the cathedral church itself as well as before the archbishop. First, Langton was led in solemn procession to the priory of Canterbury where he recited his profession of obedience and placed a copy of the same upon the high altar 'as if on that day he had been consecrated there', and then, ten miles away at the archbishop's manor of Teynham, he repeated the profession before Winchelsey. The pope may have prevented Winchelsey from consecrating this royal clerk, but he could not prevent the archbishop from making the most of the rights that remained both to himself and to his cathedral chapter. After this dispute with Langton the archbishop held firm to his policy of insisting upon consecration at Canterbury, except, of course, for those bishops-elect who were consecrated while at Rome because of appeals to the pope concerning their elections. But an exception was made during Winchelsey's suspension. This concerned the bishop-elect of Bangor, Gruffydd ab Iorwerth. After confusion concerning the granting of the licence to be consecrated elsewhere to the bishop-elect of Bangor, and after abortive plans, first for the consecration to take place at Leicester and secondly for it to be performed by none other than Walter Langton, eventually Gruffydd ab Iorwerth was consecrated at Carlisle on 26 March 1307 by Cardinal Peter of Spain.[72] Immediately after Winchelsey's return from suspension Walter Stapledon, bishop-elect of Exeter, tried to gain permission to be consecrated away from Canterbury, apparently along with the bishop-elect of Worcester, Walter Reynolds.[73] They both failed and were consecrated at Canterbury on 13 October 1308.

That Winchelsey and Walter Langton represented fundamentally different political standpoints within the English Church is not in doubt. But it has become an accepted part of the story of the careers of each man to point out that there was a bitter clash between them beginning in 1301. Winchelsey, we are told, demanded Langton's dismissal as treasurer at the Lincoln parlia-

---

[72] Le Neve, *Fasti 1300–1541*, XI. 3, *Reg. Woodlock*, p. 169, LRO Reg. Dalderby (III), fo. 112r, *Literae Cantuar.*, I. 32–3, CUL Ee. v. 31, fo. 106v, *Reg. Greenfield*, v. 65–7, Cant. D. & C., Reg. A, fos. 75v–76r, 251r and Sede Vacante Scrapbook, I. 178.
[73] *Reg. Stapeldon*, pp. 8–12, 16–17.

ment of 1301.[74] In the same year John Lovetot brought a savage case against Langton, accusing him, for example, of adultery, murder and intercourse with the devil. This attack, we learn, was 'really at Winchelsey's instigation'; the archbishop's agents at Rome 'supported the monstrous charges' brought by Lovetot; Winchelsey was 'attempting to strike at the king through Langton'; he showed throughout the case 'a strong animus against the accused'; and Langton's acquittal 'was one more rebuff for the painstaking Archbishop of Canterbury'.[75]

For all this there is a lack of firm justification. While there is no reason to discredit Langtoft's account of an attempt to remove Langton at the Lincoln parliament, yet there is no mention of Winchelsey in this account.[76] As for the Lovetot scandal Stubbs in his introduction to the *Chronicles of Edward I and Edward II* misunderstood the letters relating to the case, though elsewhere he admitted that 'there is nothing to show positively' whether Winchelsey had any share in the attack.[77] There are no grounds for disbelieving the archbishop when he reported to the pope in June 1301 that, until he had received a papal mandate issued in February, he knew nothing of the charges being made against the bishop of Coventry and Lichfield.[78] Far from being Langton's chief opponent it was he who secured his absolution and return to England. The responsibility for a full inquiry into the allegations against the treasurer was given to Winchelsey and Thomas Jorz, provincial prior of the Dominicans in England, and they completely cleared Langton's name. Letters from the king in support of Langton are to be expected; but John Dalderby, bishop of

[74] T. F. Tout in *DNB*, XXXII. 130a and LXII. 159a, H. Johnstone in *Cambridge Medieval History*, VII (Cambridge, 1932), 412, *Reg.*, p. xv, Powicke, *Thirteenth Century*, p. 718 and Emden, *Oxford*, p. 2058b.
[75] See *Liber de Bury*, p. 316, N. Denholm-Young, *The Country Gentry in the Fourteenth Century* (Oxford, 1969), p. 73, T. F. Tout, in *DNB*, XXXII. 130b and LXII. 159b, Lunt, *Financial Relations*, p. 503 and Boase, *Boniface VIII*, p. 328.
[76] Langtoft, II. 329–31.
[77] *Chronicles of Edward I & II*, I. ciii, cvi and Stubbs, *Constitutional Hist.*, II. 161. For details of the case see Beardwood, 'The trial of Langton', pp. 7–8, N. Denholm-Young, *The Country Gentry*, pp. 73–4, and Bellamy, *Law of Treason*, pp. 55–6.
[78] *Reg.*, p. 602. A letter of Feb. 1300 concerning 'negotiis de Langton' (*Reg.*, p. 377) refers to the case of John Langton, not to that of Walter (cf. Beardwood, 'The trial of Langton', p. 7 n. 26).

Lincoln, also sent a long defence of his fellow bishop to the pope dated 4 June 1301.[79] There is, in fact, no evidence at all of personal antagonism and bitterness between Winchelsey and Walter Langton.[80]

In his relations with the bishops of his province Winchelsey staunchly and persistently fought for his rights and the rights of the church of Canterbury. He was severe in his control of individual bishops and thwarted only by papal intervention; John Salmon gained papal support for the collection of first-fruits, John of Pontoise a bull of exemption and Walter Langton the concession enabling him to be consecrated outside the province of Canterbury. But there was never organised opposition from any bishops as a group, and, for his part, the archbishop did not allow individual disputes to blossom into open personal wrangles. He was severe, but also judicious. He saw no need to visit the dioceses of the scholar-bishops who adhered closely to him, and chose not to visit the dioceses of those bishops whose prime loyalty was unmistakably to the Crown. But whatever efforts he might make to prevent discord, a deep political division within the episcopate is plain to see: some bishops were descendants of Grosseteste, others were descendants of Burnell.

[79] See *CCR 1296–1302*, pp. 603–4, *CCR 1302–7*, pp. 81–2, *Liber de Bury*, pp. 43–4, 316–17 and LRO Reg. Dalderby (III), fo. 31r.
[80] A badly ox-galled letter in *Reg. Corbridge*, II. 161–2 (for the subject-matter of which see *Reg.*, pp. 713–15) seems to suggest a special friendship between Langton and Winchelsey. There may be confusion here with the close friendship between Bek and Winchelsey; but it is, in any case, unclear what the scribe intended to write at the crucial point, for the 'a' of the suggested 'amicus' is a minim. I am grateful for the assistance of Dr D. M. Smith and Dr R. Swanson.

Chapter 3

TAXATION AND POLITICS 1294–1296

SPIRITUALITIES AND TEMPORALITIES

The political relationship of Winchelsey and the Crown can be best understood if the spotlight rests on the problems of clerical taxation. Two 'extraordinary' taxes – taxes, that is, for which the Crown had no customary right based on feudal or tenurial relations – had grown to a position of outstanding importance by the closing decades of the thirteenth century: the taxes on personal property, or 'lay movables', and the taxes on clerical income. The two were quite distinct in the processes of granting, assessing and collecting. Consent was given to taxes on lay property in parliament.[1] Taxes on clerical income granted directly to the king were, naturally, the concern of the clergy. Sometimes the clergy granted taxes in parliament (as for the tenth granted in November 1295 and the fifteenth in October 1307), and sometimes they met separately but by the king's direct summons (as for the half granted in September 1294). But more usually, and to the greater satis-faction of those fighting for the preservation of ecclesiastical liberty, the clergy assembled in independent councils summoned by the archbishop (as when there was acquiescence in the imposed fine of a fifth in March 1297, when a tenth was granted in November 1297, and also when taxation was delayed in 1302 and was refused in January and August 1297 and in 1311). Study of the occasions when taxation was discussed in clerical assemblies of the southern province will be one of the central concerns of the following chapters.

In the history of public finance, and of the development of parliament, the taxes on lay movables have occupied a special place. But it is worth noting that the taxation of the clergy was as

[1] See now Harriss, *King, Parliament and Public Finance*, esp. pp. 27–48.

55

important in monetary terms as the taxation of the laity. For the years of Winchelsey's archiepiscopate we can estimate the total from lay movables (including the clerical contributions to these taxes) as in the region of £365,500[2] and the total drawn by the Crown from taxes upon the income of the English clergy as approximately £363,000.[3] Although there is included in the latter total the seizure of £33,000 by the king in 1294 from papal tenths already collected, there is very little difference in total yield between all the lay taxes and all the clerical taxes, and the clergy contributed significantly to the lay subsidies. In proportion to their numbers the clergy were certainly being taxed very heavily indeed. But, excluding purely procedural considerations, can we firmly distinguish clerical taxation from lay taxation? In one vital respect we can. Spiritualities were never taxed in lay subsidies. Virtually all taxable wealth, whether described as movables or income, was derived from the land.[4] Clerical possessions, however, were divided into temporalities and spiritualities. While it may be difficult, in many contexts, to understand clearly the contemporary view of the dividing line between things temporal and things spiritual,[5] in terms of clerical wealth and taxation of it the spiritualities of the English Church are by the end of the thirteenth century relatively easy to define and to distinguish. When tithes were sold, then in the judgment of the Crown 'things spiritual became things temporal'.[6] This was a distinction to aid legal processes. It should not be allowed to cast doubt upon the established nature of the contemporary understanding of what comprised spiritualities. Spiritualities were all that constituted the

---

[2] Including the tenth and sixth granted in 1294, but excluding the twentieth and fifteenth granted in 1313. For the assessment lists see Willard, 'Taxes upon movables of Edward I', pp. 517–21, idem, 'Taxes upon movables of Edward II', pp. 317–21 and J. H. Ramsay, 'Statistics from Subsidy Rolls of Edward II', *EHR*, xxiv (1909), 319.

[3] Including the half granted in 1294, but excluding the papal tenths collected soon after Winchelsey's death. See Appendix. For the years 1313–16 see Denton, 'Reynolds and ecclesiastical politics', p. 256 n. 50.

[4] For the goods assessed as lay movables see Willard, *Parliamentary Taxes*, pp. 73–7; and for sources of clerical income see Lunt, *Valuation of Norwich*, esp. pp. 153–8.

[5] See, for example, M. Wilks, *The Problem of Sovereignty in the Middle Ages* (Cambridge, 1963), pp. 65–83 and R. L. Benson, *The Bishop-Elect* (Princeton, 1968), pp. 55, 179, 207–9, 222–6, 248, 339–41.

[6] See *Councils*, pp. 875, 1209 and *Stat. Realm*, i. ii. 171 (Articuli Cleri, c. 1).

income of individual parish churches and parochial benefices; they were tithes, oblations and income from glebe-lands.

Stubbs offered a definition of spiritualities and temporalities: 'The taxable property of the clergy was either in land, which, whether held by the usual temporal services or in free alms, shared the liability of the rest of the land, under the name of temporalities, or in tithes and offerings, technically termed 'spiritualia', spiritualities.'[7] Lunt was certainly right to point out that this rigid distinction between land on the one hand and tithes and oblations on the other is misleading, for the income from land when attached to parish churches was certainly classed as spiritual income.[8] But he surely carried his criticism too far when he argued that even some lands described as 'of lay fee' were classed as spiritualities.[9] It is true that some prebends listed under spiritualities in the 1291 *taxatio* were noted as 'of lay fee', but this was a specific indication that, although these prebends were included for convenience with prebendal churches, they were in fact temporalities. Spiritual income was the whole of the income appertaining to parish churches. Temporalities were the baronies,[10] manors and lay tenements belonging for the most part to prelates and religious institutions.

After 1291 virtually all taxation of the clergy's income, for the remainder of the middle ages, was based upon the *taxatio* of that

[7] Stubbs, *Constitutional Hist.*, II. 179–80.
[8] Lunt, *Valuation of Norwich*, pp. 76–8.
[9] Ibid., pp. 77 n. 8 and 78 n. 6. The phrase 'of lay fee', at least in the context of clerical taxation, had apparently come to mean the same as 'temporalities': see, for example, Willard, *Parliamentary Taxes*, pp. 101–2. The examples which Lunt cited (*Valuation of Norwich*, p. 78 nn. 8 and 9) do not support the case that, by the latter part of the thirteenth century, some lands held in free alms were for that reason regarded for taxation purposes as spiritualities: the inquisitions of 1303 concerning the possessions of the abbey of Biddlesden (BL Harl. Charters 84 E 31 and 32) deduced that their lands and goods in the counties of Bucks. and Northants. were 'mere spiritualia et in puram et perpetuam elemosinam data', but they had been included in the 1291 *taxatio* under temporalities (*Taxatio Nicholai IV*, pp. 47, 55b); and the manor of Brooke held in pure and perpetual alms by the chamberlain of Bury St Edmunds was included under spiritualities in an assessment early in the thirteenth century (BL Harl. 3977, fos. 55v–56r) but clearly under temporalities in 1291 (*Taxatio Nicholai IV*, p. 110b). Frankalmoign lands were, however, undeniably spiritualities if annexed to a parish church (as in *CCR 1313–18*, p. 158). Cf. Kimball, 'Frank Almoign tenure', pp. 7–8, following Lunt.
[10] See Chew, *Ecclesiastical Tenants-in-Chief*, pp. 165–71.

year, and according to this assessment the spiritual income of the English Church was not far short of double its temporal income.[11] When the English clergy sought, as they often did, to protect their income from royal taxation they must frequently have seen themselves as defending essentially spiritual possessions from secular usurpation.[12] This perhaps applied more to the lower clergy than to the higher clergy, for the income of the lower clergy was exclusively from spiritualities.[13] It should not be forgotten, however, that the regular clergy as well as the secular clergy were directly concerned with taxes upon spiritualities since a large part of the income of many monasteries was derived from appropriated churches.

In the 1291 *taxatio*, continuing the trend set by the valuations for the papal tenths of 1266 and 1274, the temporal income of the clergy was systematically assessed along with the spiritual income. This had not been the case with the valuation 'of Norwich' of 1254.[14] The clergy had frequently opposed, during Henry III's reign, the inclusion for taxation purposes of their temporalities with their spiritualities, and when this happened the result was certainly a considerable increase in the proceeds from the papal tenths, which had become mandatory by the end of the reign.[15] But despite the dislike, in this context, of temporalities being regarded as 'ecclesiastical',[16] the clergy cannot have believed that part of their wealth could be legitimately regarded as quite separate from their 'spiritual' wealth. An item in a list of objections to a proposed subsidy in 1269 shows without question that

---

[11] The calculations of Stubbs (*Constitutional Hist.*, II. 580, facing table) can be used as a guide to the 1291 assessment as printed in *Taxatio Nicholai IV*. The study of the assessment by Graham, 'The taxation of Nicholas IV', should be read in conjunction with Lunt, *Valuation of Norwich*, pp. 107–67.

[12] See, for examples, F. M. Powicke, *Stephen Langton* (Oxford, 1928), p. 158 and *Vita Edwardi II*, pp. 76–8.

[13] For the opposition of the lower clergy to taxation see *Councils*, pp. 288–92, 398–401, 506–9, 798–800, 1156–7, Lunt, 'Consent of lower clergy', pp. 130, 135–6, 139, 160–3, Denton, 'Reynolds and ecclesiastical politics', pp. 273–4 and idem, '*Communitas cleri* in early fourteenth century', pp. 72–8.

[14] Lunt, *Financial Relations*, pp. 292–346 and idem, *Valuation of Norwich*, pp. 70–1, 79–80, 122–3.

[15] Lunt, 'Consent of lower clergy', p. 169.

[16] Lunt, *Valuation of Norwich*, pp. 68–9. See G. Olsen, 'The definition of the ecclesiastical benefice in the twelfth century: the canonists' discussion of *spiritualia*', *Studia Gratiana*, XI (Collectanea Stephan Kuttner, I), 439–41.

they regarded their temporalities as in some respects very distinctly 'ecclesiastical': 'The archbishops, bishops, abbots and priors are oppressed in that their manors and the rest of their temporalities are taxed by laymen in contravention of the provisions of canon law (contra formam iuris canonici). . .indeed, if it is right that these manors be included along with ecclesiastical income (inter proventus et redditus ecclesiasticos), it is not right that they be taxed by laymen, since the power of administering ecclesiastical goods does not belong to the laity.'[17]

For taxes granted directly to the king, as distinct from the papal tenths of 1266 and 1274, the temporalities had continued before the 1290s to be linked, if in varying degrees, with lay property in lay subsidies, and clerical subsidies had been granted essentially on spiritualities as assessed in the valuation 'of Norwich'.[18] In Edward I's reign the clergy paid papal tenths on the whole of their income with remarkably little dissent; ecclesiastical liberty was in no way threatened by them. But after 1291 clerical subsidies to the king were also paid on the whole of their income: spiritualities and temporalities. For these taxes Edward I and Edward II never consulted the pope, but had to consult the clergy, with whom rested the responsibility of protecting their own rights. Since the papacy could tax by mandate and grant the proceeds to the Crown, the English clergy had no ultimate protection in strictly monetary terms; but they could fight to protect themselves from lay en-croachments. It was necessary for the Crown at times of need to seek direct aid from the Church, and the king no doubt aimed to exercise as much control as possible over clerical wealth. Winchel-sey was a formidable opponent. In 1294, for the first time, and as a rule thereafter, the clergy contributed to lay subsidies granted in parliament only on lands acquired since the 1291 assessment and not included in it. Thus, when they discussed royal requests for subsidies in their assemblies the clergy sought to protect both their spiritual and their temporal income. After they had shown, under Winchelsey's guidance, that their right to consent could be strongly enforced, there are clear indications that the Crown came

---

[17] *Councils*, p. 798.
[18] Lunt, *Valuation of Norwich*, pp. 72–3, 167–9, Willard, *Parliamentary Taxes*, pp. 96–7 and Deighton, 'Clerical taxation 1279–1301', pp. 161–71.

to regret the fact that temporalities had become so firmly linked with spiritualities. Edward I's seizure of all the clergy's temporalities in 1297, although much less effective politically than has sometimes been assumed, was a remarkable show of strength. And when, later in that year, he attempted to tax the clergy by mandate and without consent he offered a choice of a third of their temporalities or a fifth of both their spiritualities and temporalities.[19] He may well have thought that he had a better chance of forcing the former upon them. In 1301, still faced with Winchelsey's opposition, he adopted the expedient of reverting to the earlier practice of taxing the clergy's temporal goods with the laity's. But he succeeded in doing so only after a struggle.[20] To Winchelsey, there can be no doubt, the whole of the Church's property was ecclesiastical. It had been given to God. It had to be defended. To study the events of 1294, the year before Winchelsey's return to England as archbishop, is to understand why the Crown was regarded by many in the Church as the aggressor.

THE FINANCIAL EXACTIONS OF 1294

It has long been recognised that the political and constitutional crisis of 1297 had its beginning in 1294, and recognised too that the new dispute between the kings of France and England was the lighting of the touch-paper. A period of relative calm for Edward, following a temporary settlement of the Scottish question, was threatened in May 1293 when a fleet of the Cinque Ports proved more than a match for a Norman fleet in a battle off the coast of Brittany. Philip IV hit back in Gascony. Lengthy negotiations failed and on 19 May 1294 Philip declared Edward contumacious and passed a sentence of forfeiture on the duchy of Gascony. Emergency measures followed immediately, and in the autumn the situation was worsened by a new rebellion in Wales.[21] Royal resources were strained to their limit. The bitter problems concerning royal taxation in England and in France – the most pressing problems of the last years of the thirteenth century, entangling

---

[19] Below, p. 151.   [20] Below, pp. 201–4.
[21] See esp. Cotton, pp. 233–50 and *Book of Prests*, pp. xxvi–liii; and see Prestwich, 'New account of Welsh campaign 1294–5', pp. 89–94.

king, baronage, pope and clergy alike – stemmed from the outbreak of war in the early summer of 1294.[22]

In England during the second half of 1294 every form of
financial pressure available to the king was put upon the clergy.
All emergency measures to raise more in taxation affected the
Church in one way or another. Some measures concerned the
clergy alone. There can be no doubt that the Church in particular
was made to bear the burden of the new war-effort. Naturally one
of Edward's main concerns was to prevent England's export trade
from being of any benefit to the enemy,[23] and one of his first
actions was to order, on 12 June 1294, the seizure of wool,
woolfells and hides.[24] Each sheriff was instructed to take into
custody all wool and hides wherever they were to be found,
liberties and religious houses being specifically included. The king
had gathered his advisers round him, and, with the consent of his
council and 'magnates of the land, prelates, earls and barons', he
further elaborated the procedure for the seizure on 18 June 1294,[25]
emphasising the need for speed in obtaining the money which was
required to resist the enemy. Rolls were ordered to be prepared
with details of each owner or merchant and details of the value of
the goods seized, and guarantees were given against loss. The wool
and hides were then to be conveyed to the nearest sea-ports.
How money was actually to be raised from the seizure was not
revealed until the order of 26 July.[26] This order imposed an extremely harsh new customs duty, which was the result of an
agreement with the merchants. Normal trading, except for the
French merchants, was to resume. The seized wool and hide was
to be reclaimed and immediately transported by the merchants to

---

[22] For the excessive pressure upon the king's resources between 1294 and 1297
see R. W. Kaeuper, 'Royal finances and the crisis of 1297' in *Order and
Innovation in the Middle Ages: Essays in Honor of J. R. Strayer*, ed. W. C.
Jordan, B. McNab and T. F. Ruiz (Princeton, 1976), pp. 103–10, and
J. R. Strayer, 'The costs and profits of war: the Anglo-French conflict of
1294–1303' in *The Medieval City*, ed. H. A. Miskimin, D. Herlihy and
A. L. Udovitch (New Haven and London, 1977), pp. 269–91.
[23] See esp. PRO E159/68 mm. 82–9 for royal policy 1294–5 ('De lanis et bonis
mercatorum extraneorum'), and *Lincs. Assize Roll 1298*, ed. Thomson,
pp. xxvi, xxxvi–xxxviii.
[24] *Rôles Gascons*, iii. nos. 3429–31.
[25] Ibid., iii. p. cxxxi, no. 2676, and see no. 2683.
[26] Cotton, pp. 245–7.

specified ports. There the duty of five marks for each sack of good wool, three marks for inferior wool and five marks for each last of hide was to be paid. In the autumn the rate for wool was standardised at three marks; even so, the severity of this duty – called the *maltote* and soon to be much complained against – can quickly be seen when it is compared with the old rate of half a mark for wool and one mark for hide.[27] Nor was it a measure for 1294 alone. It was ordered to be collected 'for two or three years if the war lasts so long'. In the event it was collected for three years, and the total customs yield for this period was approximately £110,000.[28] It seems clear that the growers were hit especially hard by the *maltote*, for the prices paid by the merchants were driven low. The whole community was affected by this, but the monasteries must have borne a disproportionately high share of the cost. Their hatred of the *maltote* can be seen in the reaction of the chronicle of the priory of Dunstable to the drowning of the celebrated merchant, Laurence of Ludlow, late in 1294: the chronicler blamed Laurence for persuading the merchants to grant the new duty to the king, and claimed that he was drowned because of his sins against the wool-growers.[29]

The seizure of wool had been first ordered on 12 June. On 14 June Edward summoned his feudal tenants to be at Portsmouth on 1 September fully equipped for service abroad.[30] As had become normal, especially for the 38 bishops, abbots and priors,[31] many tenants-in-chief bought themselves out of the duty of providing armed knights. The fines in lieu of service were agreed with the king soon after the issue of the summons. But Edward's

---

[27] See E. Power, *The Wool Trade in English Medieval History* (Oxford, 1941), pp. 70–9, Fryde, 'Resources in the Netherlands 1294–8', pp. 1179–85, Prestwich, *War, Politics and Finance*, pp. 195–9, Harriss, *King, Parliament and Public Finance*, esp. pp. 423–4 and Lloyd, *English Wool Trade*, pp. 75–86, 95–6.

[28] Ibid., p. 80. Prestwich gives £116,000 (*War, Politics and Finance*, p. 197) and adds 'rather more than the yield of the lay subsidies in the same period'; but this does not square with the £150,000 he suggests for the lay taxes of 1294–7 (p. 191), which also falls short of the total of about £173,000 for the three taxes of 1294–6 (p. 179). This variation is not explained by the difference between assessment and yield, for 'the evidence shows that the yield of the taxes did not fall far short of the assessments' (p. 181).

[29] Dunstable, p. 389.

[30] *Parl. Writs*, i. ii. 259–64, 391.

[31] Chew, *Ecclesiastical Tenants-in-Chief*, pp. 32–3.

plans were soon in disarray. In the event, the main army was diverted to Wales and a full muster of the feudal host never took place. For the rest of Edward's reign there was dispute about the payment of the fines, which in the next reign the exchequer at last agreed to remit. In the summer of 1294 the right of the king to demand fines was not of course in question. The problem at that time was a financial one, for the fines required by the king were based upon a new and exceptionally high assessment, that is, 100 marks for each fee on which service was otherwise required. This assessment was out of all proportion to other known assessments during Edward's reign: 1282, 50 marks; 1290, 60 marks; 1303, 30 marks; and 1306, 20 marks.[32] But there is a simple reason why this never became a major grievance. The charge, for example, of 600 marks upon the abbot of Bury St Edmunds was not paid immediately.[33] The tenants-in-chief no doubt awaited the outcome of the summons. Because there was no full muster of the host and because the king never set out for Gascony it is improbable that many of the fines were ever paid. When they were at length remitted it was as unpaid debts.

Then followed, on 16 June, the order for the scrutiny of money which was to cause much concern: all money in churches or religious houses or elsewhere was to be examined with a view to the confiscation of any that was clipped or counterfeit. To this scrutiny we shall return. On 18 June Edward requested prayers throughout the land for the successful outcome of the war,[34] and on this same day he instructed his sheriffs in his second major policy for raising money. This was the seizure from religious houses of the money collected from the crusading tenths which had been ordered by Nicholas IV in 1291 and which had now been collected for three years.[35] To understand the implication of this seizure, which brought to the royal coffers within three months more than £29,000, we must look back at the history of the crusading tenths.

Treasure collected by papal command and lying idle in

---

[32] Ibid., pp. 70, 99–101.
[33] Bury, p. 121.
[34] *Rôles Gascons*, III. no. 3451, and *Councils*, p. 1129 n. 2.
[35] See esp. Lunt, *Financial Relations*, pp. 339–40, 346–65 and idem, "Collectors' accounts", pp. 102–19.

monastic stores had already been a great temptation to Edward.[36] The tenths imposed for six years in 1274 had been conditional upon Edward taking the cross, and the money was to be delivered to him when he was ready to depart. Within a few years it became clear that he was too heavily committed at home to be able to undertake the crusade; and yet he needed the money. When his need increased in 1283 because of the Welsh war, he seized that part of the Church's treasure which had not passed into the hands of Italian bankers. But the Welsh war was quickly over and the protests from the pope and from Archbishop Pecham were sharp.[37] Edward returned the money, most of it completely untouched. The wrong was put right, but this first seizure in 1283 proved to be the thin end of the wedge.

Edward then tried by negotiation to gain possession of the money which he had returned, and also to obtain the grant of further tenths. In 1287 he took the cross; and a final agreement concerning the financial backing for his projected crusade was reached in 1291. Part of the agreement was the papal grant of a new sexennial tenth to be collected on the basis of a new assessment of clerical income. This was the *taxatio* of 1291. As much money as had been collected from these new tenths would be paid to the king when he set out on crusade. But a further and extremely important part of the agreement was the grant to the king of all the proceeds of the earlier sexennial tenth, to be paid in two halves, on 24 June 1291 and 24 June 1292. This concession marks the triumph for Edward of a long period of negotiation. Whatever the king's intentions towards the crusade, he had been granted a financial bonanza, a total of 200,000 marks. In fact only the first half was paid; but £66,000 (given without any specific conditions and simply on the understanding that preparations for a crusade would proceed) was after all more than three tenths of the assessed income of the clergy of England and Wales. Edward had thus secured for himself more than half the yield from England and Wales of the first of the crusading tenths, and collection of the second of the crusading tenths, also granted for six years, began in 1292. What had been achieved with the earlier

[36] Lunt, *Financial Relations*, pp. 335–41.
[37] Douie, *Pecham*, pp. 256–7, and see *Liber de Bury*, pp. 30, 36, 351.

tenths could perhaps be achieved with the later. Edward had shown dislike for the procedure of passing some of the money into the hands of Italian bankers and thus out of his reach, and much more than half of the money collected between 1292 and 1294 was being stored in religious houses.

Edward's interest in the stored money is understandable. He had come to regard the tenths as largely his own. In June 1294 he flew in the face of papal authority, taking full advantage of the divided allegiance of the English clergy. His seizure of the stored money was a relatively simple business, for he gained possession – perhaps directly from the papal collectors, the bishops of Winchester and Lincoln – of a list of the religious houses where the money was stored and the exact amount that was known to be there.[38] He was able from the first to order the arrest of more than £26,000 in specific sums from specific houses, 33 in all. The details which he had to hand cannot have been quite up-to-date, for the total seized within three months was £29,000 rather than £26,000, and the total in the end was £33,000.[39] The seizure of the papal tenths was not without its difficulties: St Mary's York was unable to produce immediately the required £1,902 15s 8¼d, and the goods and chattels in London of the abbot of Basingwerk were taken into custody in order to raise the money which the abbot owed.[40] The priory of Barnwell was also unable at first to produce the money, and was taken into royal custody for two weeks;[41] in the surviving account of this episode there is no hint that anyone disputed the king's right to seize the papal tax. The records concerning the seizure refer to the money as tenths of the king or as crusading tenths conceded to the king.[42] The king had demanded and the monasteries had given. Some sober churchmen cannot have failed to view the confiscation with grave disquiet. But Edward's position was a strong one. The clergy's bitterness concerning the crusading tenths had been largely directed against the pope. Since the money was already gathered in, Edward no

[38] *Rôles Gascons*, III. nos. 2679–82.
[39] Lunt, *Financial Relations*, p. 363. Surviving lists of the receipts of the tenths show most of the money being received between June and September: PRO E401/129 and /1620–2, 1625–8.   [40] PRO E159/68 mm. 58d, 65.
[41] *Liber de Bernewelle*, pp. 231–3.
[42] E.g. PRO E159/67 m. 65 and /68 m. 18d.

doubt believed that an outcry from the clergy was most unlikely. The money, after all, had been collected for the king. The possibility of a crusade, not to say a successful crusade, must have seemed remote indeed, but in 1294 the king's need, and the country's need, was manifestly great.

In accordance with the agreement of 1291 no money should have been paid to the king until the day of his departure on crusade.[43] That day had been fixed for 24 June 1293. But Nicholas IV had died in April 1292 and still in June 1294, when Edward ordered the seizure of the money, no successor to him had been elected. The successor, the hermit-pope Celestine V, was elected on 5 July. The unsuitability of Celestine for the post was soon apparent, and his disastrous pontificate demonstrates the extent to which papal government relied upon the directing hand of its monarch. Edward took advantage of the prolonged vacancy at Rome, and escaped censure and embarrassment because of the administrative incompetence of the new pontiff. In 1300 Boniface VIII was to review the crusading tenths, and to conclude an agreement with the king about the proceeds.[44] But Edward had made a *fait accompli* of the seizure. He had taken the law into his own hands. That is not really to be wondered at; the lack of resistance and protest from the clergy is more surprising. The money, we must suppose, was generally regarded as the king's in any case, and while the English clergy had suffered by its collection, they suffered nothing by its seizure.

The seizure created a difficult situation at least for the papal collectors, the bishops of Lincoln and Winchester. A series of bulls from the new pope, Celestine V, gave new instructions to the collectors about the handing over of the money.[45] The instructions were sent at a time when much more than half of the sum already collected from the tenths was in fact in the king's hands. On 25 October Celestine ordered that the proceeds of the tenths should be paid to the Friscobaldi merchant-bankers, indicating also his intention that, in accordance with a request from Edward, 30,000 marks should be kept in the country by these bankers. The request from the king may have been an attempt to gain some kind of

[43] Lunt, *Financial Relations*, pp. 339–40.   [44] Ibid., pp. 343–5.
[45] *Reg. Pontissara*, pp. 501–6.

sanction for the seizure. On 5 November the pope instructed the collectors to pay 60,000 marks to further named merchants of Florence. An order of 19 November asked that the 30,000 marks which were to remain in England should be paid to merchants of Pistoia, and this was followed by a mandate, dated 25 November, to pay a further 10,000 marks to other merchants of Florence. The total sum of 100,000 marks corresponds with the sum for which the collectors could be regarded as responsible. These were Celestine's feeble attempts to sponsor a new crusade. That he had no official news of the confiscation of the proceeds for the crusade is abundantly clear. The papal collectors could not obey the papal mandates. As English bishops they had acquiesced in the royal intervention, but, more than this, they had acquiesced also in the complete abandonment of the papal tenths. Collection had ceased. Already, before Celestine issued the first of his orders, the papal tax had been replaced, as we shall see, by an enormous royal tax. And the royal tax used the same new papal assessment of clerical income. Taxes by papal mandate for the use of the king were, it is true, well established long before the last decade of the thirteenth century. In the middle years of the century an important stage in the development of these taxes had been marked by the Anglo-papal alliance designed to secure the throne of Sicily for Henry III's son Edmund. But in 1294 the king needed no Anglo-papal agreement. The Roman taxes were turned into English taxes; the money for a crusade became money for the English wars.

Before we examine the new royal tax we must return to the scrutiny. The outcry in 1294 was not against the seizure of tenths, but rather against the forced entry by royal agents into religious houses and churches and the forced scrutiny and sealing of all money stored there. Edward had made this order on 16 June with a view to the arrest of all debased and false coinage.[46] Although the scrutiny revealed unexpected stores of the papal tenths (for example, £263 8s 6d at Kirkham priory),[47] there seems to have been no confusion either in the mind of the king or in the minds of the chroniclers between the two procedures. The procedure for

---

[46] *Rôles Gascons*, III. no. 2677. The writ, known to Powicke, was overlooked by Prestwich, *War, Politics and Finance*, p. 214.

[47] PRO E159/68 m. 18d (and E368/66 m. 5d).

the scrutiny of all money throughout the country – 'in churches or religious houses or elsewhere, no matter where it is and no matter who has custody of it' – caused many more problems than the seizure of the tenths.

Five independent chronicles give an account of the scrutiny and record the shock of the clergy at the king's act.[48] The forced entry of churches by royal agents was, of course, a breach of ecclesiastical immunity. The Dunstable annalist comments that so sacrilegious an act had never been heard of before. No previous king, the chronicler of Bury St Edmunds tells us, had presumed to violate the sanctuary of that monastery. The scrutiny took place throughout the country on the same day, Sunday 4 July.[49] It was clearly a thorough and carefully planned operation. But it was more than a search for false coinage; all money and treasure wherever it was found – in turrets or privies; in the houses of the clergy or of the laity; in leper-houses or cathedral churches – was inspected, recorded and sealed. In the case of Wolvesey castle there was a further inspection on 26 July.[50] There appear to have been only a few instances of resistance to the royal agents. The prioress of Little Marlow refused to allow entry to her priory; she was summoned before the exchequer for her defiance, but pardoned out of respect for the poverty of the house. A chaplain Henry de Preislande was charged with removing, in advance of the scrutiny, chests containing money from the abbey of Hyde, Winchester, and returning them after the scrutiny; he appeared at the exchequer and claimed that the chests only contained books belonging to Philip, archdeacon of Winchester.[51]

The king was taking stock of all stored money and valuables. The chroniclers scarcely refer to any actual seizure of private money, except that belonging to foreign merchants. But more than £10,000 in private treasure *was* seized. This money was not simply sealed, it was taken as an imprest or loan and paid into the

---

[48] Bury, pp. 121–2 (as *Flor. Wig.*, II. 271–2), Cotton, pp. 237–8, *Flores Hist.*, III. 274, Dunstable, p. 399 and Guisborough, p. 248; and see Cont. Gervase, p. 306 and *Liber de Bernewelle*, p. 231.
[49] The date is certain: cf. Prestwich, *War, Politics and Finance*, p. 214 n. 4. Cotton, p. 238, should read 'iiii nonas' and *Flores Hist.*, III. 274, 'prima dominica'.
[50] *Reg. Pontissara*, pp. 495–6.
[51] PRO E159/67 mm. 53d, 54 (and E368/65 mm. 66, 70d).

exchequer.[52] Although some of it was old currency, the seized money appears not to have been counterfeit or clipped. It was taken in the presence of the owner or a proctor, and royal letters patent made assurances of repayment at the request of the creditor. About forty people, not all of them clergy, made loans of this kind: for example, the prior of the Knights Hospitallers (£2,664 11s 4d); the bishop of Chichester (£2,691 18s 5d, taken from the New Temple, London); the archdeacon of Norfolk (£757 2s); and a certain Joan Charles (£139 13s 4d, deposited in the priory of Butley). There was apparently an element of consent in this taking of loans; but the difficulties experienced by some in obtaining reimbursement was to cause offence, as we can see from later petitions in parliament.[53] In 1294 it was more especially the king's show of strength throughout the country which offended the Church. Treasure had been sealed, but for the most part only sealed, *ad opus regis*. The dramatic breaking into churches, breaking open of chests and sealing of all treasure made a good story for the chroniclers. And the money was still sealed in September.

The biggest shock of all came in the clerical council which met in September. It was in this council that a tax of half the clergy's income was imposed by the king.[54] The king cannot have expected that the clergy would be passive in their response to this new tax, collected for secular purposes, upon their spiritual and temporal income. They were already under strong financial pressure. Open opposition to royal demands was not unprecedented. No doubt the king remembered the events of 1283 when the clergy refused to grant the king's request of a tenth for three years and, after long deliberations in three councils in January, May and October, offered only a twentieth for two years. They complained then that they should not be involved in a cause which would result in the

---

[52] See *Book of Prests*, p. li and Lunt, *Financial Relations*, p. 363. The evidence is found in several lists on receipt rolls, with, for example, the heading 'de denariis receptis de prestito regi facto per scrutinium quod communiter fuit factum per totam Angliam per preceptum ipsius regis' (PRO E401/129); letters patent were issued to each of those from whom money was taken (E401/1620, 1623–7).

[53] Lunt, *Financial Relations*, p. 363, *Rot. Parl.*, i. 298–9 and below, pp. 198, 239.

[54] See *Councils*, pp. 1125–34, Deighton, 'Clerical taxation 1279–1301', pp. 171–5 and Powicke, *Thirteenth Century*, pp. 670–2.

shedding of Christian blood, which was forbidden to the clergy; and they invoked the decree of the Fourth Lateran Council which protected them against royal taxation without prior consent from the pope.[55] While there is an air of unreality about both these claims, for they could be forgotten when the clergy wished to make a grant, they reflect attitudes which still formed the background to the clerical point of view in 1294. But Edward now controlled the clergy most skilfully, and there was to be little room for the airing of strictly clerical views.

The king's overriding advantage was of course the lack of a leader in the English Church. As Guisborough commented, 'the members without their head were divided in their counsel'.[56] Because of the vacancy at Canterbury the bishops and abbots were summoned to the council by direct mandates; these replaced the normal summons for the southern province through the archbishop of Canterbury and the bishop of London. It was an unusual kind of ecclesiastical council, summoned directly by the king and controlled by him. The clergy, of both provinces, met as if summoned to parliament. Some churchmen may well have regarded the council as irregular, though the king had avoided the mandatory form of summons ('venire facias') which had been used in 1283 and the clergy were accustomed to assemblies which considered mainly, if not solely, financial requests from the king. In September 1294 the king was in no mood to suffer delay; he knew that he had the upper hand. He made sure that there could be no claim that the clergy were not properly represented (as was claimed in 1283): deans and archdeacons were summoned to appear in person and the cathedral chapter and the clergy of each diocese were to be represented respectively by one and two proctors. The council must be in a position to bind the whole clerical body. The chronicler Guisborough tells of Edward's dealings with the council. He addressed the assembled gathering. It was a carefully planned speech, telling how a peaceful outcome to the negotiations had moved further from his grasp the more it had been sought. He asserted his lack of guilt for the opening of hostilities with France and stressed the very great expense of the war. But he had entered the war willing to fight to the death.

[55] Below, p. 93.   [56] *Councils*, p. 1130.

The clergy should regard it as their responsibility to assist the king from their goods, especially when they could see the earls, barons and knights both assisting from their goods and offering themselves for the field of battle. Assistance from the clergy was just and reasonable.

This far is as much as we might expect from the king. Then he proceeded, in this credible account by Walter of Guisborough, to defend his recent policies. Two things, he said, had disturbed the clergy. The first of these things, the seizure of wool, he passed over quickly, making no mention of the high tariff he had imposed and defending this seizure on the grounds of the general protection of the land. He was probably right in feeling that the second matter, the scrutiny of treasure, had caused a deeper affront. Concerned about bad currency in the country and intending no evil, he had ordered that money must hold its value. 'But in this matter,' he continued, 'it turned out as between the apostles of Jesus Christ. For among the twelve there was one evil man who betrayed Christ. Similarly, there were some who went beyond my mandate and deceived me. Therefore I am prepared to make amends.' It is important to make some sense of these words, for here we have the king in close dealings with his clergy. The remedy which was apparently in the king's mind is embodied in the first of the petitions of the clergy which were to be presented to the king as part of the agreement to pay the half or moiety.[57] The clergy's petitions on this occasion are interesting: far from being the more usual grievances in defence of the Church's liberties, they are for the most part specific requests about the moiety and the protection of the clergy during its collection. Even these requests, most of which Edward easily accepted, seem to have been put forward at the prompting of the king himself. In response to the first request he agreed to take the advice of the prelates for the restoration of all goods arrested. It is more than likely that the clergy were asking not simply for the restoration of any private money which had been carried off but also for the unsealing of the money which had been arrested throughout the country. It was because of this sealed money that the king was in so strong a bargaining position in September 1294. The king,

[57] Ibid., pp. 1132-3.

after all, now had a precise record of all clerical treasure wherever it was stored.

Edward was strengthening his position by disclaiming all responsibility for the arrest of money throughout the land. This was in some ways a remarkable disclaimer. Denial of responsibility for the scrutiny did not of course prevent the king from using the fact of the scrutiny as a bargaining counter, and Edward's own comparison, in Guisborough's account, of his betrayal with the betrayal of Christ smacks, to say the least, of special pleading. Yet, it is a striking fact that Edward seems to have succeeded in exculpating himself. The Dunstable chronicler tells of the dreadful scrutiny, but adds that it was said that the king was innocent in the matter.[58] There can be no doubt where Edward was placing the blame. His attack was directed against one of the bishops who was almost certainly attending the September council, for he was in London at the time. The culprit is identified in two chronicles as William of March, bishop of Bath and Wells,[59] to be dismissed as royal treasurer on 16 August 1295 after serving in that office for five years. The Merton chronicler of the *Flores Historiarum* is vicious in his attack. The author of the scrutiny, he asserts, was the bishop, and in this deed he should be called a tyrant rather than a bishop, an offender against the Church rather than a defender of the Church. Since he has violated the temple of God, he should beware the denunciation of St Paul: 'If any man defile the temple of God, him shall God destroy.'

It looks very much as though the king had found a scapegoat in the bishop of Bath and Wells. The Merton chronicler almost certainly went too far in blaming him for the scrutiny. The royal writ of 16 June (letters patent bearing the 'teste me ipso' formula) had itself ordered both the scrutiny and arrest of all money.[60] And since the clerical complaint was probably about the whole procedure of arresting and sealing money, and not just about the relatively few cases of actual confiscation, it is difficult to see how Edward was justified in fastening the blame on William of March. The treasurer may have been responsible for some extension of the terms of the royal mandate; perhaps he made the detailed

---

[58] Dunstable, p. 390.   [59] Rishanger, p. 473 and *Flores Hist.* III. 274.
[60] *Rôles Gascons*, III. no. 2677.

arrangements which resulted in the sudden assault on all churches throughout the country on the same day – a Sunday. Rishanger states that it was because of the part he played in the scrutiny that he was dismissed from office. If this were the case it seems odd that William was not dismissed until August 1295. And another reason for the treasurer's downfall is in fact better substantiated. He had become very unpopular in London. The king's hold over the city of London had been severely weakened by the disaffection of the citizens as illustrated in their grievances against the exchequer and specifically against the treasurer. The citizens of London had led the attack on the treasurer.[61] But his reputation was not permanently sullied; there was veneration for him in his diocese, and about twenty years after his death his canonisation was sought and was supported by Edward III.[62]

The scrutiny had been efficiently executed and had put the king in a strong position. Having presented his case to the September council, he left the clergy three days in which to decide among themselves about the tax which he required. The two main chronicle sources, Guisborough and *Flores*, present different, but not incompatible, versions of the proceedings of the council.[63] *Flores* inserts the story of the sudden death of the dean of St Paul's, William de Montfort.[64] He was sent by the clergy to discover from the king more precisely what was required of them, and collapsed and died in Edward's presence. William was probably a key figure in the negotiations between the king and the clergy. He had been prominent three years before in the negotiations with the pope concerning the papal tenths, as the Bury chronicler points out;[65] and it was those papal tenths granted by Nicholas IV which were now being superseded by a royal tax. The disagreement among the chroniclers about the rôle which William was playing in September 1294 may be an indication of his position as arbiter: the Merton *Flores* defends him as a good son of the Church who was trying to soften the mind of the king, but the chronicles of

---

[61] *Select Cases Before King's Council*, p. lvi. According to the annals of Hailes he was removed from office at the instance of Edward, the king's son: Blount, 'Annals of Hailes', p. 100 (BL Cotton, Cleopatra D iii, fo. 50v).
[62] Kemp, *Canonization*, p. 118.   [63] Both in *Councils*, pp. 1129–31.
[64] The account gains support from Bury, p. 124 and Worcester, p. 517.
[65] Bury, p. 124 and *Foedera*, I. ii. 746, 750.

Bury and Dunstable reflect the opinion that William favoured the king.[66] Indeed, the Bury chronicler was very suspicious of him: 'the principal agent and promoter of the king's schemes for the overthrow of the liberties of the English Church'. This was an extreme view. And the death of the dean of St Paul's seems in fact to have robbed the clergy of their negotiator. The Westminster *Flores* says that the king's mind now hardened, although it was still not made clear exactly how much he was expecting the clergy to pay.

At this point we can return to the Guisborough account. Although Oliver Sutton, bishop of Lincoln, appears to have been acting as clerical spokesman, the discussions revealed the lack of leadership in the Church. The silence of the archbishop of York, John le Romeyn, is explained by the fact that he was greatly in debt to the king.[67] Many different views were expressed, and at length the clerical body decided to make an offer to the king of two tenths for one year. This was no doubt regarded by most as a generous concession; it was double the yearly tax to which the clergy had now become accustomed. But the king reacted strongly; and we are left in no doubt about the action which he now took.[68] He sent knights to the council and the clergy were threatened with outlawry if they refused to give the king a half of their income. The accounts are all agreed about this threat and about the element of compulsion. The king's agent, John of Havering, ex-seneschal of Gascony, even asked anyone who intended to contradict the king to stand up and show himself so that his name could be taken as a breaker of the king's peace. With these threats the opposition, which had come from the archdeacons and the lower clergy,[69] melted away.

We should note that the prelates had been more willing than the proctors of the lesser clergy to support the king in his unusually high demands. But we should note also that the chroniclers come to a unanimous verdict: a large number of the clerical representatives consented to the grant unwillingly. They had acted out of

[66] *Flores Hist.*, III. 275, Bury, p. 124 and Dunstable, p. 389.
[67] See Jones, 'Relations of two jurisdictions', p. 147, *DNB* ('Romanus') and *Rot. Parl.*, I. 120.
[68] Cotton, p. 249, substantiates *Flores Hist.* and Guisborough.
[69] *Liber de Bernewelle*, p. 234.

fear and in the knowledge that ecclesiastical freedom was under attack, and they left the council feeling frustrated and deceived ('frustrati et quasi delusi'). In return for their grant they had obtained no worthwhile concession to strengthen the freedom of the English Church. The High-Church view is expressed by the Merton *Flores*: 'if they had first considered the issues more thoroughly and more wisely, they would not have ventured to make any concession to the king without consulting the pope.' It was easy to express this opinion after the event. There is no evidence that the clergy were especially disturbed because they had been unable to consult the pope. They were moved more by the attack on their own freedom of action. They were concerned because they themselves had been cajoled, even compelled, by the king into paying a tax on their spiritualities. Faced with the urgent financial demands of the king, they cannot have believed that the new hermit-pope was in a position to offer them protection. In any case the king himself had usually been successful in gaining the ear of the pope. But the clergy's need for protection was clear. They had been compelled to pay a new harsh tax, a much harsher tax than ever before, in a clerical assembly which had been directly convened and effectively dominated by the king.

By contrast, the clergy in France were able to take up a position which, although precarious, appeared to be much stronger. They conceded to Philip the Fair a tenth for two years, but even this tax was opposed by some clergy and they were able to gain important concessions from the king, including the grant that collection should be in the hands of ecclesiastics rather than royal officials and also that collection should cease if the war came to an end. These were two principles for which Winchelsey would have to fight in England. The French clergy also firmly stated the principle that the consent of the pope to the tax must be obtained, unless the danger to the realm was so great that consent could not be awaited.[70]

It must be stressed that the moiety was in practical terms a direct continuation of the papal taxation of the previous three years. Like the tenths, it was based on the new assessment of 1291. The chief papal assessors, the bishops of Lincoln and Winchester,

[70] Strayer, 'Consent to taxation', pp. 25–7.

were required to forward to the king their taxation rolls so that these could be used for the collection of the moiety.[71] The records of the papal assessors became essential for the administration of the royal tax; for example the nuns of Stratford-at-Bow were excused from the moiety because letters of the papal assessors showed that their income was too small.[72] With very few exceptions the diocesan collectors appointed by Edward for the moiety were the same collectors whom the bishops of Lincoln and Winchester had appointed for the papal tenths.[73] This continuation of the procedure established for the papal taxes had the effect of enabling the king to sidestep complaints. There was a rumour that in the first place the king had only asked for crusading tenths to be collected for three years, and that it was Nicholas IV who had conceded tenths for six years. This view suggests support for Edward who did after all terminate the papal tenths after three years. Complaints were often, in any case, against the actual assessments of income; Edward could wash his hands of the 1291 *taxatio*.[74]

On any showing the moiety was an enormous tax. But it was made an even greater burden, not only by being based on the new assessment, but also by the rapidity of its collection. The three terms for its collection were 1 November (only a month after the appointment of collectors, and six weeks after the granting of the tax), 17 April and 8 June.[75] Within eight months of the September council the clergy were being asked to pay to the king a sum of more than £100,000,[76] and it has been estimated that by September 1295 three-quarters of this sum had in fact been paid.[77] The contribution paid from the abbey of Bury St Edmunds was £655 0s 11¾d.[78] The payments from Dunstable priory, a total of £64 3s 6d, were only 16 days late for the first and second terms

[71] Deighton, 'Clerical taxation 1279–1301', pp. 174–5 and Lunt, *Financial Relations*, p. 354.

[72] PRO E159/68 m. 69.

[73] Lunt, *Financial Relations*, pp. 632–3 and *CCR 1288–96*, pp. 396–7.

[74] See *Liber de Bernewelle*, pp. 190–1, 203.

[75] For the collection of the tax see esp. PRO E159/68 mm. 68–71d.

[76] Lunt, *Financial Relations*, pp. 326–7; and see Bury, p. 124.

[77] Deighton, 'Clerical taxation 1279–1301', p. 175; and see *Book of Prests*, p. li.

[78] Bury, p. 124; and for the payment from the priory of Worcester see *Early Compotus Rolls of the Priory of Worcester*, ed. J. M. Wilson and C. Gordon (Worcestershire Hist. Soc., 1908), p. 24.

and 19 days late for the third.[79] Although the collection of arrears
continued for two decades at least,[80] many of the clergy could meet
the tax. As a result of the scrutiny the king could no doubt see that,
by and large, the clergy were able to pay. The continuator of
Gervase of Canterbury tells us that the clergy left the September
council rejoicing yet sorrowful, rejoicing at the half of their
income which they retained, sorrowful at the half which had been
extorted.[81] To have rejoiced at all is remarkable. Of course, we
must remember that the assessments of income were always well
beneath the actual, gross or net, income of a benefice or manor;
one of the guiding principles in assessing the spiritual and temporal income of the clergy appears to have been the price at which
a church or the land attached to a church could be farmed out.[82]
Nonetheless, the priory of Dunstable, and no doubt many other
monasteries and other members of the clergy, had some difficulty
in meeting all their obligations in 1294.[83] It is no surprise to find
evidence of opposition and delay: for example, in the spring of
1296 Oliver Sutton excommunicated the incumbents of 29
churches in the Lincoln diocese, many of which were valuable
churches, for their failure to pay the moiety.[84] But there are many
indications of the king's great concern that the tax should be
rapidly and efficiently collected. Although he had conceded to the
clergy that benefices which did not exceed 10 marks in value
should be exempted from the tax, he instructed the collectors that
he did not mean by this to exclude the churches which were
actually valued at 10 marks.[85] Edward badly needed ready money.
But how should the clergy measure his need against his extortion?

The final burden of 1294 came in November. At the November
parliament the king imposed a tax on lay movables of a tenth and
sixth.[86] The clergy were not represented in the parliament; yet it is

[79] Dunstable, p. 392.
[80] *Reg. Kellawe*, I and II, passim.
[81] *Councils*, p. 1132.
[82] Graham, 'The taxation of Nicholas IV' and Lunt, *Valuation of Norwich*,
pp. 107–67.
[83] Dunstable, pp. 387–8.   [84] *Reg. Sutton*, v. 149–54.
[85] *Councils*, p. 1132 and PRO E159/68 m. 69.
[86] Willard, *Parliamentary Taxes*, pp. 96–7; and for documents concerning the
collection see *Lancs. Lay Subsidies*, ed. Vincent, pp. 180–7, PRO E159/68 mm.
72–76d, *Parl Writs*, I. ii. 27 (*CPR 1292–1301*, pp. 103–4). For the *forma
taxationis* see E159/68 m. 72 and Cotton, pp. 254–6.

clear that they were to be taxed on those temporal goods which were not included in the 1291 assessment of their income. Any temporalities which were not regarded as 'annexed to churches' and had escaped the 1291 *taxatio*, and thus the moiety, must now be assessed and taxed at a tenth. In later years the practice became established that all new temporal possessions were to be taxed with the taxes on movables; but in 1294 the clerical assessment was so recent and the collection of the moiety was put into operation with such vigour that probably few temporalities remained to be taxed. This impression is confirmed by an inspection of the surviving taxation roll of 1294 for the county of Hertford.[87] The religious houses, for example, appear to have been totally excluded from the lay taxation; they obtained royal writs protecting them from any payment, in accordance with the terms of the *forma* of the taxation.[88] Yet the master of the Knights Templars and the prior of the Knights Hospitallers each made a payment for their orders of 500 marks.[89] Individual members of the clergy were taxed on their personal possessions, but it is unlikely that the clergy contributed more than a tenth of the whole yield of the tax (that is, about £8,000), and it may well have been less.

The news of the election of Celestine V as pope, which would at last make possible Winchelsey's consecration, must have reached England in late July 1294. It had been clearly to Edward's advantage to exact the maximum amount from the clergy for the coming year before the return of the archbishop. Winchelsey was to provide the firm guidance so demonstrably lacking in 1294, and was never, even at the time of greatest national need, to consent to anything more than the collection of a tenth in his province. As a result of the events of 1294 the clergy were committed to paying a vast sum in taxation to Edward during 1295, a total of approximately £78,000, and this after the taxation of the clergy (excluding the *maltote*) had already provided the king with over £60,000 during the second half of 1294.[90] These amounts can be given some kind of perspective by the fact that during the next eighteen years, the span of Winchelsey's primacy,

[87] PRO E179/120/3.
[88] *Parl. Writs*, I. ii. 391 (*CCR 1288–96*, p. 439), Cotton, p. 256 and PRO E159/68 mm. 73d–75.   [89] Ibid., m. 73d.   [90] See Appendix.

the average amount to be demanded of the clergy in taxation for the king *per annum* was in the region of £15,000 to £17,000.

The year before Winchelsey's return to England had been a critical one for the English Church. The events of that year mark an important stage in the Crown's attempt to establish greater control over clerical taxation. After the suspension of the papal tenths ordered in 1291 the responsibility for the taxation of the clergy had certainly come to rest mainly with the king. The payment of Peter's pence of course continued, although the clergy were eager to resist the attempts being made to increase the yield,[91] and procurations were still to be authorised both for papal collectors and for papal nuncios;[92] but the clergy were not required to pay a charitable aid to the pope until 1326,[93] and, more important than this, the greater part of the yield of the so-called papal tenths granted by Boniface VIII and Clement V was in fact to go into the royal coffers. In establishing control in 1294 the king had made full use of the vacancy of the papal see. This vacancy lasted from April 1292 until December 1294, excluding, that is, the fiasco of Celestine V's pontificate. This short pontificate had been no less advantageous to Edward than the vacancy. The king had secured from Celestine a grant of first-fruits for three years from churches in the province of Canterbury, which was to be shared between Edward and his spokesman at the papal curia, the cardinal deacon of S. Maria in Via Lata, James Colonna.[94] It was fortunate for Winchelsey that the general revocation of all Celestine's acts by Boniface VIII included the revocation of this grant of first-fruits to the king.[95] From the death of Archbishop Pecham (December 1292) until the consecration of Archbishop Winchelsey (September 1294) papal control was minimal, and the lack of leadership in the Church as a whole had produced a situation particularly favourable to the Crown. But the election of a strong-willed pope preceded by eight days the return of a strong-willed archbishop. While neither Boniface VIII nor Robert Winchelsey was to show

[91] *Councils*, p. 1184 c. 4; and p. 1183 c. 4, where the petition includes a protest against the papal claim on the goods of intestates, a claim not made by the pope between 1296 and 1327 (see Lunt, *Financial Relations*, p. 511).
[92] Ibid., pp. 545–9, 553–64.   [93] Ibid., pp. 238–9.
[94] Cotton, pp. 261–5 and *CPR 1288–96*, p. 442.
[95] *Reg.*, pp. 513–17 and Cotton, pp. 165–71, 177–9.

his mettle immediately, both, in their different but in some ways allied spheres, were to provide opposition to Edward's financial policies.

'CLERICIS LAICOS'

Winchelsey was consecrated at Aquila on 12 September 1294 and returned to England as archbishop, landing at Yarmouth on 1 January 1295. He had waited sixteen months in Italy for the appointment of a successor to Nicholas IV; but there had been no opposition to his election as archbishop from any quarter. Considering the severe financial pressure which the English Church had suffered during his long absence, some immediate clash between the archbishop and the king might well have been expected. It is clear that Winchelsey had been well received at the papal curia;[96] it was apparently the belief at Canterbury that the new pope, Celestine V, had wanted to make him a cardinal.[97] Boniface VIII was crowned pope in succession to Celestine on 23 January 1295. If Boniface had become pope before Winchelsey left Italy, it is very likely that the new archbishop would have returned to England carefully briefed on papal policy concerning the war between France and England and on the closely allied question of papal policy concerning taxation of the clergy. Under papal instructions Pecham had acted rapidly, indeed impetuously, as soon as he became archbishop in an attempt to inaugurate a new reform movement. According to one chronicler Winchelsey did sharply rebuke the king for his sacrilegious policy in 1294 towards the Church.[98] But Winchelsey was more patient and more calculating than Pecham, and a study of 1295 reveals only a few signs of any imminent crisis between the archbishop and the king. The chroniclers, many of whom wrote as contemporaries or near contemporaries, have, in fact, little to say about Winchelsey until the dramatic events of 1297.

Immediately after his arrival in England Winchelsey travelled to the king at Conway in Wales, and the temporalities of his see were restored on 4 February.[99] The oath of fealty to the king was

---

[96] *Reg.*, pp. 1279–80.   [97] *Anglia Sacra*, I. 12.   [98] Rishanger, p. 473.
[99] *CPR 1292–1301*, p. 129. See Graham, 'Winchelsey: from election to enthronement', pp. 173–5.

taken on 2 February, and a mistaken interpretation of what took place on that occasion has taken root: 'The archbishop did not take the oath in the form demanded by the king, and confined his obligation to his temporalities.'[100] The source of our information is an account in a Canterbury register.[101] Here we learn that the archbishop paused to consider the oath he was required to take and, *having taken it*, he added his own 'declaration and proviso': 'The oath which my predecessors, the archbishops of Canterbury, were wont and bound to take to you and your ancestors for the temporalities of the archbishopric I understand and take and offer it loyally, so God and the saints help me.' The king, we are told, was very surprised by this statement. It may be, as Rose Graham pointed out, that the conflict between the king and Winchelsey was thus foreshadowed at Conway.[102] The archbishop had chosen to stress that the king was his temporal lord, and certainly in the ensuing conflict concerning taxation the obligations of the clergy to their spiritual and their temporal lords, and the distinction between the Church's spiritualities and its temporalities, became issues of crucial importance. But Winchelsey had sworn the due oath to be faithful and loyal to his king.

If all went according to plan the archbishop then moved south to meet John of Pontoise, bishop of Winchester, on 23 February at Mortlake.[103] One item of business related to a loan made to Winchelsey when he was in Italy.[104] The second matter for discussion concerned certain papal letters to Pontoise which the bishop regarded as virtually impossible to obey. There seems little doubt that these were the letters of Pope Celestine dated October and November 1294 in which the papal collectors of the tenth granted in 1291 (Pontoise and Oliver Sutton, bishop of Lincoln) were ordered to pay all the money due from the tenth to Italian bankers, including 30,000 marks owing to the king which was to be kept in England by the bankers.[105] This demand could not be

---

[100] Powicke, *Thirteenth Century*, p. 673 n. 1 and Prestwich, *War, Politics and Finance*, p. 258, following Miss Graham's misleading account.
[101] Cant. D. & C., Reg., Q., fos. 36v–37r.
[102] *Reg.*, pp. vi, x.
[103] *Reg. Pontissara*, pp. 190, 766–7.
[104] Ibid., pp. 505–6 and *Reg.*, pp. ix–x, 56, 1284–5.
[105] *Reg. Pontissara*, pp. 503–5. See Lunt, *Financial Relations*, p. 361.

met, for the king had already seized much more than half the proceeds of the tenth. When discussing these letters, if not before, Winchelsey must have been made fully aware of the king's financial policies of the previous year. The repercussions of those policies were, of course, still felt. The collection of the second and third instalments of the moiety continued through 1295.

Winchelsey gave support to the king's campaign against the Welsh by using his powers of excommunication and absolution in the opposition to Madoc[106] and by endeavouring to establish a strong bishop in the south Wales diocese of Llandaff which had been vacant since March 1287.[107] Winchelsey's efforts to ensure the peaceful and efficient administration of this diocese dated from before his arrival in England, and, although he was never to show the concern of his predecessor for the problems of the Welsh dioceses,[108] the new archbishop was nevertheless genuinely disposed to assist the king's conquest and subjugation of the Welsh, at least from afar. The war against France was always much more difficult for Edward I to justify than the wars against the Welsh or the Scots. Boniface VIII was quick to intervene in 1295 in a determined effort to restore peace between Edward and Philip IV.

Celestine V had pleaded with Edward not to go to war with France and had made diplomatic representations through his nuncio Bertrand de Got, future Pope Clement V.[109] Boniface VIII viewed the hostilities with extreme gravity. Appeasement in western Europe was essential to him in order to gain assistance from France in Italy,[110] and the deplorable state of the Holy Land was, as so often, the papal rallying-cry. One of Boniface's first acts as pope was to appoint, in February 1295, Berald de Got, cardinal bishop of Albano (brother of Bertrand, and like Bertrand one of

---

106 *Reg.*, pp. 1–4 (and see *Councils and Eccles. Documents*, ed. Haddan and Stubbs, I. 606–9).
107 See Douie, *Pecham*, pp. 269–70, *Reg.* pp. 5–11, 513–14 and *Councils and Eccles. Documents*, I. 610–12.
108 Douie, *Pecham*, pp. 235–71 and G. Williams, *The Welsh Church from Conquest to Reformation* (Cardiff, 1962), pp. 35–45.
109 Denton, 'Clement V's early career', pp. 310–11.
110 Boase, *Boniface VIII*, pp. 65–72. In what follows I have benefited from the use of G. W. Burn, 'The Issue and Publication of "Clericis laicos": a Study in the Early Policies of Boniface VIII' (Manchester B.A. thesis, 1972).

the king's clerics in Gascony)[111] and Simon de Beaulieu, cardinal and bishop of Palestrina, as papal nuncios carefully chosen for the very difficult task of negotiating peace between the kings of France and England. Berald took special responsibility for England and Simon for France, and soon nuncios were also sent to Adolf, king of Germany, who had declared war on France in August 1294.[112] The appointment of Berald pleased Edward.[113] It is essential to appreciate the pope's eagerness to prevent hostilities and the degree to which in doing so he believed that he was protecting the interests of the universal Church. A letter from Boniface to Edward dated 30 March 1295 is particularly instructive, for here is evidence of the pope's reaction to the Crown's financial exactions.[114] 'But would that these disturbances, dissensions and scandals which constantly arise among the kings and princes of the world did not happen, particularly since they will not keep within the limits of their own authority and fail to restrain their unlawful ambitions; they assail churches and monasteries and other holy places dedicated to divine worship with all manner of injuries, involve them in losses, oppress them with afflictions, burden them with taxes, and treat them vexatiously, showing themselves thereby to be ungrateful to God from whom they acquire dominion over their lands and attain their majesty of office.' Boniface begged, exhorted and advised Edward, as a father, a friend, and one who loved him dearly, to end the war and bring peace to his own kingdom and to Christendom as a whole, and to treat with greater favour all the churches of his kingdom. Here the pope showed his understanding of the link between the Anglo-French hostilities and the exactions imposed by the king upon the English Church. Boniface's aim was to terminate both.

The summer of 1295 brought political developments: the arrival of the cardinals in England on 25 June, the meeting of Winchelsey's first ecclesiastical council on 15 July, and the return of the king to the south-east in late July, followed by the meeting

---

[111] See J. A. Kicklighter, 'La carrière de Béraud de Got', *Annales du Midi*, LXXXV (1973), 327–34.
[112] *Reg. Boniface VIII*, nos. 697–732, 865–7, 875–8 and Cotton, pp. 280–93.
[113] *Foedera*, I. ii. 821 (*CCR 1288–96*, p. 444).
[114] *Foedera*, I. ii. 817, from PRO SC7/6/18.

in August of the first parliament of the year.[115] The archbishop escorted the cardinals on part of their journey to London, bulls for the payment of procurations to them were published in the ecclesiastical council, and they preached concerning peace in the parliament.[116] Unfortunately there is no record of any discussions between the archbishop and the papal nuncios, but we cannot doubt that Winchelsey was fully appraised of their aims and intentions. Affairs apparently passed peaceably. The ecclesiastical council (of bishops and their proctors only) was summoned, as Winchelsey explained, because of the critical situation arising from recent events, and it apparently concerned itself especially with the customs and liberties of the church.[117] It is unlikely that ancient laws and other decrees were revived in the council, as one chronicler maintained, but there may well have been talk of re-enacting legislation and Winchelsey, it is clear, sought to establish himself as the defender of ecclesiastical rights. Although there is no indication of a direct and concerted attack upon the king's financial impositions, the petitions to the king which have been plausibly assigned to this council contain, along with longstanding complaints, quite pointed grievances concerning the entry of the king's bailiffs into ecclesiastical property and the occupation and sequestration of ecclesiastical goods by the lay power.[118]

In a letter sent to his cardinal nuncios Boniface had ordered that a year's truce between France and England must be observed from 24 June.[119] The reaction of the cardinals to this instruction is interesting, especially considering the delay in publishing 'Clericis laicos' in the following year. They did not reveal the pope's command to Edward or Philip, a decision which Boniface later accepted;[120] rather, they continued to make every effort to arrange

[115] Cont. Gervase, pp. 311–12 (as *Anglia Sacra*, ii. 50), and see Graham, 'A petition to Boniface VIII', pp. 35–6; *Councils*, pp. 1134–47; and Gough, *Itinerary*, ii. 131.
[116] *Councils*, p. 1138, Worcester, p. 522 and Guisborough, p. 256.
[117] *Councils*, pp. 1135–8.
[118] Ibid., pp. 1138 c.1, 1143 c.31. A set of grievances, ascribed to October 1294 and sent apparently from the diocese of Angers to Philip IV, has similar complaints, but in much stronger and more directly critical terms: C. Port, 'Livre de Guillaume le Maire' in *Collection de Documents Inédits sur l'Histoire de France, Mélanges Historiques*, ii (Paris, 1877), 322–31.
[119] *Reg. Boniface VIII*, nos. 870, 872.
[120] Marrone and Zuckermann, 'Simon de Beaulieu', p. 217. See this article for

a voluntary truce. Edward was only too willing to go along with these efforts since he was not yet prepared for a continental war.[121] As an indication of the gravity of the situation Dover suffered very badly from a French assault on 2 August;[122] a monk of Dover, Thomas de la Hale, was killed and there quickly developed a cult concerning his martyrdom and sanctity.[123] Edward negotiated with the cardinals during the second week in August at the time of the parliament and then sent his own nuncios with them to the French court.[124] The king had no difficulty in agreeing to a cessation of hostilities until 1 November 1295, conditional upon the acquiescence of the king of France.[125] It was, of course, also necessary to obtain the consent of the king of Germany. But Edward cannot have believed that an agreed truce was possible; and Philip continued to make preparations for war, including the conclusion of an alliance with the king of Scotland in October.[126] The attempts of the cardinals at mediation were proving altogether fruitless. Both sides fortified themselves with war alliances. Edward was now faced with a war against Scotland, and the need for more money was very pressing. Alliances, as well as troops, had to be paid for.[127]

There was great fear of a French invasion. Emergency measures were called for, including elaborate plans for coastal defence and the seizure of the lands and property of lay aliens and of alien priories.[128] The summoning of the 'Model' parliament, which

criticism of J. A. McNamara, 'Simon de Beaulieu and *Clericis laicos*', *Traditio*, xxv (1969), 155-70 and eadem, *Gilles Aycelin: the Servant of Two Masters* (Syracuse, 1973), pp. 40-9.

[121] See Barraclough, 'Edward I and Adolf of Nassau', pp. 231-9 and *Book of Prests*, pp. xlvi-liii.

[122] *Book of Prests*, p. xlvii, Guisborough, pp. 253-4, Cont. Gervase, p. 313, *Flores Hist.*, iii. 94 and *Reg.*, pp. 41-2.

[123] Kemp, *Canonization*, pp. 123-4 and P. Grosjean, 'Thomas de la Hale, moine et martyr à Douvres en 1295', *Analecta Bollandiana*, LXXII (1954), 167-91.

[124] See the detailed expense account of William Greenfield: PRO E101/308/16.

[125] Guisborough, pp. 257-8, Cont. Gervase, pp. 313-14, *Flores Hist.*, iii. 94, 279-80, *Chronicles of the Reigns of Stephen, Henry II, and Richard I*, ed. R. Howlett (RS, 1884-9), ii. 580, Digard, *Philippe et le Saint-Siège*, i. 251-2 and Salt, 'Embassies to France 1272-1307', p. 271.

[126] *Foedera*, i. ii. 830-1.

[127] Fryde, 'Resources in the Netherlands 1294-8', p. 1170 and *Book of Prests*, p. 1.

[128] A. Z. Freeman, 'A moat defensive: the coast defense scheme of 1295', *Speculum*, XLII (1967), 442-62; Cotton, pp. 302-3, *CFR*, i. 362-5, Matthew, *Norman Monasteries*, pp. 81-4 and *Councils*, p. 1218 n. 1.

met at Westminster from 27 November to 9 December, was itself
an emergency measure. The king had directly ordered the clergy
to meet in assemblies in 1283 and 1294, but never before had the
diocesan clergy been summoned to meet in a parliament along
with the prelates, magnates, knights and burgesses. They were not
summoned by enforceable mandates to what was, after all, a
secular court;[129] but rather each of the archbishops and bishops
was ordered to forewarn ('premunientes') his cathedral prior,
or dean, and his archdeacons to be present personally and
his cathedral chapter to be represented by one proctor and his
diocesan clergy by two proctors.[130] The clergy could not take
exception to this procedure even though it was unusual; it was a
convenient way of combining a meeting of magnates and prelates,
as barons, with a meeting of representatives of all the clergy,
usually summoned by archiepiscopal writ. This was little different,
in strict legal terms, from the accepted procedure of the king
requesting the archbishops of Canterbury and York to summon
their clergy to meet. But to bring representatives of all the clergy
into parliament was a significant move nonetheless. To judge from
his later policies, Winchelsey probably considered that to treat
concerning the taxation of ecclesiastical wealth in a parliament
rather than in a purely ecclesiastical council was a dangerous
precedent. But it is clear that he understood that emergency
measures were necessary, and, in any case, the clergy, though
certainly exposed to reprimands and threats from royal justices,
met as a clerical assembly separate from the laity.[131]

Edward was again eager to exact the greatest possible amount
from both laity and clergy; and the first significant evidence of
conflict between the king and the archbishop dates from this
second parliament of 1295. The final part of the 1294 moiety
had become due in August.[132] The statement by the continuator of
Florence of Worcester that the king now tried to obtain the grant
of another moiety is supported by no other source. If he did begin

---

[129] In 1283 the clergy *had* been ordered to meet by legally binding writs
('venire faciatis') and would be summoned again in that way in 1314–16:
see Denton, 'Reynolds and ecclesiastical politics', pp. 257–9, 262.
[130] *Councils*, p. 1148.
[131] *Flores Hist.*, III. 283 and Worcester, p. 524.
[132] Deighton 'Clerical taxation 1279–1301', pp. 174–5.

the proceedings with such high aspirations he soon reduced his request to a quarter or a third.[133] Cotton emphasised the tenacity of the clerical resistance to these royal demands and felt that for the king to obtain any grant at all marked a defeat of clerical policy. But Cotton does not provide as full an account of the proceedings of this parliament as do both the Merton chronicler and the Worcester annalist, who agree that the archbishop himself, after full conference with the representatives of the clergy, offered the king a tenth, and that the cause of the ensuing conflict was the royal dissatisfaction with this grant.[134] That the offer came from the clergy is an indication of Winchelsey's genuine concern for the problems of national defence. The Worcester annalist quotes him as instructing his prelates to remember that without help the king could not defend the country against its enemies. Winchelsey described the tenth as a tax 'for common defence from the gravest dangers', a tax which had been granted by the clergy because of 'urgent and unavoidable necessity'.[135]

Winchelsey presented the clergy with positive advice but in no way compelled them to accept his own assessment of the situation. They discussed the king's needs at length. They recognised their responsibilities. But consent to direct taxation by the Crown was not obligatory. The grant depended upon the clergy's concerted opinion. That this opinion was united in a firm policy is a mark of their confidence in the archbishop. The tenth was offered with unanimous assent, and, after it had been rejected, Winchelsey addressed the clerical assembly: 'God forbid that there should be any division between the head and the body; let each man's will be directed to one and the same end' (Worcester). All attempts at persuasion by the king were opposed, and the clergy won the day largely because their offer of a tenth was in no way unreasonable. Since the laity were being taxed with an eleventh on their movable goods (a seventh if they lived in a town or on royal demesne), it was hardly to be expected that the clergy would submit to the suggested quarter or third, especially considering the severity of the moiety, arrears of which were still outstanding, and the possibility,

---

[133] *Flor. Wig.*, II. 277, *Flores Hist.*, III. 283 and Bury, pp. 129–30.
[134] Cotton, p. 299, *Flores Hist.*, III. 282–3 and Worcester, p. 524. Also see Deighton, 'Clerical taxation 1279–1301', pp. 176–7.
[135] *Reg.*, pp. 69–70.

even if remote, that a treaty with France would follow from the work of the cardinals. With this work in mind, and wishing no doubt to soften the blow of a much lower tax than Edward had desired, the clergy made an important promise which they would be forced to consider later. They declared that they would help the king as much as possible in the following year if the war continued without hope of peace.[136] Moreover, the grant which they proposed was to be paid in very short terms (1 March and 20 May 1296), and the reduction of the limit of taxable income from 10 marks to 6 marks must have caused some hardship among the lesser clergy. As is emphasised in the Worcester annals, a major factor in the clerical resistance was the degree to which their coffers had already been drained by royal taxation. According to Cotton the clergy were not alone in resisting the king's demands, but the opposition of the laity had apparently been short-lived and of no consequence. The machinery for the collection of the tenth was immediately set in motion;[137] and at this stage the archbishop accepted what he would later oppose: the Crown's direct control over the collection of ecclesiastical taxation. At the same time plans for the Scottish campaign were put into operation.[138]

In 1296 Edward, occupied in Scotland from the end of March until the middle of September, continued to give his support to the papal nuncios' efforts to effect a truce. Despite the expedition to Gascony of Edmund of Lancaster, Edward was on the defensive in his relations with France throughout the year. Naturally he wanted a truce at least until he had dealt with the Scottish threat.[139] On 1 January he requested that special prayers should be said in every diocese of England and Wales both for Lancaster's expedition and for the successful outcome of the peace negotiations. Winchelsey, rejoicing at the king's request, issued strict and detailed orders to his commissary that the clergy and the laity throughout his diocese should be urged to take part in 'prayers, alms-giving, fasts and other pious acts', with the grant that a

---

[136] Worcester, p. 524 and Cotton, p. 299.
[137] For this tenth see *Parl. Writs*, I. ii. 46-7 (*CPR 1292-1301*, pp. 172-3), Deighton, 'Clerical taxation 1279-1301', pp. 177-8, PRO E159/69 mm. 63-64, 69-70 and BL Cotton Vesp. E xxii, fo. 2v.
[138] *Parl. Writs*, I. ii. 275-7.
[139] See Powicke, *Thirteenth Century*, pp. 613-17, 649, 661-2 and Barraclough, 'Edward I and Adolf of Nassau', pp. 239-41.

period of penance could be reduced by forty days for anyone responding to this urgent appeal.[140] A meeting of the cardinals with representatives from England, France and Germany was arranged for mid-January at Cambrai. William of Louth (bishop of Ely), Walter Langton (to be elected bishop of Coventry and Lichfield on 20 February 1296) and Henry Newark (to be elected archbishop of York on 7 May) were among those who crossed to France to treat for peace. Also, John of Pontoise, bishop of Winchester, along with a large company numbering more than thirty, all of whom were granted the king's protection for two years, was given the royal licence both to negotiate at Cambrai and to move on to the Roman curia.[141]

'Clericis laicos', banning all ecclesiastical taxation without papal licence, bears the date 24–25 February 1296.[142] It was two months before the pope ordered the bull to be published by his cardinal nuncios, but the first problem that 'Clericis laicos' poses concerns its composition in February. The meeting at Cambrai had broken up by the end of February.[143] Once again negotiations were proving fruitless. Could it be that early news of the difficulties had led to the drawing up of 'Clericis laicos'? At all events, the extreme problems which the nuncios had faced must have been

[140] *Foedera*, I. ii. 834, *Reg. Halton*, I. 70 and *Reg.*, pp. 65–6.
[141] *Foedera*, I. ii. 834–5, *CCR 1288–96*, p. 505, *CPR 1292–1301*, pp. 177–80, 182. For Langton's continuing involvement in diplomacy in 1296 see *Foedera*, I. ii. 837–40, 848–50 and Cuttino, 'Langton's mission for Edward I', pp. 147–83; and for the progress of Pontoise's mission see *Reg. Pontissara*, pp. 793–4, 802–3 (at the Roman curia he presented the final accounts of the papal tenth: *Reg. Pontissara*, pp. 798–801 and Lunt, "Collectors' accounts", pp. 103, 106–10).
[142] See Santifaller, 'Zur Original-Überlieferung der Bulle..."Clericis laicos"', pp. 71–90 and *Councils*, p. 1149 n. 3. There seems little doubt that in the papal chancery the 'sixth kalends of March' in a leap year referred to the two days 24 and 25 February as though they were one: see Extra 5. 40. 14 in *Corpus Iuris Canonici*, ed. E. Friedberg (Leipzig, 1879–81), II. 915 (counting the two as one in a leap year was also the practice by 1256 in English courts of law: *Stat. Realm*, I. ii. 7). A copy of 'Clericis laicos' printed in C. E. Du Boulay, *Historia Universitatis Parisiensis* (Paris, 6 vols., 1665–73), III. 514–15 (see Potthast, no. 24397) bears the date 21 Sept. 1296, but almost certainly in error.
[143] Cardinal Albano returned to England for three months, along with Walter Langton and others, to have further discussions with Edward; and eight of the nuncio's men were apparently killed by the Scots: *Reg. Pontissara*, p. 794, *Flores Hist.*, III. 96, 287, Guisborough, p. 258 and PRO E159/69 m. 40d and /70 mm. 74, 77.

a major factor leading to Boniface's conviction that tougher measures were necessary to secure peace. Another factor which must be examined was, of course, the extent of the recent taxation of the clergy in both France and England.

In the first place, however, it must be stressed that this bull, although in political terms related especially to the policies of the kings of France and England, was a general constitution of universal legality. It did not represent a revolutionary method of protecting papal and ecclesiastical revenues and of counteracting the increase of secular power. As has often been pointed out, it has its antecedents in two decrees of the Lateran Councils of 1179 and 1215; and the statement of the complete hostility of the laity towards the clergy had a long canonical history.[144] The interests of the papacy and of the Church were being defended, firmly and decisively. 'Clericis laicos' was promulgated, and largely accepted, throughout western Europe, in the Italian cities of Parma, Pisa, and Lucca, from Ireland to Majorca, Sicily and Cyprus, from Aragon and Castile to Bohemia. Licences were sought for the taxation of the clergy; and absolution was granted for transgressions of the terms of the bull.[145] Originals of the bull survive in archives at Milan, Munich, Vienna and Budapest; copies were made everywhere.

Yet no one doubts that 'Clericis laicos' was directed especially at the kings of France and England. It was composed with France and England in mind. In its catalogue of impositions upon the clergy there is the statement that the laity exact 'a half, or a tenth, or a twentieth or some other portion of the clergy's income or goods'; and the pope forbade the clergy to pay 'a tenth, twentieth or hundredth or any other portion'. It is likely that the 'hundredth' was the 1295 property tax in France.[146] But much more

---

[144] Le Bras, 'Boniface VIII, symphoniste et modérateur', p. 387, and see C.-J. Hefele, *Histoire des Conciles*, new edn by H. Leclercq (Paris 1907–38), VI. i. 359.

[145] *Reg. Boniface VIII*, nos. 1523, 1744, 2609, 3110, 3128, 3248, 3271, 4144, 4149, 4612, 5022, 5203, *Reg. Benoît XI*, no. 1062, H. K. Mann, *Lives of the Popes in the Middle Ages* (London, 1925–32), XVIII. 242, Boase, *Boniface VIII*, pp. 155–6, Digard, *Philippe et le Saint-Siège*, I. 257–9, and J. A. Watt, *The Church and the Two Nations in Medieval Ireland* (Cambridge, 1970), pp 167–9.

[146] See Marrone and Zuckermann, 'Simon de Beaulieu', p. 213 n. 51.

pointed is the reference to 'a half', which under any circumstances was a very large and most unusual tax. Surely this was an allusion to the moiety imposed by Edward in 1294. It should be noted that, unlike the French hundredth, the moiety was exclusively a tax upon clerical wealth. More important perhaps than these particular references, however specific they may appear to be, is the fact that it had become the practice in recent years for the kings of both France and England to tax ecclesiastical income and goods with no regard for the pope's consent, and, as in England in 1294, at times with scant regard for the consent of the clergy.[147] Both kings had come to rely very heavily on direct taxation of their respective Churches. But Edward I's recent taxation of the clergy had been especially harsh and there are strong reasons for thinking that 'Clericis laicos' was directed more against the king of England than against the king of France. This possibility is strengthened rather than weakened by the fact that it was many months before the bull was promulgated in England. It must have been recognised that 'Clericis laicos', once received, would be seen to apply directly to the policies of Edward. The inhibition of the arrest or seizure of treasure deposited in holy places could not fail to remind all in England of the scrutiny of ecclesiastical stores of money and the seizure of papal tenths in 1294. The most recent taxes in both countries (the English tenth on income in late 1295, and the French fiftieth on property in late 1295 and early 1296)[148] were not unusually harsh, but it could be significant that the English tax, of which the pope had probably learned by January 1296, was Edward's first imposition upon the English clergy since Boniface VIII's accession. In granting this tenth the English clergy promised further aid to the king if the war continued, but 'Clericis laicos' now forbade not only payments without papal licence but also promises of payments.

It is thus hardly surprising that a chronicler, writing not before the middle of the fourteenth century, should have assumed that Winchelsey had himself petitioned for 'Clericis laicos'.[149] On the

[147] Strayer, 'Consent to taxation', pp. 7–8, 25–8, Deighton, 'Clerical taxation 1279–1301', pp. 163–78 and Boase, *Boniface VIII*, pp. 134–6.
[148] For the latter see Marrone and Zuckermann, 'Simon de Beaulieu', p. 215 n. 53, Digard, *Philippe et le Saint-Siège*, 1. 255–6 and Strayer, 'Consent to taxation', pp. 48–9.   [149] 'Rishanger', p. 168.

basis of this late chronicle evidence Prynne declared that the arch-bishop 'most perfidiously and trayterously procured an Anti-christian Bull'.[150] There is no precise evidence to support this belief. But the very first letter that Winchelsey wrote to Boniface, dated 24 March 1295, is suggestive, if quite inconclusive.[151] The archbishop stressed that he had returned to an England which was oppressed by severe starvation and unexpected wars. He continued: 'greatly hindered in the prosecution of my affairs and the affairs of my Church by a burden of financial debt, I now reside among the English people, suffering with them in their misfortunes and in my own humble way making every effort to bring about more favourable circumstances. Indeed, because pastoral care thrives the better when it is honoured with many privileges, so it is that I have decided to send to the apostolic see by the bearer of this letter certain petitions, separate from this letter and sealed with my seal, pleading for a favourable hearing'. We know nothing more about these 'petitions', and it would be rash to guess as to their content. If Winchelsey had sought papal assistance in the combating of royal exactions, he had done so quietly, indeed, secretly.

In France, characteristically, there had been a vigorous and outspoken appeal to the pope, inspired, it seems, by the Cistercians but avowedly from the abbots, canons and clergy of the whole of France, recalling the principles of clerical immunity, especially the need for papal consent to taxation.[152] Franco-papal relations produced a welter of trenchant literature, of propaganda and of documentation, of which this appeal is an example. But the fact that no comparable body of extant material emanated from England is not in itself a reason for believing that the issues raised by 'Clericis laicos' were less critical in the one kingdom than in the other. The clergy of both France and England, and especially the lower clergy, had certainly not forgotten the protection afforded

---

[150] Prynne, III. 690.   [151] *Reg.*, pp. 11–12.
[152] Kervyn de Lettenhove, 'Études sur l'histoire du XIIIe siècle', *Mémoires de l'Académie Royale des Sciences, des Lettres et des Beaux-Arts de Belgique,* XXVIII (1854), 13–17, thence Digard, *Philippe et le Saint-Siège,* I. 257 and Boase, *Boniface VIII,* p. 136; and reprinted (with erroneous reference to *Mémoires,* XXVII, 1853) in *Patrologiae…Latina,* ed. J. P. Migne, CLXXXV, cols 1843–5.

by the requirement in canon law of papal consent to ecclesiastical taxation. The need for papal consent, except in cases of urgent necessity, had been reiterated by some of the French clergy in 1294 in relation to the grant to Philip of a tenth of clerical income for two years.[153] In 1269 and 1270 the decree of the Fourth Lateran Council requiring papal licence had been cited by the English clergy, and the question of papal consultation concerning taxation had been raised in England in 1283.[154] There had been no need during most of the reign of Henry III for the English clergy to stress the necessity of a papal licence, for the Crown and the papacy had been repeatedly involved in consultations concerning the taxation of the clergy.[155] The position had changed in Edward I's reign. 'Clericis laicos' was certainly in some degree a response to the declared desire of provincial or local clergy for papal protection in the matter of taxation.

It was not until 21 April that the pope instructed the papal nuncios to publish 'Clericis laicos' in France and England.[156] This order was forwarded at about the same time as letters concerning the pope's new proposals for a truce. A new mandate to enforce a truce had been drawn up on 13 April, with instructions to publish it dated 16 April, but in a letter of the following day the pope carefully directed his nuncios to defer publication if there was a possibility of a voluntary truce.[157] The mandate was an essential weapon for the nuncios, should they think fit to call a truce, but the publishing of it was left to their discretion. The cardinals were continuing their efforts to bring the kings to peace, and Edward once again declared his willingness to cease hostilities if Philip would agree.[158] The nuncios did not publish the enjoined truce, judging that it would not aid their negotiations. It was for the same reason no doubt that the publication of 'Clericis laicos'

[153] Strayer, 'Consent to taxation', pp. 26–7 and Digard, *Philippe et le Saint-Siège*, I. 256.
[154] *Councils*, pp. 800 and n, 950, and Lunt, 'Consent of lower clergy', esp. pp. 160–2.
[155] Lunt, *Financial Relations*, pp. 187–238 and Gibbs and Lang, *Bishops and Reform*, pp. 132–4.
[156] *Reg.*, p. 161 and BL Cotton Vesp. E xxii, fo. 7v (Potthast, no. 24321). For what follows see Marrone and Zuckermann, 'Simon de Beaulieu', pp. 211–20. [157] *Reg. Boniface VIII*, nos. 1584–6 (*CPL*, II. 567–8).
[158] *Foedera*, I. ii. 837 and *Reg. Halton*, I. 67–8; and see *Foedera*, I. ii. 837–40, 844, 848–50.

was also delayed; it was not published in France before the middle of July. Boniface sent more letters, dated 18 August,[159] very similar to those sent in April, once again giving discretionary powers concerning the truce and also ordering the publication of 'Clericis laicos'. It was perhaps at about the same time, mid-August, that the bull was released in France, probably because Philip was already negotiating for a further clerical tax.[160] The first bitter conflict between Philip and Boniface followed, with the king's prohibition of the export of money and precious metals and the pope's famous bull 'Ineffabilis amoris'; the dispute was to be healed in part by the papal concessions of 1297.[161]

The crisis in England between king and clergy was to be just as bitter and perhaps of more consequence, but it was for the most part internal. John Balliol of Scotland surrendered to Edward in July 1296,[162] and in late August the king's writs went out for a parliament, with the clergy again fully represented, to meet at Bury St Edmunds on 3 November.[163] More money was the king's aim, and a twelfth and eighth was to be granted by the laity. Probably knowing full well that the king intended to ask for another clerical subsidy, the nuncios wrote from Paris on 10 October ordering the archbishops of Canterbury and York to publish and observe 'Clericis laicos'.[164] The bull had long been expected in England, in some quarters at least. As early as 30 May Winchelsey replied to an inquiry from Godfrey Giffard, bishop of Worcester, telling the bishop that he was wrong to believe that he had obtained any official notification of papal statutes concerning taxation. He assured Giffard that he would obey the statutes to the full when he was formally apprised of them, having regard as far as possible to the interests of the bishop.[165] It is tempting to associate two writs from the king dated 16 October with the arrival of 'Clericis laicos': Edward ordered inquiries concerning certain letters brought into England by a clerk called Nichodemus and by

---

[159] *Reg. Boniface VIII*, nos. 1642–5.
[160] Marrone and Zuckermann, 'Simon de Beaulieu', p. 216.
[161] See esp. Digard, *Philippe et le Saint-Siège*, pp. 263–97.
[162] See E. L. G. Stones and M. N. Blount, 'The surrender of King John of Scotland to Edward I in 1296: some new evidence', *BIHR*, XLVIII (1975), 94–106.
[163] *Councils*, pp. 1148–9.   [164] *Reg.*, pp. 159–61.
[165] *Concilia*, II. 218 and Wake, *State of the Church*, app. p. 23.

evil men because he wanted to prevent the letters getting into the hands of his enemies.[166]

It is quite certain that 'Clericis laicos' was received either before or during the meeting of parliament at Bury St Edmunds in early November,[167] and that, having been fully discussed by the separate clerical assembly there, it provided the essential reason for the postponement of a final answer to the king about another subsidy until further discussion had taken place. But this was the reaction of the southern rather than the northern clergy, for we have the explicit statement in a royal letter of 6 April 1297 that the prelates and clergy of the whole province of York granted a fifth to the king in this parliament.[168] The clergy of the northern province were not afraid to ignore the papal constitution, and it is thus clear that the chronicle accounts refer only to the response to the king of the clergy of the Canterbury province. The continuator of Gervase of Canterbury claims that the clergy did not wish to make a final reply at Bury since they had been called there at the order of the king and not by the authority of the Church; this must, indeed, have influenced the proceedings to some extent. As in the Westminster parliament of the previous year full consideration was given by Winchelsey to clerical opinion, though it is clear that it was once again through his leadership that the southern province displayed a unity of purpose and put forward an independent policy. It is indicative of the archbishop's appreciation of the broad issues involved that he should have advised his clergy to discuss the practical matters (the danger from France and the burden of taxation) as well as the considerations of principle and duty (the promise to the king and the bull itself). Debate took place in four separate groups and the conclusions of each were brought together in one assembly: the conclusion was that no way

---

[166] PRO E159/70 m. 99.
[167] Cotton, p. 314 (the most detailed account, also in *Councils*, p. 1150), Langtoft, II. 268–75, Cont. Gervase, p. 315, Guisborough, p. 286, Trivet, p. 352 and 'Rishanger', p. 165. The Bury chronicle (p. 135) alone claims that the bull was actually published ('publicavit') in the parliament.
[168] PRO E159/70 m. 110d: 'Cum venerabilis pater J. Karliolensis episcopus in ultimo parliamento nostro apud Sanctum Edmundum nobis per se quam pro toto clero episcopatus sui iuxta promissum et concessionem quas ei prius fecerant quintam partem bonorum suorum sicut prelati religiosi et ceteri clerici de provincia Eboracense in certo loco deponendam ad defensionem ecclesie et regni nostri gratanter concessisset. . .'.

of circumventing the demands of 'Clericis laicos' could be found. Consequently the archbishop persuaded the king to allow the clergy until 20 January before coming to a final decision.

Edward was beginning to lose patience. He had suffered the opposition of the clergy in 1295 'with a calm face',[169] but he did not accept so calmly the opposition at Bury St Edmunds. The Bury chronicler states that as soon as the king heard of the clergy's refusal to make a grant 'he ordered the archbishop, the other prelates and the whole clergy of England to be oppressed and harried from that day'. Winchelsey was immediately harried. He had been allowed three years in which to pay a debt to the king of £3,568 arising from the purchase of produce on the archiepiscopal estates at the end of the vacancy of the see, but Edward now demanded that it should be paid by 14 December. Winchelsey replied on 7 December that this was completely impossible, but considering the king's great financial need he would pay with all possible speed.[170] Apart from this indication of anger, Edward's coercive policies against the clergy were being reserved until after the January council.[171]

On what basis were the clergy rejecting the king's request that their promise of further aid should now be honoured? It was not, it must be stressed, a simple question of following the letter of a papal decree. If that had been the case there would have been no need to discuss the political issues, as, for example, in the words of Cotton, 'the imminent danger to the whole kingdom of England from our enemies of the kingdom of France'; and Winchelsey had not yet ordered 'Clericis laicos' to be published. His central concern was to formulate a policy which would protect the interests specifically of the English, not specifically of the Roman, Church. The bull now in his hands was a prohibition in the most extreme terms. Its novelty was not only the directness with which lay powers were instructed of the limits of their powers, but also the emphasis upon the *ipso facto* excommunication of all offenders, whether those responsible for receiving or those responsible for giving ecclesiastical subsidies without papal consent. Boniface

---

[169] Worcester, p. 524.
[170] PRO E159/68 m. 52 and/70 mm. 7d–9d and *Reg.*, pp. 149–50.
[171] Cf. *Flores Hist.*, III. 98, 289.

admitted that the canonical penalties were new.[172] But, more than this, the bull, described by the pope repeatedly as in defence of liberty, denied to local clergy the right to give consent to taxation independently of the pope. The bull is specific: the clergy incur excommunication if they consent to pay ('vel se soluturos consenserint'). Thus 'Clericis laicos', in making the pope sole judge, appeared to strike a blow at the widely accepted document of 'necessitas', that is the right to tax and to be taxed in an emergency.[173] In this particular and crucial respect the English clergy may well have eyed the bull with suspicion, for they only ever argued for the need to seek a papal licence for royal taxation when they did not wish to give consent.[174] They prized highly their own right to judge 'necessitas'. But, even so, they knew that it was from the king that they had recently been under the severest pressures in attempting to exercise this right and to prevent large and arbitrary taxation. The granting of subsidies was much less of an obligation for the clergy than for the laity. It was, after all, a very important aspect of their 'liberty' that they should maintain an independent control of ecclesiastical resources. To the clergy consent really meant consent: they could certainly refuse. But events since 1294 revealed, more than ever before, the extent to which this 'liberty' ran counter to a powerful opinion which had emerged in the course of the thirteenth century: the belief in the common obligation upon all subjects to give aid in defence of the realm. Here was a collision of political views. Winchelsey was quick to see that 'Clericis laicos' gave him the protection he needed. When the clergy judged that the problems of the realm did not merit a favourable response to the king's demands, they could cite the papal decree as the reason for their inability to pay. In addition, they were soon to find in 'Coram illo fatemur' of 28 February 1297 an assurance of the freedom of action they desired,[175] for Boniface VIII here firmly accepted the legality in

---

[172] In 'Ineffabilis amoris': *Reg. Boniface VIII*, no. 1653.
[173] See Harriss, *King, Parliament and Public Finance*, pp. 22–4, 33–4, 46, 60, 63, idem, 'Parliamentary taxation and the origins of appropriation of supply', pp. 169–71, Rothwell, 'Confirmation of the charters', pp. 18–23, J. B. Hennemann, *Royal Taxation in Fourteenth Century France* (Princeton, 1971), pp. 22–5, and Brown, 'Taxation and morality', esp. pp. 3–9.
[174] Lunt, *Financial Relations*, p. 407 n. 4.   [175] Below, pp. 123–4.

an emergency of clerical aids freely offered without papal consultation.

The strength of Winchelsey's personality and the firmness of his beliefs are beginning to reveal themselves. He intended to stand aloof from all involvement in royal government. In a letter of August 1296 he had revealed his fear to Anthony Bek, bishop of Durham, that the cardinal nuncios had nominated him to take part in the negotiations for peace in France, and he urged Bek to have him excused, if the opportunity arose, before the king and his council.[176] He gave his severe financial straits as the excuse,[177] but he also felt that he should not desert the arduous work of cure of souls to which he had been unable to devote himself having so recently assumed office. Cure of souls took firm precedence over royal diplomacy. Yet he had shown his grave concern for the king's difficulties, and, despite the primacy for him of spiritual matters, it would be misleading to regard his political outlook as notably papalist, for there is no evidence of a special relationship of confidence and trust between him and Boniface VIII. There was no inexorable subservience to papal policy among the English clergy, who had their own traditions, their own independence, to guard. It is important to note the bitter complaints from the clergy against the procurations levied for three years towards the expenses of the cardinal nuncios, who spent most of their time outside England. Some chroniclers emphasised the wealth of the cardinals as they left for France in 1295, and bitterness was caused not merely by the procurations themselves, against which Winchelsey was to lead protests to the pope in 1297, but also by the numerous gifts which the nuncios required.[178]

By the end of 1296 the archbishop had shown the first signs of determination and the king the first signs of annoyance. Extreme financial demands from Edward and a papal constitution from Boniface had paved the way for the crisis of 1297. Although papal

[176] *Reg.*, pp. 126–7.
[177] See *Reg.*, pp. ix–x. Pecham had also faced financial problems especially during the first years of his primacy: D. Sutcliffe, 'The financial condition of the see of Canterbury, 1279–92', *Speculum*, x (1935), 53–68.
[178] Cotton, pp. 283–93, *Flores Hist.*, iii. 280, *Liber de Bernewelle*, pp. 235–6, Guisborough, p. 258, Thorne, p. 326, Lunt, *Financial Relations*, pp. 553–7, *Reg.*, pp. 524–5 and Graham, 'A petition to Boniface VIII', pp. 36–9.

explanations concerning 'Clericis laicos', and concessions, became necessary – addressed to Philip or the prelates of France, for the direct pleas to the pope came from them – yet this bull was no 'castle in the air'. It was to occupy an important place in the development of the constitutional relationship of the English clergy to the Crown. The assumption that it was ineffective in England and that the king successfully ignored it has been a serious misjudgment;[179] it gave authority and strength to Winchelsey's policies concerning taxation for the rest of his primacy, and this despite the modification of it by Benedict XI and the annulment of it by Clement V.[180] In 1297 Boniface VIII became conciliatory towards Philip concerning taxation. The main reason for this was a major development which took place on 7 January and which changed the balance of power: the conclusion of the Anglo-Flemish alliance.[181] Edward was now in a strong position and he planned to gain the necessary support at home in order to put to good effect his alliance with Germany and his alliance with Flanders.

[179] E.g. Lunt, *Financial Relations*, pp. 363–4.
[180] Denton, 'Reynolds and ecclesiastical politics', pp. 250–2.
[181] *Foedera*, I. ii. 850–1.

Chapter 4

TAXATION AND POLITICS 1297

The ecclesiastical council, at which a decision had to be made about a grant to the king, met at St Paul's London on 13 January 1297.[1] That Winchelsey had issued mandates for the publication of 'Clericis laicos' before the council[2] serves to emphasise his acceptance of the bull. But he had proceeded with caution. Although the bull had been discussed in the parliament of early November, the surviving mandates of the archbishop for its publication in the dioceses of his province are dated 10 December, 5 and 11 January. And the responsibility for publication had apparently been handed down from the bishops to the archdeacons and from the archdeacons to the rural deans so that the bull, in some dioceses at least, may have received hardly any proper publication.[3] One main reason for reluctance to publish is clear enough. Could the bishops actually enforce the bull? There are no indications that Winchelsey in any way questioned that the bull *should* be obeyed, but he knew of the dangers which lay ahead. He no doubt realised that he would get some support from the prelates and clergy of his province. Bishop Sutton of Lincoln, on 26 December, ordered that the collection in his diocese of the arrears of the moiety of 1294 and of the tenth of 1295 should cease.[4] But how much support could the archbishop rely upon? How much support were the clergy willing to give in the struggle to establish their liberty in the matter of taxation? On 19 Decem-

---

[1] See esp. *Councils*, pp. 1150–62 and Deighton, 'Clerical taxation 1279–1301', pp. 178–81.
[2] *Councils*, p. 1149 n. 6 and *Councils and Eccles. Documents*, ed. Haddan and Stubbs, i. 620.
[3] Cotton, p. 316.   [4] *Reg. Sutton*, v. 198.

ber Winchelsey had written to Henry of Eastry, prior of his cathedral church, telling him that it was apparent from the king's preliminary moves that the English Church was about to suffer many and grave tribulations. He had received letters from his bishops which clearly led him to doubt whether some of them were prepared to stand by him, and he asked the prior to sort out the documents concerning the professions of obedience to the church of Canterbury made by each of the bishops of the province and to bring them with him to the council soon to meet in London.[5]

The reason for the January council was well known: the king required an answer to his request for a subsidy. There is no mention of this request in the summons to the council. The eloquent generalities which form the preambles of the formal summonses often hide the actual reasons for the convoking of the clergy to councils, and a commitment to the interests of the English clergy had to be firmly placed in the context of a commitment to the interests of the kingdom. This understood, the summons for the January meeting of prelates and clergy is nonetheless revealing.[6] It suggests a definite attitude by Winchelsey to England's predicament at the end of 1296. For the king it was a time of new and vigorous preparations.[7] Hostilities had already broken out between Philip IV and Edward's ally the count of Flanders. The campaigns in Wales and then in Scotland and the payment of large subsidies to his allies in Brabant and Flanders meant that Edward's financial needs were greater than ever. Winchelsey's summons to the January council presented in hopeless terms the state of war in which the kingdom found itself. The archbishop pointed out that, while the country had faced the vicissitudes of war before, it had previously enjoyed an increasing recruitment of men and plentiful supplies. Now the men and the provisions had dried up. While not in any way underestimating the dangers from the enemies of the kingdom, the archbishop suggested that a new remedy should be sought for this new predicament. 'New and virulent diseases need new medicines.'[8]

[5] *Reg.*, p. 1317.   [6] *Councils*, pp. 1152–5.
[7] See Barraclough, 'Edward I and Adolf of Nassau', p. 241.
[8] Quoting St Augustine: see Post, *Studies in Medieval Legal Thought*, p. 534 nn. 95, 98.

Winchelsey can only have meant that he opposed going to war
with France. The new remedy was to support the negotiations for
peace initiated by the pope. And 'Clericis laicos' was part of that
remedy.

Winchelsey knew his own mind. The question was whether he
could carry his clergy with him in the January council. After the
council had been opened with a sermon from the archbishop, the
dangers facing the kingdom were expounded both by the archbishop and by one of the king's nuncios, John Berwick, who
asserted that the defence of the kingdom was not possible without
the financial assistance of the clergy. Winchelsey then ordered
'Clericis laicos' to be read to the whole assembly. The other royal
nuncio, the knight Hugh le Dispenser, reacted to this by speaking
on behalf of the king, his earls, barons, knights and other faithful
men. The clerk John Berwick was, it seems, spared the presentation of the lay point of view. Hugh's message was a threat: the
clergy must provide a subsidy lest the king, the earls and the
barons take into their own hands the control of ecclesiastical
possessions.[9] The threat associated the interests of the lay magnates
with the interests of the king and sought to isolate the clergy.
The clergy were presented with a clear choice. No compromise
was open to them. They can never have been more conscious of
their double allegiance.

As in the Bury parliament the gathering was divided into four
groups, each commissioned to reach its own conclusions after full
and open discussion. Debate continued for several days. A surviving report from the proctors of the lower clergy may come
from this council or from the Bury parliament.[10] Either way, it
presents important evidence of the attitude of one section of the
clergy. The lower clergy, who had been more inclined than the
prelates to oppose the king in 1294, provided what was probably
the strongest body of opinion in support of 'Clericis laicos'. They
had least to lose both in terms of land and possessions and in terms
of individual reputation by a policy of opposition to the king, and,
at the same time, with their lack of resilience and their limited
powers of redress, they had probably been hit particularly hard by
taxation. They pointed out that the previous tax, the tenth of

[9] Cotton in *Councils*, p. 1160.   [10] *Councils*, pp. 1156–7.

1295, had been granted on condition that ecclesiastical liberty as expressed in *Magna Carta* be restored and on condition that there be no further exactions upon the possessions of the clergy, with no prises of goods from unwilling owners unless a just price be paid before the goods were taken away. Neither condition had been met. Indeed, for twenty years and more the Church had been burdened by making subsidies in the hope of obtaining a restoration of its freedom. The clergy showed an awareness of the change which had been taking place in the rôle of the Church within the kingdom. There had been a time, after all, when the accepted way of securing divine aid was to *give* to the Church. The clergy looked back and recommended that the king should glory in God's name, for, through the prayers of the Church, God had strengthened his arm against his enemies, and to maintain this divine propitiation he should restore the liberty of his Church and return the possessions which had been taken from the clergy by the royal ministers. The king should note, claimed the lesser clergy, that they were always prepared to give some assistance to him when it was not against ecclesiastical canons, and they argued that in the present situation he should procure for them a favourable attitude from the pope about their financial difficulties. This was an interesting point of view. The clergy saw themselves burdened by king and pope alike; the king should be working for them, not against them. But they made it clear that they felt that they had no choice but to obey the papal decree. To make a grant without the pope's licence would be for the whole clerical body to fall into a trap. It would bring the Church and the faith into disrepute, for they could not as excommunicates administer the sacraments without irregularity. All would follow the law of men and abandon the priesthood and rule of Christ. Here was the *sacerdotium* at its most defensive, demanding respect for its rights and its laws. The proctors of the diocesan clergy, two summoned from each diocese, showed an awareness of the stronger position in which 'Clericis laicos' had placed them vis-à-vis the king. Their report was an impassioned plea to the bishops to stand firm.

But there was also opposition to Winchelsey's policy. In the first place, the clergy of the whole province of York had already conceded a fifth to the king at the Bury parliament.[11] No leading cleric in the north made a stand like Winchelsey. In the wake of the Scottish war and with the royal adviser, Anthony Bek, as bishop of Durham, and the royal servant, Henry Newark, as archbishop-elect of York, this is hardly surprising. Yet, it should be noted that the clergy of the north did not all follow submissively the lead of their episcopal superiors. To obtain the fifth, action had to be taken by the king against the clergy of the Carlisle diocese and against some of the canons of York.[12]

The bishops of the northern province were not alone in supporting the king. It is certain that some bishops failed, either totally or in part, to execute the orders from the bishops attending the council for the excommunication of violators of ecclesiastical property.[13] The bishop of Coventry and Lichfield, Walter Langton, was royal treasurer, the bishop of Winchester, John of Pontoise, was an active royal servant, the bishop of Bath and Wells, William of March, was an ex-treasurer and the bishop of Ely, William of Louth, was ex-keeper of the wardrobe. From these prelates dissent from Winchelsey's policy could be fully expected.[14] All of them, including William of March who might well have felt bitter after his dismissal from the office of treasurer in 1295, were very quick

---

11 PRO E159/70 m. 110d. See above, p. 95. For the submission of Henry Newark, archbishop-elect of York, and John Halton, bishop of Carlisle, for themselves and the clergy of their dioceses, and of Anthony Bek, bishop of Durham, see also Prynne, III. 708, *Cal. Chanc. Warr.*, p. 75, *CPR 1292–1301*, p. 237, *Cal. Var. Chanc. Rolls*, pp. 38–9, Dunstable, p. 406 and Guisborough, p. 288. The January council summoned by Winchelsey cannot *in itself* have been also a council of York clergy (cf. *Councils*, p. 1151). There survives, among the parliamentary proxies of the public records a proxy issued by the abbot of Meaux on 6 Jan. for a 'convocation or council of clergy' in London on 13 Jan.: PRO SC10/1/11A. The king thus appears to have summoned the York clergy to what was, in effect, a prorogued session of the clergy in parliament. In doing so he perhaps wanted the continuing support of the York clergy in his attempt to obtain a fifth from the clergy of the whole realm. The clergy of the two provinces had been summoned as though to separate assemblies; whether or not they actually met in one gathering, the northern clergy seem to have had little influence upon the southern.

12 PRO E368/68 m. 26 and E159/70 mm. 19, 101, 110d, 114d.

13 *Councils*, p. 1193.

14 Pontoise was in Rome: *Reg. Pontissara*, p. 842. Whether the others attended the council is not known. Six days before the council assembled the bishop of Coventry and Lichfield and the bishop of Ely were with the king at Ipswich (along with the bishop of Durham): PRO C53/83 no. 19. But Langton *was* in London on 14 Jan.: Cuttino, 'Langton's mission for Edward I', p. 180.

to submit to the king's policy of coercion. Their opinion was represented by a few at the council whom Winchelsey noted as disagreeing with the decision that a subsidy should not be offered to the king.

Nevertheless, the archbishop for the most part obtained from the clergy of his own province a common view-point. There is a significant difference in tone between the report of the lower clergy and the controlled statement of policy which the archbishop sent to the king.[15] The archbishop's statement reveals that the clergy's decision, although it was a clear choice between two courses of action, was necessarily based upon an assessment of the king's predicament and upon judgment of the extent to which they felt bound to observe the new papal decree. Winchelsey naturally stressed that the clergy faced grave dangers if they offended against the constitutions of the Church, and he could not hide from the fact that it was 'Clericis laicos' that lent authority to the clergy's policy of obstruction. Yet, it was clearly not a question of blind obedience to the bull. The clergy were agreed that if the kingdom were faced in the future with the unavoidable risk of subversion they would all oppose the enemy with every lawful means within their power. Although the bull forbade them to make a promise[16] of financial aid, Winchelsey stated that it ought not to prevent the kingdom from being defended if the danger to it was great enough. The archbishop believed that the English clergy should make up its own mind about the circumstances in which a grant should be made. 'Clericis laicos' had not, after all, changed the law of the Church in any fundamental way, and the English clergy in the making of subsidies on their income to the king had very often set aside the need for papal consent. It was the greater allegiance of the French clergy to the principle of papal consent that made them in these years more dependent than the English clergy upon papal decisions concerning taxation.[17] 'Clericis laicos' had put Winchelsey in a strong position to fight for the independence of the English Church. He was denying that the threat from Philip the Fair was great enough to merit a subsidy.

[15] *Councils*, pp. 1157–9.
[16] 'Promissio' is a better reading than 'provisio': *Councils*, p. 1159 n. l.
[17] Strayer, 'Consent to taxation', pp. 24–32.

The line between supporting the papal decree and fighting for an independent policy was a fine one. Certainly the archbishop felt that he could not turn his back on the pope. He was giving full support to 'Clericis laicos', and, as if to emphasise the direct relevance of the bull to the situation in England, the archbishop and bishops at the council determined that sentences of major excommunication should be pronounced in churches throughout the dioceses of the province against all those who had attacked and removed ecclesiastical goods.[18] According to Guisborough, Winchelsey stated his willingness to request the pope's consent to make some payment or at least to ask him what the clergy should do,[19] and it is possible that the archbishop did seek the pope's advice.[20] But Guisborough goes on to show that the archbishop's willingness to consult the pope was in fact taken by the royal envoys as tantamount to a refusal of the royal demand. The envoys were surely right.

Winchelsey knew the consequences of the clergy's decision, though he perhaps hoped that Edward's coercive intentions would be thwarted because of the extent of the clerical opposition. He asked the king to consider what an incomparably greater danger it was for the clergy to offend against their sacred laws than for them to lose all their goods and the temporal aspects of their lives. But his letter ended with a plea, not about the probable confiscation of clerical possessions, but about the recent prises of corn. The depredations of men claiming to be royal ministers were such, he said, that unless the king in his piety thought fit to provide a speedy remedy many of the clergy would be so poor that they would be driven to begging. It was, no doubt, especially the recent exactions of the king, not least the prises,[21] which stiffened the opposition to Edward in January 1297. This must be borne fully in mind before we imagine that the clergy as a whole accepted all the implications of Winchelsey's own opinion, as stated by Guisborough, that the clergy were bound by a greater allegiance to the spiritual than to the temporal power. Until the king's threats of confiscation and outlawry were changed into actual policy it

[18] *Councils*, p. 1193.
[19] Guisborough, p. 287. According to Langtoft's account (p. 273) Winchelsey had shown his willingness at the Bury parliament to consult the pope.
[20] Below, pp. 122–3. [21] Bury, p. 137.

was still convenient for the clergy to stand firm with Winchelsey.

In the account by Guisborough the king's envoys at the council told the prelates to send their own messengers to announce the decision of the clergy, for they feared his wrath. But Cotton notes that they in fact brought him the news in advance of the deputation commissioned by the clergy.[22] We can assume that the members of this deputation were supporters of the council's decision. They were the bishops of Hereford, Exeter and Norwich, the archdeacon of Norfolk and the abbots of Ramsey and Colchester, and they found the king at Castle Acre, where he was staying between 28 January and 1 February. Naturally, they were given a cool reception. To their statement the king replied that they were not now bound by the homage and oath sworn to him for their baronies and nor was he bound by the same homage and oath. It is more than likely that the king had, in fact, known of the clergy's decision on or before 26 January when the writs were issued for the lay parliament to meet at Salisbury on 24 February.[23] An independent account, from Evesham, tells us that having heard of the clerical reply the king agreed to accept the suggestion of his chief advisers to summon a parliament of earls, barons and knights to discover how he could take vengeance on the clergy.[24] The clergy would have to accept the judgment upon them of the laity.

In fact, the king determined the main lines of his policy in advance of the lay parliament at Salisbury. He determined to carry out his threats. On 30 January he decided to put the clergy outside the protection of himself and the common law and to seize their lay fees.[25] Understandably, the chronicles fully reveal the bitterness which this policy created within the Church.[26] The king's act, considered worthy of a second Nero or Pilate, was widely accepted as the direct cause of the defeat of the English army in Gascony on the same day and, if we are to believe Cotton, at the same hour.[27] 'The mother Church which has been accustomed for a long time

[22] Cotton, p. 318.   [23] *Parl. Writs*, I. ii. 51.   [24] Evesham, p. 568.
[25] Cotton, pp. 318–19 and Worcester, p. 530.
[26] For particularly indignant accounts see *Flores Hist.*, III. 291–3 and *Anglia Sacra*, I. 14–16.
[27] Cotton, p. 319, Worcester, p. 530, Guisborough, p. 287, *Flores Hist.*, III. 291–3 and Bury, pp. 137–8.

past to rule over her sons is made a servant and a slave.'[28] Cotton states that the king expressly empowered laymen to seize the horses of clergymen, and this statement finds some support in other chronicles.[29] The Bury chronicle notes that the king's 'edict' against the clergy was reported by some as specific protection for those laymen who attacked and robbed clerks; and the chronicler refers to the 'edict' in terms which echo the papal bull ('Clericis laicos infestos'): 'edictum ne laycos clericis infestos. . . censura iusticie civilis cohiberet'.[30] The king's attack upon the clergy appeared as confirmation of the enmity of the laity towards the clergy as stated in 'Clericis laicos'. Edward, comments the Evesham chronicler, was deliberately setting the laity against the clergy.[31]

The king thus began a policy of using force in order to insist on his right to tax the clergy's income. He sent his instructions to the exchequer, telling his ministers in a letter dated 9 February to do as Hugh le Dispenser instructed them. On 13 February Hugh presented the king's orders before Walter Langton, Anthony Bek, Philip Willoughby (chancellor of the exchequer), John of Cobham, Peter of Leicester and John de Insula (barons of the exchequer), and John Droxford (keeper of the wardrobe).[32] No clerk was to be admitted to plead in the exchequer or to continue a hearing already begun there and no writ on behalf of any clerk was to be issued in the exchequer, unless he could produce royal letters of protection. Naturally, cases in which a clerk was the defendant were not affected. A public statement to the same effect was made by John of Mettingham, justice of the king's bench.[33] The outlawry included from the first the confiscation of the clergy's lands and possessions. And a 'fine' of a fifth, already conceded by the northern clergy, was fixed as the price to be paid to regain possession. Far from being a compromise[34] this was direct defiance

---

[28] Guisborough, p. 287.

[29] *Flores Hist.*, III. 99, 291, Dunstable, p. 406, Bury, p. 137, Evesham, p. 569, Blount, 'Annals of Hailes', p. 107 (BL Cotton Cleo. D iii, fo. 52r); and see Rishanger, p. 474. For the scarcity of horses see Morris, *Welsh Wars*, p. 82.

[30] Bury, p. 137.

[31] Evesham, p. 571.

[32] PRO E159/70 m. 17 and E368/68 m. 23.

[33] Worcester, p. 530 and Guisborough, p. 287.

[34] Cf. Deighton, 'Clerical taxation 1279–1301', p. 181.

of the papal bull. The 'fine' was a forced tax upon the income of the clergy. Also, in what appears to have been a deliberate attempt to isolate the clergy, the king had ordered on 31 January that no one should leave the realm without the king's licence and that any letters seized at the ports should be sent to him for his inspection.[35]

We need have no doubts about describing the king's action against the recalcitrant clergy as a sentence of outlawry. In the king's words they had betrayed their liege lord, their own nation and the kingdom.[36] They were accused of treason and put outside the law: 'exleges et laesae majestatis rei censebantur'.[37] The outlawry of virtually all the clergy of the southern province was, nonetheless, an action *sui generis*. It cannot be closely equated with the sentences of outlawry which carried the liability of the death penalty, nor with the process whereby laymen, and sometimes clerks, abjured the realm.[38] But the ancient process of outlawry had comprised essentially the confiscation of rights and goods, and the restoration of both only by the grace of the king;[39] and in more recent times it had become to a large extent a process of law for the contumacious, very similar in this respect to excommunication.[40]

The earliest writs to the sheriffs concerning the sequestration of the clergy's lands and possessions were dated 12 February,[41] and they specified that the lay fees and temporal possessions of the

---

[35] Prynne, III. 729–30 (*CCR 1296–1302*, p. 81 and see 86–7). Part of a draft statement of 9 March 1297 by the proctor of Christ Church Canterbury (Cant. D. & C., Sede Vacante Scrapbooks, II. 170) refers to this prohibition, but it is probably unrelated to another document pasted on to the same page (cf. *Councils*, p. 1151 n. 5). This second document is an undated appeal of the constable of Dover against his excommunication by Winchelsey; he was excommunicated in 1302 for the incarceration of the abbot of Faversham (see Cant. D. & C., Reg. I, fo. 243 and *Reg.*, pp. 1322–3).

[36] PRO E368/68 m. 27d.

[37] Dunstable, p. 406.

[38] See A. L. Poole, 'Outlawry as a punishment of criminous clerks', in *Historical Essays in Honour of J. Tait*, ed. J. G. Edwards, V. H. Galbraith and E. F. Jacob (Manchester, 1933), pp. 239–46 and Cheney, 'Punishment of felonous clerks'.

[39] A. Réville, '*L'abjuratio regni*: histoire d'une institution anglaise', *Revue Historique*, L (1892), 5–8.

[40] Pollock and Maitland, *English Law*, I. 49, 476–8, II. 449–50, 581, 593.

[41] Worcester, p. 530, Cotton, p. 320, Evesham, p. 569 and Prynne, III. 694–5 (*CCR 1296–1302*, p. 14).

clergy should be seized. This meant, as the chroniclers insist, the confiscation of almost all ecclesiastical land other than that actually occupied by churches and their cemeteries.[42] According to the Evesham chronicler the royal officials exceeded the king's orders. Possessions on manors belonging to monasteries were carried off, even though the king's mandate was for the *safe* custody of the clergy's lands and goods.[43] How much the king regretted the depredations of his agents, and how much the chroniclers exaggerated, it is difficult to judge. The king's policy, it is undeniable, was a very severe blow to the clergy. It put them in an intolerable position. They had already been greatly concerned about prises, but now corn, or any goods, could be much more easily confiscated and without any possibility of redress.[44]

Individual bishops on occasions had their temporalities confiscated by the Crown. It was a means of coercion against prelates who showed contempt. The seizure of a bishop's barony could be threatened if he claimed men charged with felony as clerks when they were in fact laymen and if the king was unable to levy debts from clerks under his jurisdiction.[45] In a notable case Edward I seized the temporalities of Thomas Corbridge, archbishop of York, in 1304, and he seized the franchise of the bishop of Durham in 1302–3 and 1305–7.[46] When a bishop's temporalities were in the king's hands the Crown exercised patronage rights as during a vacancy of the see.[47] But the seizure of the temporalities

[42] Cotton, p. 320, Dunstable, p. 405 and Guisborough, p. 287.
[43] Evesham, pp. 568–9.
[44] For prises see *Lincs. Assize Roll 1298*, ed. Thomson, esp. pp. lii–lxxxviii and Maddicott, *English Peasantry*, esp. 15–24, 57–8; and for the prise of wool in April 1297 see G. O. Sayles, 'The seizure of wool at Easter 1297', *EHR*, LXVII (1952), 543–6 and Lloyd, *English Wool Trade*, pp. 87–93.
[45] See *The Eyre of Kent 1313–14*, ed. F. W. Maitland *et al.*, I (Selden Soc. XXIV, 1909), 86 and *Reg. Geynesborough*, pp. 182–93. And for the imposition of fines upon prelates see R. B. Pugh, *Imprisonment in Medieval England* (Cambridge, 1968), pp. 37–8 (for escapes from bishops' prisons), *CPR 1281–92*, p. 10 and *CFR*, I. 134 (for proceeding with an election without royal licence), *CPR 1301–7*, p. 110 and *Councils*, p. 1227 (for admission of a bull of provision injurious to the Crown).
[46] *Select Cases Before King's Council*, p. lx, *Select Cases King's Bench*, III. 136–7, Guisborough, pp. 358–9, *The Historians of the Church of York*, ed. J. Raine (RS, 3 vols. 1879–94), II. 411–12, Deeley, 'Papal provision and royal rights', p. 506, *Hemingsby Register*, p. 19 and Fraser, *Bek*, pp. 161–2, 164, 194, 221.
[47] See W. E. L. Smith, *Episcopal Appointments*, pp. 86–94 and Cheney, *Pope Innocent III and England*, p. 91.

of all the recalcitrant clergy in England in 1297 was as unusual as
the withdrawal of the protection of the law. It naturally resulted
in the recording of the size of the clergy's estates and the valuation
of their lands and possessions.[48] A value was put on their goods,
comments the author of *Flores*, so that they could be sold as
quickly as possible.[49] The dramatising of the events of February
and March in the chronicles is only to be expected. The Evesham
chronicler, for instance, asserts that 'the king took great delight in
the plundering of the monasteries and ordered, it was said, the
imprisonment of anyone who resisted this plundering'.[50] This was
the truth from the clerical point of view. But, although the
violentia against the clergy no doubt varied from area to area,
documentary evidence gives support to the chronicle accounts at
almost every point.

Two notarial acts tell the story of what happened at Christ
Church Canterbury.[51] On Ash Wednesday (27 February), a fortnight after the issuing of the writs to the sheriffs, the king's
nuntius, John Dynnoke, along with the sheriff of Kent and some
of the sheriff's men, took possession of the priory, locking up the
cellars and storehouses, the larder, the guest-house, and the
granary. A new janitor was installed. Henry de Tychfield, notary,
was called in on the same day by the monks to witness the
sequestration. He secretly inspected, from door to door, the locked
offices, noting the details of the seal affixed to the locks, with its
image as though of a predatory lion ('quasi leonis rapacis') and its
device 'Ci Repos'. His notarial act states that 'ecclesiastical liberty
had been set aside'. Only a week after the sequestration, on
6 March, the notary was called to the priory once again, this time
by the monastic keeper of the granary, who feared the loss of the
corn stored in the granary because of overheating. The notary
testified that he saw and touched the steaming and putrefying

---

[48] Dunstable, p. 405 and Evesham, p. 569.

[49] *Flores Hist.*, III. 291.

[50] P. 571. Having described the seizure of the clergy's horses by laymen, the
annalist of Hailes commented 'unde multum gaudebat rex': Blount, 'Annals
of Hailes', p. 107 (BL Cotton Cleo. D iii, fo. 52r).

[51] Cant. D. & C., Cartae Antiquae X3 and C169. The former is wrongly cited
as X6 in *Historical MSS Commission: Fifth Report* (1876), p. 433a and
Councils, p. 1149 n. 7; for C169 see Cheney, *Notaries Public*, p. 70. The
sequestration of Christ Church is described in *Anglia Sacra*, I. 14–15.

grain and witnessed the obstruction by the king's custodians of workmen who were spreading the grain in an attempt to save it.

The sequestration was certainly very damaging to the life of Christ Church Canterbury. Cotton, Thorne and the archbishop's biographer noted that following the seizure the monks had nothing to eat or drink from their own stores and relied upon the charity of friends.[52] The biographer interpreted the attack on Christ Church as a deliberate attempt to prevent the archbishop from obtaining support from his cathedral church. He tells us that the eighty monks had to sleep in the chapel of St Nicholas in the priory church and that when the food stored in the priory was returned to the monks it had all gone to waste. It was probably as a result of the king's seizure of the priory that the number of monks sank to less than thirty.[53] The monk's notary had mentioned the belief of some of the members of the priory that the king's policy of sequestration was designed essentially to undermine their morale. But the events at Canterbury illustrate that, even if sequestration was carried out with less harshness elsewhere, considerable loss must have been caused to the English clergy's property and wealth.

In the face of the king's complete opposition Winchelsey had little hope of holding to the policy for which he had fought successfully at the January council. He made the strongest possible attempt to maintain support for 'Clericis laicos'.[54] At Canterbury on 10 February, after the consecration of John of Monmouth as bishop of Llandaff, he had publicly excommunicated all those who contravened the terms of the bull in any way. John of Monmouth was the scholar-bishop whom Winchelsey himself had appointed to the see of Llandaff, and the archbishop chose the important occasion of his consecration to make clear his continued and firm intention of enforcing 'Clericis laicos'. The continuator of Gervase of Canterbury dates the period of the seizure of the archbishop's lands and possessions from 17 February.[55] On this same day Winchelsey wrote to the bishop of London ordering the full

[52] Cotton, p. 322, Thorne, p. 327 and *Anglia Sacra*, I. 14–15.
[53] *Reg.*, pp. 257–8 and see R. A. L. Smith, *Canterbury Cathedral Priory* (Cambridge, 1943), p. 3.
[54] *Councils*, p. 1151.   [55] Cont. Gervase, p. 315.

publication of 'Clericis laicos' throughout the province of Canterbury. He saw the bull as a decree which followed the tradition of earlier decrees, for example the legate Ottobono's protection of ecclesiastical property and the similar mandate of Archbishop Boniface of Savoy; and he told the bishop of London that the prelates had been remiss concerning the publication of these statutes. This was Winchelsey's answer to the seizure of the clergy's lands and possessions. Four days later in a letter perhaps not unconnected with these events the archbishop asked the vice-chancellor of Boniface VIII for assistance against the assaults and torments of his adversaries.[56]

The Evesham chronicler, while he is extremely sympathetic to the clergy, nonetheless shows knowledge of the king's side of the story. Forewarned by the bishop of London, Richard Gravesend, that the archbishop had ordered the general sentence of excommunication embodied in 'Clericis laicos' to be promulgated in all the dioceses of the province, the king forbade the execution of the archbishop's mandate.[57] Edward interpreted Winchelsey's action as an attack upon his ministers, both lay and clerical, especially those who had sought royal protection. This is clear from an important letter dated 27 February (that is, during the lay parliament at Salisbury), which apparently survives only in the Evesham chronicle and which is probably addressed solely to the bishop of London ('venerabili in Christo patri episcopo etc.'). Edward informed the bishop that he had prohibited the archbishop from promulgating the sentences of excommunication because they were prejudicial to his 'Crown and dignity'. Since, he claimed, the subversion of the realm could follow from the promulgation of these ecclesiastical sentences, he prohibited the bishop of London from executing the archbishop's mandate to publish them. Battle was joined.

It is important to estimate how many of the clergy of the southern province submitted to the king as soon as the policy of coercion became a reality. There is no doubt that the royal clerks

---

[56] *Reg.*, pp. 525–6.
[57] P. 571 ('per predictum [episcopum] Londoniensem premunitus'). The writ which follows in the chronicle is printed as in MS but should probably read (lines 4–5): 'proponebat promulgare et per suam provinciam facere promulgari'.

submitted immediately to the king's demands. The author of *Flores* describes the officials in the king's service who had supported the king's request for a subsidy at the January council as false clerks, and the ecclesiastics ('prelati') of the royal court who immediately succumbed to Edward's coercion as manifest Pilates. And the Bury chronicle confirms that the royal courtiers and clerks rapidly made peace with the king.[58] The many lists recording the submission of the clergy to the king are difficult to use because the date recorded on them often appears to be that of the first entry. But they can be put into some order. There is a list of restitutions of lay fees and goods and a list of protections which both have the initial date 16 February and which almost certainly reveal the first batch of clergy from the Canterbury province to submit to the king.[59] Most of the names, totalling 130, appear in both lists, and a very large number are undoubtedly royal servants and clerks. They include John Droxford, Walter Langton, William of Louth, William of March and John of Pontoise. There was, therefore, in the first place, a division between the clergy of the northern and the southern provinces, and, in the second place, a division between the clergy in royal service and the rest.

But the royal clerks were quickly followed by some clergy who were certainly outside royal service. The next list of protections survives under the date of 22 February at Odiham in Hampshire,[60] for the king was on his way to Salisbury. This list should be studied along with three other lists, two of which are concerned with the restitution of goods and with the protection of spiritualities from inclusion in the current lay tax of a twelfth.[61] The third has no title but is undoubtedly a list of clergy who had submitted. These three lists were being added to as the days passed and they soon include entries which date from after the beginning of March; but a large number of the early entries coincide not only with each other but also with the entries on the list of protections.

[58] *Flores Hist.*, III. 291 and Bury, p. 138.
[59] Prynne, III. 740 (*CPR 1292–1301*, pp. 235–7) and *Cal. Var. Chanc. Rolls*, pp. 17–20. It was decreed in the exchequer on 20 Feb. that writs of protection be issued to clergy who submitted and letters close for the restoration of seized possessions be sent to sheriffs: PRO E159/70 m. 10d and E368/68 m. 23d.
[60] Prynne, III. 709–11 (*CPR 1292–1301*, pp. 260–4).
[61] *Cal. Var. Chanc. Rolls*, pp. 22–5 and 39–42, and *CCR 1296–1302*, pp. 88–93.

Taking the lists together, they record about 230 submissions which probably took place up to the beginning of March, that is, the end of the Salisbury parliament. They do not represent any particular group, although, as the Evesham chronicle stresses,[62] many were regular clergy (including the Hospitallers and Templars),[63] and it is noticeable that many came from Salisbury itself and the surrounding area, including the bishop of Salisbury, Nicholas Longespee (who died two months later), but not including Master Simon of Ghent, canon and prebendary of Salisbury and of York, and archdeacon of Oxford, who was elected bishop of Salisbury on 2 June. And one further bishop apparently submitted at an early stage to the king: the ageing bishop of Worcester, Godfrey Giffard, who had served in early life in the royal household and had been royal chancellor 1266–8.[64] Thus, within three weeks of the first royal writs to the sheriffs concerning outlawry, six out of the thirteen English bishops of the southern province, excluding Winchelsey, had made their peace with Edward. But this figure is somewhat deceptive. The bishops who stood firm were very influential within the clerical body; and the rest of the clergy did not succumb as readily as the bishops. Yet, when a bishop had submitted, others in the diocese could follow all the more easily. About fifty religious houses had already obtained protection, and the vast majority of the ones recorded for the southern province came from the dioceses of Bath and Wells, Salisbury and Winchester.

The surrender of some important clerics, if still only a minority, helped to determine royal policy. The king's plan for securing the submission of the whole of the clerical body is embodied in mandates of 1 March.[65] Just how far this policy arose out of discussion at the lay parliament is not apparent; but there is certainly no indication that the earls, barons and knights in any way opposed Edward's determined stand against the clergy.[66] The mandates set in motion an administrative process whereby the

---

[62] Evesham, p. 570.   [63] Prynne, III. 696 (*CCR 1296–1302*, p. 16).

[64] Gibbs and Lang, *Bishops and Reform*, p. 192.

[65] *Parl. Writs*, I. ii. 393–4 (*CPR 1292–1301*, pp. 239–40); and see Cotton, p. 321 and Evesham, p. 570.

[66] The Evesham chronicle claims (p. 570) that the final date for the buying of royal protection, viz Easter, was determined by the barons and knights.

clergy were able to buy back their seized land and property. For each county a knight was appointed to work with the sheriff to receive recognisances from the clergy before Easter (14 April) at the latest, and in the articles added to the mandates the price to be paid for royal protection was confirmed as double the aid previously given by the clergy (that is, a fifth of clerical income) since the king's need in defending his kingdom was now so much greater. The king, admitting his 'rancour and indignation' that the clergy had refused him financial aid, was clearly eager that they should submit without delay and without further obstruction.

Edward realised that he was faced with a potentially dangerous situation. Disaffection had to be held in check. Winchelsey's strength was based partly on the clergy's close involvement in the whole process of disseminating information on affairs of state. In one of the mandates of 1 March[67] Edward hit out at the inventors of rumours ('troveurs de novelles'), declaring that they appeared to be creating discord among the ruling members of society – the king, the prelates, the earls and the barons – and that they were no less responsible for attempting to disturb the peace and subvert the realm than those who attacked the country by force of arms; he assigned the named knights and sheriffs to seek out all the evil men who were spreading rumours and working to prevent the execution of royal mandates. The evil men included, Edward declared, those who 'utter sentences of excommunication and issue monitions' against royal ministers or subjects who were obeying royal orders or against members of the clergy who had put themselves under royal protection in order to defend themselves and their churches. All those found guilty of these malicious practices were to be arrested and put in jail awaiting the king's will.

Was there much subversion to be discovered? We know that there had been great reluctance among the clergy to publish any of the ecclesiastical decrees, let alone to attempt to pronounce sentences of excommunication. So the king's letter may at first appear more as a threat than as a piece of administrative control.

---

[67] *Parl. Writs*, I. ii. 393b and Prynne, III. 699 (*CPR 1292–1301*, p. 239); and see Evesham, p. 572. This writ echoes c. 34 of the first Statute of Westminster (1275): see T. F. T. Plucknett, *A Concise History of the Common Law* (London, 5th edn 1956), pp. 485–7.

But this is to undervalue the force of the king's writ. His concern for the spreading of rumours is perhaps illustrated by his order to the exchequer on 4 March for the imprisonment in the Tower of London of a clerk accused of forging papal bulls;[68] and the king, we must remember, had forbidden on 27 February the publishing of the sentences of excommunication arising from the infringe-ments of 'Clericis laicos'. The mandate of 1 March is the follow-up to that prohibition. It is a thinly veiled attempt to prevent alto-gether the execution of the terms of 'Clericis laicos'. Anyone pub-lishing the bull could certainly be regarded as 'uttering sentences of excommunication and issuing monitions'. There is clear evi-dence that the royal ministers took action against members of the clergy specifically for publishing the bull. From Cornwall we have the names of thirty-four clerks, mostly vicars and chaplains, who were imprisoned at Launceston for the 'publication of a papal letter'. Clerks were imprisoned also in Devon and in East Anglia.[69]

Yet, can Edward's fears, at the beginning of March, have been very great? The submission of some clergy probably encouraged him to strike out openly and uncompromisingly against the policies of his archbishop. He had been confident enough to demand from the clergy a fine twice as great as the tax which he might well have had to accept if the clergy had made an offer in November or perhaps in January. On the other hand, the clerical opposition was as yet far from crushed. And the king now had cause for apprehension about developments in another sphere. It was the lay opposition which he encountered at Salisbury that some chroniclers stressed.[70] In excluding the clergy from the parliament the king had opened the door to opposition from elsewhere, and the parliament marks the beginning of overt conflict between Edward and both his constable and his marshal (Humphrey de Bohun, earl of Hereford, and Roger Bigod, earl of Norfolk).[71] The issue was that they refused to fight in Gascony

---

[68] PRO E159/70 m. 118 and E368/68 mm. 32, 53; and see *CCR 1296–1302*, p. 56.
[69] Prynne, III. 700–1, *CCR 1296–1302*, pp. 25–8 and PRO E135/21/77.
[70] Bury, p. 138, *Flores Hist.*, III. 100, Trivet, p. 354, 'Rishanger', p. 169 and esp. Guisborough, pp. 289–90.
[71] For earlier relations of Edward with both earls see Morris, *Welsh Wars*, pp. 158, 222, 233, 250, 274–5.

unless the king went there too.[72] It was at this parliament, in Guisborough's account, that an argument with the earl marshal resulted in the king's declaration to Bigod: 'By God, earl, either you will go or you will hang.' To which the earl replied. 'By the same oath, king, I shall neither go nor hang.' What had been regarded by some as a lay parliament intended to sit in judgment on the clergy became in fact a parliament which produced disagreement between the king and some of the lay aristocracy. This was a significant turning-point. There is no evidence of collusion between the archbishop or the clergy and the earls, but there was almost certainly a common belief that the projected war in Gascony was foolhardy. Perhaps Edward's mandate of 1 March against the spreading of rumours is an indication of this; newsmongering, the king had said, seemed to be creating discord 'between ourselves our prelates our barons and our great men'.

The chroniclers report that the king at the Salisbury parliament issued a cruel 'edict' against the clergy: 'fecit statutum', 'crudele edictum statuit', 'fuit propositum hoc edictum', and 'statuit... subscripta'.[73] But they are not referring to any known royal edict. The contents of the 'edict' are related in brief in the Worcester annals and by Cotton and at greater length in the Evesham chronicle, but it is nowhere cited in writ form. We may doubt whether it ever was a published edict. Both Cotton and the Evesham chronicle use the tell-tale 'ut dicebatur', and Cotton's note of it is chronologically later than his description of the Salisbury parliament. Nonetheless, the 'edict' is in all probability a completely accurate record of the king's known, and perhaps openly stated, intentions: if the clergy did not submit before Easter (14 April) they would forfeit all the goods which had been seized by the king, and all their 'fees' would be held by the king for a year, after which they would be recovered as escheats by the lords of the fees or the patrons of the churches. And all those disobeying the king's will should be treated as outcasts and should not be

---

[72] See Prestwich, *War, Politics and Finance*, p. 77 and Chew, *Ecclesiastical Tenants-in-Chief*, pp. 99–100. Bury and Guisborough agree on the constable's presence; but see Rothwell, 'Confirmation of the charters', p. 25 n. 4.

[73] Cotton, p. 323, Dunstable, p. 405, Worcester, p. 530 and Evesham, p. 570. A number of chancery clerks were paid for writing 'secret letters and ordinances' at Clarendon: BL Add. 7965, fo. 16v.

communicated with in any way. Thus, without payment of the fine, outlawry was to become permanent.

The Evesham chronicle, and very briefly Cotton, tell us of a meeting between the king and Winchelsey which has gone unnoticed. Winchelsey visited the king at Salisbury early in March. Before he set out to meet the king he had already summoned another ecclesiastical council to meet at St Paul's on 24 March, stressing the need to assemble quickly to discuss the critical situation facing the English Church.[74] Leaving Canterbury for Salisbury the archbishop was watched over by an armed guard of the sheriff of Kent. The archbishop and his household came to Maidstone,[75] and since his manor there had been seized by the king along with all his other manors he spent the night in the rectory.[76] There he was put under siege by armed men who were his own tenants and their accomplices, as though, in Winchelsey's own words, he and his clerks were robbers and enemies of the state ('tanquam fures et hostes rei pupplice'). The king's ministers confiscated the archbishop's horses and left him to make his way to the king as best he could. Cotton believed that the archbishop failed to obtain the release of his horses or of those of other clergymen. Almost certainly at the same time the prior of Christ Church Canterbury, also at Maidstone and also travelling to the king at Salisbury, had two horses seized by the sheriff of Kent.[77] On 9 March Edward gave instructions that the horses seized at Maidstone belonging to the servants of the archbishop should, by special grace, be delivered, along with the stable boys who were looking after them, to the archbishop's lay servants if they could show that they were their own.[78] On a strict interpretation of the order, if the horses belonged to Winchelsey they were not to be returned. The return of his horses was presumably dependent upon the archbishop's submission. On 17 April Edward ordered the return of the prior's two horses if, as was the case by that time, he had bought the king's protection.[79]

[74] *Councils*, pp. 1162–4.
[75] Cotton, p. 322 (see also *Flores Hist.*, III. 293).
[76] *Reg.*, pp. 216–17 (see Graham, 'Siege of Maidstone rectory', pp. 2–3).
[77] PRO E159/70 m. 23d.
[78] PRO E159/70 m. 15d and E368/68 m. 32.
[79] PRO E159/70 m. 23d.

Winchelsey arrived in Salisbury on 7 March.[80] There was a show of good will between the king and the archbishop, Winchelsey giving Edward the kiss of peace during the celebration of mass and accepting Edward's invitation to dine with him. On the following day the archbishop had a private interview with the king and spoke with courage and firmness ('audaci constantia'). Edward listened patiently but was unmoved: he replied to Winchelsey that if the pope had temporal possessions in England, like the archbishop, the king would have every right to seize them for the defence of the kingdom and of the English Church. He stressed the seriousness of the crisis facing himself and his kingdom, his willingness to die in support of his policies, and his belief that he was doing nothing unlawful. Winchelsey said that he did not see that the crisis ('necessitas') was so great that either the king or himself or anyone else could be excused the penalties of 'Clericis laicos' if a contribution were made, and he asked the king to consider seeking and awaiting a papal declaration on the question of 'necessitas' and other doubtful matters relating to 'Clericis laicos'. The king was unwilling to do this without taking full advice, and since this could not be accomplished before the ecclesiastical assembly on 24 March they agreed that the king should send members of his council to that assembly to discuss with the clergy there this possibility of seeking papal advice or to discuss any other suggested policy. The king expressed a willingness in the meantime to be less severe in his dealings with the clergy. He ordered that the seized lands should be sown without delay; and this order was noted by Cotton as the king's sole concession.[81]

There is nothing obviously incongruous or overdrawn about the Evesham chronicler's account of this private meeting. While neither side made important concessions, compromise was becoming essential for both. Edward, on the one hand, was faced with opposition from the earls; on the other hand, many of the clergy were already contravening Winchelsey's policy as set out in the January council. The archbishop had shown courage in facing up to the king. Although his hand was being forced by Edward's coercive policies, he continued to press his own judgment of the

[80] For what follows see Evesham, pp. 571–2.
[81] Prynne, III. 695 (*CCR 1296–1302*, p. 19) and Cotton, p. 322.

needs of the king, the kingdom and the English Church, and, while there was to be consultation in the forthcoming council with some of the king's ministers, the clergy were still in a position to arrive at a decision in their own assembly.

During March the king sought the best means of obtaining the fifth from the clergy. On 14 March further instructions were sent to the sheriffs and bannerets appointed to obtain the clerical fines.[82] The king's ministers were enjoined to inform any clergy making recognisances before Monday 25 March to pay half the sums owed directly into the exchequer at Westminster on that day or the Monday following, and if they made recognisances after 25 March to pay a half of the fine without delay at the exchequer. The aim was perhaps to persuade the clergy and the clerical proctors attending the ecclesiastical council to bring money with them. A new procedure was adopted in an order of 20 March.[83] This mandate instructed the royal agents to receive the first half of the fine in the counties and to transport it to the exchequer before 7 April.

How many of the clergy of the southern province had submitted to the king before the ecclesiastical assembly of 24 March? The lists certainly show that more clergy during March defied 'Clericis laicos' by paying the fine to the king.[84] Although it is difficult to date the submissions precisely, the frequent inclusion on the lists of the names of the king's agents, appointed on 1 March to assist the sheriffs,[85] indicates that some were taking place during the early weeks of March. But, unless the lists are very incomplete, the number of submissions during March was not large: about two to three hundred clergy appear to have sought royal protection following the three to four hundred in February. The king's attempt to obtain the submission of the clergy in the shires was apparently only a qualified success. Robert de Tateshale, appointed to assist the sheriff of Norfolk and Suffolk, had summoned all the clergy in the county of Norfolk to appear before him at Norwich on a certain day. A number turned up, but only a

---

[82] PRO E368/68 m. 90d.   [83] PRO E159/70 m. 109d.
[84] Prynne, III. 711–12 (*CPR 1292–1301*, pp. 264–9), *CCR 1296–1302*, pp. 94–7 and *Cal. Var. Chanc. Rolls*, pp. 24–7, 42.
[85] *Parl. Writs*, I. ii. 393–4.

few bought protection.[86] And no further bishops appear to have submitted before the meeting of the ecclesiastical council, so that, along with the four Welsh bishops, the bishops of London, Lincoln, Chichester, Hereford, Norwich, Exeter and Rochester were awaiting the lead of their archbishop.

We need to assess, too, what kind of interpretation Winchelsey was putting upon 'Clericis laicos'. The bull, of course, concerned England quite as much as it concerned France. Yet, all Boniface VIII's bulls glossing 'Clericis laicos' were addressed to Philip of France or the prelates of France. It is hard to ascertain how much direct contact existed between Winchelsey and the pope, but certainly a lack of papal pronouncements addressed to England does not argue for a complete lack of communication. Although Edward had prohibited anyone from leaving the realm without his licence,[87] it seems unlikely that there was no correspondence at all on the matter of 'Clericis laicos' between Winchelsey and his proctor at Rome, Walter of Dunbridge.[88] In his description of the January ecclesiastical council Guisborough states that Winchelsey announced his willingness to send special nuncios to the pope to seek a licence to make a grant, or at least to obtain advice about what the clergy should do.[89] We can give full credence to the willingness to seek advice, but there is no other evidence for a desire on Winchelsey's part to request a papal licence to make a grant. If we are prepared to believe the words put into Winchelsey's mouth by Guisborough, we should note that they are in the context of a statement of the greater allegiance of the clergy to their spiritual lord than to their temporal lord. The archbishop's reply to the king following the January council in fact makes no mention of any desire to consult the pope.[90] At Winchelsey's meeting with the king on 8 March, as described by the Evesham chronicler, the archbishop suggested to Edward that he should seek and await a statement from the pope about the doctrine of 'necessitas' and other doubtful matters relating to 'Clericis laicos'. Edward did not wish to make such a move. He was clearly unwilling to take any step which might imply an acceptance of the principle of papal consent for all ecclesiastical taxation. The

[86] Cotton p. 321. [87] Above, p. 109. [88] *Reg.*, pp. 517–19.
[89] Guisborough, p. 287. [90] *Councils*, pp. 1157–9.

Dunstable annalist, in a passage concerned with the council proceedings at the end of March, says that the archbishop was awaiting a papal remedy ('remedium a domino papa super huiusmodi
angustiis expectabat') and that the nuncios from the pope did not
arrive.[91] But it would be rash to assume, on this slender evidence,
that a particular 'remedy' had been sought from the pope. The
archbishop continued to believe that the problems facing the
kingdom were not such that they merited a grant. He wished to
solve the crisis with the king his own way and in the interests of
the liberty of his own provincial church.

It is unlikely that the archbishop received no news from the
papal curia or from France during February and March. What
interpretations of 'Clericis laicos' may have reached him? On the
crucial question of 'necessitas' it was not until 31 July, with the
bull 'Etsi de statu'[92] that the pope clearly conceded that in France
the king possessed the right to judge what constituted a national
crisis. However we understand this remarkable gloss upon 'Clericis
laicos', the attitude and policies of the English clergy ensured that
it could not be regarded as relevant to the situation in England.
But earlier papal pronouncements concerning France may well
have influenced the English clergy,[93] especially perhaps 'Ineffabilis
amoris' (20 September 1296),[94] 'Romana mater ecclesia' (7
February 1297),[95] and, above all, 'Coram illo fatemur' (28
February 1297).[96] The latter, along with the French prelates'
petition of 31 January for a licence to make a grant, was copied
into at least four English bishops' registers, including Winchelsey's.[97]

In 'Ineffabilis amoris' Boniface VIII stressed that it was not his

[91] *Councils*, p. 1166 (cf. n. 2).
[92] *Reg. Swinfield*, p. 346 and Cant. D. & C., Reg. I, fos. 182v–183r.
[93] See Rothwell, 'Confirmation of the charters', pp. 18–21 (on p. 26 Rothwell
confuses 'Ineffabilis amoris' with 'Coram illo fatemur') and Digard, *Philippe
et le Saint-Siège*, I. 273–310.
[94] *Reg. Boniface VIII*, no. 1653 (see Potthast, nos. 24398, 24404).
[95] Refs. to texts in Potthast, no. 24468 (calendared in *Reg. Boniface VIII*, no.
2312).
[96] *Reg. Boniface VIII*, no. 2333 (Potthast, no. 24475).
[97] After a number of items dated May and June 1297 in *Reg.*, pp. 174–9, after
two items of May in *Reg. Halton*, I. 99–104, between items of July and May
1297 in *Reg. Giffard*, p. 485 and after items for 1298 and 1299 in *Reg.
Swinfield*, pp. 350–5; and also between bulls of May 1296 and Feb. 1297 in
Cant. D. & C., Reg. I, fos. 178r–179r.

intention to prevent the French king's taxation of the clergy when it was necessary for defence and essential for the king and kingdom, but he continued to insist upon his own rôle as arbiter and the need for papal consent. 'Romana mater ecclesia' certainly went a stage further, for here the pope declared that, in a situation in which a grant had been obtained from the clergy and delay would cause grave danger, the procedure of seeking the pope's licence could be dispensed with. In such circumstances the fact that the clergy themselves had consented to the grant was regarded, no doubt, as all-important. Before 'Romana mater ecclesia' had been issued the French prelates had appealed to the pope for permission to assist the king with an aid. Their appeal was urgent and convincing because of the Anglo-Flemish alliance. An appeal at this time from England would have been correspondingly unconvincing. The pope authorised a grant from the French clergy in 'Coram illo fatemur' of 28 February. How quickly this bull reached England is not known, but it was clearly considered to be a pronouncement of importance. Over twenty years later a statement purporting to be Boniface VIII's reply to the English prelates concerning 'Clericis laicos' was entered into a Canterbury register:[98] it is identical with the passage in 'Coram illo fatemur' which glosses 'Clericis laicos'.[99] It had been copied, too, into the annals of Worcester. There is nothing strikingly new in this passage. The pope continued to point to the need for a papal licence, despite 'Romana mater ecclesia'. But in stressing that subsidies could only be given freely and spontaneously ('libero arbitrio ac sponte') the pope was acknowledging that the clergy must themselves assess the justice of a claim for an aid. Clerical consent to clerical taxation is Boniface VIII's firm claim. The archbishop was making this claim very much his own.

Far from feeling secure in the knowledge that some clergy had already submitted to his will, Edward was aware of the danger that the clergy might decide in its assembly to continue to use 'Clericis laicos' to support a policy of defiance. Would Winchelsey be able to continue his insistence upon the publishing of the bull and the excommunication of all infringers? The king took steps to

---

[98] Denton, 'Reynolds and ecclesiastical politics', p. 251.
[99] *Reg.*, p. 178: 'Licet enim constitutionem'; and Worcester, p. 531.

avert this possibility. He issued letters forbidding the clergy about
to assemble in London from ordaining anything prejudicial to the
king, his ministers and those under his protection, and appointed
Hugh le Dispenser as his proctor to deliver this royal prohibition
in the clerical council. Hugh was instructed to choose other
members of the king's council to be there with him. The annalist
of Worcester refers to three knights and three clerks as the royal
nuncios in the assembly. In addition, the king appointed Itier
Bochard of Angoulême, king's clerk and archdeacon of Bath, to
make an appeal ('provocatio et appellatio') to the pope against
any action which Archbishop Winchelsey and his suffragan
bishops and other prelates might take against the king and against
those who were 'of his faith and in his peace and under his protection'.[100] These included, of course, the clergy who had already
obtained royal protection by paying the fine. Itier Bochard made
this appeal to Rome on 24 March (the day on which the archbishop had ordered the clergy to congregate at St Paul's) in the
house ('aula') of the bishop of London, and in the presence of this
bishop, the archbishop of Canterbury, and the bishops of Lincoln,[101] Hereford, Norwich, Exeter, Bath and Wells, Rochester
and St David's.[102] Of these, it seems that only the bishop of Bath
and Wells had already paid the fifth. The king's appeal to the pope
– though there is no evidence that it was ever sent to the pope –
was against the possible actions of the archbishop and the clergy in
the assembly at St Paul's, and it included the accusation that
Winchelsey and those who supported him, contrary to their oaths
of fealty, had worked to undermine the king's laws. The appeal was
a threat lest the archbishop should try to continue his policies:
'lest you should attempt to order, admonish, cite, decree, ordain
or determine, declare, denounce, publish, suspend, excommunicate, interdict, or execute or otherwise undertake anything with or
without legal process against the king, his kingdom, his subjects
and his adherents'. Whatever the clergy decided, the contingent
appeal of the Crown to the pope had already been proclaimed.

[100] *Councils*, pp. 1164–7.
[101] Oliver Sutton, bishop of Lincoln, was in London until 4 April: *Reg. Sutton*, v. 212–14.
[102] PRO E159/70 m. 117. Walter le Noreys, notary public, was paid a mark for drawing up the documents concerning the appeal: BL Add. 7965, fo. 16v.

From the names of those present when the king's appeal to Rome was made, we can confidently assume a large attendance of bishops of the Canterbury province at the assembly in St Paul's. There is no evidence of the presence of the bishop of Ely, ex-keeper of the wardrobe, who is found at the king's side witnessing royal charters in January 1297 and again in June, July and August.[103] The bishop of Coventry and Lichfield was at Brussels on the king's business,[104] and the bishop of Winchester was at Rome.[105] The bishop of Worcester was clearly too ill to travel.[106] There remain, of the English bishops, two unaccounted for: the bishop of Chichester, and the bishop of Salisbury (who died on 18 May). Eight out of fourteen of the English bishops were present; of these eight only Bath and Wells had yet submitted. Probably very few of the clergy who had gone against the decision of the January council attended in March. In the story told by the Lanercost chronicler the abbot of Osney, who had submitted, was rebuked by Winchelsey and soon afterwards died of heart failure.[107] As previously, the gathering divided into four estates (the bishops, the monks, the canons, and the lesser clergy) and the debate lasted for several days.[108] A large majority of the clergy, according to Cotton, believed that a grant had to be made to the king and that 'necessitas' excused them from the general sentence of excommunication. It was believed by some that the royal claim for aid was just and could be defended before the pope. The Evesham chronicle states that some of the clergy decided that they should agree to the tax of a fifth, establish control over its collection and keep the money in safe custody to be used only for the defence of the kingdom. But the bishops advised against this policy, partly because they feared the dangers of building up deposits of money in this way. Winchelsey, with a few supporters, wished to stand firm. He had a solution to the dilemma facing the clergy: each man, he determined, should follow his own conscience. This was a wise move. The clergy could now buy the king's protection and

---

[103] PRO C53/83 nos. 1–5, 7–10, 19, 20.
[104] Cuttino, 'Langton's mission for Edward I', p. 180.
[105] *Reg. Pontissara*, p. 842.   [106] *Reg. Giffard*, p. liv.
[107] *CPR 1292–1301*, p. 265 and Lanercost, pp. 162–3.
[108] For the chronicle accounts see *Councils*, pp. 1166–8, Bury, p. 139 and Evesham, p. 574.

bring virtually to an end this damaging quarrel with the Crown. But the archbishop and a small number of adherents could continue their opposition and demonstrate the firmness of their beliefs. Above all, the clergy in its council had not given full and common consent to a subsidy. The king had failed to compel them to do that. It is clear that many of the clergy continued to oppose the war, for which Edward was making elaborate preparations.

Immediately after the council the clergy in large numbers individually bought back their seized lands and possessions. Many who attended the council submitted before leaving London; others, like the priory of Dunstable, sought to avoid the penalty of confiscation by buying protection before Easter (14 April).[109] On 26 March the subprior and chapter of Christ Church Canterbury recommended to their prior that he should take advice from Winchelsey. They were hopeful that the communal decision of the clergy in the ecclesiastical council would enable them both to appease the king and to avoid the 'sword of St Peter who was threatening to strike'.[110] The prior wrote to inform them of the choice open to them, and on 1 April they determined on the lesser of the two evils and appointed a proctor to obtain the king's protection and the return of their lands, tenements, goods and chattels.[111] But the continued threats to the archbishop's lands and possessions were naturally viewed with fear by the prior and chapter; they appointed a proctor to safeguard their interests, pointing out that, although the lands and goods of the archbishopric were divided from their own ('quoad usum et in personis'), they belonged 'pleno iure' to the cathedral priory.[112]

The Evesham chronicler described the clergy as sheep without a shepherd: the royal ministers jeered at them and reproached them, saying that it would have been better if they had bought the king's protection earlier rather than incurring his wrath. Having submitted, many of the clergy, because of the sentence of excom-

---

[109] Dunstable, pp. 406–7. The £34 promised from the priory of Dunstable was not paid into the exchequer until 10 Sept.: PRO E401/1653 m. 19.
[110] *Concilia*, ii. 225, from CUL Ee. v. 31, fo. 72r.
[111] CUL Ee. v. 31, fo. 72r. £200 from the prior and chapter of Canterbury was paid into the exchequer on 25 May: PRO E401/1653 m. 9. The priory's account book records the payment to the king of £284 7s 5d in 1297 'per manus R. de Wylingham pro maneriis redimendis': Cant. D. & C., Miscellaneous Accounts Book 1, fo. 210r.   [112] Cant. D. & C., Reg. I, fo. 155r.

munication in 'Clericos laicos', now abstained from celebrating mass.[113] The lists on the chancery rolls of the clergy buying protection are once again difficult to date. Perhaps a list on the patent roll, and part of a close roll list, relate to the first weeks of April.[114] Included here is the bishop of Exeter. These lists do not in fact give the impression of the sudden submission of the majority of the clergy, as stated, for example, by Cotton.[115] There are many protections recorded as having been granted after Easter.[116] But the lists were not systematically compiled, and we can expect in most cases a time-lag between the submission and the enrolment of grants of protection and orders for the restoration of temporalities; and the surviving lists for this period are certainly incomplete, for they do not include any further bishops except the bishop of Exeter and the bishop of Bangor. The bundles of bills that have survived, attesting payment of fines or promise of payment, probably give a more accurate impression of what had ensued. A very large proportion of the bills that are dated belong to the first fortnight of April.[117]

The king's intention had been stated in the so-called edict of Salisbury: first the clergy would forfeit all their goods if they had not submitted by Easter, and, secondly, their lands and advowson rights would be held for a year before escheating to the lords of the fees or the patrons of the churches. It becomes clear that the order for the forfeiture of goods and lands related to all clergy

[113] Evesham, p. 575.
[114] Prynne, III. 713–20 (*CPR 1292–1301*, pp. 271–86) and *Cal. Var. Chanc. Rolls*, pp. 42–53.
[115] *Councils*, p. 1167.   [116] *Cal. Var. Chanc. Rolls*, pp. 27–38, 53–65.
[117] The bills, approaching 700, are in four files: PRO C81/1660B, C and D, and E163/2/6 (the old ref. of C81/1660D was C47/21/1). Prynne (III. 701) printed examples. In addition, E163/2/7 is a roll of recognisances of Kent clergy seeking protection; and E135/10/7 is a roll of fines paid by the clergy, from which Prynne printed the whole of m. 2 and part of m. 3: Prynne, III. 702–6. E401/1653 (of which E401/1654 is an incomplete duplicate) contains day by day entries of money actually paid into the exchequer from the close of Easter to mid-September (though the roll is deficient at the beginning). There are over 1400 items, mostly individual payments sometimes by instalments but including lump sums collected by sheriffs, and the roll records payments for this whole period totalling £22,810, more than half the expected return of a fifth of clerical income. Also, the alien priories paid their annual fine to the king as ordained in the autumn of 1295 (see *Councils*, p. 1218 n. 1); E401/1655 is the record of the payments from the alien houses, item by item, between April and Sept. 1297 (cf. Matthew, *Norman Monasteries*, p. 85) amounting to the large sum of £22,908.

with benefices valued at 40 shillings or more.[118] The details of the royal action can be traced from privy seal letters sent to the exchequer and copied on to the memoranda rolls.[119] In early April the king wrote to the exchequer to ensure that the policy for the selling of all goods, except those necessary for making a living, was about to be put into effect. A prise of the grain found in the clergy's possession, as much as possible of it to be shipped to Gascony, had already been ordered on 25 March. The order for the forfeiture of goods was reiterated on 11 April in more urgent terms because of the king's increasing need of money, and on 13 April the king, foreseeing that the clergy's goods might be sold at less than their value, added the warning that his ministers should take care not to sell the goods back to the clergy, nor to anyone through whom the clergy could regain possession. By 14 April news of the outcome of the ecclesiastical council had reached Edward at Plympton (Devon), for he wrote on that day (Easter Sunday) that he had heard that the clergy were communally ('communeaument') more willing to pay the fine and were coming in greater numbers to the exchequer. Because of this the king gave instructions that the clergy should be allowed a three weeks' extension of the term, so that, in cases of failure to pay the fine, the forfeiture of goods would not now take place until after 5 May. A further letter of 15 April ordered that the later the clergy were in yielding to the king's will the more they should pay, and, indeed, it becomes clear from later evidence that a fine of a quarter rather than a fifth was to be levied on the goods of the recalcitrant bishop of Llandaff and bishop-elect of Salisbury.

Winchelsey was now much more isolated. His courageous stand against the Crown was naturally highlighted by the chronicles: he was prepared to die rather than to concede, wrote Guisborough. He can have had no doubts about the justice of the clergy's case, for he was staking his position as head of the English Church upon it, not knowing how long the king would compel him to remain dispossessed and outside the protection of the law. Yet, any further molestation of him by the Crown would have weakened the king's political position, not his own, and the continued loss of his

---

[118] See Cotton, p. 324 and Evesham, pp. 570, 575.
[119] PRO E159/70 mm. 18, 19d, 23 and E368/68 m. 27d.

temporalities may have caused hardship, but probably not severe hardship. There is no record of any correspondence from him during April, but during May and June he continued the administration of the Canterbury province apparently undeterred. Some of the letters despatched in his name during these months concerned, for example, the maintenance of episcopal jurisdiction in the diocese of Salisbury *sede vacante*, and they were dated at Chartham (three miles from Canterbury) where he lived, in the rector's house, with a very small household, spending a large part of his time preaching in the surrounding parishes.[120] The archbishop's patience is emphasised by his biographer;[121] he was willing to await events, and avoided any dramatising of his situation.

The archbishop had a few notable adherents. The bishop of Lincoln, Oliver Sutton, was probably one of the last of the English suffragan bishops to submit; according to Guisborough, friends of the bishop acted without his consent in raising the fine from his possessions and gaining the restoration of his lands.[122] There were late submissions too from some monasteries, for among the lists probably of May and June we find, for example, the priors of Boxgrove, Chirbury, Burscough and Merton.[123] Another significant supporter was Simon of Ghent, Winchelsey's friend, from whose seized goods the tax was levied by an order of 31 July;[124] Simon had been elected bishop of Salisbury on 2 June. But particularly strong support appears to have come from parts of Wales. The newly-appointed bishop of Llandaff, and also apparently the bishop of St Asaph, continued to oppose the king.[125] As late as 22 June the Crown was attempting to gain safe custody of the lay fees of all the recalcitrant clergy of South Wales; this further order for the seizure of temporalities was sent to the king's keeper of the land of Glamorgan and to the bailiffs of franchises in the area, including the bailiff of Roger Bigod at the castle of Striguil

---

[120] Thorne, p. 327 and Guisborough, p. 288. [121] *Anglia Sacra*, I. 14–16.

[122] Dunstable, p. 407 and Guisborough, p. 288. A royal letter dated 14 April instructed the treasurer and the barons of the exchequer that in respect of the bishop of Lincoln they should act as instructed by John Droxford, keeper of the wardrobe: PRO E368/68 m. 27d. The receipt roll E401/1653, mm. 9, 11–15 records payments to a total of £150 from the sale of the goods of the bishop of Lincoln.

[123] *Cal. Var. Chanc. Rolls*, pp. 36–8, 65. [124] *CFR*, I. 389.

[125] Cant. D. & C., Reg. Q, fo. 40, printed in Somner, *Antiquities*, pt II. app. p. 31.

(Chepstow) and the bailiff of Humphrey de Bohun at Breck-nock.[126] Here, at least, there appear to be clear connections between the recalcitrance of the clergy and the recalcitrance of the earls.

On 15 May the king requested all who held land worth £20 or more a year to muster in London on 7 July; and the bishops were ordered, also, to provide their *servitium debitum*.[127] The latter writs were sent to all the English bishops who held in chief, with the exception of the archbishop of Canterbury.[128] It seems likely that private talks between the king and the archbishop took place early in June. Edward travelled from Devon to London, calling at Mayfield (in the Canterbury peculiar of South Malling), Charing (where there was an archiepiscopal manor) and Canterbury, where he stayed from 1 to 10 June.[129] In the household account of the king's oblations for the whole year, totalling £427, we learn of payments made during his stay in Canterbury at the altars of St Augustine's abbey and Christ Church priory, including offerings at the *corona* of St Thomas, at the saint's cloak, at the sword which killed him, at his first tomb, and three offerings at his shrine.[130] On 12 June Edward gave instructions that Winchelsey should be allowed accommodation in the houses on his manors.[131] This enabled the archbishop to travel once again, and he was in London during the second week in July at the muster of forces for the army which the king was to lead to Flanders.[132] A reconciliation with Winchelsey had become a political necessity.

The reconciliation probably took place on 11 July, the date of the king's order for the complete restoration of the archbishop's lands and goods;[133] the order apparently took effect on 19 July.[134]

---

[126] *CCR 1296–1302*, p. 41. For further writs of 11 July sent to Roger Bigod, Henry of Lancaster (the king's nephew), John Hastings and the sheriff of Glamorgan see PRO E159/70 m. 103 (and 36).

[127] For a detailed account of the political events of July see Rothwell, 'Confirmation of the charters', pp. 25–9; and see Powicke, *Thirteenth Century*, pp. 678–82.

[128] *Parl. Writs*, I. ii. 283 (*CCR 1296–1302*, p. 113). Archbishops of Canterbury had been in practice exempt from military service or commutation from the middle of Henry III's reign: Chew, *Ecclesiastical Tenants-in-Chief*, p. 61.

[129] Gough, *Itinerary*, II. 153–4.   [130] BL Add. 7965, fo. 7v.

[131] PRO E159/70 mm. 26, 104 and E368/68 m. 50d.

[132] Cotton, p. 325 (see J. G. Edwards, '*Confirmatio Cartarum*', p. 149 n. 1).

[133] Prynne, III. 721 (*CCR 1296–1302*, p. 42).

[134] Cont. Gervase, pp. 315–16 (as *Anglia Sacra*, I. 51 and Cant. D. & C., Reg. Q, fo. 40, printed in Somner, *Antiquities*, pt II. app. p. 31).

The meeting of magnates, prelates and landowners in London became a gathering of political importance.[135] A ceremony for the swearing of fealty to young Edward took place outside Westminster Hall on 14 July, in the presence of Winchelsey (moved to tears according to the Merton *Flores*), as well as the archbishops-elect of York and Dublin, and the bishops of Durham, Lincoln, Ely, Norwich, London, and Bath and Wells.[136] At this ceremony the reconciliation was thus made public, and the archbishop declared obedience to the king and his heir. It was the king who had given way, for Winchelsey, it is clear, did not pay the fine of a fifth. None of the archbishop's lands and goods had been sold as threatened, and all were restored 'simpliciter et absolute', or 'cum dampnis', or 'gratis', or 'sine protectione seu alicuius dati conditione'.[137] This was an open-handed concession to Winchelsey. The following May the sheriff of Kent accounted at the exchequer for £400 as income obtained from the archbishop's reeves while the temporalities were in the king's hands, and he accounted in addition for over £127 owing to the archbishop for prises, during the same period, of corn, barley, oats and timber (oak and beech); these sums, less £80 paid on behalf of the archbishop in alms to the hospitals of Harbledown and Northgate, were, by the king's special grace, set against the amount which Winchelsey owed to the Crown.[138] It had been essential for Edward to secure, as far as possible, a stable political situation before he departed for Flanders; as we shall see he tried to use Winchelsey to mediate with Bigod and Bohun who had become openly hostile to the king. New developments followed quickly after the reconciliation with Winchelsey, developments which begin a new chapter in the clergy's relations with the Crown and lead directly to the confirmation of the charters.

With the reconciliation of Edward and Winchelsey, superficial though it proved to be, the outlawry of the clergy was virtually at

---

[135] Described as a parliament in Bury, p. 140, Cotton, pp. 327, 330 and Trivet, pp. 357–8. The king had certainly held a parliament on 8 July: PRO E368/69 m. 16.

[136] *Lancs. Lay Subsidies*, ed. Vincent, p. 200, *Flores Hist.*, III. 101–2, 295 and Guisborough, p. 291.

[137] See above, n. 134, *Flores Hist.*, III. 295, and Evesham, p. 577.

[138] Prynne, III. 787 (*CCR 1296–1302*, p. 157) and PRO E159/71 mm. 34, 39 (as E368/69 mm. 76, 81d).

an end. The king continued his efforts to raise the fifth. Some lesser clergy had no lands or goods seized, for they possessed no lay fees and no goods except those which formed part of their ecclesiastical benefices. But these clergy were not excluded from the fine, and writs had been issued on 22 June for the seizure and sale of goods and chattels found outside sanctuaries and belonging to clergy who had not paid the fine and who possessed benefices of 40 shillings or more in value.[139] It is difficult to see which possessions, if not spiritualities, were now being ordered to be seized and sold. The difficulty was a real one, for it had to be made clear, in writs of 1 August,[140] that it was not the king's intention to seize possessions which were unquestionably spiritualities (glebe land, tithes, and oblations). This elucidation itself signifies the easing of royal policy. In any case, by the beginning of August there can have been very few remaining recalcitrants. The archbishop and the bishops of the province had pleaded for the London clergy, and gained the restoration of their temporalities.[141] The archbishop had pleaded, too, for the bishop of Llandaff (who by 22 July had joined the other bishops in London)[142] and a writ of 18 July had ordered a fine of a quarter for the bishop's disobedience to be raised from his temporalities before they were returned to him.[143] Thus, the threat to sell temporalities had not in general been carried out; but a higher fine was paid by the bishop of Llandaff, as also by the bishop-elect of Salisbury,[144] because of their protracted refusal to submit. The Bury chronicle appears to have been broadly correct in reporting the reconciliation as including all who had defied the king by obeying 'Clericis laicos';[145] but all except Winchelsey were compelled to pay the fine.

However much we may regard compromise and conciliation as essential in 1297 for the clergy, for the Crown, and also for the papacy, it is undeniable that the issue of sovereignty in relation to clerical wealth had been at the heart of the conflict between the

[139] PRO E159/70 m. 121d and Cotton, p. 325.
[140] PRO E159/70 m. 107d.
[141] Prynne, III. 721 (*CCR 1296–1302*, pp. 120–1).   [142] *Reg.*, p. 181.
[143] PRO E159/70 m. 33. Some small payments from his goods are recorded in E401/1653 mm. 18, 19.
[144] *CFR*, I. 389.   [145] Bury, p. 141.

Church and the king. Guisborough is misleading when he wrote that the clergy who paid the fine did not incur the sentence of excommunication in 'Clericis laicos'.[146] This was not the case. Many clergy abstained from divine service and were concerned to obtain absolution.[147] Guisborough himself, a few lines later, noted that Winchelsey chose to incur the wrath of the king rather than the sentence of excommunication. The king's policy of extorting a fine for protection, far from providing a means of avoiding the penalties of 'Clericis laicos' or the issue of sovereignty, was a largely successful, if precarious, means of compelling the clergy to pay a tax. The king, and indeed almost all the clergy (by force of circumstance and for most of them after due deliberation with their archbishop), flew in the face of the papal ban. Winchelsey's outstanding success was to use this difficult political situation actually to strengthen the position of the English clergy in relation to the Crown.

The pope had excommunicated; the king had outlawed. Both used, within their respective powers, the 'last and most terrible weapon against the obstinate offender'. Neither legal process brought the terrors of old; 'but, at least in this world, the consequences of the temporal were far more severe than those of the spiritual ban.'[148] Indeed, the English clergy could be forgiven for believing that the events of 1297 were a demonstration not only of the effectiveness of the king's coercive authority but also of the accuracy of Boniface VIII's statement that the laity were hostile to the clergy. The Dunstable annalist wrote of 1297 as a year of persecution of the clergy by the laity ('de persecutione...per laicos clero facta').[149] 'Clericis laicos' was a statement of immediate and continuing relevance for the English clergy. There is no direct evidence to suggest that they were influenced by the papal concessions to the clergy and king of France, though 'Coram illo fatemur' of 28 February was certainly regarded as a pronouncement of importance. The papal concession had no doubt made it

---

[146] Guisborough, p. 288.
[147] *Councils*, pp. 1172–3 (Worcester), 1182 and n. 3, 1184, Denton, 'Reynolds and ecclesiastical politics', p. 250 n. 21, Prynne, III. 870–2 (printing from Lincoln's Inn MS Hale 185, fos. 105v–106v), and BL Add. 10374, fo. 88v (calendared in Hill, *Ecclesiastical Letter-Books*, p. 162).
[148] Pollock and Maitland, *English Law*, I. 478–80. [149] Dunstable, p. 407.

easy for Winchelsey to recommend at the March council that the English clergy should follow their own consciences, but it is an exaggeration to suggest that it was 'news from France that won even Winchelsey over'.[150]

The Rochester version of the *Flores* lavished praise upon Winchelsey as the new Thomas, 'a man of no less constancy than the saint', triumphing over the persecutors of the English Church.[151] The theme is echoed time and again by the archbishop's biographer.[152] This is a moving story of the undaunted archbishop, resisting all the entreaties of Edward's counsellors to persuade him to yield, and excluded even from his own cathedral priory. Those clergy who believed in the defence of the privileged and independent position of the clergy had every right to regard the resistance of Winchelsey as a triumph. Despite the deep division between the royal clergy and the learned sacerdotalists, Winchelsey had maintained a spirit of unity within his provincial Church. He had acted through representative councils summoned and controlled by himself. He had held firmly and unflinchingly to the principle of clerical consent to taxation, and there is no question that his policies were of long-term practical significance. Edward's direct control of the clergy in 1294, and his great exactions of that year, could not be repeated. 'Clericis laicos' had served Winchelsey's purposes well. The will of the clergy had been stiffened; and the king could hardly resort to the seizure of all temporalities on every occasion of clerical opposition to taxation. The clergy had to be persuaded and bargained with, and not in parliament. Edward must himself have known better than to think, like Prynne, that by his strenuous opposition to Winchelsey he had 'crushed this cockatrice in the shell'.[153] But the major concession to the king's opponents, the confirmation of the charters, was yet to come.

[150] Rothwell, 'Confirmation of the charters', p. 26.
[151] *Flores Hist.*, III. 292–3.
[152] *Anglia Sacra*, I. 14–16.
[153] Prynne, III. 721.

WINCHELSEY AND 'CONFIRMATIO CARTARUM'

The king's reconciliation with Winchelsey in the middle of July was part of a new strategy.[154] Urgently planning his departure for Flanders, Edward required new subsidies from both the laity and the clergy. For the successful collection of a lay subsidy it was clearly important that the reconciliation with the archbishop be extended to Bohun and Bigod, who had established themselves outside London and had declared that they did not consider themselves bound by the king's order to fulfil their duties as marshal and constable.[155] In an attempt to establish peace with them Winchelsey agreed to act as mediator; and in response to the request for a clerical subsidy, between 15 and 17 July the archbishop issued summonses to the third ecclesiastical council of the year, to meet on 10 August at the New Temple in London.[156] The king made it known that in the event of further subsidies he would reaffirm the terms of *Magna Carta* and of the Charter of the Forest.[157] He had set the bait for establishing internal concord and for obtaining more money. Yet it must be remembered at the outset that both the laity and the clergy had already been under the severest financial pressure. And since there was no time to summon shire representatives to London, a lay subsidy could not be obtained by what was by now the accepted process of gaining consent.[158]

In summoning the clergy to discuss the matter of a grant in return for an affirmation of the charters, Winchelsey had made no promises to Edward. He was making efforts to assist the king to establish peace in the realm, but there are no indications that this amounted to a significant change of policy. His willingness to treat with the recalcitrant magnates was not a *volte face*, though

---

[154] For the events of the second half of July see esp. Rothwell, 'Confirmation of the charters', pp. 27–30.

[155] As revealed in the royal Manifesto of 12 Aug.: *Foedera*, I. ii. 872–3 and *Eng. Hist. Documents*, III. 478. See Rothwell, 'Confirmation of the charters', pp. 25–6.

[156] *Councils*, pp. 1168–70.

[157] As stated in Winchelsey's summons and confirmed in the clergy's reply after discussion in the Aug. council: *Councils*, pp. 1171–2; and see Cotton, p. 327.

[158] See Harriss, *King, Parliament and Public Finance*, pp. 52–3 and Prestwich, *War, Politics and Finance*, p. 273.

it involved him in affairs of state to an unusually direct extent. He cannot have failed to realise that negotiations with Bohun and Bigod, and all that such negotiations were bound to entail concerning taxation and the charters, had a very close bearing on the affairs of the Church. All the bishops who had been present at the public oath-swearing to the young Edward on 14 July[159] conferred with the king concerning the means of arriving at a peaceful settlement with the opposing magnates, and Edward left the bishops, under the leadership of Winchelsey, with the responsibility of arranging a meeting with Bohun and Bigod, though the king insisted that the negotiations should be completed by Sunday 28 July, otherwise the matter must be left to his own judgment. After a rapid exchange of letters between 19 and 23 July a meeting was arranged for 26 July at Waltham.[160] The bishops, including Winchelsey, appeared, but the earls sent as their representatives Robert FitzRoger and John de Segrave.[161] We know nothing of the discussions. The two knights – and perhaps the prelates too – came to the king at St Albans on 28 July, but the only outcome of this, as far as we know, was the granting by the king, so he claimed, of safe-conducts for the earls to come to him.

Winchelsey's failure to negotiate a settlement with the earls was the first set-back following his conciliation with the king. It is not clear why the earls were unwilling to take part personally in the discussions at Waltham. There was probably a fair balance of viewpoints and sympathies among the mediating bishops, especially since the bishop of Llandaff had by 22 July taken the place of Anthony Bek, bishop of Durham.[162] Those most likely to have had pronounced royalist allegiances (the bishops of London,[163] Ely, Bath and Wells,[164] and the archbishop-elect of Dublin[165]), none of whom currently occupied high office in royal

[159] See above, p. 132.
[160] See *Reg.*, pp. 180–2 and J. G. Edwards, *'Confirmatio Cartarum'*, p. 151.
[161] See *Foedera*, i. ii. 873, *Chartes des Libertés*, ed. Bémont, p. 82 and *Eng. Hist. Documents*, iii. 478–9.
[162] *Reg.*, pp. 180–1.
[163] Above, p. 113. And the bishop of London, along with the bishop of Ely, was with the king on 26 June, 4, 13, 23 July, 20, 21 Aug.: PRO C53/83 nos. 2–5, 7–10; and see below, p. 157 n. 247.
[164] For both see above, pp. 104, 114.
[165] See *Councils*, p. 1167 n. 2, Hinnebush, *Early English Friars Preachers*, pp. 485–6 and Roensch, *Early Thomist School*, pp. 28–34.

government, were balanced by prelates who had in the previous months stood firmly against the king (Winchelsey, the bishops of Lincoln, and Llandaff, and probably Norwich[166]). But towards the end of July Bohun and Bigod were apparently more convinced than the bishops that a strong line must still be taken with the king. Their reply to the mediators, as explained by Guisborough, was that the king oppressed the whole community, not them alone, by unjust taxation and by a failure to rule with respect for the liberties of *Magna Carta*.[167] It was at this time, during late July or early August, that the Remonstrances were formulated: these provide the reasons for the continuing opposition to the Crown. Following the failure of the negotiations with the earls the king took decisive action about a new lay tax and a new prise of wool, both ordained by him on 29 or 30 July,[168] and the Remonstrances were certainly drawn up before this new policy of enforced taxation had become known.[169] The Remonstrances show that the opposing magnates were now strengthened rather than weakened in their cause, and one of the reasons for the failure of the negotiations with them could well have been that they were, in fact, gaining some sympathy for that cause from the non-royalist bishops.

Indeed, the Remonstrances were presented as the grievances of archbishops, bishops, earls, barons and all the community of the realm.[170] This statement in the preamble tells us nothing about the actual drafters of these representations to the Crown, and the Bury chronicler was probably correct when he wrote that the earls and barons replied to the king's request for subsidies without the agreement of the clergy and the archbishop of Canterbury.[171] But, at the very least, the Remonstrances demonstrate the belief of the earls that they had widespread support. These grievances are, indeed, the first convincing indication of a uniting of lay and clerical interests, and doubt must be immediately expressed in the commonly held view of the continuing, if not increasing, separation of lay and clerical opposition to the Crown. This view was

---

[166] Above, pp. 107, 129–30.   [167] Guisborough, p. 291.   [168] Below, p. 143.
[169] J. G. Edwards, '*Confirmatio Cartarum*', p. 156. For the Remonstrances see ibid., pp. 147–71 and Denton, 'Worcester text of the Remonstrances'.
[170] The text in Guisborough, p. 292, adds abbots and priors.
[171] Bury, p. 140.

stated firmly, for example, by Galbraith: 'after July the baronial opposition entirely lacked the support of the Church'.[172] The magnates would in all probability have liked more direct and open support from the Church; but there has been a failure to realise just how superficial, and short-lived, the king's reconciliation with Winchelsey in fact was. It is quite wrong to suggest that the opposition to the Crown in the latter part of 1297 had nothing to do with the fight for the liberties of the Church.[173]

Although the complaints listed in the Remonstrances came, it seems certain, directly from the lay opposition, they included nothing which did not concern the Church to some extent. Many of the clauses were of the most pressing concern to the clergy, and relate closely to their own grievances against the Crown. How much positive support Bohun and Bigod were receiving from the clergy we cannot ascertain, but the clear acceptance by them that support existed was surely not at all unrealistic. In the disaffected Welsh Marches the lay magnates had seemingly resisted royal orders concerning the recalcitrant clergy,[174] and it is more than likely that the clergy's opposition to the king on the matter of excessive taxation – and, in turn, the king's coercive methods in compelling them to pay a heavy fine because they refused to give their consent to taxation – had greatly helped to stimulate the discontent of the earls and their followers. Winchelsey and his supporting prelates, it is true, held back from open alliance with the lay faction. They had a concern for peace and a primary interest in the affairs of the Church. Also, Winchelsey's leadership of the clergy was largely dependent upon the strength of his claim that he had the interests of the king and of the kingdom at heart. However much he sympathised with the grievances of the earls, as a sacerdotalist he shunned close association with the particular interests of rebellious laymen. He could support their cause, and benefit from it, without being directly linked with it. Any likelihood of an open alliance had, in any case, been forestalled by the fact that being brought into royal favour, if only temporarily, was a political triumph for Winchelsey.

Nonetheless, the reconciliation had put Winchelsey in a difficult

---

[172] Galbraith, *Studies in the Public Records*, p. 148.
[173] Gray, 'The Church and Magna Charta', p. 33.   [174] Above, pp. 130–1.

position. Working closely with the king during the last two weeks of July can only have been acceptable to the archbishop because he was not in any essential way compromising his own objectives as head of the English Church, a position in which he was even more firmly established by the reconciliation with Edward. It is impossible to know how committed he was during July to the policy of reconciling the earls with the king. There is certainly no indication that he actually supported the king's Flanders campaign; indeed Langtoft tells us that Winchelsey advised the king to suspend his passage to Flanders.[175] He could not fail to see that in the Remonstrances the lay opposition were taking up the clergy's own complaints against royal exactions. In the earls' attempt to speak for the whole community we have an interesting reaction against Edward's policy, earlier in the year, of stirring up the laity to act against the recalcitrant clergy. But, with 'Clericis laicos' to guide him, a uniting of clerical and lay interests was certainly not in itself a major aim in Winchelsey's mind.

The section of the Remonstrances concerning military service was the one which probably least affected the Church, although the clergy were linked with the laity in claiming that there was no precedent for service of the king in Flanders,[176] and ecclesiastics had reason for complaint since, unlike the magnates, they had been specifically ordered to provide their *servitium debitum* (with commutation if they wished).[177] It was on the question of service abroad that the earls had opposed the Crown at the Salisbury parliament in February,[178] but the issue then had been service in Gascony without the king. Edward had not pressed the matter. In opposing service in Flanders, the earls now attacked the form of the writs by which they had been summoned, with no place of service specified. Once again this was a short-lived bone of contention, for Edward undermined the opposition by deciding to pay all those who gave service, and he had, in any case, in the initial writs, requested rather than demanded that the magnates provide service.[179] The other transient, though very grave, complaint in

---

[175] Langtoft, ii. 288.
[176] 'avis est a tote la comunalte ausi byen des clers com de lays' (Denton, 'Worcester text of the Remonstrances', p. 520).
[177] Rothwell, 'Confirmation of the charters', p. 25 n. 3.   [178] Above, pp. 117–18.
[179] Cotton, p. 327. See Rothwell, 'Confirmation of the charters', pp. 25–6,

the Remonstrances stressed that it was unwise to go to war in Flanders without greater assurances about the Flemings and at a time when the Scots were rising up against the king even before he left his kingdom. No doubt, on this general issue of political strategy there was widespread concern in England, for the failure of the Flemish campaign was foreseeable, especially in view of the crumbling of the Anglo-German alliance.[180] But complaint on this score was soon not only ineffectual but also irrelevant.

At other points the specific grievances embodied in the Remonstrances were of direct and long-term significance to the clergy as well as to the laity; and these grievances, all of them related to taxation and to the defence of liberties, formed the basis of the reform programme of the opposition to the Crown during August and September. In the complaints concerning taxation the clergy were linked throughout with the laity as the aggrieved. The Remonstrances stressed the impoverishment of the complainants because of tallages, aids, prises and mises.[181] The prises (without any payment) of corn, oats, malt, wool, hides, oxen, cows and salted meat were specifically noted, and prises had, of course, affected all sections of the community.[182] But the general complaint was clearly against all recent and uncustomary exactions. To list recent extraordinary subsidies, on lay movables or clerical income, granted to the king in parliaments or ecclesiastical councils, is to show that in this the most important sphere of uncustomary taxation the clergy had contributed at least as much as the laity.[183] This was so because of the enormous moiety of 1294 and the fine of a fifth of 1297. Another tax specifically complained against was the customs duty on wool, or the *maltote*, which had been imposed since 1294 at six times the previous rate, and the cost of which, at this stage in the history of the duty, was being passed down from the merchants to the sheep-farmers.[184]

Prestwich, *War, Politics and Finance*, pp. 85–6, 251, Harriss, *King, Parliament and Public Finance*, pp. 24, 55–6, 62 and B. C. Keeney, 'Military service and the development of nationalism, 1272–1327', *Speculum*, XXII (1947), 541, 543.
[180] Barraclough, 'Edward I and Adolf of Nassau', esp. pp. 244–7, 252–3.
[181] Clauses 2 and 3 in the Worcester text (clauses 1 and 2 in the text in J. G. Edwards, '*Confirmatio Cartarum*', p. 170). On the clauses concerning taxation see J. G. Edwards, '*Confirmatio Cartarum*', pp. 153–61.
[182] See Harriss, *King, Parliament and Public Finance*, pp. 57–8 and above p. 110.
[183] See Appendix.
[184] C. 7 in the Worcester text (c. 6 in J. G. Edwards, '*Confirmatio Cartarum*',

Monasteries were among the worst sufferers. It was claimed in the Remonstrances that the money from the *maltote* represented a fifth of the annual wealth of the whole land. The mitigation of the amount first demanded on wool in 1294 (5 marks per sack of good wool and 3 marks per sack of inferior wool) to a standard 3 marks for each sack may, it seems, have lapsed at Christmas 1297;[185] certainly, the earls were complaining against the extremely severe duty of 5 marks and 3 marks. The final grievance[186] expressed the fear of the clergy and the laity that the various tallages, aids, prises and mises might be used as precedents and bring disinheritance to the Church and to themselves and their heirs, and enduring bondage to the whole people. In his opposition to Edward in 1297 Winchelsey openly fought in support of the clergy's right to give consent to taxation in their own councils. While he had been concerned especially with subsidies on clerical income, other royal exactions, including prises of goods without payment, had greatly concerned the clergy in recent years.[187] The widest expression of Winchelsey's political aims was the statement of ecclesiastical freedom enshrined in *Magna Carta*, and the relation of that freedom to taxation was clarified for him in 'Clericis laicos' and in 'Coram illo fatemur'. But the matter was taken a stage further, and ecclesiastical freedom put firmly in the context of the issues of the day, by the Remonstrances. Just as 'Clericis laicos' had directly served Winchelsey's purposes, so did the Remonstrances. Although there was a vital issue unmentioned in the Remonstrances – the issue of consent – yet there was nothing among these grievances with which the archbishop can have disagreed, and, fortunately for him, the king was compelled to take

p. 171). For the *maltote* see J. G. Edwards, '*Confirmatio Cartarum*', p. 158, Prestwich, *War, Politics and Finance*, p. 255, Harriss, *King, Parliament and Public Finance*, esp. pp. 424–5 and above, p. 62.

[185] See M. Hale, 'Concerning the custom of goods imported and exported', p. 155 in F. Hargrave, *A Collection of Tracts Relative to the Law of England*, I (London, 1787), cited in Stubbs, *Constitutional Hist.*, II. 551 n. 1. But no wool appears to have qualified for the 5 mark duty (Lloyd, *English Wool Trade*, p. 77); there are no examples in the account for Newcastle-upon-Tyne: see J. Conway Davies, 'The wool customs account for Newcastle-upon-Tyne for the reign of Edward I', *Archaeologia Aeliana*, 4th ser. XXXII (1954), 223, 275–98 and *Eng. Hist. Documents*, III. no. 128.

[186] C. 9 in the Worcester text.

[187] See *Councils*, pp. 1138–9, 1148, 1156.

much greater notice of the grievances of the earls in 1297 than he was inclined to take of purely clerical complaints.

At the end of July the attempt at reconciliation with the earls had failed, and the king, having returned to London from St Albans, acted decisively in order to obtain the money he urgently needed for the Flanders campaign. What he had failed to gain by negotiation with the opposing magnates, he now attempted to force upon the realm.[188] Necessity, in his view, justified emergency measures; but his actions very greatly aggravated the political situation. On 29 or 30 July he obtained the consent of those with him[189] in his chamber to a lay tax of an eighth and a fifth. In return for this subsidy the king at the same time agreed to confirm *Magna Carta* and the Charter of the Forest, as promised; Winchelsey was present and, according to a later statement by the king, announced this confirmation in the king's presence and on the king's behalf.[190] But would this concession be acceptable to or sufficient for either the laity or the clergy? As yet it remained a promise in return for subsidies; no written confirmation was issued. At the same time, Edward ordered a prise of 8,000 sacks of wool as a forced loan from 'the archbishops, bishops, abbots, priors, and all other clerks and other important people'.[191] This was to be paid for out of the proceeds of the lay subsidy, but it was clearly a compulsory loan, taken especially from the clergy. The king hoped that by skilful administration of the lay tax, and by persuasive statements of policy, he could steal a march on the recalcitrant earls. It was a remarkably confident, but dangerous, course to take. The orders for the prise of wool were issued immediately, and the orders for the lay subsidy were ready by 8 August.[192] The barons of the exchequer were now describing the subsidy as actually having been granted by the earls and barons.[193] But open opposition both to the prise of wool and to the forced lay tax was very soon apparent.

[188] See Rothwell, 'Confirmation of the charters', pp. 30–2.
[189] *Plebs* according to *Flores Hist.* (III. 102, 296); *graunt seygneurs* according to the king (Manifesto of 12 Aug.: *Foedera*, I. ii. 873).
[190] See *Statutum de Finibus Levatis* (April 1299): *Stat. Realm*, I. ii. 126, *Chartes des Libertés*, ed. Bémont, p. xlvi and *Eng. Hist. Documents*, III. 491.
[191] *Parl. Writs*, I. ii. 395 and *Eng. Hist. Documents*, III. 475. See Lloyd, *English Wool Trade*, pp. 90–5.　　　　[192] PRO E159/70 mm. 36, 118.
[193] Rothwell, 'Confirmation of the charters', p. 31 and *Eng. Hist. Documents*, III. 477.

The clergy were yet to consider their position in the council summoned for 10 August. In agreeing to confirm the charters the king was assuming that a large grant was to be forthcoming from the Church. The Bury chronicler even maintained that he was asking for another moiety;[194] but he asked the northern province for a fifth and certainly cannot have asked the southern province for more.[195] Before the clergy met, the barons of the exchequer firmly stated in the instructions to those taking the oaths of the taxors for the lay subsidy that the archbishops, bishops, abbots, and priors had already granted the king an aid,[196] and, although this was wrong and deceptive, it is certainly true that Winchelsey had made encouraging noises at the time of his reconciliation with Edward. The archbishop had, however, also made it clear that no grant could be made without a meeting of prelates and clergy.[197] Winchelsey had done nothing positive as yet to upset his reconciliation with the king; but he still had all his cards to play. His policy of non-committal co-operation had paid dividends. On 31 July, as the king left London on his way to Winchelsea and embarkation, the temporalities of those London clergy who had still not bought royal protection by paying the fine of a fifth were restored,[198] and, on the same day, the king's assent was given to the election of Simon of Ghent, Winchelsey's friend and ally, to the bishopric of Salisbury.[199]

In summoning the clergy Winchelsey had stressed the urgency of the situation: there was fear, he wrote, of a state of terrible disorder in the community and realm.[200] By 10 August the position was even more critical. In letters dated 7 August the king had stressed the justice of his case against Philip of France, and the necessity of his campaign, and had requested the bishops to arrange prayers for him in their dioceses.[201] But the clergy, having refused to give consent to a tax since the November parliament of 1296, and having been joined in their opposition to the king's financial exactions by an influential and determined lay faction,

[194] Bury, p. 140.   [195] *Reg. Newark*, p. 292.
[196] Rothwell, 'Confirmation of the charters', p. 31 and *Eng. Hist. Documents*, III. 477.
[197] *Councils*, p. 1172.   [198] Above, p. 133.
[199] *CPR 1292–1301*, p. 301.   [200] *Councils*, p. 1169.
[201] *Foedera*, I. ii. 872 (*CCR 1296–1302*, p. 124) and *Reg. Sutton*, VI. 21–3.

were in a stronger position than ever to continue the fight to control their own taxation and to decide upon cases of necessity for themselves.

The archbishop instructed the clergy meeting in council to discuss the issues under four headings:[202] whether a grant could be made; how large a grant; what should be sought concerning ecclesiastical liberty; and the nature of the crisis facing the king. The reply, apparently from all sections of the clergy, was an emphatic denial that the needs of the king excused them from the penalties of 'Clericis laicos'. It is clear that they regarded the granting of their own consent as the essential factor, more impor-tant to them, we can scarcely doubt, than the licence of the pope, for, although they recognised that it was pointless petitioning the king about the rights of the Church unless they were offering an aid, yet they declared, as explained by the Worcester annalist, that if the king relieved the oppressed state of the Church they would freely and willingly give him financial assistance by some lawful means ('per aliquam viam licitam'). The lawful means existed, for 'Romana mater ecclesia' and 'Coram illo fatemur' had placed the emphasis upon clerical consent.[203] If they had wished to give aid, believing that it was necessary for the kingdom and the Church, they could have done so; because they did not wish to give aid, they answered that the pope's licence was required. The clergy were intransigent.[204] Their reply to the king can be easily misunderstood, for the decision of the council, as conveyed to the king by the bishops of Exeter and Rochester, was that the clergy were willing with the king's permission to seek the pope's licence to grant a tax. And it is true that two learned clerks, to be sent to Rome, had been named in the council. But the clergy were concerned at this time to petition the pope on other matters, even though in fact the departure of their nuncios was delayed until later in the year.[205] It was fully realised, no doubt, that the king

---

[202] For what follows see *Councils*, pp. 1171-2.

[203] Above, pp. 123-4.

[204] Cf. Rothwell, 'Confirmation of the charters', p. 33 and Deighton, 'Clerical taxation 1279-1301', p. 185.

[205] *Reg.*, p. 200. One set of petitions which has been assigned to the Nov. council (*Councils*, pp. 1183-5) could well belong to the Aug. council, and it was perhaps re-drafted to form the second set at the later council. Cf. *Councils*, p. 1178 and n. 3.

would not submit to the terms of 'Clericis laicos' by agreeing to seek the pope's licence. Was there, in any case, the remotest possibility that Boniface VIII would respond favourably in the summer of 1297 to such a request? The English clergy, in short, continued to maintain that there was no urgent crisis facing the realm. The account of the decisions of the council in the Worcester annals indicates another vital consideration: it was regarded as neither proper nor expedient for the prelates to negotiate without the magnates concerning matters that so touched the whole community. The clergy, we can be sure, were aware that they must do nothing to put the Remonstrances in jeopardy.

Winchelsey was not content simply to refuse a grant. He proceeded also with his policy of excommunicating those who attacked ecclesiastical property: 1 September was arranged as the day for pronouncements of excommunications in the cathedral church, or some other important church, of each of the dioceses of the province.[206] It was ordained, also, that on the feast days immediately following 1 September the bishops should denounce the excommunicates in person at the more important places of their dioceses and by deputies at other places. These denunciations were to take place between the celebration of masses, the bells having been rung and the candles lit. All those who violated ecclesiastical property or persons were to be denounced, including, following the terms of 'Clericis laicos', all those who exacted taxes from the clergy without apostolic authority. Despite all the obstacles in the way of making general sentences of excommunication effective,[207] Winchelsey was endeavouring once again, and with even greater determination, to execute 'Clericis laicos' throughout his province. By his actions the reconciliation with the king was firmly and decisively robbed of all significance. Edward had completely failed to mollify his archbishop. Lest these general denunciations should be ineffective, it was ordered that all the evildoers, revealed by the evidence of their deeds or by diligent inquiries, should be excommunicated publicly by name, and those who persisted in their evil-doing were to be denounced, according

---

[206] *Councils*, pp. 1173–5 (Worcester and Cotton), *Reg. Gandavo*, pp. 1–2 and *Reg. Sutton*, VI. 27.

[207] Gray, 'The Church and Magna Charta', pp. 23–30, 34; and see Gray, 'Pecham and the decrees of Boniface'.

to the nature of their misdemeanours, from day to day with full solemnity. Anyone disobeying these orders incurred excommunication *ipso facto*, and in the public denunciations it was to be expressly forbidden that any churchman should do anything to contravene 'Clericis laicos'. By these decisions at the August council the conflict between the clergy and the Crown was revived in earnest.

While the ecclesiastical council was in session Edward, now at Udimore near Winchelsea, in an attempt to undermine the arguments of the opposition, issued the Manifesto of 12 August to all sheriffs for publication.[208] This was a defence of royal policy and a circumstantial account of the recent 'withdrawal' of the earls and of the attempts at mediation. It was skilful propaganda. While it is impossible to imagine that Edward 'knew nothing' of the Remonstrances, he had apparently not been presented with a copy by the earls. He could thus deny all knowledge of the written grievances, yet answer the main complaint of crippling taxation. He emphatically refuted any suggestion that he had turned his back upon petitions for the common profit of the realm. This was an understandable and deliberate attempt to cover up the deep division between himself and his opponents. Urgent necessity, he stressed, had forced him to burden his people, but he promised future amends after the campaign. He pleaded for acquiescence in the new lay tax, for he was fighting for a long-lasting peace with France. Edward, no doubt, genuinely feared serious internal discord. He warned against false rumours, and meant, it seems clear, all expressions of opposition. But the Church was at this very time in the process of discussing and determining a policy of opposition.

The king ended his Manifesto by his own statement of the excommunication of all those who disturbed, or gave assistance in the disturbance of, the peace of the realm. He claimed papal support for this declaration, citing a bull, not, of course, of Boniface VIII, but rather of Clement IV (1265–8): 'from the

---

[208] For which see *Foedera*, I. ii. 872–3 (*Chartes des Libertés*, ed. Bémont, pp. 79–85, *CPR 1292–1301*, p. 305 and *Eng. Hist. Documents*, III. 477–80), Cotton, pp. 330–4 and Cant. D. & C., Reg. I, fos. 211r–212r. And see *CCR 1296–1302*, p. 123.

sentence of excommunication against disturbances of the peace no
one can be absolved without special order of the pope, except at
the point of death, as appears from a bull that the king has of the
time of Pope Clement, which a great many of the prelates and
other great lords of this land have well understood'. The implication of this last remark must be that there were other prelates and
lords who took a different view. Edward is apparently referring
here to the excommunication of Simon de Montfort and all his
supporters by Clement IV. This denunciation was first made by
Clement as papal legate in 1264,[209] and, after he became pope,
further orders for the publishing of sentences of excommunication
were issued on 15 September 1266 and 15 July 1267.[210] These
two bulls excommunicated all those who disturbed the peace of
the realm and Clement prohibited any absolution from the sentences without a special papal mandate, except on the point of
death. Edward clearly had in mind one of these bulls, and one,
though it is not clear which, was among the collection of the
king's bulls calendared by Walter Stapledon in 1323.[211] It was the
bull of September 1266 that was, during Edward's reign, copied
into the Registrum Munimentorum Liber A.[212] But Clement IV's
bulls were, of course, concerned with the particular problems of
the baronial revolt of the previous reign. If Edward was attempting to persuade the readers and hearers of his Manifesto that a
previous pope had excommunicated, in general and until revoked,
all those who disturbed the peace of the kingdom by opposing the
Crown, with arms or without as the two bulls had specified, then
it is not surprising that the king found himself indirectly admitting that there was not full agreement on this point. Clement's
bulls were mandates to the legate Ottobono in pursuance of papal
policy in relation to a particular rebellion against a particular king.

[209] *Councils*, p. 694 n. 6.
[210] 15 Sept. 1266: *Foedera*, I. i. 469–70 (Potthast, no. 19810, calendared in
Les Registres de Clément IV, ed. E. Jordan (École française de Rome, 1945),
no. 426 and *CPL*, I. 434; and see *Chartes des Libertés*, ed. Bémont, p. 85n).
15 July 1267: *Reg. Clément IV*, no. 483 (*CPL*, I. 434).
[211] *Antient Kalendars*, I. 15.
[212] Ibid., I. lxxxix–xc, and *Foedera*, I. i. 469–70 (from Liber A: PRO E36/274,
fo. 138). But neither of the bulls survives among the originals now in the
PRO; for related bulls, one directly concerned with the excommunication of
de Montfort, see *PRO: Lists & Indexes*, XLIX (HMSO, 1923), p. 257 (esp.
Foedera, I. i. 469).

In 1297 it was not those who disturbed the peace that were under a papal ban of excommunication, rather it was those who supported the Crown by contravening 'Clericis laicos'.

On 13 August a safe-conduct to come to the king was issued for the earls and their retinues,[213] and we learn from Guisborough, and the related chronicles of Trivet and 'Rishanger',[214] that envoys of the earls came to the king at Udimore and presented him with the Remonstrances. The king's reply was that no answer could be given to the petitions without his full council, part of which was in London and another part of which had gone ahead to Flanders. He said that he would be pleased if the earls themselves would come to him, but, failing this, he asked that they should not harm the kingdom in his absence. At about the same time, during the second week in August, the bishops of Exeter and Rochester brought to the king the firm decisions of the ecclesiastical council. The king, as was predictable, refused to allow the clergy to seek a papal licence to make a grant.[215] He declared that he would override the decision of the clergy to refuse him a subsidy and would ignore the need for consent. The situation was so critical that he would use his royal authority to compel the clergy to pay a tax, but, according to Cotton, he claimed that it would be so moderate a tax that the clergy would not consider themselves oppressed. The order for a subsidy of a fifth or a third, hardly moderate in view of the taxation of recent years, was, as we shall see, issued on 20 August. The king also reacted strongly to the clergy's decision to publish sentences of excommunication against invaders of ecclesiastical property. He prohibited the excommunications, gave letters of prohibition to all the bishops present with him, and sent out letters to Winchelsey and all other bishops. He had issued a similar prohibition, probably to the bishop of London as dean of the province, in late February;[216] but Edward's political position had been severely weakened during the intervening months. The royal prohibition now sent to all the bishops and dated 19 August[217] included the statement that the king would make appropriate

---

[213] *CPR 1292–1301*, p. 302.
[214] Guisborough, pp. 293–4, 'Rishanger', pp. 175, 177 and Trivet, pp. 360, 362.
[215] For Edward's replies to the clergy see Cotton in *Councils*, p. 1175.
[216] Above, p. 113.
[217] *Foedera*, i. ii. 875 and Prynne, iii. 698–9 (*CCR 1296–1302*, p. 124).

and sufficient satisfaction for the enforced taxation, specified as the seizure of corn and other goods. But this call for trust came at a time when trust had very largely broken down. His plea of necessity had been denied by the clergy. He claimed that if the denunciations against his lay and clerical ministers, obeying his mandates, were carried out, these excommunications would very clearly redound to the grave impairment of the king's dignity and Crown and to the shame of the people, and from this could follow the destruction of the Church and the subversion of the whole kingdom. The king reminded his prelates of their oaths of fealty. There was no mention now of outlawry or of the seizure of temporalities: this policy had been tried and had had a temporary success, but it had failed to lessen the resolve of the clergy and was too difficult and damaging a process to repeat. The struggle was no longer between excommunication on the one hand and out-lawry on the other, but was rather a struggle about whether the Church or the king had ultimate and overriding control over the process and effectiveness of excommunication. Without the Crown's support excommunication could not be carried through to imprisonment; but the power of excommunication, especially perhaps over men of standing, went beyond the procedures of bodily coercion.

Immediately after issuing the letters of prohibition Edward sent to the exchequer, on 20 August, his orders for the taxation of the clergy.[218] Because of the clergy's firm refusal Edward could not even nod in the direction of consent, as he had done with the forced lay subsidy. He was ordering taxation of ecclesiastical wealth by direct royal authority, with no regard for Boniface VIII's pronouncements on taxation. The king's instructions for the tax began with a statement of royal rule by divine right: 'As the king by the ordinance of God has received the government of the realm, by which he is bound to defend that same realm and all his subjects clerk and lay'. And this was followed by a statement of the common responsibility of the clergy and laity for subsidising the king's campaign. The instructions for the subsidy

---

218 *Parl. Writs*, I. ii. 396 (*CPR 1292–1301*, p. 300) and PRO E368/68 mm. 58d–59; see *Eng. Hist. Documents*, III. 480–1; and see Prynne, III. 765–6 (*CCR 1296–1302*, p. 56).

reveal something of Edward's thinking on clerical taxation. He gave the clergy a choice. They could if they wished give a fifth of their income, both spiritual and temporal, appertaining to their benefices – no doubt as assessed in 1291, though this is not specified. But what the king clearly preferred and suggested was an important departure in the process of clerical taxation. He wanted to make a clearer dividing line between temporalities and spiritualities, a dividing line which had the potential of giving him much greater control over the Church's wealth. He proposed that the Church should pay nothing on its purely spiritual income: specified as all tithes, oblations, obventions, mortuaries, or income assigned to lights or to church ornaments. But on the temporal income of the clergy, income from the lands appurtenant to churches and monasteries, a third was suggested. It was the temporalities of the clergy, lands and possessions attached to churches, church offices, and monasteries, that had been seized in February and March; now Edward wished to reinforce his control over the Church's temporalities by taxing them directly and entirely by his own authority. This was a stage in the bid to control the temporal wealth of the English Church; and there was little substance in the king's vague promise, at the end of his instructions concerning the tax, that he would make satisfactory amends to the clergy, who, of course, in fighting for the liberty of the Church regarded the whole of ecclesiastical income as independent of lay or royal interference.

There can be no question that the king still had some firm supporters among the prelates. Walter Langton had been in Flanders and Brabant since March.[219] But in the king's presence at Winchelsea on 20 and 21 August, along with Anthony Bek, were two bishops whose sympathies, though they had attended the recent ecclesiastical council, were clearly with the king: William of Louth, bishop of Ely, and Richard Gravesend, bishop of London. Their support, however we judge it, was insufficient. It was more and more difficult, as Edward was discovering, to tax the clergy without their common consent. The king's orders for the forced tax of a third or a fifth were unrealistic. The exchequer was

[219] Cuttino, 'Langton's mission for Edward I', pp. 180–1.

probably unable even to begin to put the orders into effect, and the tax was certainly not collected.[220]

The lay subsidy was never paid either, even though there were initial attempts to undertake the process of assessment and collection.[221] On 22 August, two days before the king finally embarked, Bohun and Bigod with a company of knights and others appeared in London at the exchequer and challenged the king's financial ministers on behalf of both the laity and the clergy.[222] They stressed again their grievances as expressed in the Remonstrances, and now complained specifically that the lay subsidy was being quite erroneously described in exchequer writs as having been granted by the earls, barons, knights and the commonalty of the realm.[223] Nothing sooner puts men in bondage, they said, than being compelled to pay tallage and merchet ('being tallaged at will and redeeming their own'). As to the latter, the king had declared that the prise of wool would be paid for out of the lay subsidy, and it was precisely buying back their own that the clergy had, earlier in the year, been compelled to do by outlawry. The earls declared that they would not suffer the lay subsidy or the prise of wool to be taken, nor, Guisborough added, the fifth from the clergy, and they pleaded for the support of the citizens of London.[224] There was widespread fear of an uprising against the Crown.

220 Deighton ('Clerical taxation 1279–1301', p. 187) assumed that it was, at least in part, levied. But the *secunda quinta*, which as he noted is referred to in the receipt rolls (as PRO E401/144), is the fifth granted by the York clergy at the end of Nov. 1297 (*Councils*, p. 1185). For the account of the two fifths, granted by the York clergy in Nov. 1296 and Nov. 1297, see PRO E 372/155B mm. 27–8, E 159/73 m. 78d and E159/80 m. 28. The reference to the 'third and fifth' in the list in the PRO (*List of Subsidy Rolls: Clerical Series*, i. 15) is based on the evidence of the king's order for the tax, not on the evidence of taxation returns, of which there are none.

221 *Taxation of 1297: Bedfordshire Rolls*, ed. Gaydon, p. ix, Willard, *Parliamentary Taxes*, p. 16, and see Worcester, p. 534.

222 *Eng. Hist. Documents*, iii. 482–5, from PRO E368/68 m. 28d (printed in *TRHS*, new ser. iii (1886), 284–91) and E159/70 m. 125.

223 Rothwell ('Confirmation of the charters', pp. 18, 34) accused them with insufficient justification of being unwilling to challenge the king directly. The terms of the exchequer writs (above, p. 143), to which they refer, support their claim that the exchequer was acting, to some extent, without the knowledge of the king.

224 Guisborough, p. 294; and see G. A. Williams, *Medieval London* (London, 2nd edn 1970), p. 260 and *Flores Hist.*, iii. 102–3.

Edward was informed immediately of the challenge from the earls, and he instructed the barons of the exchequer to proceed undeterred. In an effort to allay the fears of bondage and disinheritance, he ordered the barons of the exchequer to have it proclaimed in the counties that the lay tax would not be drawn into a custom. He also ordered young Edward and his council and the royal chancellor, John Langton, to issue letters patent to this effect: the letters are dated 28 August.[225] The essentials of the crisis can be viewed in simple terms. The lay and clerical opposition parties pleaded the principle of consent; the king pleaded the principle of necessity. The breakdown of confidence in royal government was such that concerning the crucial issue of taxation an unbridgeable gulf had developed by the end of August preventing the actual execution of royal orders. To base an assessment of the king's situation as he left for Flanders upon the king's own letters is to give the impression that he had retained a strong position of authority.[226] This was hardly the case.

As a final indication of the strength of the opposition to Edward, the clergy of the York diocese, previously compliant to the king, refused in a meeting held on 23 August to offer him a subsidy.[227] The king's promises to the clergy of future satisfaction had been altogether ineffectual. And the confirmation of *Magna Carta* and the Charter of the Forest (or rather promise of confirmation, for it was dependent upon a grant), apparently reiterated while the king was at Udimore between 9 and 18 August,[228] had been ineffectual too. When royal ministers demanded the eighth and fifth in the county of Worcester, they were told that Henry III had promised to confirm the charters in return for a grant, but having received the money he forgot about the charters: 'So when we are in possession of the liberties, we will give the tax.'[229] Concessions more concrete than promises to abide by the charters were now required to quieten the opposition to the Crown of both the laity and the clergy.

That Edward's 'old dominance was gone' has been rightly

[225] *Foedera*, I. ii. 877 (*CPR 1292–1301*, p. 307).
[226] Rothwell, 'Confirmation of the charters', pp. 34–5.
[227] *Councils*, p. 1185 n. 3.
[228] See *Statutum de Finibus Levatis*: above, p. 143 n. 190.
[229] Worcester, p. 534.

stressed by Deighton,[230] who also wrote that the attitude of the clergy in August 1297 'might well have precipitated another crisis'. It did precipitate another crisis. Rothwell commented that the king was 'strong enough to ignore, it seems, this last display of conscience by the clergy'.[231] But the clergy, we might retort, were strong enough to ignore the king's order for a new subsidy and to proceed to the excommunication, on 1 September and after, of infringers of 'Clericis laicos'. If this seems like the 'last' display of conscience, it is because Edward I never repeated the extreme demands of 1294 to 1297. As we have seen, the king had prohibited, on 19 August, the planned excommunications. On 29 August, the royal clerk, Master Itier Bochard of Angoulême, brought into the exchequer the record of the appeal to Rome which he had made on 24 March, under royal instructions, against any acts of the archbishop and clergy that were prejudicial to the Crown.[232] In view of Winchelsey's decision to promulgate new sentences of excommunication, described in the royal memorandum as sentences 'against the king', it was now determined by the regency council that appeals should once more be made to the apostolic see. On 31 August Hugh of Yarmouth and Thomas de Boyvil were appointed to renew the citations and appeals to Rome, in order to prevent the archbishop and others from making denunciations that were prejudicial to the king and the realm.[233] Hugh of Yarmouth proceeded to Canterbury, along with Itier Bochard, and there on Sunday 1 September he directly challenged the authority of the archbishop of Canterbury before the high altar of the cathedral church. He recited his proctorial appointment and made formal declaration of the appeal to Rome, stating that it had become abundantly clear to the king and his council, from the reports of faithful men and from Winchelsey's own sayings and deeds, that the archbishop proposed to make prejudicial and defamatory pronouncements against the king, his councillors, his justices, his clerks and his ministers. These proposed denunciations, he declared, would contravene the king's earlier appeal to Rome concerning certain papal bulls which, in

230 Deighton, 'Clerical taxation 1279–1301', pp. 185–6.
231 Rothwell, 'Confirmation of the charters', p. 34.
232 PRO E159/70 m. 117 (and see *Antient Kalendars*, i. 97). See above, p. 125.
233 PRO E159/70 m. 117 and Prynne, iii. 698 (*CCR 1292–1301*, pp. 307–8).

accordance with the canons of the saints and other divine laws, could claim no force when the realm was placed in a state of emergency.[234] Hugh's appeal to the apostolic see was made openly and publicly before, and directly to, the archbishop, who was at the time, as the record states, engaged in preaching in his cathedral church. It was an unusual and dramatic confrontation. But the king's council had not chosen very eminent men to make the appeals, and Winchelsey probably reacted with his usual studied calm. Soon afterwards, on 12 September, two other royal clerks, Alan of Kent and John of Boreham, were appointed to make similar appeals in the other bishoprics throughout the realm.[235]

The king's *provocationes et appellationes*, first in March and now in September, were proclamations made in England, where they were clearly intended to have an impact upon the political situation. They were formal statements of appeals made to the court of Rome: 'ad sedem apostolicam in hiis scriptis provoco et appello et apostolos peto'. There is no means of ascertaining whether they were actually delivered to the papal curia, though it may seem unlikely that Edward believed that there was anything to be gained by making an appeal to Boniface VIII for a judgment against the execution by the English clergy of 'Clericis laicos', and there is no indication that any of the proctors appointed to make the appeals in 1297 were in fact sent to Rome. Be that as it may, we can guess that diplomatic representations had been made at Rome against 'Clericis laicos' and were perhaps being made already against Winchelsey. The archbishop himself, we do know, wrote letters dated 20 August in support of his own special envoy sent to Rome.[236] But these royal appeals to the pope were certainly, and maybe primarily, in the nature of propaganda statements, to convey especially the belief that divine law itself, and, indeed, the apostolic see, supported the doctrine of necessity. The king had a strong case.[237] But who was the interpreter in England of 'divine

---

[234] 'ipse, spretis dictis appellationibus de quibusdam sedis apostolice constitutionibus et aliis, que regno Anglie in necessitatis articulo in quo positum est existente hiis diebus secundum sanctorum regulas et iura alia infinita locum sibi vendicare non possunt, sumpto colore quedam prejudicialia et infamatoria dicto regi, consiliariis, justiciariis, clericis et ministris suis proponit promulgare': PRO E159/70 m. 117.

[235] Prynne, III. 697 (*CPR 1292–1301*, p. 308) and PRO E159/70 m. 117d.

[236] *Reg.*, pp. 526–8.   [237] See above, p. 97 n. 178.

law'? Was it the pope, or was it the archbishop, or was it the king?

There can be no doubt that the archbishop ignored the royal prohibition and the Crown's appeal to Rome. Cotton is explicit: 'On 1 September in his cathedral church at Canterbury the archbishop excommunicated in the prescribed way all invaders of ecclesiastical goods.'[238] But we cannot believe the Bury chronicle when he states that a general sentence of excommunication was fulminated by every bishop on 1 September.[239] The king's prohibition had had some effect, for Cotton goes on to explain that while there were some others who also at the set time pronounced the sentences of excommunication, taking care to make an exception of the king himself and his sons, there were those (apparently like the bishop of Worcester)[240] who delayed until they had been given further advice by the archbishop, and there were yet others who did little or nothing to implement the decisions of the ecclesiastical council. There is nothing surprising in the discovery of a divided episcopate. We can feel confident that Bishop Ghent of Salisbury was one of the prelates to follow Winchelsey's lead closely: the bishop had given his instructions on 29 August for the carrying out of the denunciations.[241] Also, Bishop Sutton of Lincoln did not hesitate, for there is in his register an account of the ceremony he performed in the prebendal church of Buckingham, and this is followed by orders for denunciations to be made by his archdeacons throughout his diocese.[242] Of great interest is the evidence in this account of the terms in which the king and young Edward were excepted from the sentence of excommunication.[243] Sutton stated that young Edward was certainly innocent. As for the king, the bishop declared: 'It seems desirable to say out of respect for the king that, if perhaps he believes in all conscience that he has excuse for his mandates and is not alive to the peril to souls which could ensue, or perhaps thinks himself to be protected by some privilege or reason which, he supposes, saves him from having incurred the sentence in question, we do not intend any

[238] *Councils*, pp. 1175–6.   [239] Bury, p. 141.
[240] *Councils*, p. 1173.   [241] *Reg. Gandavo*, pp. 1–2.
[242] *Reg. Sutton*, VI. 24–8.
[243] The suggestion (ibid., VI. 25 n. 3) that the brackets round this section in the MS were intended to indicate that it was not part of the published statement seems a little doubtful.

prejudice to him by our declaration and publication.' The bishop
added that it must be stressed that the king had been warned that
it would be necessary to proceed with the denunciations and had
been assured of the desire of the clergy to assist him if their
position permitted it ('si hoc permitteret status noster'). Their
good will, he said, was quite apparent from the fact that they
thought fit to send envoys to seek a papal licence to make a grant
('nuncios duximus specialiter destinandos'). This was a forceful
argument, but, if Sutton believed that papal permission to pay a
subsidy was actually being sought by the clergy in August 1297,
he was certainly mistaken, and however much the bishop had
tried to soften the blow, the king stood accused. The prelates were,
of course, well aware that sentences of excommunication could
not, by papal privilege, touch the person of the king,[244] nor indeed,
by royal order, the persons of the king's ministers,[245] but the terms
by which the bishop of Lincoln excepted the king from the denunciations were laboured and clearly, to himself, somewhat unconvincing. It may not have been the direct aim of the clergy to
bring Edward to his knees, but it is difficult to believe that
Winchelsey and his supporters positively wished to spare him from
political embarrassment.[246]

Winchelsey no doubt still considered that there must be negotiations with Bohun and Bigod and their supporters, but, whatever
his opinion in July, he cannot possibly in September have believed
in mediation on the king's terms. He was certainly not one of the
prelates now working with the regency government: prominent
among these were the bishops of London and Ely,[247] and also the

---

[244] Except, of course, excommunication by the pope himself: see Gray, 'The
Church and Magna Charta', p. 26 and Denton, *Royal Chapels*, p. 61.
[245] See Gray, 'The Church and Magna Charta', pp. 25, 34, *CCR 1302–7*, p. 90
and the statement in PRO E159/67 m. 29d: 'Cum citationes, summonitiones,
denuntiationes vel alieque executiones sententiarum excommunicationis vel
interdicti seu executiones alie que ad forum spectant ecclesiasticum in
scaccario regis nec infra palatium suum fieri non debeant. . .'.
[246] Cf. *Reg. Sutton*, VI. 25 n. 3.
[247] Trivet, p. 365 (and 'Rishanger', p. 179), *CCR 1296–1302*, pp. 71, 73, 138,
142 and *CPR 1292–1301*, pp. 296, 301, 315–16, 323. In the following year
Winchelsey wrote to console the bishop of London when he was ill (*Reg.*,
p. 287); but there was clearly tension between them, for the archbishop assured
his suffragan that censures in councils were not made, as the bishop suspected,
with him in mind.

bishop of Coventry and Lichfield who returned from overseas for the crucial autumn parliament.[248] In the weeks after Edward's departure for Flanders, his government worked for the enforcement of royal control and the restoration of political stability.[249] Preparations were made for preventing an armed rebellion: a further 56 knights were summoned to gather on 8 September at Rochester, with horses and arms, to supplement the 170 already summoned; then, on 9 September, a smaller company of knights, under the earl of Arundel, were ordered to come to young Edward and his council on 22 September. This was apparently an armed guard assembling in preparation for the Michaelmas parliament. On 16 September an even greater concentration of troops was ordered to be in London for 6 October. The king's government intended to negotiate from a position of strength. The show of force may indicate a determination to support and pursue the king's policies; but it amounts also to recognition that the opposition presented a real threat to the authority of the government and the peace of the realm.

A meeting with four of the knights who supported Bohun and Bigod had been arranged for 4 September; this was perhaps an unsuccessful attempt to bring them into line with other armed knights who were supporting the Crown. Then, on 5 September, came the first mandate for the parliament: in a clear attempt to rally the most important supporters of the king, a number of the leading men of the realm were summoned to meet with young Edward and the council in London on 30 September. The men summoned included the earls of Cornwall and Warwick (both later ordered to come with horses, men and arms), the archbishop-elect of York and the bishops of London, Ely, Worcester and Carlisle. The first three of these prelates were certainly of strong royalist sympathies and the other two had apparently taken no active part in the clerical opposition to the Crown. Thus, twenty-five days' notice of the parliament was given to some of the king's prominent adherents. The next writs to be sent out, on 9 September, are of special interest, for they were addressed to the king's

[248] See *Reg.*, pp. 203, 205.
[249] See esp. Rothwell, 'Confirmation of the charters', pp. 178–80, J. G. Edwards, '*Confirmatio Cartarum*', pp. 287–90 and *Parl. Writs*, i. ii. 55–6, 296–300 (*CCR 1296–1302*, pp. 125, 127–30 and *CPR 1292–1301*, p. 309).

158

opponents.[250] The 'afforcing' of the king's council was now being extended to the opposition parties, both clerical and lay: Winchelsey was summoned, with the bishop-elect of Salisbury, and the bishops of Lincoln, Norwich, Hereford, Rochester and Bath and Wells,[251] and, with these, twenty-three regular prelates of various orders; and eight knights, many of whom we know to be important members of the rebellious faction;[252] and, last in the list, Bohun and Bigod, the latter still described as marshal of England, but surely erroneously in view of the king's replacement of him in office. It seems a little unlikely that there can have been a deliberate policy of excluding from the parliament the bishops of Exeter and Chichester (as also the Welsh bishops, two of whom, the bishops of St Asaph and Llandaff, had given strong support to Winchelsey earlier in the year); but these bishops certainly do not appear in the enrolled lists of those summoned. On 15 September knights of the shire were ordered to be present on 6 October, a week after the rest; but the lower clergy were not to be represented.

In this situation of internal crisis, and without any possibility of support from Winchelsey, there was nothing that the king could immediately do to lend weight to his orders for the clerical, as distinct from the lay, subsidy. The intention was, as the writs summoning the knights of the shire make plain, to gain consent in the parliament to the lay tax which the king had already ordered to be collected. To be specific, the knights of the shire were summoned to come to receive the confirmation of the charters (as already promised in return for a grant) and also the letters patent giving assurances that the tax would not be drawn into a custom (as already issued on 28 August).[253] This amounted to seeking consent to the taxation, and it was, of course, the failure to seek consent that had caused strong resentment. The regency

---

[250] We can be more certain of the distinction between the list of adherents and the list of opponents than J. G. Edwards assumed: 'Confirmatio Cartarum', pp. 288–9. See Morris, *Welsh Wars*, pp. 281–4.

[251] The position of William of March, bishop of Bath and Wells, in relation to the king's government is now uncertain (see above, pp. 72–3); but he was, in fact, included in an extended list of the king's councillors at the parliament, though not in a shorter list (*Reg.*, pp. 203, 205).

[252] See Prestwich, *War, Politics and Finance*, p. 250.

[253] Above, p. 153 n. 225.

government, acting under Edward's instructions, was therefore attempting to regularise the king's direct order of a subsidy. The very summoning of the parliament amounted to a significant concession. But would the confirmation of the charters and the king's assurances in letters patent prove to be sufficient to secure consent?

The bishops who followed Winchelsey's lead had been making their protest by declarations of excommunication against all who infringed the Church's own control of its property and wealth. Yet, the prelates were still giving no overt support to the lay opposition to the Crown. To have done so would surely have increased the possibility of extensive civil disorder during these dangerous weeks in late August and September. Despite the efforts of the king's government to prevent it, an assembly of the magnates who had withdrawn their allegiance from the Crown met at Northampton, apparently on 21 September.[254] We know nothing of the outcome of this illegal assembly and can only guess that Bohun and Bigod, like the king's council, were planning how to proceed in the imminent parliament. The parliament was their opportunity to obtain redress for the petitions embodied in the Remonstrances. When they came to London, just over a week later, they were armed, and they insisted upon posting their own guards at the gates of the city.[255] News of the defeat of the English troops at Stirling Bridge on 11 September had arrived before the meeting of the parliament.[256] Both the laity and the clergy must now have regarded the threat from Scotland with serious alarm. The need for subsidies was no doubt immediately recognised, for here was an unmistakable threat to the security of the realm; but the crisis in the north, which had been foreseen, probably served to strengthen rather than weaken the bargaining power of the opponents of the Crown.

Little is known of what took place during the negotiations in the Michaelmas parliament. But there can be no doubt that Winchelsey played a leading rôle, almost certainly *the* leading rôle, in securing a peaceful settlement, with major concessions

---

[254] See *Foedera*, I. ii. 878, *CCR 1296–1302*, pp. 129, 131, Bury, pp. 141–2 and J. G. Edwards, 'Confirmatio Cartarum', pp. 290–2.
[255] Guisborough, p. 308.
[256] Rothwell, 'Confirmation of the charters', p. 180.

from the Crown. Edward's bitterness against Winchelsey, culminating in his suspension in 1306, was certainly related to the archbishop's success in this parliament.[257] Guisborough noted that the archbishop acted as mediator in the long discussions,[258] and Winchelsey himself revealed the position very clearly in a letter, dated 9 January 1298, to Anthony Bek: he informed Bek that he had worked with sincere devotion to quell the dangerous dissension in the realm and to bring the negotiations to a successful conclusion, and yet he knew that certain sons of the devil were interpreting his actions in a sinister and evil way and were daily spreading malicious stories about him in their letters to the king.[259] This letter to Bek is, incidentally, an indication of the support which the bishop of Durham appears to have given to the movement that gave rise to *Confirmatio Cartarum*. During the period of the king's clash with the earls and with Winchelsey between 1297 and 1301, Bek seems to have adopted a policy of compromise and conciliation. Although he showed no intention of following Winchelsey's lead early in 1297,[260] and even gained a reputation for oppressive methods in persuading his clergy to redeem their temporalities from the king,[261] yet when the earls of Norfolk and Hereford came into conflict with the king later in the year there can be little doubt that Bek was to show some sympathy for their cause. Tradition soon had it that he acted as arbiter after the earl marshal and his adherents left the July parliament; he apparently persuaded the king not to arrest Bigod.[262] The account given by Robert de Graystanes of the clash between Edward and Bek, even if it is inaccurate as to dating, points at least to the high regard which the bishop had for the protest of the earls.[263] In letters to Rome in 1302 the archbishop described his indebtedness to Bek

[257] See below, pp. 229–30. [258] Guisborough, p. 308.
[259] *Reg.*, p. 218. For Winchelsey's close friendship with Bek see above, pp. 43–4.
[260] Above, p. 104. [261] *Reg.*, p. 537.
[262] See *Chronica de Melsa*, ii. 266 and Bridlington, pp. 38–9, cited in Fraser, *Bek*, p. 70.
[263] *Historiae Dunelmensis Scriptores Tres*, ed. J. Raine (Surtees Soc., ix, 1839), p. 78, and Fraser, *Bek*, p. 152 n. 2. But this account stands on its own and can only be accepted with caution; Emden, however, concludes that Bek 'fell into disfavour in 1297 owing to the support that he gave to archbishop Winchelsey, the earl marshal, and the earl of Hereford in their opposition to the king' (Emden, *Oxford*, p. 152).

in the tribulations he had suffered: of all the prelates of England Bek especially had given him assistance and support.[264]

In late 1297 and early 1298 Winchelsey was already taking the blame for the way in which the granting of *Confirmatio Cartarum* was forced upon the king. Some of the malice perhaps stemmed from the fact that Winchelsey had been primarily responsible for the exposure in 1297 of the chamberlain of the exchequer, Richard of Louth, a clerk, who had supervised the recent prises in the county of Kent and, on his own admission, had been responsible for the purveyance of the archbishop's corn in Kent and elsewhere.[265] Louth was sentenced in November 1297 by the king's council for contempt of the king and of the king's court, by the treasurer and barons of the exchequer for corruption in the administration of the prise of corn in the county of Kent, and, later, by the archbishop's court for marrying when in orders, for immorality and for perjury.[266] The prominent part that Winchelsey played in the downfall of the chamberlain of the exchequer cannot have endeared him to other royal clerks, or to the king. It had been the aim of the promulgation of sentences of excommunication early in September to reveal and to name just such men as Richard of Louth.

Winchelsey occupied a commanding position in the Michaelmas parliament not only because he stood apart from the king's council, but also because he had not been drawn into openly giving his allegiance to Bohun and Bigod. Yet there can be no doubt where he stood; bringing an end to excessive and arbitrary taxation was as important to the clergy as it was to the laity. The chronicle evidence for what took place at the parliament is very much less helpful than we could have hoped. Cotton and the chroniclers of Worcester and Bury tell us nothing that we do not know from the official records.[267] They give us the correct general impression that the petitions of the barons were granted by the king, though, as we shall see, in some particulars the barons wanted more than was actually conceded. We are left with two instructive, if not altogether accurate or precise, accounts in Guisborough and in the

[264] *Reg.*, pp. 617–18.   [265] See Rothwell, 'Disgrace of Richard of Louth'.
[266] *Reg.*, esp. pp. 236–7.
[267] Cotton, pp. 337–8, Worcester, p. 335 and Bury, p. 142.

chronicle of Evesham.[268] We must rely very largely upon the documentary evidence, especially the unofficial *De Tallagio Non Concedendo* (as given by Guisborough and, in part, by Evesham),[269] and, of course, the official *Confirmatio Cartarum* (of 10 October and confirmed by the king on 5 November), as well as the two letters concerning amnesty for the earls, both of 10 October, one from young Edward and the other from the king's council (upon which the king's pardon of 5 November was based). The official letters concerning the outcome of the negotiations, those of 10 October and those of 5 November, are to be found, significantly, in Winchelsey's register.[270]

But we must first return to the Remonstrances, for we have been taught to see this document as the principal and authoritative statement of baronial grievances.[271] That these petitions were still relevant and were used in the negotiations of early October is apparent, as Edwards showed,[272] from a comparison of them with *Confirmatio Cartarum*. The text of the Remonstrances in the register of Bishop Giffard of Worcester[273] reinforces the link, for the final clause of this text, concerning the possible use of recent taxes as a precedent because they might be found enrolled, was directly answered in clause 5 of the *Confirmatio*.[274] The words of the *Confirmatio* ('peussent tourner en servage a eux e a leur heyrs') reflect even more closely than Edwards realised[275] the words of the Remonstrances ('eus e lor successours e lor heyrs pussent entrer en grant servage'). In addition, and contrary to Edwards's belief,[276] the Remonstrances refer to 'aydes' and 'mises' as does the

---

[268] Guisborough, pp. 308–13 and Evesham, pp. 578–9. Trivet (pp. 366–8) and 'Rishanger' (pp. 180–2) provide identical abbreviated versions of Guisborough.

[269] Esp. Rothwell, 'Confirmation of the charters', pp. 300–15, Denton, 'Crisis of 1297 from Evesham chronicle', pp. 565–7 and Denton, 'Worcester text of the Remonstrances', pp. 514–18.

[270] *Reg.*, pp. 201–9.

[271] J. G. Edwards, '*Confirmatio Cartarum*'.

[272] Ibid., pp. 162–9.

[273] Denton, 'Worcester text of the Remonstrances', pp. 520–1.

[274] On the content of this clause see Harriss, *King, Parliament and Public Finance*, p. 67. For the standard editions of the *Confirmatio* see *Stat. Realm*, I. ii. 123–4, *Chartes des Libertés*, ed. Bémont, no. XIV, and *Select Charters*, ed. Stubbs, pp. 490–1 (translated in *Eng. Hist. Documents*, III. no. 74), and see *Lancs. Lay Subsidies*, ed. Vincent, pp. 207–9.

[275] J. G. Edwards, '*Confirmatio Cartarum*', p 168.

[276] Ibid., pp. 163–5.

Confirmatio. With certain modifications, including inevitably the rejection of the term 'tallage' with its close associations of servility and the addition of salvos concerning the king's customary aids and dues, the *Confirmatio* conceded substantially, and often directly, the petitions in the Remonstrances.

That the Remonstrances concerned the clergy just as much as the laity has already been stressed.[277] The recent excommunications promulgated by at least some of the bishops had included the denunciation of all who seized the goods of clergymen, from the archbishop down to vicars of parish churches, without their consent, as well as the denunciation of all involved in any kind of taxation paid to laymen without papal licence.[278] We have seen how the granting of their own consent (rather than the pope's) was especially important in practical terms (rather than as a legal principle), to the English clergy. The allowance in *Confirmatio* of consent to all forms of extraordinary taxation (aids, mises, prises and *maltote*) was a concession to Winchelsey and the English Church as well as to the magnates and the laity. The clergy, after all, had suffered outlawry only seven months earlier for refusing to grant consent to an aid. The *Confirmatio* was, in effect, an admission by the Crown of the unwarranted, if not unlawful, nature of the king's demands upon the clergy in recent years, from the seizure and scrutiny of money and forced moiety of 1294, and from the *maltote* and prises of 1294 to 1297, to the fine of a fifth in lieu of an aid in 1297. All had been imposed upon the clergy despite the lack of 'common assent' and 'good will', to use the terms of *Confirmatio*. *Confirmatio* provided not simply clauses additional to *Magna Carta*: it provided a gloss upon the liberty of the English Church as granted in the first clause of *Magna Carta*. Small wonder that Winchelsey, as Langtoft tells us,[279] rejoiced at the outcome of the Michaelmas parliament.

The Remonstrances must certainly be regarded as a principal source for what transpired at the Michaelmas parliament. The Remonstrances were answered. All the same, it should not be overlooked that this set of grievances was, by the beginning of

[277] Above, pp. 138–42.
[278] *Reg. Gandavo*, I. 1–2 and *Reg. Sutton*, VI, 26.
[279] Langtoft, II. 302–3.

October, already out of date in some respects. The petition concerning the inadvisability of the Flanders campaign and the petition concerning the form of the writs by which service in Flanders had been requested were no longer of direct relevance. Neither required a specific answer in October. The granting of amnesty to those who refused to serve in Flanders was a safeguard against possible royal retaliation rather than an answer to the particular petition of the Remonstrances.[280] Also, the Remonstrances had been drawn up before the king's most recent and most blatant attempts at compulsory national taxation had become known. The document in its taxation clauses was concerned with the extent and the burden, and by direct implication the frequency, of the king's financial demands; but the *Confirmatio* is directly and notably concerned with consent. This important development arose partly because of the changed situation caused by the king's attempt to force new subsidies upon both the laity and clergy. It is noteworthy that the need for consent was in the minds of the earls when they protested at the exchequer on 22 August.[281] But the change was probably also brought about by the influence of Winchelsey and his supporters, who were throughout unmistakably preoccupied with the principle of consent.

This concern to compel the king to admit the need for consent to all extraordinary taxation is clearly reflected in *De Tallagio Non Concedendo*, which contains the baronial demands at about the time of the Michaelmas parliament. If Guisborough and the chronicle of Evesham are sufficient testimony, *De Tallagio* as a draft-charter was sent to the king, as also was the *Confirmatio*. In its insistence upon consent *De Tallagio* gives a better indication than the Remonstrances of what most concerned the opponents of the Crown in October.[282] There was no need at this time to press for the confirmation of *Magna Carta* and the Charter of the Forest, as such, for Edward had already promised confirmation in return for a grant, and the confirmations were indeed forthcoming on 12 October without further reference to Edward.[283] *De Tallagio* successfully highlights the demands and concessions of greatest

[280] Cf. J. G. Edwards, '*Confirmatio Cartarum*', p. 166.   [281] Above, p. 152.
[282] See Harriss, *King, Parliament and Public Finance*, pp. 63–5.
[283] *Stat. Realm*, i. ii. 114–22 and *Foedera*, i. ii. 879.

importance: the pardon for the lay rebels, and the need for consent to any future subsidies for the king, and to prises, and to any *maltote*, that is, any duty upon wool and hides beyond the customary half a mark and one mark. We should not be surprised that this baronial draft-charter, whether drawn up shortly before, during, or shortly after the parliament, reveals something of the aims and aspirations of the baronial opposition rather than the actual terms conceded by the king's councillors and later by the king himself. It refers not simply to 'common assent' for subsidies and for prises, but rather to 'the will and common assent of the archbishops and other prelates, earls, barons, knights, burgesses and other free men of the realm' and to 'the will and assent of whoever the goods belonged to'.[284] On this last point it is interesting that Winchelsey, interpreting *Confirmatio* in the terms of *De Tallagio*, was to emphasise in 1298 the need for the consent of each clergyman or his bailiff before any prises could be made upon his goods.[285] The lay opposition was fighting for the freedom from arbitrary taxation of all free men, just as Winchelsey was fighting for the freedom of all the clergy. But the Crown avoided any specific written commitment to the recent regular procedure of consulting shire and borough representatives. Since it was very much in the king's interests to continue this procedure, the issue of shire and borough representation in parliament, and also the interpretation of what was meant by 'common assent' to prises,[286] were matters of underlying, but not crucial, importance in 1297. If the earls and barons had been able themselves to agree in July that the king's continuing need for money was a necessity for the defence and well-being of the realm, there would have been no major political crisis. Most magnates and prelates no doubt still believed that they represented as king's councillors the common interest of all the realm.[287] It is interesting that Cotton glossed 'common assent' as 'the consent of the archbishops, bishops, prelates, earls and barons'.[288]

[284] See Prestwich, *War, Politics and Finance*, pp. 254, 260 and Harriss, *King, Parliament and Public Finance*, p. 66.
[285] *Councils*, p. 1194.
[286] Harriss, *King, Parliament and Public Finance*, p. 68.
[287] See ibid., pp. 30, 38, 42, 53, 76 and the general argument of W. A. Morris, 'Magnates and community of the realm in parliament 1264–1327', *Medievalia et Humanistica*, 1 (1943), 58–94.   [288] Cotton, p. 337.

In another, perhaps more crucial, matter *Confirmatio* differed from *De Tallagio* and failed to represent the true intentions of both lay and clerical opponents. When Winchelsey drew up his new sentence of excommunication against infringers of the charters, probably immediately after the agreement with the king's council early in October,[289] he was concerned to defend not just the charters, but the *Confirmatio* too, against all infringements. Likewise, *De Tallagio* in its final clauses was concerned with the maintenance of the terms of the new agreement: it was 'this present charter' that was to be read in all cathedral churches; and anyone who contravened the terms of 'this present charter' was to be denounced as an excommunicate twice a year in parish churches throughout the land. Yet the *Confirmatio* in fact provided for the reading twice a year of *Magna Carta* and the Charter of the Forest in all cathedral churches and for the denunciation twice a year of contravenors of only these two charters.[290] The sentence of excommunication laid down in the *Confirmatio* was thus unlike Winchelsey's new sentence of excommunication which certainly concerned infringers of the new additions to the charters. It is difficult to believe that Winchelsey, or those who sent *De Tallagio* to the king, misunderstood the actual terms of the agreement set down in the *Confirmatio*, especially on so crucial an issue as the maintenance and defence of the king's concessions. Here the royal councillors appear to have had a final say in the wording of the agreement. They avoided making the clauses of *Confirmatio* firm additions to the clauses of *Magna Carta*. While the *Confirmatio* was an addition to *Magna Carta*, it was certainly supplementary to, and separate from, *Magna Carta*. As a result, it would be easier in due course to obtain its revocation. Even so, Edward's opponents apparently still accepted that their rights were enshrined in *Magna Carta*. And it must be stressed that whether the *Confirmatio* was later revoked or not was of less consequence than we might imagine. The political forces which had given birth to this commentary upon *Magna Carta* were not of a temporary nature.

---

[289] For the text see *Reg.*, pp. 204–5 and *Stat. Realm*, I. ii. 126 from BL Harl. 667, fo. 14r, where the sentence follows Edward's confirmation of the charters of 28 March 1300. Also see *Councils*, p. 1193 and Rothwell, 'Edward and the struggle for the charters', p. 322.

[290] See Prestwich, *War, Politics and Finance*, p. 260.

The king's admission of the need for consent to all but customary taxation even in situations which he judged to be of urgent necessity was a major defeat on a vital issue. It was a defeat of long-term consequence, whether or not the actual terms of the *Confirmatio* were read twice a year in churches, and whether or not they were rescinded by the pope.

The granting of *Confirmatio Cartarum* was a political humiliation for Edward I. He had compelled Archbishop Pecham to *revoke* excommunications of infringers of the charters.[291] Now he ordered Archbishop Winchelsey and the archbishop of York and all the bishops to *carry out* excommunications on a regular basis. The rôle of the Church as the guardian of liberties was reasserted. Winchelsey had succeeded in establishing as a constitutional principle the right of the clergy to be consulted, and to arrive at their own conclusions, about the necessity for any royal taxation of their income and wealth. This was a political advantage to which the archbishop would cling tenaciously. The clergy had suffered even more than the laity from the extent and nature of the king's exactions; by the same token, they were to gain more than the laity because of this new protection from arbitrary royal taxation. 'Clericis laicos' had borne fruit.

Indeed, if we take a general view of the course of the crisis in 1297 with the clergy and the lay magnates it is difficult to avoid the conclusion that the clergy under Winchelsey's leadership had played a major part in determining the content of *Confirmatio Cartarum* and in compelling the king to accept this concession. From the time of the Remonstrances the coalescence of the clerical and lay interests greatly strengthened the hand of the king's opponents. The clergy had vigorously opposed the king's financial demands since 1294, the laity only since July 1297, for the laity had a greater sense of the subject's obligation to aid the king for defence, as the apparent lack of significant opposition to taxation upon lay movables in the parliaments of 1294, 1295 and 1296 bears witness.[292] It was, after all, the clergy much more than the laity who were fighting for the right of real consent, that is, the right of free refusal. The capacity of the laity to bargain and to

291 Douie, *Pecham*, p. 119.
292 See Harriss, *King, Parliament and Public Finance*, pp. 32, 49.

withhold consent was, however, increasing, as the events of 1300–1 and 1309 will show. Opposition to the Flanders campaign was no doubt an important factor in bringing the question of consent to the fore as a crucial issue for the laity in August and September 1297, as well as the increasing effects of very high taxation; but the persistent claims and the pervasive influence of the clergy must not be overlooked. The magnates spoke for the whole community, including the clergy. At the same time, it must be stressed that the clergy – prelates and lower clergy – had shown their capacity through their representative assemblies to speak firmly and decisively on their own behalf.

It was primarily the laity who had bought the new agreement, giving consent to a subsidy before Edward himself had set his seal to the *Confirmatio* and to the amnesty for the earls. The issuing of the promised confirmations of *Magna Carta* and the Charter of the Forest on 12 October[293] provides the evidence that a lay subsidy had been granted in the parliament. The enforced tax on lay movables of an eighth had been replaced by an agreed ninth in return for the confirmation of the charters.[294] The collectors of the new tax were assigned on 14 October. The lay goods (not annexed to churches) of the clergy were, as usual, included in this tax on movables; but the clergy had gained the concessions of the charters and the *Confirmatio* without making, or even formally promising, a subsidy to the king on their income. They were free now to consider their position independently.

The archbishop had openly disobeyed the king's orders not to proceed with the denunciations of early September, and he had worked against the king's orders concerning taxation. Yet, the formal amnesty which was part of the agreement of October 1297 concerned only the lay opponents of the Crown. It was a grant of pardon to all who did not obey the king's request to go with him to Flanders, and a pardon to Bohun and Bigod and their followers for failure to obey orders to come to the king and orders to refrain from organising armed assemblies. In that Edward was to take no

[293] Above, p. 165 n. 283.
[294] *Parl. Writs*, I. ii. 62–4 (*CPR 1292–1301*, p. 313). Soon, after negotiation, the tax was extended to the cities and boroughs and ancient demesne: Mitchell, *Taxation in Medieval England*, p. 381 and *Taxation of 1297: Bedfordshire Rolls*, ed. Gaydon, p. x.

legal action against the offenders specifically because of their disobedience in 1297, the amnesty was apparently respected. But it is nevertheless clear that the king found no reason to forgive the perpetrators of this successful revolt against his policies. Like the chronicler Langtoft, Edward no doubt felt, and with some justification, that his war-effort against Philip of France had been critically weakened because of the treacherous behaviour of some of his leading subjects.[295] Barraclough is of a similar opinion and blames the English clergy: 'The effect of the publication of *Clericis laicos*...was to rally the French clergy round their king, and from this junction of royal interests and clerical opposition to papal centralisation the birth of Gallicanism can be dated. In England, on the other hand, the clergy under Winchelsey sought to obey Boniface's prohibition, and Edward's plans were crippled at the critical moment.'[296] The king very soon, and most effectively, pursued the houses of Bohun and Bigod.[297] Other than these two leading earls the only man actually named in the amnesty was John Ferrers, whose father Robert Ferrers, earl of Derby, had been denied the benefits of the Dictum of Kenilworth and had lost his earldom.[298] In fact, there is no other evidence that John Ferrers had involved himself in opposition to the Crown in 1297. Presumably he had not responded to the call to go to Flanders with Edward. Winchelsey certainly saw the king's long-term vindictiveness against the house of Ferrers as unjust, and he referred to John Ferrers in 1301 as his special friend.[299] It seems very likely that the archbishop was influential in having his name included in the 1297 amnesty: perhaps there was already a link of close friendship between him and John Ferrers. At about this time Ferrers claimed in a letter to Boniface VIII that he had the support of many clergy and prelates.[300] Is the case of Ferrers an indication of a closer bond between the clerical and lay opposition to the Crown than we had suspected? We know of support by Winchelsey for John Ferrers; but the evidence is certainly not substantial enough to undermine the predominant impression of the archbishop's aloofness from the opposition magnates (however sym-

[295] Langtoft, II. 296-7.
[296] Barraclough, 'Edward I and Adolf of Nassau', p. 259.
[297] McFarlane, 'Had Edward I a policy towards the earls?', pp. 154-5.
[298] Ibid., pp. 149-51.   [299] *Reg.*, p. 566.   [300] See below, p. 205 n. 120.

pathetically he may have viewed their cause and however influential his position in the October parliament) and of his corresponding commitment to supporting *ex officio* the interests of the clergy as distinct from the interests of the laity.

Immediately after the parliament Winchelsey summoned the clergy of the southern province to the fourth council of the year, stressing the very recent and sudden threat from Scotland to the realm, the Church and the clergy.[301] If this emergency had not arisen, it is most unlikely that Winchelsey would have considered discussing once again with the clergy the possibility of making a grant. But the crisis in Scotland had also, of course, been a major factor in compelling the king to concede *Confirmatio*. It is important to stress that the archbishop had consistently followed both a hard-headed and a high-principled policy. The clergy were summoned again to judge the case of necessity. There was no question of them offering a grant specifically in return for the king's concessions. For Winchelsey it was not a matter of bargaining with the king. The clergy in making their decisions must remain as free as possible from external political pressures. This new council was summoned to meet at New Temple, London, on 20 November. But an important gathering took place at Westminster, probably just before the ecclesiastical council met, though Cotton wrote that it was at the same time and place as the ecclesiastical council, and an anonymous chronicler believed that the clergy were already meeting in council.[302] At this gathering the *Confirmatio* and the amnesty, both sealed by the king, were received and recited. Before endorsing the concessions the king had hesitated and had looked for assurances that the earls would fight for him either in Flanders or in Scotland;[303] but Edward was in no position to open further negotiations, and at length the sealed documents were brought to England, apparently by the treasurer, Bishop Langton.[304] Present at the formal reading of the

---

[301] *Councils*, pp. 1178–80. The king, had, however, been warned in the Remonstrances of the danger from Scotland.

[302] Cotton, p. 339, and BL Cotton Domitian A xii, fo. 36v ('Et istud scriptum [i.e. the *Confirmatio*] traditum fuit archiepiscopo Cantuariensi vidente toto clero in capitulo Westmonasterii in consilio ibidem convocato.')

[303] Guisborough, p. 313.

[304] Langtoft, II. 306–7.

agreement were young Edward and a company of earls, barons and magnates, and, noted Cotton, the documents (he wrote simply the 'charters') were handed over to the custody of Winchelsey. The effects of the sealing of *Confirmatio* were soon felt: new perambulations of the king's forest were ordered on 16 October; further orders for the observance of *Magna Carta* and the Charter of the Forest were issued on 17 November; and on 27 November the *maltote* was abolished.[305]

The southern clergy met on 20 November to reassess the question of necessity, and they must certainly, in view of the receipt of the sealed *Confirmatio*, have felt more amenable to the suggestion of a new subsidy. There had been another development which must also have influenced discussion at the council. Boniface VIII had conceded to Philip IV by his bull 'Etsi de statu' (31 July) the right to tax the French clergy at a time of urgent need without consulting the pope. As an interpretation upon 'Clericis laicos', and certainly a severe weakening of the force of 'Clericis laicos', 'Etsi de statu' clearly had relevance outside France. It became well known in England,[306] and the annalist of Worcester gives abstracts from it immediately after his note of the November council. Yet, even though 'Etsi de statu' may well have made it easier for the English clergy in November to make a grant without first securing the pope's licence, this bull in fact had very little influence upon the situation in England. 'Clericis laicos' had seemed to deny the long-standing and widely accepted doctrine of necessity; but Winchelsey and the English clergy had not given it that interpretation. They had insisted that, in the case of ecclesiastical taxation, they should decide whether or not the claim of necessity applied in a given situation. Now they believed that the gravity of the crisis in Scotland obviated the need for papal consultation.[307] However much they had used the extreme statement of clerical liberty in 'Clericis laicos' to their advantage, they had been well aware that their discussions centred upon the needs of the realm. And the

---

[305] *CCR 1296–1302*, pp. 134, 137, 187, 190–1, *CPR 1292–1301*, pp. 312, 323 and *Eng. Hist. Documents*, III. no. 78.

[306] *Councils*, p. 1177 n. 3, and for other copies in English sources see, for example, *Reg. Swinfield*, p. 346, BL Harl. 3911, fos. 185r–186v, and BL Royal 11 B v, fo. 10r.

[307] *Reg. Sutton*, VI. 46.

English clergy would continue to cite the authority of 'Clericis laicos', in 1298 and later.[308]

What was new about 'Etsi de statu' was the explicit concession that the right to judge whether or not a situation was one of urgent necessity belonged to the king of France himself. Boniface VIII was thus prepared to admit that in France at a time of emergency there was no need for the clergy themselves to debate the question of necessity. Here was the pope's *volte face*. This was an acceptance that clerical consent, as well as the pope's licence, was at times unnecessary. Any such concession to the king of England would have been a betrayal of the English clergy. Not only was the tradition of consent to taxation too strong in England. It was now reaffirmed in *Confirmatio Cartarum*. To compare 'Etsi de statu' with *Confirmatio Cartarum* is to reveal a striking contrast between the kind of control which the king of France had over taxation and the constitutionally limited rights of the king of England.[309]

There was one overriding factor which required the clergy to make a grant: the need to defend the realm against the Scots. Even so, the grant of a tenth in the council of 20 November was not an open-handed concession. It was a grant with a difference.[310] The lower clergy were given some protection by paying on the Norwich assessment rather than on the much harsher 1291 assessment. More important, there was to be no return to the royal administration of ecclesiastical taxation as in 1294 and 1295. While the assessment of ecclesiastical subsidies had never been the responsibility of royal agents, the collection of the taxes had come more and more under the control of the exchequer working in conjunction with the diocesan bishops.[311] But Winchelsey had achieved his aim of freedom from lay interference. He himself, as his register bears witness,[312] kept a strict control over the whole

---

[308] *Councils*, p. 1191 and Denton, 'Reynolds and ecclesiastical politics', pp. 250–2.
[309] See Strayer, 'Defense of the realm in France', pp. 289–96; not forgetting that Boniface revoked all his concessions to Philip in 'Salvator mundi' of Dec. 1301: *Reg. Boniface VIII*, no. 4422.
[310] For the tax see *Councils*, p. 1181, Graham, 'Ecclesiastical tenth for national defence in 1298', pp. 200–5 and Deighton, 'Clerical taxation 1279–1301', pp. 189–91.
[311] Powicke, *Thirteenth Century*, pp. 508–9.
[312] *Reg.*, pp. 210–15, 229–30, 232–6, 238–9, 243–7, 250, 260–2, 530, 686–8, 767–8; and see *Reg. Gandavo*, pp. 3–5, 73–4, 117–19.

process of collection and distribution of the new tax of November 1297. It was the archbishop who now supervised the supply of money. Accordingly, payments could be withdrawn as soon as the king's need was considered insufficient to merit further aid, and, in fact, by the decision of the June council of 1298, the final payments from the tax never reached the king.[313] This control of appropriation of supply was a major achievement, beyond the hopes and dreams of the laity, for whom appropriation was 'inherent in the grant of taxation and inseparable from consent'.[314] Winchelsey withdrew the control of the clerical aid from the administration of the exchequer.

While the archbishop acknowledged the need at this time cautiously to give aid, for the laity alone did not have the wherewithal to defend the realm against the great dangers of invasion, yet he was vigorously protecting the clergy's freedom. The English Church was being taxed by the authority of each diocesan, without the petition, imposition, summons, or assessments of any lay power. In this respect, as in others, Winchelsey's statement concerning the tax was modelled upon 'Coram illo fatemur'.[315] It was this bull, and certainly not 'Etsi de statu', that the English clergy were using as their gloss upon 'Clericis laicos'. Thus, the archbishop stressed in his letter to the pope that they had granted the tax by their own decision and without any coercion from the laity.[316] It was precisely for this liberty that Winchelsey had suffered loss of his temporalities and outlawry. He had by perseverance and political skill achieved his primary aim. After November 1297 Winchelsey never again agreed to a direct tax for the Crown upon the spiritualities of the English clergy: the fifteenth collected in 1303 was upon temporalities only and the fifteenth of 1307–8 was granted to Edward II while Winchelsey was suspended from office.

Edward I had tried in 1294 and 1295 to control the clergy's taxing assemblies; in fact, he had taxed the clergy in parliament.

[313] *Councils*, p. 1191, and see Rothwell, 'Edward and the struggle for the charters', pp. 321–2.
[314] Harriss, 'Parliamentary taxation and appropriation of supply', p. 178.
[315] Above, p. 124.
[316] *Reg.*, p. 530: 'deliberato consilio, proprioque arbitrio, libere ac sponte, absque petitione, impositione, exactione, et coarctione cuiuscumque laicalis potestatis'.

But Winchelsey had reasserted the separate and independent character of ecclesiastical councils. The policies of the English Church during one of its worst crises had been determined by the archbishop of Canterbury in four councils, in which he consulted with representatives of all the clergy. Councils of the southern province had met with exceptional frequency, summoned by the archbishop himself and not, as in 1294, by the king.

For this reaffirmation of political and constitutional freedom in relation to taxation there was a price to be paid. While 'Clericis laicos' had been cited time and again, it would be wrong to assume that Winchelsey and his supporters had based their actions upon unthinking obedience to the pope and his decree; the archbishop's view of the rights and customs of the English clergy very largely determined his policy. The point is underlined by the clergy's petitions to the pope from the November council. They included complaints against the severity of the 1291 assessment, against the procurations of the papal nuncios (the bishops of Albano and Palestrina), and against the exactions of the papal collector, Geoffrey de Vezzano.[317] Boniface VIII's name had been on the lips of many in 1297, but both the Crown and the English clergy had remained notably aloof from the pope. Relations between Crown and papacy would, however, improve, even before the remarkable alliance of interests in 1305. The clergy had placed their reliance upon papal protection against lay exactions. But who was their protector against papal taxation? Papal taxes had developed into mandatory taxes. Here there was no process of consent. When the pope taxed, as he did, each year between 1301 and 1304, 1306 and 1307, 1309 and 1313, the king increasingly obtained the proceeds. The pope's taxation, it is true, never reached anything like the proportions of the king's direct taxation between 1294 and 1297; but the pope had consolidated his power to tax the wealth of the English Church. The king greatly needed and often received the support of the pope for taxation. But the Crown, even so, remained deeply unhappy about the separateness of the clerical estate within the realm.

This critical year clearly reveals a division between the clergy

---

[317] *Councils*, pp. 1178 n. 3, 1182–5 and Graham, 'A petition to Boniface VIII', pp. 35–46; and see above, p. 145 n. 205.

and the laity in England, as well as a division between the royal clergy and bishops and the supporters of the archbishop. Even the common political programme embodied in the Remonstrances failed to bring the earls and barons and the bishops, abbots and clergy into an open political alliance. The Church supported its own interests. The declaration of the enmity of the laity for the clergy in 'Clericis laicos' had touched a sensitive nerve in England. As for the archbishop, Rothwell's conclusion is perceptive: Winchelsey 'emerges from the contest with his stature increased, moderate himself and a true moderator, a political prelate who can marry principle with opportunity without sacrificing either: who, while keeping universals before him in the profound conflict of the *lex divina* and the *lex terrena* raised by 'Clericis laicos', is statesman enough to recognise and accept a local situation for them'.[318] Certainly Winchelsey had realised the need to negotiate and at times to compromise: he was in politics a moderator. But was he 'moderate'? All, including his supporters, must have recognised him rather as a conscientious and determined leader with an immovable political viewpoint.

[318] Rothwell, 'Confirmation of the charters', p. 189.

Chapter 5

TAXATION AND POLITICS 1298–1313

CONFLICT WITH THE CROWN 1298–1305

The period between the crisis of 1297 and the archbishop's suspension from office in 1306 was one of intense activity for Winchelsey. It was during these years that he undertook long visitations of the dioceses of Rochester, Chichester, Worcester, London, Norwich and Winchester. His meticulous examinations of these dioceses led him into conflict with Edward I notably concerning cases which posed the problem of the non-residence of royal clerks in their churches and the problem of the exemption from ordinary jurisdiction claimed by royal free chapels. Discussion of these issues, important for an understanding of the archbishop's relations with royal government, must await the last chapter.[1] The critical constitutional issues of 1297 continued to figure large in the relations of king and Church, just as they did in the relations of king and magnates, and the themes which have been analysed in previous chapters relating to taxation and *Magna Carta* must be traced through to the suspension of Winchelsey, which was, by Edward's clear admission, an act of retribution for the part the archbishop played in the rebellion of 1297. The issues of 1297 did not die.

But there were other problems that involved the archbishop and the Crown during this period, problems which were not related to these constitutional questions, nor related to the rights of royal clerks and royal chapels. The claim of archbishops of Canterbury to the custody of their fiefs during the minority of a subtenant was in question in 1299–1300; and Winchelsey involved himself in Anglo-Scottish relations by delivering Boniface VIII's remarkable bull, claiming papal overlordship of Scotland, to the king at Sweetheart Abbey in Galloway in 1300; and the bitter dispute

---

[1] See below, pp. 279–93.

177

between the archbishop and St Augustine's abbey, a royal foundation, naturally engaged the attention of the Crown. The first of
these issues was the least important. The Meinill family held their
lands in Yorkshire of the archbishop of Canterbury, with the
exception only of Castle Levington which was held of the king in
chief, and when Nicolas de Meinill died early in 1299 the
escheator was ordered to take all these lands into custody, in
accordance with the established royal right over lands of tenants-
in-chief; but Winchelsey immediately claimed the privilege enjoyed by archbishops of Canterbury to custody of all their fiefs.[2]
The archbishop had as precedents evidence of cases concerning
lands held by the earl of Gloucester and by Warin de Munchesny;
and, in addition, the first clause of that enigmatic legal declaration,
the *Prerogativa Regis*, which appears to date from the early years
of Edward I's reign, provided a clear statement that the special
right to the custody of lands of all tenants, even of tenants who
held some land of the king, was enjoyed by the archbishop of
Canterbury, as well as the bishop of Durham between Tyne and
Tees and the earls and barons of the March.[3] After a series of
inquests, and letters from Winchelsey to Anthony Bek and Walter
Langton pleading for their assistance, the decision in the archbishop's favour came at the end of March 1300.[4] Winchelsey's
claim had been strong, and there had been no great delay in
obtaining recognition of it. The episode demonstrates that over
the 'temporal' aspects of his office, as over the 'spiritual', the
archbishop exercised firm control, additional evidence for which is
provided by the fact that an unusually large part of his register
was devoted to 'temporal' concerns.[5]

In the matter of the pope's intervention against Edward on
behalf of the Scots, there is insufficient evidence to be certain of

[2] *CFR*, I. 415 and *Reg.*, pp. 338–9. See Cokayne, *Complete Peerage*, VIII. 627–8
and Du Boulay, *Lordship of Canterbury*, p. 90.
[3] *Reg.*, pp. 878–9, 881, 1255. For the nature and date of *Prerogativa Regis*
(*Stat. Realm*, I. ii. 226) see F. W. Maitland, 'The "Prerogativa Regis"', *EHR*,
VI (1891), 367–72 (reprinted in *The Collected Papers of F. W. Maitland*, ed.
H. A. L. Fisher (Cambridge, 1911), II. 182–9) and *Select Cases King's Bench*,
III, xliv, lii.
[4] *Reg.*, pp. 339–40, 694–7, 699, 880, 988, *Cal. Inq. P. M.*, III. 427–30, *CPR
1292–1301*, p. 498 and PRO E159/72 mm. 35, 43.
[5] Du Boulay, *Lordship of Canterbury*, p. 249.

Winchelsey's attitude. That Boniface VIII favoured the Scots was demonstrated forcefully in his bull 'Scimus fili', which, although dated 27 June 1299, was probably not dispatched until the spring of 1300 when Edward's campaign against the Scots was about to be renewed.[6] Boniface ordered Winchelsey to deliver the bull to the king under pain of suspension from office.[7] It was not an order which he could lightly ignore; and we should beware of accepting the archbishop's own statement to the pope that he had urged the king to obey the bull as evidence that Winchelsey fully sympathised with the severe admonitions and overriding claims of the apostolic see. It may well be that a better indication of the archbishop's viewpoint can be found in the advice to the king, critical of Boniface's pretensions, of the archbishop's clerk Master William of Sardinia, official of the court of Canterbury and ex-dean of the Arches, who had been appointed by Winchelsey as his vicar-general during his mission to Scotland.[8] William's discussion of the 'dangers' of 'Scimus fili', although directed towards the particular issues raised by this bull, can, in its distrust of the notion that the pope was the king's judge in temporal matters, be related to a deeper and wider opposition to extreme papal claims, as found notably, and only shortly afterwards, in the tract of French provenance *Rex Pacificus*.[9] Even so, because of the hazardous journey undertaken by Winchelsey, which he described in detail to the pope, the archbishop may have been identified, if only for a short time, with the papal case against the king; and it is difficult to deny the possibility that 'the whole incident widened a little further the breach between the king and the primate'.[10] At the Lincoln parliament of 1301 over a hundred magnates sealed a protest to Boniface VIII against his attack upon the king's policy in Scotland;[11] the prelates chose not to have their names linked

---

[6] *Anglo-Scottish Relations*, ed. Stones, nos. 28–9, and see Boase, *Boniface VIII*, pp. 208–11 and G. W. S. Barrow, *Robert Bruce* (London, 1965), pp. 85–6, 163.

[7] *Reg.*, pp. 569–77, 713–16, *Annales London.*, pp. 104–12, *Documents Illustrative of the History of Scotland*, ed. J. Stevenson (Edinburgh, 1870), ii. 376–7, Prynne, iii. 879–83 and *Reg. Boniface VIII*, nos. 3342–3.

[8] Emden, *Oxford* ('Sarden'), *Reg.*, p. 392 and Churchill, *Canterbury Admin.*, ii. 2.

[9] See W. Ullmann, 'A medieval document on papal theories of government', *EHR*, LXI (1946), 180–201.

[10] Boase, *Boniface VIII*, p. 211.   [11] *Foedera*, i. ii. 926–7.

with the protest. To any who were inclined to see the issue of allegiance to pope or king in stark terms, and no doubt there were some, it might well have seemed that the archbishop's obedience to the bishop of Rome determined and governed all his actions.

Winchelsey's relations with the king were without question strained as a result of his dispute with St Augustine's Canterbury. This dispute was a revival of an age-old conflict.[12] We should take care not to dismiss it as a petty local squabble. The issue turned on the archbishop's jurisdiction over the abbey's churches; and if the abbey had been successful in the struggle the diocese of Canterbury would have been 'cut in two'.[13] There were two notable cases in England of monasteries which had secured an exemption by papal privilege which extended to their parish churches: Evesham acted as virtually its own bishop in the deanery of the Vale of Evesham, which comprised ten or so churches, and St Albans enjoyed the full exercise of spiritual jurisdiction in fifteen of its churches.[14] The abbot of St Augustine's planned to establish an unusually large area of peculiar jurisdiction: three rural deaneries containing a total of about forty churches. Indeed, in 1300 Abbot Findon actually announced the creation of the rural deaneries of Sturry, Minster and Lenham.[15] He did so as a result of a papal privilege in

[12] E. John, 'The litigation of an exempt house, St Augustine's, Canterbury, 1182–1237', *Bulletin of the John Rylands Lib.*, xxxix (1956–7), 390–415. It flared up again c. 1329–33: see W. A. Pantin, 'The letters of John Mason: a fourteenth-century formulary from St Augustine's, Canterbury' in *Essays in Medieval History Presented to Bertie Wilkinson*, eds. T. A. Sandquist and M. R. Powicke (Toronto, 1969), pp. 192–219.

[13] B. L. Woodcock, *Medieval Ecclesiastical Courts in the Diocese of Canterbury* (Oxford, 1952), pp. 23–4 and Denton, *Royal Chapels*, pp. 16–18. For a detailed survey of the dispute see Graham, 'Winchelsey and St Augustine's', pp. 37–50. Should the story be retold there is much additional manuscript evidence: see, for example, Cant. D. & C., Cartae Antiquae A29, A56, A208, A210–A213, A215, A216, M375, N25 and Reg. I, fos. 215r–217r, 228v–229v, 251, 253v–254r. Thorne's account of the events of Edward I's reign, though compiled late in the fourteenth century, was probably based not only on extant documentary evidence but also on earlier chronicles, as Cambridge Corpus Christi College MS 301, pp. 45–140, and see PRO E164/27, esp. fos. 172r–179v (see Thorne, pp. xx–xxxiii). A version of the events of 1300–3 from the point of view of Christ Church Canterbury is provided by BL Harl. 636, fos. 225r–230r.

[14] See, for Evesham, Haines, *Administration of Diocese of Worcester*, p. 17 n. 2; and, for St Albans, *Taxatio Nicholai IV*, p. 219b and Sayers, 'Monastic archdeacons', pp. 181–2, 201–2. For the unusual rights of the monastic archdeacon of Glastonbury over seven parishes see ibid., pp. 182–5, 291–2.

[15] Graham, 'Winchelsey and St Augustine's', p. 41.

the abbey's favour dated 27 February 1300.[16] This grant was un-
acceptable to Winchelsey and resulted in an increased effort on his
part to ensure control over the churches appropriated to the house.

Already in early 1299 the king's support for the royal abbey
had been clear. Following the abbot's appeal to Rome, Boniface
had apparently written to the king seeking his assistance in protecting St Augustine's which as an exempt abbey was subject in
spiritual matters immediately to Rome. In a letter of 11 April
1299 the king admonished the archbishop to await the outcome
of the appeal and not to continue molesting the abbey in any way
concerning its churches. Edward declared that he was willing to
defend the abbey 'so far as justice permits'.[17] Later, rectors and
vicars of churches belonging to St Augustine's, imprisoned following excommunication by the archbishop, were released by the
king's mandate and ordered to present their case to the king at the
Lincoln parliament of 1301, at which the king determined upon
a policy of support for the abbey.[18] The king granted protection to
the abbot and his men and ordered the release from prison of
others, now regarded as of the abbot's jurisdiction, who had been
signified as excommunicates by the archbishop.[19] Edward's action
was, as he recognised, entirely in accordance with the terms of the
new exemption, which determined that the abbot was – though
temporarily, as it transpired – ecclesiastical ordinary over the
abbey's churches and their parishioners.

His vigorous protests having failed, the archbishop sought in
vain the imprisonment following excommunication of rectors,
vicars and parishioners of St Augustine's churches.[20] In a letter
from the abbot to the king's chancellor, John Langton, the claims
of the abbey were stated precisely: the abbot attacked not only
Winchelsey's right to excommunicate any subjects of the abbey but
also his right to summon any of them to appear before his court of

---

[16] *Reg. Boniface VIII*, no. 3466 (*CPL*, I. 585–6) and *Scriptores Decem*, pp. 1971–4
(Thorne, pp. 335–9).
[17] Prynne, III. 823–4 (*CCR 1296–1302*, pp. 308–9) and Thorne, pp. 346–7.
[18] *CCR 1296–1302*, pp. 427, 472 and Prynne, III. 905–6.
[19] *Cal. Chanc. Warr.*, p. 149. And see Prynne, III. 927–9, 932.
[20] See *Reg.*, pp. 393–4, 455–7, 567–9, 578–85, 592–5, 604, 608–16, 637–41,
CCR 1296–1302, pp. 427–8, 472–3, 512, 522, 569, *CCR 1302–7*, p. 11, and
for the extant significations of excommunication of the archbishop relating to
the dispute see PRO C85/5/34, C85/6/6, /51, /19, /21, /26, /53, /54.

audience.[21] During 1302 and 1303 there was violence and bloodshed at Faversham, Kennington, Selling and at three churches in Canterbury.[22] The Crown was closely involved in the struggle. In September 1302 the king summoned the sheriff of Kent and the bailiffs of Canterbury to defend their policies towards St Augustine's before the archbishop and his proctors and in the presence of the king and his council.[23] There is no doubt that it was the abbot rather than the archbishop who had the king's ear. Winchelsey heard that the king's nuncios at Rome were pleading the case of the abbot and he challenged the king to this effect, but Edward denied ordering his nuncios to do anything other than seek a speedy and fitting outcome to the dispute. The archbishop conveyed this reply to the pope lest the king's agents were exceeding their brief.[24] In March 1303 Boniface in effect rescinded the privilege of 1300 and decided in favour of the archbishop.[25] When the king learnt of the new papal declaration he could no longer deny the archbishop's authority over the abbey's churches, but he insisted that there should be no caption of excommunicates 'on account of anything done before the publication of the declaration'.[26] The dispute continued to simmer. Winchelsey sued writs *de laica vi amovenda* from chancery, and commissions of oyer and terminer were ordered (1303, 1304, 1305) against those who had attacked the archbishop's house at Canterbury and assaulted the dean of Ospringe.[27] The archbishop attempted to bring to justice the sheriff of Kent, Henry of Cobham, and his bailiffs for acting against the men he had appointed to St Augustine's churches and for reinstating excommunicates into their benefices, but the Crown issued a writ of prohibition on the grounds that the king's

[21] PRO SC1/26/141, dated 18 March 1301.
[22] Graham, 'Winchelsey and St Augustine's', pp. 44–7.
[23] PRO SC1/13/183: sheriff and bailiffs were summoned to be at St Radegund's Abbey, near Dover, on 23 Sept. 1302 to answer to the charges of the archbishop or his proctors. On 26 Sept. the king again requested Winchelsey's presence, this time for 28 Sept., to hear some news to be brought by royal messengers from abroad (SC1/14/94): the news may have concerned St Augustine's.
[24] *Reg.*, pp. 647–8.
[25] Graham, 'Winchelsey and St Augustine's', pp. 47–50.
[26] *Cal. Chanc. Warr.*, p. 180.
[27] PRO KB27/171 mm. 72, 76, /172 mm. 24, 37 and in later rolls, and *CPR 1301–7*, pp. 197–8, 274–5, 403–4.

ministers had been executing royal orders.[28] Winchelsey was
charged in the king's bench, with adjournments from term to term
until the end of the reign, for suing pleas in court christian and
fulminating sentences of excommunication against the bailiffs
(William de Cotes and John de Helles) to the king's prejudice and
against the king's prohibition. The king could claim that he had
acted throughout within the bounds of established legal practice.
But can we doubt where his sympathies lay? He had clearly wished
to give all possible assistance to the abbey of which he was patron.[29]

To return to the weightier issues raised by the 1297 crisis, we
must consider the main features of the English Church's constitutional relationship with the Crown as revealed in its primary
political campaign of fighting for ecclesiastical liberty. What
happened to the grant embodied in *Confirmatio Cartarum* that
the Church should defend *Magna Carta* and the Charter of the
Forest by sentences of excommunication against offenders? And
what happened to the protection from arbitrary taxation which
was the central concession of *Confirmatio*? But first, without
direct reference to the influence of the Church and the archbishop,
we must trace the main stages of what has been aptly described as
'the struggle for the charters'. The granting of *Confirmatio* was
a substantial defeat for the king. Yet, even in the autumn of 1297,
it had not gone quite far enough for the opponents of the Crown,
whose aims, as we have seen,[30] are found in *De Tallagio*. The
conceded *Confirmatio* was supplementary to, and separate from,
Magna Carta; the desired *De Tallagio* was intended to be added
to, and form part of, *Magna Carta*. The distrust between king
and barons which had increased in the course of 1297 was temporarily eased, but certainly not dissipated, by the concessions of
November.[31] This is clear from the evidence concerning the meeting of earls and magnates at York in mid-January 1298.[32] At this

---

[28] *Reg.*, pp. 455–7, Prynne, III. 985 (*CCR 1302–7*, p. 90) and PRO KB27 esp.
/177 m. 61d, /179 m. 81d.
[29] See Prynne, III. 905 (*Cal. Chanc. Warr.*, p. 124).
[30] Above, pp. 165–7.
[31] See Galbraith, *Studies in the Public Records*, pp. 147–8.
[32] Guisborough, p. 314 (and the related Trivet, pp. 368, 370 and 'Rishanger',
pp. 182–3, 184) and Langtoft, II. 306–9. Rothwell's doubts (Guisborough,
p. xxx) concerning the accuracy of the passage in Guisborough, have been
allayed a little by Powicke (*Thirteenth Century*, p. 688 n. 4). The additional

congregation, along with the earl of Gloucester, the king's son-in-law, and many magnates, there were the protagonists of 1297, Bohun and Bigod, and the earl of Arundel, who had attended the meeting of discontented barons in the spring of 1297,[33] and also at least one of the knights who had supported Bohun and Bigod, John de Segrave. On 21 January the bishop of Carlisle excommunicated violators of *Magna Carta* in York Minster, and it is perfectly clear that Guisborough believed that *Magna Carta* along with the 'inserted articles' of *De Tallagio* was read out.[34] For this there is no corroboration, but it is likely that *De Tallagio* was at this stage still in the forefront of the reform programme of the opposing magnates. There was great concern that the concessions of 1297 – and, indeed, *Magna Carta* and the Charter of the Forest themselves – would be unpublished and would not be maintained. And there was room for concern.

Edward returned from Flanders in March 1298 and quickly travelled to Scotland. Bohun and Bigod made known their suspicions that the king had changed his mind about the confirmation of the charters and that he was excusing himself on the grounds that the confirmation had been made in a foreign land. Before the two earls proceeded further on the Scottish campaign they required guarantees concerning 'certain articles' and concerning disafforestment. The bishop of Durham and the earls of Surrey, Gloucester and Lincoln took an oath for the king that when he returned victorious from Scotland he would fulfil his promises.[35] Later in the year the earls were involved in a further

evidence from Langtoft is significant, for he provides an account of Edward I's reign which is of unusual interest and is often independent of known chronicles, and, since he was writing at the priory of Bridlington, he was likely to be in touch with events at York (see T. Wright in Langtoft, 1. xix and M. D. Legge, *Anglo-Norman in the Cloisters* (Edinburgh, 1950), pp. 70–4 and *Anglo-Norman Literature and its Background* (Oxford, 1963), pp. 278–9); yet, at some points there is a close similarity between Guisborough and Langtoft and they may have used a common source (Gransden, *Historical Writing*, pp. 475–6, 483). It need be no surprise that the gathering is noticed neither in the Bury chronicle, which is never comprehensive, nor by Cotton, who in drawing to a close refers to only a few of the events of 1298.

33 Evesham, p. 576.
34 *De Tallagio* was specifically 'articuli inserti' (Guisborough, pp. 311, 314), whereas *Confirmatio* was described officially as 'articuli additi' (Rothwell, 'Confirmation of the charters', pp. 190–1).
35 Guisborough, p. 324.

squabble with the king and left Scotland,[36] but the opposition was no doubt weakened by the death of Bohun on 31 December 1298.[37] Edward apparently intended, as far as possible, to sidestep the concessions of 1297. On the other side, it becomes clear that his opponents had wide support and that they aimed to obtain concessions which went beyond, and were more specific than, the clauses of *Confirmatio Cartarum*. A parliament met in March and the chroniclers tell us that the king was retreating from his promises.[38] There was talk of rebellion. The opposition magnates were moved especially by the king's failure to implement the grant of a perambulation of the forests. Far from being concerned with additions to the charters, Edward, in the statute *De Finibus Levatis* of 2 April 1299,[39] omitted five clauses in his recital of the Charter of the Forest. At the following May parliament, which Bigod seems to have attended with an armed force, the king again made promises; but he was playing for time, for in June he sent a proclamation to all the counties, to be read publicly in cities, boroughs and market towns throughout the realm, protesting that he *did* intend to keep the charters, giving as his excuse for further delay the continuing negotiations concerning Gascony.[40]

But in 1300 Edward was unable to hold out against the demands for concessions, especially since he was greatly in need of a subsidy and was planning a major campaign in Scotland to begin in the summer. The parliament of March 1300 was of wider composition than any parliament since 1296.[41] The charters were

[36] Ibid., p. 329. And see the note in an allied chronicle BL Harl. 3860, fo. 21v, in J. Stevenson, *Documents Illustrative of Sir William Wallace, his Life and Times* (Edinburgh, 1841), p. 38. The rights and duties of the earl marshal and the constable were still in question: see Prestwich, *War, Politics and Finance*, p. 263 and PRO E159/72 mm. 7d, 14d, 21d, E159/73 m. 16d.

[37] Cokayne, *Complete Peerage*, VI. 466. Both Guisborough, p. 329, and Langtoft, II. 317–19, must be in error in noting Bohun's presence in London in 1299; Langtoft, at least, *was* referring to Bohun the father not Bohun the son and heir.

[38] Bury, p. 151, Guisborough, p. 330 and *Flores Hist.*, III. 297 (as Prynne, III. 780). The account in *Flores Hist.*, *sub anno* 1298, certainly relates to the March parliament of 1299.

[39] Rothwell, 'Edward and the struggle for the charters', pp. 323–4; for the text see *Stat. Realm*, I. ii. 126–30 and *Eng. Hist. Documents*, III. 491–4, and see *Chartes des Libertés*, ed. Bémont, pp. xlv–xlvi.

[40] Bury, p. 152, Rishanger, pp. 391–2, Guisborough, p. 330 and Prynne, III. 810–11 (and *CPR 1292–1301*, p. 424).

[41] For this parliament see Rothwell, 'Edward and the struggle for the charters',

confirmed afresh, now in charter-form with the attestation of an impressive list of witnesses.[42] And the king granted an ordinance 'to the people of his realm for the alleviation of their grievances sustained by reason of the late wars'.[43] This was the statute known as *Articuli super Cartas*.[44] Rothwell, we now know, exaggerated the extent to which the *Articuli* represented a successful defence of the royal prerogative by the Crown.[45] In fact, in 1300–1 Edward was once again under strong pressure from the magnates. Consent to a new lay tax, the first since 1297, and to new national prises, was not easily obtained. The twentieth discussed in the parliament was dependent, it seems quite clear, upon assurances concerning the maintenance of the charters and the actual implementation of new concessions, including a perambulation of the forests,[46] and, in the event, a tax was not agreed until the following year. *Articuli super Cartas* made two notable grants: specific provisions for the hearing of complaints against infringements of the charters, and a systematic process for the regulation of prises, which was intended to ensure not only payment for prises but also the need for the consent of those providing goods. Both issues, of course, concerned laymen and clerks.

The March parliament of 1300 was followed by another important parliament, at Lincoln in January 1301.[47] The king had

pp. 325–9 and especially now the decisive corrective to Rothwell in Harriss, *King, Parliament and Public Finance*, pp. 99–106. Also see *Lancs. Lay Subsidies*, ed. Vincent, pp. 225–33, Prynne, III. 845–54, Rishanger, pp. 404–6 and Guisborough, p. 332.

[42] *Stat. Realm*, I. i. 38–44 (*Eng. Hist. Documents*, III. 495–6), BL Harl. 3911, fos. 171r–174r, and see *Parl. Writs*, I. ii. 86–7, 398–400 and *Foedera*, I. ii. 919.

[43] *CCR 1296–1302*, p. 410.

[44] *Stat. Realm*, I. ii. 136–41 (*Chartes des Libertés*, ed. Bémont, pp. 99–108 and *Eng. Hist. Documents*, III. 496–501), and see *Foedera*, I. ii. 920. For another copy see BL Harl. 3911, fos. 174r–180v. The different version of the *Articuli* among the Acland-Hood MSS may have been a draft; an edition of it is needed (see *Historical MSS Commission: Sixth Report* (1877), p. 344; the roll is now Somerset Record Office, MS DD/AH, and I am grateful to Dr J. R. Maddicott for the loan of his photocopy).

[45] See Harriss, *King, Parliament and Public Finance*, esp. pp. 99–106 and Prestwich, *War, Politics and Finance*, esp. pp. 265–6; and see Maddicott, *Lancaster*, pp. 97–8, 103, 106–7.

[46] Langtoft, II. 323, Rishanger, pp. 404–5 and Worcester, p. 544.

[47] For which see *Lancs. Lay Subsidies*, ed. Vincent, pp. 233–4, Prynne, III. 855–6, Rothwell, 'Edward and the struggle for the charters', pp. 329–30, Prestwich, *War, Politics and Finance*, pp. 266–8 and Harriss, *King, Parliament and Public Finance*, pp. 105–6. The fact that there are three important

bound himself more closely than ever to the charters,[48] and he was still under great pressure. In somewhat bitter terms he asked the prelates and magnates attending the parliament whether they, in truth, wished to agree to disafforestation following the new peram-bulation of the forests, for he clearly believed that he would thereby be infringing his coronation oath and disinheriting the Crown. The king wanted them to find a more moderate course, so that the dignity of the Crown would be protected.[49] Apparently a committee of twenty-six was appointed to discuss the matter,[50] and the famous 'bill' of twelve articles was the outcome.[51] The com-mittee carefully avoided making a direct answer to Edward's challenge, for they could have been accused of passing judgment upon the Crown. Nevertheless, their response was decisive. They made severe demands on behalf of the whole community of the realm, and the king submitted, by and large, to these demands: above all, he granted (c. 4 of the 'bill') the disafforestment of all districts which lay outside the boundaries found in the recent perambulations;[52] he reaffirmed (c. 5) the concessions of *Articuli super Cartas* in relation to prises and the transgressions of royal officials against the terms of the charters; and he accepted (c. 9) that a fifteenth on lay movables to be collected in the autumn would be conditional upon the grievances having been remedied.[53] Also (c. 2), Edward conceded, as part of his reaffirmation of the

accounts of this parliament has been largely overlooked: Langtoft, ii. 329–35, *Flores Hist.*, iii. 108–9, 303–4 and Rishanger, pp. 453–65.

[48] In October he had ordered the barons of the exchequer to observe *Magna Carta* in every article and had sent *Articuli super Cartas* to the justices of the bench (*CCR 1296–1302*, p. 410 and PRO E159/74 m. 6d).

[49] *Parl. Writs*, i. ii. 104 from Cant. D. & C., Reg. I, fo. 214v (*Eng. Hist. Documents*, iii. 510).

[50] Langtoft, ii. 331: the speech put into the king's mouth here is in part very similar to the recorded statement of the king (previous note).

[51] *Parl. Writs*, i. ii. 104–5 from Cant. D. & C., Reg. I, fos. 214v–215r (*Eng. Hist. Documents*, iii. 510–12). There appear to be only a few small errors of tran-scription in *Parl. Writs*, i. ii. 104–5; the MS shows that the king's replies (printed in italics in *Parl. Writs*) were added later, though perhaps in the same hand.

[52] *Select Pleas of the Forest*, ed. G. J. Turner (Selden Soc., xiii, 1901), p. cv, and as noted in the annals of Hailes: Blount, 'Annals of Hailes', p. 115 from BL Cotton Cleo. D iii, fo. 53v. For the king's orders of 14 February con-cerning disafforestment see BL Lansdowne 402, fos. 121r–122r (for Notting-hamshire) and BL Egerton 3663, fos. 33r–34v (for Huntingdonshire).

[53] For the fifteenth see *Parl. Writs*, i. ii. 105–8, 401, 403, Willard, *Parliamentary Taxes*, pp. 22–5 and BL Lans. 402, fos. 121r–122v.

charters, that any statutes which were contrary to the charters would be amended or annulled.[54] In assessing the developments of 1300 and 1301 Rothwell was too concerned that the actual terms of *Confirmatio Cartarum* were not reiterated. After the uncertainties of 1298 and 1299, and when the king's need for money compelled him to negotiate, concessions were obtained by the magnates and prelates which built upon, and went beyond, the achievements of 1297. By dint of necessity, and however reluctantly, Edward had become conciliatory.

How far had Winchelsey, and the English prelates and clergy, been involved in this 'struggle for the charters'? The answer must be: closely and directly. But there is much more to be said than that, for the clergy were more closely involved in some respects than in others. Like the opposition magnates Winchelsey had every intention of building upon the successes of 1297. The clerical tenth granted in November 1297 for the war in Scotland was controlled, as we have seen, both in its collection and in its distribution by the archbishop himself.[55] The king cannot have been at all happy with this procedure. Edward and Winchelsey met at St Albans towards the end of April 1298,[56] and the archbishop agreed to summon another council to consider the matters which would be put to the clergy by the king's representatives. The council was summoned for 25 June, and we learn from the recorded decisions of the council that the king sent to the assembly the knights John de Insula and William of Sutton, who conveyed four requests.[57] Two of the requests, for prayers and for the excommunication of the marauding Scots, were easily granted. But the answers to the other requests show how resolute the clergy

---

[54] *Stat. Realm*, I. i. 44, *Foedera*, I. ii. 927, *Chartes des Libertés*, ed. Bémont, p. 109 (*Eng. Hist. Documents*, III. 512), and BL Eger. 3663, fo. 32v.

[55] Above, pp. 173–4.

[56] *Councils*, pp. 1187, 1197. Edward was at St Albans between 23 and 29 April: Gough, *Itinerary*, II. 164. We know that Winchelsey was there on 26 April (PRO C53/84 m. 2, no. 9), and it was on this date at St Albans that the king made orders to the exchequer concerning the hearing of the final account for income received from the archbishop's lands while they were in the king's hands in 1297: see above, p. 132 n. 138.

[57] For the council see *Councils*, pp. 1187–99 and Rothwell, 'Edward and the struggle for the charters', pp. 321–2. Can there be some truth in the Bury chronicler's statement (Bury, pp. 149–50, as *Councils*, pp. 1198–9) that it was the king's son who presented the requests to the clergy?

had become in their defence of ecclesiastical income. In an attempt
to placate the clergy Edward explained through his representatives
that he was not asking for a further subsidy, nor would he do
so unless he faced great need. The king knew that there was no
chance of another subsidy. He declared – and this was an indication of the impact and effectiveness of *Confirmatio Cartarum* –
that in fighting the Scots he would as far as possible live of his
own. But he asked that some promise be given of a future subsidy
from the clergy in the event of the war continuing and the king
being unable without aid to defend the realm and the Church.
Just such a promise had been made by the clergy in 1295. But in
1298 they refused, for, as they pointed out, 'Clericis laicos' forbade, on pain of excommunication, the giving of promises of aid
without papal licence. The tenth which had been eventually
granted late in 1297 had been conditional upon the continuing
needs of the Crown, and now the king asked, also, that what
remained of the tenth should be paid. Again, the clergy refused.
They declared that the residue of the tax would be retained and
given to the king only if it proved to be necessary for the defence
of the Church and the kingdom against the Scots. Following the
principle of 'cessante causa',[58] the clergy declined to pay the whole
of the tax. Some of the residue was, in fact, used to expedite the
business of the Canterbury clergy at Rome.[59] And it is apparent,
as the Bury chronicler explicitly stated,[60] that while the clergy
believed in contributing towards the *defence* of the realm they
were reluctant to support wars beyond the borders of the realm.
Thus, there began in 1298 a determined protection, by the secular
and regular clergy led by Winchelsey, of their hard-won freedom
from royal interference concerning taxation.

Other decisions of constitutional importance were taken at the
June council. The clergy discussed what was for them a vital aspect
of *Confirmatio Cartarum*: the excommunication of offenders
against the charters.[61] Winchelsey was determined that excommunication in defence of the charters, the 'Great Sentence',

[58] For which see Brown, '*Cessante causa* and the taxes of the last Capetians'.
[59] *Reg.*, pp. 300–3.   [60] Bury, p. 147.
[61] *Councils*, pp. 1192–6 (and see *Reg. Orleton*, pp. 288–92, and N. R. Ker,
Medieval MSS in British Libraries, 1 (Oxford, 1969), 36–7 citing Corporation
of London Records Office, Liber Ordinationum, fos. 30v–32).

should be more than a threat. Part of the problem, as the terms of *Confirmatio* indicate, was that there was no certainty that bishops would carry out the publication of sentences of excommunication. *Confirmatio* provided that negligent bishops should be reprimanded by their archbishop and that the sentences of greater excommunication should be pronounced twice a year by each bishop against all who contravened in any way, or assisted in the contravention of, the clauses of the charters. Although it was now being overlooked that Winchelsey, in his sentence of excommunication of October 1297, had included infringers of the new agreement, that is of *Confirmatio* as well as the charters,[62] yet it is clear that the clergy in June 1298 were reinforcing, and certainly not retreating from, the concessions of 1297. Decisions were now taken, in Winchelsey's words, 'so that what had been so satisfactorily ordained for so great a common good should not fail, through neglect, to be made effective'. It was determined that the two occasions for the denunciations by the bishops should be the week before Easter and 1 November. Concerning prises Winchelsey was interpreting *Confirmatio* in the terms of *De Tallagio*, for he stressed that goods should not be taken from the clergy without the permission of the owners of the goods or of the owners' bailiffs; and, because it would be difficult and often detrimental for the clergy who suffered from attacks always to be compelled to proceed by having recourse to their bishops, it was decided to grant to the lesser clergy, to rectors, vicars and chaplains, the right themselves to name and denounce malefactors publicly.

Thus, a procedure was laid down for the immediate excommunication of anyone seizing the goods of the clergy without their consent. And if any cleric should be jailed for making these denunciations, as it was feared might happen, the diocesan bishop was enjoined to put an interdict upon the place where he was detained and upon the four churches nearest to that place; and those who had captured him, or had given authority for his capture, were to be declared as excommunicates on Sundays and feast days in all the churches of the diocese, following the same procedure as for the earlier denunciations, that is, in English and with full solemnity, the ringing of bells and the lighting of candles.

[62] Above, p. 167.

In addition, the sentences against all who invaded ecclesiastical property, which had been enjoined upon the bishops in January 1297,[63] but which, as the archbishop regretfully pointed out, some bishops had omitted to execute, partly or wholly, were now renewed, with the order that they should be published in churches throughout the dioceses of the province. Winchelsey was attempting to consolidate the achievements of the previous year, and it is no surprise that the bishops of Lincoln and Salisbury, Oliver Sutton and Simon of Ghent, were among those who responded to the archbishop's mandate.[64] By an effective process of excommunication the wealth of the Church should thus be protected from all incursions upon it made without the clergy's consent. The archbishop's mandate raised, perforce, the issue of the king's protection from excommunication of his ministers, as well as the clergy's reliance upon the secular arm for the capture of obdurate excommunicates. But the power of excommunication was weakened rather than nullified by the king's customary protection of royal officials; and excommunication did not depend solely upon bodily coercion for its effectiveness.

There were, no doubt, large obstacles in the way of the enforcement of the 'Great Sentence' protecting the charters.[65] But it is too extreme a judgment to suggest that we look in vain for any effective action upon the 'Great Sentence' as a result of *Confirmatio Cartarum*, and too extreme, also, to reduce the promulgation of the general sentences to a 'pious gesture' of negligible importance in temporal politics.[66] The fact that the *Articuli super Cartas* in their official form overlooked ecclesiastical sanctions and provided for the election of three men of standing in each county to supervise the observance of the charters was, indeed, an indication that sentences of excommunication were not an adequate defence of the charters. But there is nothing to suggest that the procedure established for ecclesiastical denunciations was in any way set aside.[67] Indeed, the sentences were renewed by the king's order

[63] Above, p. 104.
[64] *Reg. Sutton*, vi. 187–8 and *Reg. Gandavo*, pp. 70–2.
[65] See Gray, 'The Church and Magna Charta', pp. 23–38.
[66] Ibid., pp. 34–5.
[67] Rothwell, 'Edward and the struggle for the charters', p. 328 and Harriss, *King, Parliament and Public Finance*, p. 101.

at the Lincoln parliament,[68] and at least some bishops continued to promulgate them and to seek out malefactors.[69] The protection of royal officials from excommunication and the protection of the temporal rights of the Crown was one side of the story. But the reiteration of the 'Great Sentence' was a means of defending the practical concessions of 1297 by moral pressure applied far and wide. In effect, it brought the *ipso facto* excommunication embodied in 'Clericis laicos' into the context of English political life. And, extremely important for the archbishop as head of a Church whose prelates were not always united in their attitude towards the Crown, it served to emphasise to the whole clerical body, including the bishops, the need for continuity of action in the defence of ecclesiastical property and wealth.

In thus continuing the struggle of 1297 Winchelsey held to his belief that he was defending the common interests of the realm. Wherever possible he was intent upon assisting the king. In 1299 the main initiative in the parliaments of March and May for gaining fresh concessions, especially concerning the perambulation of the forests, came from the opposing magnates: Winchelsey acted as mediator and at Edward's request stood surety for the king's promises to the earls and barons.[70] The king had, it seems, decided, for the time being, to accept with patience the opposition of the clergy as revealed in 1298; and the archbishop briefly undertook once again the responsibility of intercession between king and barons. Edward was making efforts to restore political stability. In 1298 he had instituted the country-wide commission of inquiry, as promised before the Flanders campaign, into the grievances of both the laity and the clergy against the acts of royal agents since the beginning of the war with France in 1294; the inquiry was concerned especially with the maladministration of prises.[71] Early in 1299 Winchelsey was apparently drawn into assisting the king, for a short time and unusually, in his diplomatic relations with France by taking part in negotiations at Canterbury.[72] And on

---

[68] *Flores Hist.*, III. 109 and Rishanger, p. 461.
[69] *Reg.*, p. 409 and *Reg. Gandavo*, pp. 70–2.
[70] Rishanger, p. 392 and Bury, p. 152.
[71] Prynne, III. 734–5 (and *CPR 1292–1301*, pp. 338–9) and esp. *Lincs. Assize Roll 1298*, ed. Thomson.
[72] *Cal. Chanc. Warr.*, p. 100 and *Reg.*, pp. 306–7.

10 September 1299 the archbishop officiated at the king's marriage to Margaret, sister of Philip IV of France, in Canterbury cathedral.[73]

In a few small ways during 1299 there was a lessening of tension between king and archbishop, but it was a very insecure and short-lived interlude. A new chapter of conflict begins with another ecclesiastical council which met late in 1299. There had been secret discussions in the June 1298 council and certain royal clerks who had had the effrontery to try to attend the meeting had been expelled by Winchelsey.[74] Secret discussions continued in the council of 4 November 1299.[75] As in March 1297 the king sent his agents to appeal against any decisions at this council which might impugn his Crown and dignity. There can be no doubt that the king's need for money for the Scottish war was still well known; and an aid was to be requested of the clergy in 1300.[76] Although there is no evidence of this request being made in 1299, it was perhaps to try to influence the clergy at least to make financial promises (as well as to offer up prayers for the king)[77] that Edward also sent to the assembly his treasurer, Bishop Langton. All the indications are that this most influential royal minister, although summoned, of course, as a bishop to Winchelsey's councils, chose not to attend them in person; and on this occasion Langton may well have been present only to convey the king's wishes. But can discussions in the council, in fact, have been successfully hidden from royal clerks like Langton? We can only speculate. It is clear, at all events, that Winchelsey was attempting to organise closed clerical meetings insulated from royal influence. It may be that the secret discussions of 1299 concerned the granting of a subsidy to the archbishop for his own requirements, for in the first order for the collection of this subsidy Winchelsey emphasised the need to proceed without attracting the king's attention.[78] This grant of a tax of a fortieth for Winchelsey

---

[73] Worcester, p. 542, Blount, 'Annals of Hailes', p. 111 (BL Cotton Cleo. D iii, fo. 53r), Cont. Gervase, p. 317 (9 Sept.) and Rishanger, p. 395 (11 Sept.); the assignment of dower is dated 10 Sept. (*Foedera*, I. ii. 912–13), and concerning the dowry see PRO E159/74 mm. 12, 14d, 22–23.
[74] *Councils*, p. 1199 (as Bury, p. 150).   [75] *Councils*, pp. 1199–1204.
[76] Worcester, p. 544.   [77] *Reg.*, p. 695.
[78] *Reg.*, pp. xiii–xiv, 719–20, and see Du Boulay, 'Charitable subsidies', pp. 149–53.

is an indication of the clergy's support for the archbishop in his fight for clerical rights.

But the archbishop may well also have wished to prepare in secret in 1299 the revised set of grievances which were presented to the king in the two important parliaments of March 1300 and January 1301.[79] Here was the archbishop's attempt, continuing the work of his predecessors, to bring greater reality to the declaration of ecclesiastical liberty embodied in *Magna Carta*. In these specifically ecclesiastical complaints we have the clearest evidence that in matters directly relating to the protection of ecclesiastical jurisdiction the clergy's opposition to the Crown was quite separate from the baronial opposition. Winchelsey, according to Rishanger,[80] was the first to petition in the March parliament of 1300 for a new confirmation of *Magna Carta*, but his interests were not linked as closely with the interests of the magnates as they had been in 1297. Disafforestation, no doubt, concerned the prelates, but it did not concern the whole clerical body. And the archbishop's interests were concentrated rather less now upon taxation and prises, for the protection of the English Church from arbitrary and direct royal taxation had been largely secured. Although the *Articuli super Cartas* granted in 1300 concerned the clergy as well as the laity, the archbishop's ecclesiastical programme of reform was to be found not in the *Articuli* but rather in the grievances of the prelates and clergy which had been drawn up in all probability in 1299.

These petitions for remedies presented to the king in parliament were for the most part long-standing complaints. Although related in a more or less direct way to particular cases and to the particular practices and procedures of royal ministers, royal justices and royal courts, these complaints were couched in general terms, as had been the tradition for sixty years or more. For the most part the specific cases giving rise to anxiety among the clergy lie hidden behind the generalised grievances; and the complaints were directed very often at accepted and continuing practices which churchmen saw as infringing or weakening their rights. The

---

[79] *Councils*, pp. 1205–18. Cant. D. & C., Cartae Antiquae K11a is another copy of the *gravamina*, without the royal replies and later additions.
[80] Rishanger, p. 404.

issues cannot usually be studied in relation to particular conflicts, of say 1298 and 1299, but only in the context of long-term developments. This is true of the complaints against royal interference in the operation of ecclesiastical courts and ecclesiastical jurisdiction (cc. 5–9, 17, 19–21, 24–5, 33); against the procedures concerning criminous clerks and imprisoned clerks (cc. 10–13, 16); against the treatment of fugitives in churches (cc. 14–15); against the fining of bishops who failed to ensure the appearance of clerks summoned before royal justices (c. 22); against the disregard of liberties enjoyed by particular churches (cc. 26–8); as well as the complaints against the terms of the Statute of Westminister II and the Statute of Mortmain (cc. 23, 32). While there was much recapitulation of earlier grievances, the complaints had been reworded, rearranged and extended. Although this repetitious pleading, in many instances over a very long period, gives a strong impression of ineffectiveness, yet there can be no doubt that these matters were seen by the clergy as important, if not always burning, issues of the day. Specific references to the clauses of *Magna Carta* are rare (see cc. 30, 31), but the whole petition represents the clergy's view of what was required for the maintenance of the first clause of *Magna Carta*: 'that the English Church may be free and may have its rights undiminished and its liberties unimpaired'.

There was a continuing concern[81] about the seizure by royal ministers of horses and carts belonging to the clergy and about distraints made by royal bailiffs upon ecclesiastical property (cc. 30, 31). These clauses perhaps reflect the contemporary interest of the clergy in securing protection from arbitrary prises. Also, conflict with the Crown arising from the exercise of regalian right during the vacancy of the bishopric of Ely (March 1298 to October 1299) may well be reflected in the three petitions against the unlawful incursions of the custodians of vacant sees, abbeys and priories (cc. 1–3). Part of the clergy's complaint was that royal custodians unjustly took possession of goods belonging to chapters and convents and that the king during a vacancy presented to appropriated churches. These grievances concerning regalian right

[81] See c. 13 of the 1280 and cc. 1, 3 of the '1295' complaints: *Councils*, pp. 882, 1138–9.

were not distinctly new,[82] but they are particularly detailed, and it is noteworthy that during the vacancy at Ely, when both king and archbishop were taking a very close interest in the appointment of a new bishop for this diocese,[83] the priory of Ely had been taken into custody along with the bishopric and the king had presented during the vacancy to the churches of Wisbech and Foxton, which churches were, the archbishop claimed, appropriated to the prior and convent and provided the monks with resources vital for the maintenance of the house.[84] Yet, by the time the general grievances were formulated, probably in November 1299, the particular conflict at Ely had been resolved by the acquisition, in return for a fine of 500 marks, of a licence for the appropriation of the churches of Wisbech and Foxton and also by the acquisition, in return for a fine of 1000 marks, of a charter granting that the priory would not be taken into custody when the bishopric was vacant.[85] On another issue, concerning the premature delivery from jail of excommunicates (c. 18), there was the case, late in 1300, of the release by the king's order of the excommunicated rectors and vicars of the churches of St Augustine's abbey, who were summoned to appear at the Lincoln parliament.[86] This notable case arose after the grievance was drawn up; but at the Lincoln parliament the case and the grievance might well have been seen as significantly juxtaposed.

The relationship of the grievances to current and pressing cases appears to be direct and unmistakable in only two instances, and in both these cases separate petitions by the parties involved were also presented to parliament. The clergy complained of the king's treatment of the alien priories (c. 34). At about the same time, some of the priors of alien monasteries petitioned individually for the reduction of the fines imposed upon them by the Crown, and in eleven cases the fines were reduced by a third.[87] Secondly, the dispute between the king and the bishop of Chichester about the

---

[82] See, for example, c. 12 of 1280 and c. 29 of '1295': *Councils*, pp. 881, 1143.
[83] Above, pp. 41–2.
[84] See Graham, 'Administration of Ely during vacancies', pp. 52–4, 60, *Reg.*, pp. 253–4, 258, *CPR 1292–1301*, p. 347 and Howell, *Regalian Right*, pp. 69–70, 114–16.
[85] *CPR 1292–1301*, p. 365 and *CFR*, I. 419.
[86] Above, p. 81.
[87] *Councils*, p. 1218 n. 1, *Rot. Parl.*, I. 144, Matthew, *Norman Monasteries*, p. 85; and see PRO E159/74 mm. 63–64.

collation to the prebends, with cure of souls, belonging to the college of Hastings, claimed by the king as a royal free chapel, is specifically referred to in the clergy's general complaint (c. 4).[88] We know of the specific petitions to the king of the bishop of Chichester, Gilbert of St Leofard.[89] A long series of prorogations of this important case between the bishop and the Crown began at the parliament of 1300.[90] The complaint of the prelates and clergy cited Hastings only as an example. The so-called royal free chapel of Blyth was in a similar position to Hastings, and the archbishop of York petitioned the king in the parliament at Lincoln about the usurpation of his rights over the Nottinghamshire churches associated with the chapel of Blyth.[91] The disputes concerning both Hastings and Blyth became *causes célèbres*.

Thus, the grievances of the clergy against the Crown were reduced to general and therefore comprehensive complaints, which, although formulated, it seems clear, by a council of the southern province, were presented as the petitions of the prelates and clergy of England. Other clerical petitions to the Crown remained individual and particular, and the king's memoranda roll for his 29th year provides evidence of an unusually large number of petitions to the Lincoln parliament of 1301. Many of these petitions were related to the king's policies earlier in the reign for raising money. Edward and Boniface VIII were negotiating concerning the proceeds from papal tenths and, as we shall see, concerning the imposition of a new series of tenths. In 1285–6 the king had taken loans from papal money deposited in England which formed part of the revenue from the tenths decreed at the Council of Lyons in 1274; but in February 1300 the pope required the release of this money.[92] Consequently, some of the depositaries – the monasteries of Ramsey, Merton, Osney, Peterborough, Abingdon, Crowland, Westminster, Ely, Thorney and Bury – petitioned the king singly at the Lincoln parliament for satisfaction to be done to them concerning money, totalling

---

[88] And see c. 39 of '1295': *Councils*, pp. 1144–5.
[89] See *Rot. Parl.*, I. 144 (and Prynne, III. 856–7), PRO SC8/E620, /E668 and /E1368 and PRO E159/74 m. 36d.
[90] See below, p. 292.
[91] PRO E159/74 m. 35d and below, pp. 289–91.
[92] See Lunt, *Financial Relations*, pp. 342–5.

8,500 marks, which they were now required to pay to the pope.[93] Their claims were acknowledged by the Crown, but, despite the initial promise of repayment within two months, recovery was very slow indeed. There were, too, petitions in the parliament concerning satisfaction for loans taken from private treasure in 1294, and the king ordained at Lincoln that reimbursements of these loans should be made.[94] Also payments were being made to some religious houses in 1301 for earlier prises of wool and corn.[95] While in all these instances debts of the Crown were recognised, repayment was in general by a long-term process of allowances. Wherever possible the Crown, in fact, continued to play a waiting game; the abbess and convent of Canonsleigh, for example, were still petitioning in 1331 for the reimbursement of the loan to the king in 1294 of £672 5s 10½d.

For the most part there was a firm distinction between these individual petitions of the clergy and the general petitions or *gravamina*. The individual complaints usually represented more or less distinct injustices of royal government; redress, if long in materialising, might well be expected. The general complaints were directed against established, often long-established, procedures of government; here, redress called for changes in the practices especially of the king's justices and of the king's courts. The royal replies, formulated almost certainly in 1301, to the *gravamina* are an indication of the great difficulties which the clergy faced in attempting to gain satisfaction for what *they* regarded as unreasonable infringements of ecclesiastical liberty. The king or his officials took full advantage of the tradition of clerical grievances, for almost half of the material constituting the royal responses of 1301 is a verbatim repetition of royal replies to the clergy first made in 1280.[96] The responses were a defence of royal policies. In only a few cases do they amount to an acknowledgement of maladministration: if clerks, for example, were

---

93 Ibid., p. 344, PRO E159/74 mm. 9–11, 13–19, 24 and E159/75 m. 4d, and see Prynne, III. 907–8, 924.
94 PRO E159/74 mm. 20–21 and above, pp. 68–9.
95 PRO E159/74 mm. 11, 25d.
96 For the 1280 replies see *Councils*, pp. 874–86: the reply to cc. 5 and 6 in 1300–1 is derived directly from the reply to c. 2 in 1280, c. 7 from c. 1, c. 9 from c. 2, c. 10 from c. 15, c. 13 from c. 19, c. 15 from c. 18, c. 19 from c. 8, and c. 31 from c. 13.

being tried again in the king's court, having been handed over to an ecclesiastical judge and having purged themselves (as complained in c. 12), then this was against the king's will; and also against the king's will was the refusal of the necessities of life to fugitives in churches (cc. 14, 15).[97] Otherwise, on the long-standing issues, concerning, for instance, writs of prohibition and control of caption of excommunicates, the king conceded nothing at all to the Church. If Winchelsey was hoping at last to achieve a breakthrough in favour of the Church's interpretation of its liberties he must have been greatly disappointed by the royal replies to the *gravamina* of 1300–1. We have seen that there was conciliation at this time from Edward on matters which had caused particular complaint during 1297 and after. The demands of the magnates and prelates, relating especially to disafforestment and prises, were being met with concessions from the Crown. Why then did the petitions of the clergy result in staunchly defensive replies?

The answer lies in part with the very nature of the grievances, which attacked set royal rights and procedures, and which, of interest exclusively to the clergy, had not the remotest chance of attracting positive and direct baronial support. It is difficult to believe that the clergy can have expected very favourable responses to their *gravamina*; perhaps they hoped, above all, by their complaints to prevent any increase in royal encroachments upon their rights. Winchelsey, no doubt, continued to bring some weight to his particular cause by his own support for the magnates who opposed the king. But the question of how much bargaining power the clergy possessed in 1301 relates, of course, to the matter of taxation. The clergy, unlike the laity, were giving no hint that they might be prepared to concede a direct subsidy on their income to Edward. They were asked to grant a subsidy to the king in 1300, but, as in 1298, they refused to give any promise.[98] Again, at the Lincoln parliament of 1301 the king requested an aid, a fifteenth, to match the fifteenth now promised by the laity in exchange for concessions; but the final clause of the 'bill' of the committee of twenty-six magnates and prelates was a refusal by

[97] Also see the replies to cc. 24, 28, 31.
[98] Worcester, p. 544.

the clergy, citing the authority of 'Clericis laicos', to accede to this request.[99] As an indication of the continuing importance of 'Clericis laicos' for the English clergy, it was copied into annals by Rishanger immediately following a detailed account of the Lincoln parliament, and it is given there the erroneous *incipit* 'Ecclesiasticis infestos' and the erroneous date 24–25 February 1300.[100] Had this up-dated copy of the bull been deliberately put into circulation in order to give greater strength to the terms of the papal decree? The English clergy's adherence in their own interests to 'Clericis laicos' had certainly been further sanctioned by the incorporation of the bull into the Sext of 1298, which had soon circulated in England.[101] But was it in the clergy's best interests now to stand so firmly against direct taxation for the king? Holding fast to the principle of immunity as stated in 'Clericis laicos' had proved to be a successful policy in 1297. Would it always be successful?

Edward had means whereby he could circumvent the clergy's resistance; and here was the main reason for the failure of the English Church to establish a permanently strong bargaining position for itself in its relations with the Crown. The sexennial tenth imposed by the pope in 1291 had been suspended in 1294, after tenths for three years had been collected and more than half the proceeds seized and retained by the Crown; in the summer of 1300 collection was renewed, in the event for only one further year.[102] The proceeds from this tenth went to the papacy. But early in 1301, following negotiations between king and pope, a new papal tax, a triennial tenth, superseded the sexennial tenth. The agreement *ab initio* was for half of the proceeds to go to the king, though the Crown eventually received about two-thirds of the money collected.[103] The papal mandate for these tenths was issued when the Lincoln parliament was in session. Although the clergy refused to pay a tax to the king, the pope had in fact already agreed to what amounted to a twentieth for three years for himself and a twentieth for Edward. Collection began in the autumn of

[99] Rishanger, p. 462, *Flores Hist.*, III. 109, 303, and see above, p. 187 n. 51.
[100] Rishanger, pp. 462–4. See above, p. 89 n. 142.
[101] Sext., 3. 23. 3. See *Reg. Swinfield*, p. 377, *Reg.*, p. 365 and Maitland, *Roman Canon Law*, p. 131n.   [102] Lunt, *Financial Relations*, pp. 357–8.
[103] Ibid., pp. 366–9, 380–1, and see Prynne, III. 921–3, 939.

1301. A bull of 12 March 1301[104] indicates Boniface VIII's new mood of friendliness towards the king: the pope remitted to Edward money seized from earlier papal tenths and absolved him from any sentence of excommunication which he may have incurred because of impositions upon churches and upon churchmen. The king, Boniface declared, had been compelled to make impositions because of poverty and necessity. With the pope, if not with the English clergy, Edward had, it appears, at last won the argument of 'necessity'. Without papal support the English clergy would be weakened in the defence of their income against royal control and also weakened in their attempt to gain further concessions from the king.

In addition to the agreement with the pope, the Crown in 1301 adopted a different policy in relation to the tax on lay movables. Very soon after the order for the collection of the fifteenth was made in the autumn of 1301, it was decided that the clergy should be required to pay on their temporalities.[105] This was a very interesting move on the part of the king and the king's council. It was an attempt to bring under royal control the taxation of the income from the lay fees of prelates and religious houses. Since 1290 lay taxes had not been collected from the temporalities assessed in the 1291 *taxatio*, and ecclesiastical taxes, whether papal or royal, had been upon both the spiritual and temporal income of the whole clergy. In broad terms temporalities comprised the resources of the higher clergy, whereas spiritualities, the income from parish churches, comprised the resources of the lower clergy. Temporalities amounted to approximately one third of the clergy's assessed income and spiritualities to approximately two-thirds. The king laid no claim now to taxation of spiritualities. But how should income from the estates of the higher clergy be regarded? Was it *ecclesiastical* income, or was it income from *lay* fees? There had been no doubt in Winchelsey's mind. In defending the income of the English Church he had been defending the whole income as assessed in 1291. On 23 November 1301 the king, in a reply to an inquiry sent from the king's council at York,[106] advised

[104] *Foedera*, I. ii. 931 and *Reg. Halton*, pp. 252–3.
[105] See esp. Willard, *Parliamentary Taxes*, pp. 100–1.
[106] PRO E159/75 m. 11, and see Prynne, III. 930.

that the clergy should pay the fifteenth on their temporalities, for the king's concessions in return for the fifteenth were as much to their advantage as to the advantage of the earls, barons and laymen of the realm. Some clergy had already petitioned at the exchequer against paying twice on their temporalities, that is, both for the papal tenth and for the lay fifteenth. The king indicated that he considered it to be against the interests of the Crown for the taxation of temporalities to be linked permanently with the taxation of spiritualities and thus within the ordaining power of the pope and of the Church. The Crown, it should be stressed, was planning the direct taxation of the temporalities of the Church even though the prelates had refused to give their consent. It is no wonder that Winchelsey strongly opposed this new development.

The king's council examined thoroughly the possibility of preventing the papal collectors from taxing the clergy's temporalities, and secured a suspension of the collection of the tenth for some months.[107] The argument which the council presented against the taxation of temporalities by papal mandate is of particular interest. It is the Crown's answer to papal claims of jurisdiction in temporal matters. 'Spiritualities can be controlled by the mandates of the pope but not temporalities, for these are subject to the royal dignity and are so separated from spiritualities that the king has cognizance over all the temporalities of the kingdom because of the nature of his rights.'[108] But it was clearly not in the king's interests to suspend for long a taxation which was of financial benefit to him, especially since the royal order for the direct taxation of a fifteenth of the clergy's temporalities proved

---

[107] PRO E159/75 m. 30 (old m. 26) and Lunt, *Financial Relations*, pp. 367–9. The king's own taxation of all the temporal possessions of the clergy is the answer to Lunt's query: 'What Edward's purpose may have been is left in the field of conjecture.'

[108] PRO E159/75 m. 30 (as cited in Lunt, *Valuation of Norwich*, p. 75 n. 7, and see Lunt, 'Testa and parliament of Carlisle', p. 339): the king's council instructed Bartholomew of Ferentino, one of the collectors of the papal tenth, 'quod ipse temporalia prelatorum, clericorum et virorum religiosorum regni Anglie pretextu alicuius mandati summi pontificis taxare seu quicquid inde levare non debet, presertim cum mere spirtualia domini pape mandatis submitti possint, temporalia vero non. Ea etenim regie dignitati submissa sunt, et a spiritualibus adeo separata quod in omnibus temporalibus regni habet ipse rex cognoscere ratione iuris sue tenoris.' (For the denial by the Crown of the pope's right to bestow both spiritualities and temporalities in bulls of provision see *Councils*, pp. 1226–7.)

difficult to enforce. Collection of the papal tenth was resumed in the early summer of 1302. The prelates and monasteries were inclined to resist the demand for the fifteenth until it was expedient to submit.[109] Winchelsey was undaunted in his opposition.

Two of the extant assessment rolls of the fifteenth indicate that in some areas clerical temporalities were under review from the start.[110] Having received complaints from the bishop of Lincoln and the bishop of Ely that the king's agents were proceeding with the taxation, the archbishop advised that proclamations should be made against the assessors of clerical property, followed if necessary by excommunication.[111] John Dalderby, the new bishop of Lincoln, immediately followed Winchelsey's advice.[112] But in February 1302 Edward reissued his orders for the collection of the tax. An ecclesiastical council was summoned to meet in June,[113] and Winchelsey issued once again in this council his mandate that the bishops of the province should publish sentences of excommunication against all invaders of ecclesiastical property.[114] At the archbishop's request in the July parliament, the collection of the fifteenth on clerical goods was deferred until Michaelmas. John Dalderby continued to experience difficulty in preventing the fifteenth from being collected from clerical goods, and in August 1302 once again ordered his archdeacons to make known the penalty of excommunication to the royal collectors.[115] After the Michaelmas parliament a further deferment was granted until the following Easter, and Winchelsey, having undertaken to discuss the matter with all speed, summoned a second council to meet in December.[116] The December council agreed that the pope's permission should be sought and representatives were sent to Rome without delay. The decision to seek papal permission

---

[109] See, for example, *Worcester Sede Vacante Register*, pp. 75–6.
[110] See especially the Yorkshire roll (*Yorkshire Lay Subsidy 30 Edward I*, ed. W. Brown (*Yorkshire Archaeological Soc.: Record Series*, xxi)), and also the local assessment roll for Colchester (*Rot. Parl.*, i. 243–65); but another extant local assessment roll, for Dartford, (R. P. Coates, 'Valuation of the town of Dartford', *Archaeologia Cantiana*, ix (1874), 285–98) specifically notes that the sum was given 'preter religiosos'.
[111] *Reg.*, pp. 757–8, 760–1.   [112] LRO Reg. Dalderby (iii), fo. 39.
[113] *Councils*, pp. 1218–22.   [114] LRO Reg. Dalderby (iii), fo. 46v.
[115] Ibid., fo. 49r.   [116] *Councils*, pp. 1222–6.

was, of course, a decision in favour of the tax. As far as we know papal consent was not forthcoming; but this was of little consequence. Collection of the fifteenth was reordered, finally, in the spring and early summer of 1303, and the king asked for the names of anyone who resisted the collection and of anyone who fulminated sentences of excommunication against the collectors.[117]

But collection of this fifteenth was no resounding victory for the king. The king's council had claimed cognisance for the Crown over all the temporalities of the kingdom. But there had been a long delay before full collection became possible, and the tax was, in the end, dependent upon the consent of the clergy meeting in their own assembly. And, before submitting to the fifteenth, the prelates had sought papal permission for the royal taxation of their temporal income. Although Winchelsey's political position had become less secure, he had held unwaveringly to the principle of clerical consent to royal taxation. The clergy, it is true, contributed on their temporal income both to the papal tenth and to the lay fifteenth, but the protracted negotiations had alleviated the burden of payment. The king's attempt to take control of the temporal income of the clergy, and distinguish it firmly from their spiritual income, was repeated with the tax of a thirtieth and twentieth in 1306, but not thereafter. Taxation of the income of the English Church, whether papal taxation or royal taxation, in fact continued to be based upon the 1291 assessment of both spiritualities and temporalities.

Despite the improved relations of pope and king, Winchelsey had lost little of his control over the English Church. Even so, the policies of pope and archbishop concerning taxation no longer coincided. Also, the policies of the opposition magnates and the archbishop had to some extent, as we have seen, grown apart. In assessing Winchelsey's position in 1297 it was necessary to strike a balance between, on the one hand, his sympathy for and influence upon the baronial movement and, on the other hand, his unmistakable emphasis upon matters of purely ecclesiastical concern. Despite this emphasis the interests of clergy and laity in 1297 had been very closely linked. This was not so clearly the case

[117] Prynne, III. 1001–2 and *CFR*, I. 474–5, 479.

after 1297. Had Winchelsey, then, become more distant from the baronial malcontents?

Concerning the leading opponents of 1297, Roger Bigod and the son and heir of Humphrey Bohun both submitted in 1302 to arrangements concerning succession to their estates which greatly favoured the interests of the king. Indeed, in the case of Bigod, because he died childless (in 1306) the earldom of Norfolk was surrendered to the Crown.[118] But a third protagonist, John Ferrers, submitted in no way to Edward and continued his long dispute with the king concerning the loss of the earldom of Derby. There can be little question of Edward's 'crude high-handedness' in his refusal to accept the justice of John Ferrers's case.[119] Ferrers appealed to the pope. In the first place he had appealed to Boniface VIII for permission to obtain contributions from prelates and ecclesiastics in order to redeem his lands by paying the required £50,000 to the earl of Lancaster.[120] But later, perhaps early in 1300, his appeal was against the earl of Lancaster for the loss of £20,000 of income from estates comprising the earldom of Derby.[121] Winchelsey certainly lent support to this appeal, for on 24 January 1300 the archbishop wrote to Cardinal Matthew de Aquasparta referring to John Ferrers as his special friend and asking the cardinal to give assistance to John who had not succeeded to the earldom because justice had been denied to his father.[122] The pope delegated Winchelsey to act as the sole judge in John Ferrers's case against Thomas of Lancaster; and in the spring of 1301 the archbishop appointed his deputies to hear the case.[123] It is difficult to believe that this attempt to use the Church courts to bring aid to Ferrers in his quarrel with the Crown ever had any chance of success. The earl of Lancaster was summoned by Winchelsey to be at St Paul's London on 24 April.

[118] It is clear that the account in *Flores Hist.*, III. 125, see n. 5, concerns Bigod, the earl marshal, not the earl of Warwick as preferred in the printed edition of the chronicle.
[119] See refs. above, p. 170.
[120] B.L. Lans. 229, fo. 24v (and see 21r). This plea to the pope must be c. 1297: it refers to 'Clericis laicos' as already issued and to the lands of the earldom of Derby, surrendered in July 1266, as in the hands of the earls of Lancaster for thirty years and more. See Cokayne, *Complete Peerage*, IV. 203 and V. 307 n. b.
[121] Prynne, III. 949.   [122] *Reg.*, pp. 566–7.
[123] *Reg.*, pp. 407, 412–13, and see *Antient Kalendars*, I. 92.

Proceedings apparently took place there on 30 May and 27 June, and the case was referred back to Rome. But a writ of prohibition had been issued by the Crown against the hearing in court christian of a plea concerning lay fees. The prohibition had been delivered to Winchelsey by one of Lancaster's messengers at Withington, Gloucestershire, on 26 May. The earl of Lancaster followed this up with an action against Winchelsey in the king's court for suing him in the ecclesiastical court in disregard of a royal prohibition, and he claimed the enormous, but notional, sum of £100,000 as damages against Winchelsey.[124]

Winchelsey was accused in the king's court of contravening his oath of fealty to the king, to the manifest disinheritance of the Crown and the subversion of the realm. The case against him was adjourned, term by term, until the end of the reign.[125] The suits initiated in the court of the king's bench were not just against the archbishop. Ferrers himself pleaded, in 1302, that he did not know that the acquisition of the papal bull militated against the king's dignity. He was accused of continuing to sue after the receipt of the king's prohibition, submitted to the king's grace and was pardoned.[126] He undertook not to sue further in the Church courts. Others were charged, with repeated adjournments, for procuring the citation and prosecuting the plea against Lancaster in contravention of the royal prohibition; only the suits against Walter of Witton and John of Aunesley were terminated with the king's pardon.[127] Winchelsey had made an open attempt to assist Ferrers: this must have been severely detrimental to his relations with the king.

The significance of Winchelsey's support of Ferrers is high-

---

[124] Prynne, III. 902–3, 948–9 and *CCR 1296–1302*, p. 571. The note in *Annales London.*, p. 137 (*sub anno* 1305) to the king's case against Winchelsey is probably a reference to a different case (cf. *Reg.*, p. xxviii, and see below, p. 213 n. 150). The king's draft of the writ to Ferrers as printed in Prynne, III. 902 is PRO SC1/32/91; it was printed again, without indication of date, in Davies, *Baronial Opposition*, p. 585.

[125] PRO KB27/167 m. 8, /169 m. 36d, /170 m. 84, /171 m. 72d, /172 m. 78d, /182 m. 82d, /184 m. 63d and /185 m. 60.

[126] PRO KB27/168 m. 10 and /169 m. 24d.

[127] The accused included John de Bloyou, Adam of Hereford, William of Fotheringay, Gilbert of Middleton, John de Haselarton, Ralph Bygot, Robert de Ros, William of Sardinia, Thomas of Sutton and Adam of Goldingham. See, for example, PRO KB27/170 m. 97d, /174 m. 65d, /176 m. 33 and /178 m. 103.

lighted by Ferrers's accusation of the king's treasurer, Bishop Langton, at the Carlisle parliament of 1307 for collusive maintenance in the king's court.[128] The acquittal of Langton at this stage through the direct intervention of Edward I led McFarlane to comment that 'in the very last years of his life Edward was still inclined to prefer his own wishes to his own laws'. The contrast between the king's attack upon Winchelsey and his support of Walter Langton during these years needs no stressing. But Winchelsey's support of John Ferrers does not make the archbishop into the leader of an opposition party in England. There is very little to suggest that the archbishop was a man of intrigue; and, indeed, after the period 1297–1301 it is not possible to discern anything so coherent as an 'opposition party'. It is very doubtful whether any political significance can be read into the legal dispute which involved Winchelsey and the earl of Warwick (whose loyalty to the king was not in question)[129] concerning the earl's marriage to Isabella de Clare.[130] And the fact that the archbishop referred to the earl of Lincoln, also loyal to Edward, as 'his very special friend'[131] should discourage us from imagining the existence of exclusive factions.

If Winchelsey was not the leader of an opposition group, he appears nonetheless to have become, perhaps ever since the Bury parliament of 1296, the king's most prominent opponent. He was closely associated with the strong and successful opposition to Edward in 1300–1; and there is no doubt that he had been a member of the committee of twenty-six which, according to Langtoft, had been appointed at the Lincoln parliament of 1301 to discuss the petitions to the king.[132] An interesting passage in the Hagnaby chronicle, relating apparently to the parliament of October 1302, tells us that thirty-five men were chosen to give

---

[128] *Select Cases King's Bench*, II. lxix–lxx, cxxxi–cxxxv, III. lvi–lvii, 165–8, 175–8 and *Records of the Trial of Langeton*, ed. Beardwood, pp. 283–90, 336–8; and see Beardwood, 'Langton's use of recognizances', pp. 60–1 and McFarlane, 'Had Edward I a policy towards the earls?', pp. 150–1.

[129] Maddicott, *Lancaster*, pp. 68–9. Guy de Beauchamp, earl of Warwick (1298–1315), was son and heir of William de Beauchamp, who had been involved briefly in the opposition to Edward I in 1297: see Evesham, p. 576.

[130] *Worcester Sede Vacante Register*, pp. 8–9, and see Cokayne, *Complete Peerage*, XII. ii. 370.

[131] *Reg.*, p. 306.   [132] Above, p. 187, and below, p. 238.

advice on the state of the Church and of the kingdom, the most important of whom was the archbishop of Canterbury.[133] Whether or not this passage is correct in detail, it accurately reflects the archbishop's political position: he was never close to the king and never a member of the king's council, but whenever the king was compelled to take counsel from outside the royal court, then among those chosen Winchelsey occupied a position of pre-eminence. This pre-eminence was a reflection not simply of his high office but also of his political strength and acumen. He could not be ignored, and certainly not directly bought off, by the king.

It was often politic, of course, for the king to treat his Church with tact and respect. But greater control over ecclesiastical wealth had become a persistent aim of the Crown. The striking events of 1303–4 are an indication of the king's opportunism and of his determination to lay claim when at all possible to taxes upon ecclesiastical income. Three weeks after Boniface's death the king ordered that all the money from the current papal tenth which was in the hands of the papal collectors, and all the money which was to be collected, should be sent to the exchequer.[134] The papal agents were compelled to obey royal rather than papal orders, and the king alleged, without any written evidence, that Boniface had agreed that in the event of his death proceeds from the tenth should go to the king. Arbitrary procedures by the Crown in relation to clerical taxes granted by the English clergy were less possible as a result of *Confirmatio Cartarum*; but a papal vacancy had offered once again a tempting opportunity for the seizure of papal money. The vacancy was very brief and the new pope, Benedict XI, attempted to oppose the Crown's audacious policy

---

133 BL Cotton Vesp. B xi, fo. 513v, *sub anno* 1302 (cited also in Prestwich, *War, Politics and Finance*, p. 90): 'Item post festum sancti Michaelis rex tenuit concilium apud London' in quo multis multa locuntur [*sic*]. Tandem ex consensu regis et regni actum est ut ex Anglia xxxv eligerentur, quorum primus et primas archiepiscopus Cantuariensis erat, de quorum consilio vel assensu status ecclesie et regni secundum defensionem et utilitatem regni ordinaretur.' While this chronicle contains much interesting material, it is a curious compilation and is not altogether reliable. See Gransden, *Historical Writing*, p. 406 n. 20, and for fos. 36v–37 of the chronicle see Prestwich, 'New account of Welsh campaign 1294–5', pp. 89–94.

134 For what follows see Lunt, 'The account of a papal collector 1304' and Lunt, *Financial Relations*, pp. 372–8. Gerard de Pecorara's report is translated in Lunt, *Papal Revenues*, I. 228–32. For the king's orders concerning the money collected in Ireland see PRO E159/79 mm. 76–77d.

by appointing Gerard de Pecorara as papal collector with authority to collect, *inter alia*, the arrears of the tenth. The office of papal collector, a foreign agent resident in the country he was commissioned to tax, could be distinctly precarious, and Gerard de Pecorara's visit to England provides a notable case in point.

Gerard failed to receive the customary letter of safe conduct from the king, who was in no mood to give way to papal pressure. Nonetheless, the collector proceeded to exercise the papal commission and, in consequence, was treated very harshly indeed. Edward ordered that Gerard's instructions to the deputy collectors should be revoked and that he should appear before the king and council in Scotland to justify himself. On his return to London the papal collector persisted in his efforts to recover the money which the king had arbitrarily seized, but his position had been weakened by the death of Benedict XI in July 1304. This ensuing papal vacancy lasted for almost a year. On 7 December 1304 Gerard was forbidden by the constable of the Tower, acting for the Crown, to collect papal revenue, compelled to revoke all his acts, and given seven days' notice to leave the country.[135] All his goods, except those which he had brought with him, were confiscated and he left England immediately. For the rest of the reign the arrears of the papal tenth continued to be collected by the Crown, with the deputy collectors using their powers of excommunication and sequestration supported by royal authority. This was the kind of direct control over the taxation of the English clergy which Edward would no doubt have preferred to exercise at all times.

This attack upon the courageous, if foolhardy, papal collector reflects a significant strengthening of Edward's position in 1303–4. Peace had been made with France in May 1303. Walter Langton, the king's chief minister, who had been summoned to Rome and suspended as bishop following John Lovetot's vigorous

---

[135] The document which contains the memorandum of the meeting in the house of the dean of St Martin-le-Grand at which the constable of the Tower of London ordered Gerard's banishment (Vatican, Archivio Segreto, Instrumenta Misc. 377) also contains notes about matters in England of which Gerard disapproved: the spoliation of the lands of his bishopric by the late bishop of Winchester, John of Pontoise; the rarity of visitations of the exempt abbeys and the absence of visitations of the royal free chapels; and the independence and war-mongering of the Scottish bishops.

appeal against him, now had his name cleared and in June 1303 he was restored by the pope to his episcopal office.[136] Boniface VIII's death in the autumn of 1303 was a distinct advantage to the king. And Edward had embarked upon a new Scottish campaign and was determined 'to make an end of the business':[137] the surrender of the Scots came in July 1304 after a three-month siege of Stirling castle. Every effort was now made to achieve a constitutional settlement for Scotland. In December 1304 the king's exchequer, resident at York since 1298, returned to London in a caravan of twenty-seven carts;[138] and on 28 February 1305 Edward himself returned to Westminster for the meeting of a full parliament, the first to include the lower clergy since the parliament of March 1300. In the hope and belief that peace on all fronts had at last been established Edward was eager to re-establish his authority in England. In the course of 1305 the strength of his determination became apparent.

There had been in recent years no healing of the tension between king and archbishop. Winchelsey had continued to defy Edward's protection of his own ministers and clerks. The protection of royal agents from excommunication as a result of activities 'by reason of their office and in respect of the king's court' was a stumbling block to the implementation of the general sentences of excommunication against invaders of ecclesiastical property. But Winchelsey, nonetheless, had made every effort to ensure execution of the sentences in relation to royal taxation. In addition, on other issues in 1302 and 1303, his attempts to bring into court christian Robert de Burghersh, constable of the castle of Dover, and Henry of Cobham, sheriff of Kent, along with his ministers and bailiffs, had been met with royal prohibitions.[139] The archbishop's concern to make beneficed royal clerks answerable to the ecclesiastical courts because of their non-residence and often, too, their failure to take orders, revealed itself notably in cases that

[136] *Foedera*, I. ii. 956–7 and *Reg. Boniface VIII*, no. 5239 (*CPL*, I. 610), and see above, p. 53.
[137] Powicke, *Thirteenth Century*, p. 706.
[138] *Annales London.*, p. 134, and see D. M. Broome, 'Exchequer migrations to York in the thirteenth and fourteenth century' in *Essays Presented to T. F. Tout*, ed. A. G. Little and F. M. Powicke (Manchester, 1925), esp. p. 291.
[139] Prynne, III. 916–17 (*CCR 1296–1302*, p. 582) and above, pp. 182–3.

arose during his metropolitical visitations of the dioceses of Worcester, London and Norwich in 1301, 1303 and 1304.[140] The king ordered the archbishop to desist from disturbing and molesting the royal clerks; but, as indicated in a series of letters to the king,[141] Winchelsey was able to offer only a postponement of the cases in his court of audience. With the highest of motives and intentions the archbishop acted in defiance of the Crown and remained a thorn in the side of the king. From 1294 to 1304 Edward had faced successive military, financial and political crises. Winchelsey was to take much of the blame.

SUSPENSION

The king's diplomat, John of Pontoise, bishop of Winchester, died on 5 December 1304. The bishop had enjoyed exemption from the jurisdiction of the archbishop of Canterbury, and only a month after his death Winchelsey visited the vacant diocese. The visitation lasted from the second week in January to the second week in February 1305.[142] Having completed this demonstration of his authority in the wealthy diocese of Winchester, the archbishop travelled to Lambeth. The first writs for the impending Westminster parliament had given 16 February as the date for the opening session, and Winchelsey had summoned a council to assemble at Lambeth two days before the parliament, with the express purpose of making preparations for what should be done in the parliament.[143] A postponement of the meeting of parliament until 28 February may have upset Winchelsey's plans, but it is possible that an ecclesiastical council did meet, for Winchelsey and at least two of his bishops were certainly in or near London well in advance of the parliament.[144] The king, having heard that the ecclesiastical council had been summoned, took no chances. He feared that the clergy were planning to present petitions and

[140] Below, pp. 281–5.
[141] *Reg.*, pp. 1336–7 (from PRO C47/22/11/75), PRO SC1/21/84 and *Reg.*, pp. 811–12.
[142] *Reg.*, p. 487.   [143] See *Councils*, pp. 1227–9.
[144] Winchelsey was at Lambeth on 14 and 17 Feb. (PRO C85/7/2 and Lambeth Palace Lib., MS 244, fo. 34r), and for the bishop of Salisbury and the bishop of Worcester see *Reg. Gandavo*, p. 644 and *Reg. Geynesborough*, pp. 15, 100.

ordered his chancellor, William Hamilton, to have at the ready the records of previous clerical grievances and the royal replies. The chancellor and the treasurer, Bishop Langton, were instructed to assemble the members of the king's council who were in London and to ensure that agents of the Crown were sent to the clerical assembly, as had become a common procedure in relation to Winchelsey's councils.[145]

It was at this Lenten parliament of 1305, which was in session until early April, that Edward mounted an attack against Winchelsey. This attack was part of a new broad political strategy. The king's institution of the trailbaston[146] inquiries shows a determination to stamp out rebellion and lawlessness. There can be no doubt that there had been a possibility of serious civil disorder, especially during the years 1297–1301. Writing about the events of 1299 Guisborough had noted that the king's councillors feared an uprising of the people.[147] An intensification of special commissions of inquiry began in 1302 and culminated in the trailbaston trials of 1305–6, aimed at the rigorous suppression of crime, such as murder, arson, robbery, vagrancy and other breaches of the peace, and perversions of justice, such as confederacy, maintenance and bribery.[148] The Ordinance of Trailbaston was promulgated in this first parliament of 1305,[149] and it specified that judges should be concerned with felonies committed between 24 June 1297 and Easter 1304. This reference to the summer of 1297, the time of the most dangerous baronial and

---

[145] *Councils*, p. 1229.
[146] The Evesham chronicler (Oxford Bodl., Laud Misc. 529, fos. 99v–100r) tells how, on returning from Scotland, the king heard of an outbreak of gang warfare. One of the members of a particular gang was a cobbler. 'Trailbaston', he explains, was a cobbler's instrument, often used for whipping thieves, and thus by association was used to describe the inquests instituted by the king: 'Traylebaston instrumentum quoddam est sutorum et inde solent manopia [*sic*] flagellari, sed inde placiti vocabulum inolevit.'
[147] Guisborough, p. 330. And see the king's writ of 2 April 1299 (*CPR 1292–1301*, p. 403): 'Mandate to the mayor and aldermen of the city of London to arrest, try and punish persons congregating by day and night, and speaking ill of the king and his subjects.'
[148] *Cal. London Trailbaston Trials*, esp. pp. 1–4 and A. Harding, 'Early trailbaston proceedings from the Lincoln roll of 1305' in *Medieval Legal Documents: Edited in Memory of C. A. F. Meekings*, ed. R. F. Hunnisett and J. B. Post (HMSO, 1978), pp. 144–68.
[149] *Rot. Parl.*, I. 178.

ecclesiastical rebellion against the Crown, can have been no co-incidence.

On 1 April the king initiated proceedings against Winchelsey for what had happened while the king was in Flanders late in 1297 and early in 1298: he declared that the archbishop had retained £4,000 of the tenth which he and the whole clergy of the kingdom had conceded to him for the war against the Scots.[150] Although there may be doubt about the exact amount, and debate about the rights and wrongs of the case, the king's claim was essentially correct. Winchelsey had determined that the grant should be paid only for as long as there was need of it, and the whole tenth had certainly not been given to the king.[151] Edward clearly believed that it was detrimental to the authority of the Crown for the clergy to control the supply of taxation in this way. He now claimed that the archbishop's policy had been against the terms of the grant, and Winchelsey was summoned before the treasurer, the barons of the exchequer and others of the king's council on 10 May 1305 to answer for his actions. But the archbishop failed to appear and wrote to the treasurer and the barons of the exchequer on 11 May seeking to be excused, since he was not well and was burdened with work, and also, a more substantial reason perhaps, since he could make no reply to the king's writ without consultation with the prelates and clergy who had conceded the tax. Nicholas of Warwick, who represented the Crown, sought judgment against Winchelsey for his default and for his contempt of the royal mandate. The sheriff of Surrey was ordered to seize all the archbishop's lands in his county and to ensure the archbishop's presence at the exchequer on 20 June to answer for the £4,000 and receive judgment for his default and contempt. But by that time the king had deferred his attack upon Winchelsey and ordered that there should be no further proceedings on this matter. The termination of this case certainly did not constitute a reconciliation between the king and Winchelsey. Perhaps Edward realised that the case was an attack upon the clergy and not just

---

[150] PRO E159/78 m. 38d and E368/75 m. 46. *Annales London.* (p. 137) tells us that the king sought £6,000 from the archbishop; this is possibly an error for 6,000 marks, though it is not clear which case against Winchelsey the annalist had in mind.

[151] Above, p. 189.

upon the archbishop; or the appointment of a new pope in June 1305 may have immediately changed the king's plans for the future.

A meeting between Edward and his council and Winchelsey took place at Kennington between 20 and 22 May.[152] One of the major issues under discussion at this specially convened meeting was the status of the Augustinian priory of St Oswald Gloucester, claimed by the Crown as a royal free chapel. The long dispute about St Oswald's was reaching a climax.[153] Winchelsey presented to the king's council his plea for the exercise of ordinary jurisdiction by the bishop of Worcester as diocesan and by himself as metropolitan. But, whatever the irregularities of the status of St Oswald's from Winchelsey's point of view, convincing evidence was produced to demonstrate that the church of St Oswald had an historically valid claim to be regarded as a royal free chapel and a right therefore in English custom to enjoy exemption from ordinary jurisdiction. Winchelsey put himself upon the king's grace. When judgment was declared against him in November, the exaction of damages was deferred. Edward was playing for time. Even so, disgrace was being heaped upon the archbishop's head by the king and his council.

Two other cases were perhaps under discussion at the meeting at Kennington in May. The first concerned another church claimed as a royal free chapel: St Mary's Hastings. This dispute, too, was of several years' duration; but here the king's claims lacked historical validity. The petition of the canons of Hastings to the Lenten parliament of 1305 provided the opportunity for Edward, on 20 April, to make a firm declaration against the archbishop's exercise of jurisdiction at Hastings, and, 'being unable to bear with equanimity such insolence and such erroneous wrongs', to summon Winchelsey to appear before him on 14 June 'to answer for the said wrongs notoriously perpetrated against us and our Crown and to answer also for other related matters'.[154] Whether or not this dispute was discussed in May, it seems clear from their

---

[152] The king was there 17–24 May (Gough, *Itinerary*, II. 249) and the archbishop 20–22 May (PRO C53/91 m. 6 no. 31 and m. 7 no. 32, and Lambeth Palace Lib., MS 244, fo. 26r).

[153] See below, pp. 286–9, and esp. *Select Cases King's Bench*, III. 140–3.

[154] See below, p. 293.

respective itineraries that there was no meeting of king and archbishop during June, though they were both at Canterbury in the
second week of July. The bishop of Chichester as diocesan and
the archbishop as metropolitan had a watertight case for the up-
holding of their rights over the prebends of Hastings with cure of
souls, and theirs was a case which the king's bench could not in
the end refute. If the Crown's position had been stronger in this
dispute, a decision would probably have been reached much
earlier. In fact, the matter was postponed from term to term, and
it was a source of added tension between Crown and archbishop.

The other notable dispute, almost certainly under review in
May 1305, concerned the church of Dodderhill in the Worcester
diocese. Important issues of patronage and jurisdiction were at
stake in this interesting case, which embroiled the prior and convent of Worcester, the bishop of Worcester, the archbishop, the
pope and the king.[155] The interest of the king and his clerks in
this church had been particularly apparent since, at least, the
autumn of 1301. The incumbent, William of Dover, king's
chaplain, had expressed a willingness to resign Dodderhill in
favour of John Bush ('Bouhs') of London, special clerk of the king
and notary public.[156] The king, and John Droxford, keeper of the
king's wardrobe, and Anthony Bek, bishop of Durham, had all
written to the prior and convent of Worcester requesting that John
Bush be presented to the church when William of Dover resigned
it. But the prior explained that he was unable to make such a
pledge because of a papal reservation of the next vacant church in
his patronage. In fact, in January 1302 the bishop of Worcester,
Godfrey Giffard, just before his death, appropriated Dodderhill to
the priory of Worcester. The first clash which followed this
appropriation was with Winchelsey, for the archbishop refused to
confirm the appropriation, and, indeed, after hearing the case in

---

[155] For what follows see *Reg. Giffard*, p. 85, Worcester, Dean & Chapter Lib.,
   Liber Albus, fos. 5, 6v, 16r (*Liber Albus*, nos. 46–52, 59, 135), Sede Vacante
   Reg., fos. 14v, 16v, 18, 20 (*Worcester Sede Vacante Register*, pp. 35, 41, 47–
   50, 57–8), Worcester, pp. 550–1, 556, *Reg. Geynesborough*, pp. 21, 85, 119,
   203, 205, 211, *CPR 1301–7*, pp. 148, 361, *CCR 1302–7*, pp. 222–3, PRO
   KB27/174 mm. 2, 57, 98d, /179 mm. 6, 71, and *Reg.*, pp. 801, 1050. See
   also Haines, *Administration of Diocese of Worcester*, pp. 245–6, 249, 257–8
   and Saunders, 'Royal Eccles. Patronage', pp. 272–7, 342–4.
[156] See refs in Cheney, *Notaries Public*.

1303, he declared Dodderhill vacant and in his gift by reason of lapse of time, and conferred the church upon his clerk, John of Middleton, brother of the archbishop's distinguished clerk, Master Gilbert of Middleton. The archbishop's actions were strongly opposed by the prior, who appealed to Rome, and also by the new bishop, William Gainsborough.

In August 1303 the king intervened, asserting *his* right of presentation to Dodderhill, since the church had been appropriated to the priory without royal assent and thus in contravention of the Statute of Mortmain. The case was brought before the king's bench.[157] In a first hearing at Michaelmas 1303, concerning the advowson, the king was awarded the writ *ut admittas*. When the prior came before the bench the following year he claimed that the appropriation was concerned entirely with spiritualities, cognisance of which belonged only to court christian. But the king's attorney argued damage to the Crown's rights by this appropriation, since, when both the bishopric and the priory were vacant, the king presented to the priory's churches. The matter was heard 'before the whole council', and although the council doubted the king's right now to present to the church and stated that there was no precedent for the seizure of the advowson of a church in such a case, yet, because the prior had trespassed against the king, the advowson of the church was declared to be forfeit 'in the name of distraint'. Thus, the king, 'notwithstanding the claim of Robert, archbishop of Canterbury', ordered the bishop of Worcester to institute the royal presentee, William Thorntoft. Middleton was removed; and Thorntoft, a royal clerk, was instituted on 3 August 1304. The archbishop was unwilling to accept this royal presentation and the consequent episcopal institution to Dodderhill. Gainsborough's political allegiance certainly appears to have been directed more towards the king than towards the archbishop. Proceedings against him were initiated in the court of Canterbury, and the bishop appealed to Rome against the judgment of this court, which he said was made 'in contempt of the king'. In October 1304 the king notified Winchelsey that to take action against Gainsborough was in derogation of royal rights, and at the Hilary term 1305 the archbishop, John of Middleton and Walter

---

[157] *Select Cases King's Bench*, III. 125–7, printing from PRO KB27/175 m. 19.

of Thorpe, dean of the Arches, were impleaded in the king's court for contravening writs of prohibition. It was almost certainly as a result of the meeting between Winchelsey and the king in May 1305 that the archbishop agreed (on 21 May) to postpone the case against the bishop of Worcester until the matter had been discussed in the next parliament (planned for 15 July), and the king agreed (on 22 May), a fine having been paid, to restore the advowson of Dodderhill to the priory of Worcester.[158] With the king's nominee in possession of Dodderhill, and the prior and convent pardoned for their appropriation of the church without a royal licence and the advowson restored to them, there was very little chance that the archbishop's case would be heard to any avail. The cases against Winchelsey and against John of Middleton were adjourned. In 1308 the archbishop was seeking another benefice for John of Middleton, claiming that the latter had been fraudulently ejected from Dodderhill by order of the king's court and with the connivance of the bishop of Worcester. So, this tangled case had become by 1305 a direct dispute between king and archbishop. Winchelsey was willing to postpone proceedings, but certainly not, on this issue, to admit the justice of the king's actions. Yet, a royal clerk, in place of the archbishop's clerk, was securely installed at Dodderhill.

Commenting upon the discord between king and archbishop in the early part of 1305, the annalist of London wrote that Winchelsey submitted to the king's grace saving the rights of his church and of his office ('salvo iure ecclesie sue et status sui') and that all matters were postponed until the next parliament.[159] We cannot know whether the annalist had precise 'matters' in mind. Although Winchelsey was, in a sense, submitting himself to the king's grace in all these cases against him *coram rege*, each of the cases, as we have seen, requires separate study. The suits against the archbishop for contravening writs of prohibition in relation to the dispute with St Augustine's Canterbury and in relation to the Ferrers plea against the earl of Lancaster were still being adjourned from term to term in the king's bench,[160] as was

---

[158] *Reg.*, p. 801 (and *Reg. Geynesborough*, p. 21) and *The Chartulary of Worcester Priory*, ed. R. R. Darlington (Pipe Roll Soc., new ser. xxxviii), no. 496 (as *CPR 1301–7*, p. 361).
[159] *Annales London.*, p. 137.   [160] Above pp. 182–3, 206.

also a suit concerning St Martin-le-Grand. We might well wonder whether there was any major political advantage to be gained by all these attacks upon the archbishop in the royal courts. Cases could be won for the king (as concerning St Oswald's and concerning the church of Dodderhill) or terminated without judgment if the king and his advisers chose (as concerning the 1297–8 grant of taxation) or delayed if the king and his advisers chose (as concerning Hastings). It is true that the archbishop's temporalities were always vulnerable – though when they had been seized in 1297, this action had, in fact, strengthened Winchelsey's political position. The London annalist was certainly right to imply that the Crown's attack upon the archbishop, launched early in 1305, had been postponed. It was difficult to find an issue upon which Winchelsey had acted blatantly and without justification, from the Church's point of view, against the rights of the Crown; and, although there was no doubt a good deal of gerrymandering in the royal courts in order to favour the interests of the king and his clerks, there are no clear indications that outlandish and unsupportable charges were being trumped up against the archbishop. The ground had been prepared for further action later in the year. Winchelsey was in disgrace. It was surely for reasons of expediency that some mercy was being shown.[161] The king had also deferred action in relation to the statute (later the Statute of Carlisle of 1307) proposed in the Lenten parliament forbidding the export of money from monasteries of the realm to their Orders or to their mother houses abroad. It has sometimes been assumed that Winchelsey successfully opposed this statute in 1305, but, as Maitland observed, 'the reasons for the delay are not obvious'.[162]

It is possible, indeed likely, that Edward was awaiting with special interest the decision of the cardinals meeting at Perugia.

---

[161] Mercy was also shown in the remarkable case of Nicholas de Segrave (an opponent of the king in 1297), who had recently left the war in Scotland in order to charge a fellow soldier to defend himself in the court of the king of France: see *Rot. Parl.*, I. 172–4, *Memo. de Parliamento*, pp. lxxvi–lxxvii, 255–64, *Flores Hist.*, III. 121–2, Prestwich, *War, Politics and Finance*, p. 250, Powicke, *Thirteenth Century*, pp. 331–3 and Bellamy, *Law of Treason*, p. 57.
[162] T. F. Tout in *DNB*, LXII. 160a and Emden, *Oxford*, p. 2058b; see *Memo. de Parliamento*, p. li, Stubbs, *Constitutional Hist.*, II. 163 and *Councils*, p. 1232.

Benedict XI had died in July 1304. There was a serious division in the Sacred College, essentially between the pro-French and the pro-Boniface VIII factions, and a protracted vacancy was the result.[163] At one point the English Dominican cardinal and royal confessor, Walter Winterbourne, was a strong candidate. The period immediately before Boniface VIII's pontificate, and the period immediately after, had witnessed the seizure by Edward I of papal taxes. But no papal tenths had been granted during Benedict XI's brief pontificate, and, although the king continued to collect the arrears of the tenths imposed by Boniface VIII,[164] there was no new papal money in England to seize during the 1304–5 vacancy. Ever since 1297 it had proved difficult for Edward to tax directly both the laity and the clergy; and he had not succeeded in his effort to 'live of his own'. From a purely financial point of view a conciliatory pope would be more than welcome to the king; and it was a decidedly conciliatory pope who was elected on 5 June 1305.

The appointment to the papal see of Bertrand de Got as Clement V was an event of far-reaching significance not simply for the Church but also for the kingdoms of France and England. Since 1299 Bertrand had been archbishop of Bordeaux, the leading prelate of Edward's continental fief. It is not known whether Edward had been involved in any underhand scheming to secure the highest office for Bertrand, or, indeed, whether he had actively supported his candidature. The evidence for negotiations between the king and the archbishop of Bordeaux in April 1305 concerning an exchange of lands and castles is intriguing, but inconclusive.[165] But the king certainly had every reason to rejoice at the papal election. In his early career Bertrand had been active as one of the king's clerks in Gascony.[166] As the new pope himself stressed in a letter to the king, he had not forgotten that he had once been among the company of Edward's councillors.[167] The

---

[163] For the sources concerning the election see *Vitae Paparum*, ed. Baluze, ii. 31 and Ullmann, 'Curial exequies', p. 28 n. 2.
[164] Lunt, *Financial Relations*, p. 376.
[165] *Foedera*, i, ii. 971 and *Rôles Gascons*, iii. no. 4774.
[166] See Denton, 'Clement V's early career'.
[167] *Foedera*, i. ii. 981, from PRO SC7/11/12: 'consiliariorum tuorum utpote ascripti consortio'.

author of *Flores* tells us that a prophecy was discovered inscribed
in gold letters on one of Bordeaux's gates, describing the city as
'altera Roma'.[168]

News of the papal appointment reached England in thirteen
days, and the king immediately sent a deputation to the papal
court. The first major concession to Edward came very rapidly:
on 1 August Clement granted a tenth of the income of the English
clergy for each of the next seven years.[169] Some of the money was
earmarked for Queen Margaret and some for Prince Edward, but
the rest was to go directly to the king. It was noted that the money
was to be used for the welfare of the Holy Land. But, despite the
frequent references to a crusade in both papal and royal correspondence,[170] and however much the king may have wished to go on
crusade, it is very difficult to believe that it was seriously in his
mind in 1305. He gave no pledges, and the pope made no requirement that the money should be restored if it was not used for a
crusade.

This especially open-handed papal taxation of the clergy for the
king was the beginning of a new chapter in Anglo-papal relations.
In the late summer and autumn there are many signs of the
king's renewed self-confidence. It was a time for strong government and the reassertion of royal authority. The conflict with
Winchelsey had been postponed, and the next parliament, first
summoned for 15 July, was to meet on 15 September. Before it
met, London witnessed, on 23 August, the trial and execution of
the Scottish leader William Wallace, described by Langtoft as
'the master of the thieves'. Wallace's execution was notably brutal.
For his treason he was drawn from Westminster to the Tower and
from the Tower to Aldgate and through the centre of the city to
Smithfield; for his robberies and killings he was hanged and dis-
embowelled; for his injuries to the Church his entrails were
burned; and for his sedition his corpse was quartered, one part
sent to Newcastle-on-Tyne, another to Berwick, another to Stirling
and another to Beverley, and his head was impaled on London

168 *Flores Hist.*, III. 322 (and cited in Johnstone, *Edward of Carnarvon*, p. 103).
169 Lunt, *Financial Relations*, pp. 382–4, Denton, 'Clement V's early career',
   p. 312 and Trabut-Cussac, *Administration Anglaise en Gascogne*, pp. 129–30.
170 E.g. *Foedera*, I. ii. 973–4.

Bridge.[171] In parliament, three weeks later, work began on the new Ordinance for the government of Scotland, which was drawn up, apparently, after twenty days.[172] It will be recalled that Edward had given his oath that, when he was victorious in Scotland, he would fulfil the promises he had made in 1297.[173] In fact, at about the same time as the 'form of peace' was being prepared for Scotland, the king was proceeding with a comprehensive policy of resumption, which was designed to overturn the concessions wrung from him during the critical years 1297–1301 and to secure the dismissal of the archbishop of Canterbury. The September parliament was a meeting of only some prelates and magnates. Of the bishops, it seems that only Winchelsey, Bek (Durham), Langton (Coventry and Lichfield), Ghent (Salisbury), Gainsborough (Worcester) and Halton (Carlisle) were summoned.[174] Winchelsey, who was apparently not involved in the preparation of the Ordinance for Scotland, must have arrived in London long after the opening of parliament, for he had arranged for the consecration of John Langton as bishop of Chichester to take place at Canterbury on 19 September. The bishop of Worcester had declared his inability to attend the consecration in person because of his summons to parliament.[175]

The writer of *Flores* comments that, the negotiations concerning Scotland being complete, the time for keeping silent was passed.[176] One by one, we are told, those who had been involved in the 'conspiracy' against the king while he was in Flanders in 1297–8 were brought before the king and fined. But we certainly cannot be sure that the chronicler's story is true in every detail. He tells us that the first to come and make his peace with the king was Roger Bigod, earl marshal; yet, we know that, even though there had been later arrangements concerning the Bigod lands, the agreement with Roger Bigod had been arrived at three years

---

[171] Bellamy, *Law of Treason*, pp. 34–9, *Annales London.*, pp. 139–42, *Flores Hist.*, III. 123–4, 'Rishanger', pp. 225–6 and Langtoft, II. 363.
[172] Powicke, *Thirteenth Century*, pp. 712–13 and *Anglo-Scottish Relations*, ed. Stones, no. 33.
[173] Above, p. 184.
[174] *Parl. Writs*, I. ii. 159–60.
[175] *Canterbury Professions*, ed. Richter, p. 90 and *Reg. Geynesborough*, p. 24.
[176] *Flores Hist.*, III. 125–6. 'Rishanger', p. 227 is apparently derived from *Flores Hist.*

before.[177] Apart from Bigod and Winchelsey those involved in the 'conspiracy' of 1297–8 are unfortunately not named. Winchelsey came before the king last of all, and the *Flores* account of this interview between the king and his archbishop, which perhaps took place in mid-October 1305, deserves to be given in full, for it is a rare piece of reporting, to be compared with the account by the Evesham chronicler of the equally dramatic meeting between Edward and Winchelsey in March 1297.[178]

'The king charged the archbishop with the same offence [i.e. conspiring against him]. Blushing with shame Winchelsey offered his cap to Edward as an act of submission of himself and of all his goods to the king. Edward said to him, "The justice of your deed and judgment upon it should be decided, not by me, but by your episcopal peers." And he added, "How many times have I written to you when you were exercising your rights of visitation and taking action against the royal clerks residing at my court, and asked you out of reverence for me not to take proceedings against these clerks until the clamour of war died down, and you did not listen to me! Indeed, without regard for the appeals of the clerks, you deprived them of their churches in their absence. I have been well aware of your arrogant attitude, your hostility and your lack of mercy, for you have always set yourself against me in a contentious way." He levelled these and many other rebukes at him. At length, the archbishop was so overcome that he sought a blessing from the king. "This is not fitting, father," said the king, "for I ought to be blessed by you." And the archbishop blessed him there and then.'

It is a little difficult to believe in this blushing and submissive Winchelsey. The story of the abject priest who must nonetheless bless his king is told with effect, and perhaps for effect. But the strong possibility of hyperbole should not lessen our interest in the account. Edward felt, it seems, that Winchelsey should be judged by the bishops; it was a convenient point of view, for there are no indications in 1305–6 that the bishops – and certainly not the new

177 See McFarlane, 'Had Edward I a policy towards the earls?', p. 155, *CPR 1301–7*, pp. 317–18, 382 and above, p. 205. A copy of the agreement, with the earl's seal, was delivered for custody to the exchequer on 19 March 1305: PRO E159/78 m. 35 (and see 40d, 67d and /80 m. 11).
178 Above, p. 120.

bishop of Rome – would give support to the archbishop. There is not even any evidence that his friends among the suffragan bishops, the bishop of Salisbury and the bishop of Llandaff, spoke up for him. The chronicler picks out Winchelsey's treatment of the royal clerks as a particular bone of contention, and it *was* certainly one of the main issues between king and archbishop in 1305.[179] This fact gives added significance to the appointment of one of Edward's clerks as pope. The problem of the plurality, non-residence and non-ordination of royal clerks appears to have become particularly acute after the archbishop's visitations of the dioceses of London and Norwich in 1303 and 1304. The archbishop defied the king by continually summoning royal clerks before him in his court of audience. For example, four clerks (John of Sheffield, Ralph of Dalton, Walter Bacon and Peter of Dunwich), whose work included purveyance for the king's armies, were prosecuted by the archbishop, and against one of them, Ralph of Dalton, the archbishop's court issued a sentence in 1305 depriving him of one of his benefices.[180] In general, cases were not terminated and Winchelsey was allowing delays and respites. But the cases certainly continued into 1306, and they show that the archbishop was unwilling to give way on matters which, as he believed, were an essential part of the exercise of his duties. The case of John of Sheffield, who became sheriff of Northumberland in 1305, is instructive. The archbishop had decided not to sell the fruits of John's benefice, the church of Foulden, and on 1 March 1306 he appeared before the archbishop and gained consent to administer the fruits of his church until 11 June when he was to be present once again in the archbishop's court. But this far from satisfied the royal clerk, who wrote to Walter Langton pleading for assistance and claiming that he had not received the fruits of Foulden, his only benefice, for a whole year.[181] He told

---

[179] See PRO C47/22/11/75 (*Reg.*, pp. 1336-7), PRO SC1/21/84, *CCR 1302-7*, pp. 88, 193 and *Cal. Chanc. Warr.*, pp. 223-4.
[180] See *List of Documents Relating to the Household and Wardrobe: John to Edward I* (PRO Handbooks VII, HMSO, 1964), pp. 37-8; refs. to these men in Prestwich, *War, Politics and Finance;* and below, pp. 284-5.
[181] See Lambeth Palace Lib., MS 244, fos. 32v, 34r, *Reg.*, pp. 806, 808-9 and Fraser, *Bek*, esp. p. 196. John's letter, PRO SC1/31/12, was probably written after 1 March 1306, for it mentions the fact that John was to appear before the archbishop in June, which had been determined on 1 March. Prince Edward

Langton that Anthony Bek was obtaining a dispensation for him from the pope. Late in 1305 or early in 1306 Winchelsey started proceedings against another royal clerk, John of London, for molesting ecclesiastical possessions in the diocese of Winchester; the king claimed that John was supervising purveyance and was simply carrying out royal orders.[182] Serving to emphasise the fact that Winchelsey was not behaving in a submissive way towards the king, the archbishop, in addition, took no account of the king's desire that the archbishop of York, William Greenfield, should be allowed to have his cross carried before him throughout England.[183]

Whatever we make of the story in *Flores*, we know from other sources that October 1305 was a time for the detailed preparation of a new and extremely important mission to the pope which was concerned, among many other things, with the removal from office of Archbishop Winchelsey. Edward now had the opportunity to establish on a new footing not only his relations with the papacy but also his relations with his own Church. The large embassy, with the bishop of Coventry and Lichfield and the bishop of Worcester among its members, set out for the papal court on 24 October.[184] Some of the concessions which they were charged to obtain can be deduced from the succession of bulls which, as we shall see, were issued in Edward's favour late in 1305 and early in 1306. The embassy had departed in order to arrive at Lyons in time for the pope's coronation on 14 November. But work continued in London in preparation for the negotiations with Clement V. One very interesting development was the making of authenticated copies from the Crown's collection of papal bulls.[185] Transcripts of thirty-six bulls were sent to the envoys making their way to the papal court, and were later returned.[186] The record of these tran-

had pleaded with Winchelsey in 1305 that John of Sheffield and one of his own clerks should be allowed to exchange benefices, but Winchelsey seems to have heeded the prince no more than the king: *Letters of Prince Edward*, ed. Johnstone, pp. 84, 93, 146.

[182] *CCR 1302–7*, pp. 427–8, as also PRO E159/79 m. 71d.
[183] See *Foedera*, I. ii. 969 (*CCR 1302–7*, p. 312), *Reg.*, pp. 506–7 and *Literae Cantuar.*, I. 31.
[184] Denton, 'Clement V's early career', pp. 312–14.
[185] See Cheney, *Notaries Public*, pp. 57–9 and refs.
[186] *The Gascon Calendar of 1322*, ed. G. P. Cuttino (Camden, 3rd ser. LXX, 1949), no. 2029.

scripts leaving the king's wardrobe gives the general date as the month of October 1305, in the king's parliament at Westminster. This date, imprecise as it is, should not preclude the possibility that these transcripts included the whole batch of surviving notarial instruments dated at Westminster on 22, 26, 28, 31 October and 6 November.[187] The termination of the work of transcription is perhaps marked by the order of 7 November that all the papal bulls granted to the king and his predecessors which were in the custody of the treasurer should be delivered to the controller of the wardrobe and lodged in the Tower of London.[188] We know of thirty-two exemplified documents, but four of the bulls were copied twice. Looking at these twenty-eight bulls, which range in date from 1215 to 1301, it might well seem that only a few were relevant to Edward I's position in 1305.[189]

But we must avoid too narrow a view. The bulls as a whole give an indication of the extent of Anglo-papal co-operation during the thirteenth century. Despite deep clashes of interest between the papacy and the Crown, popes had intervened on many issues to give support to the king of England, and papal concessions of the past were quite frequently cited by the king to further his interests. The use to which papal letters were put as political propaganda could amount to the deliberate disregard of the intended limits of former papal grants. To give only two examples: Henry III had chosen to ignore the temporary and restricted nature of an in-hibition of 1245 in favour of royal chapels; and in his Manifesto of 12 August 1297 Edward I had referred for support to a bull of Clement IV which was concerned specifically and solely with the political problems caused by the baronial war of 1263–5.[190] And in any case the direct relevance, or at any rate significance, of many of the bulls transcribed in 1305 is not, in fact, difficult to show.

At a time when the king was eager to be released from the concessions and promises made between 1297 and 1301 it is not surprising that a transcript should be made of Clement IV's bull of 13 September 1265 which was an annulment of all the

---

[187] *PRO List and Indexes*, XLIX (HMSO, 1923), 277–8 and *Reg. Halton*, I. 252–3.
[188] Prynne, III. 1074 (*CCR 1302–7*, pp. 300–1).
[189] See Cheney, *Notaries Public*, p. 58 n. 4.
[190] See Denton, *Royal Chapels*, p. 93 and above, pp. 147–8.

agreements, grants and promises made to Simon de Montfort and his adherents.[191] The notarial exemplification preserved in Bishop Halton's register is that of Boniface VIII's important bull of 12 March 1301, which was the first indication from Boniface of a new mood of conciliation between himself and the king.[192] In effect, Edward was pleading in 1305 for an extension of the spirit of this recent bull. And it is interesting, in view of the current emphasis upon papal and clerical consent to taxation, to find a bull of 12 June 1247 being copied, for here Innocent IV was urging Henry III not to prevent papal taxation of the English Church: consent was required from the king.[193] The interest in concessions for royal clerks is understandable: transcripts were made, for example, of two bulls of Innocent IV on this matter, one relaxing sentences of excommunication on the king's servants and the other granting to Henry III's clerks an extended period of exemption from molestation for absenteeism and for not taking orders.[194] The bull of 27 May 1286, whereby the king was given the faculty to grant canonries in Gascony to six of his clerks there, was possibly a concession of some significance in the early career of Clement V.[195] In addition, as we might well expect in connection with a major deputation to the papacy, the exemplified bulls indicate the great anxiety felt in England about papal provisions and the usurpation of patronage rights: a number of the 1305 transcripts were of bulls which had made concessions concerning both provisions and pluralism, and the Crown was even giving emphasis, it seems, to the 1215 papal confirmation of the famous grant by King John of free elections to churches.[196] We need not doubt that the king saw himself as defending what he regarded as the true interests not only of the Crown but also of his magnates and prelates.

This evidence relating to the mission to Clement V is particularly revealing of the thoughts of the king and his supporters on

[191] PRO SC7/10/18 and Potthast, no. 19340.
[192] Above, p. 201.
[193] PRO SC7/36/6, Potthast, no. 12559 and *Foedera*, I. i. 266.
[194] 22 June 1246: PRO SC7/36/3 and /4 (Potthast, no. 12174); and 27 Sept. 1252: SC7/36/2 (Potthast, no. 14722).
[195] PRO SC7/18/22.
[196] PRO SC7/36/1, /4, /6, /7 (a total of seven bulls of Innocent IV), and SC7/64/22 (30 March 1215).

the right relationship of the Crown and the Church. Although the opinions and beliefs of bishops like Walter Langton and William Gainsborough, two of the members of the mission, are more elusive than those of the canonical rigorists and doctrinaires we must not suppose that they were less firmly or less sincerely held. Nor must we suppose that distrust of the high-minded fight for clerical liberty was to be found among only a small minority of the English ecclesiastical hierarchy. The papal bulls that the Crown collected, preserved, cited and copied provide telling indications of the direction and aims of royal government, which was, of course, dependent for its effectiveness upon the active adherence, if not full-time commitment, of many of the most eminent clergy of the day. The patron saint of the 'royalists' was the king–saint Edward the Confessor, and four of the bulls copied in 1305 concerned the celebration of the feast days of St Edward.[197]

Another development early in November 1305 must be recorded. It appears that the Crown had its own view of the kind of English prelate who deserved canonisation, for in August 1305 the king had told Bishop Swinfield of Hereford that he intended to petition the pope for the canonisation of Thomas Cantilupe, bishop of Hereford 1275–82, who had been, as Edward pointed out, 'of our council'. Powicke succinctly described Cantilupe: 'an austere and cultivated aristocrat, lavish and courtly.... Witnesses to his sanctity during the process of canonisation recalled how he had turned the enjoyment of his pluralities into a gracious ministry.'[198] The king asked for, and of course received, assistance from the bishop and chapter of Hereford, so that the case could be prepared in the autumn parliament of 1305.[199] The timing of the king's application to the pope was no accident. In letters to Clement V and the cardinals dated 2 and 4 November the king pleaded the case of Cantilupe and, possibly at the same time, a petition was also sent from the earls.[200] There is no

[197] PRO SC7/36/2, /4 and /6.
[198] Powicke, *Thirteenth Century*, pp. 488–9.
[199] *Reg. Swinfield*, pp. 420–1, 440–1, *Antient Kalendars*, I. 83 and *Reg. Halton*, I. 235.
[200] *Foedera*, I. ii. 976 and see 985 (*CCR 1302–7*, pp. 354, 436), and *Liber de Bury*, nos. 29, 37.

indication that Winchelsey supported the petition, and this is not surprising for, although Cantilupe had enjoyed a very varied career and had been certainly a man of considerable learning and of concern for his pastoral duties, he had also been an adviser of the king and a bitter opponent of Archbishop Pecham. Despite Cantilupe's adherence to the baronial party in 1264–5, for which he was pardoned,[201] veneration for him was surely not akin to the common veneration of opponents of the Crown.[202] Here the conversion was in the direction of co-operation with the king. Cantilupe was one of the few successful English candidates for approved sanctity: he was canonised by John XXII in 1320.[203] It is undeniable that political factors affected directly the outcome of processes for canonisation, and offending an archbishop was, it seems, less damaging than offending either the papacy or the Crown.

In August 1306 Clement V instituted an inquiry into the life and miracles of Thomas Cantilupe. In the months before this the pope had been making one concession after another to Edward I. The king's person and the king's chapels were protected from all sentences of excommunication, suspension or interdict except on the pope's own mandate and by the pope's special licence; and a whole batch of bulls gave dispensations for plurality, non-residence and non-ordination to clerks in royal service.[204] One notable dispensation for plurality was granted on 7 February 1306 to Walter Reynolds, treasurer of the wardrobe of Prince Edward, future bishop of Worcester, royal chancellor and archbishop of

[201] *CPR 1258–66*, p. 549.
[202] See Russell, 'Canonization of opposition to the king' and above, pp. 20–1.
[203] See *Acta Sanctorum: Octobris*, I (Antwerp, 1765), 539–705, *Vitae Paparum*, ed. Baluze, II. 240–1, III. 198–9, L-H. Labande, 'Le cérémonial romain de Jacques Cajétan', *Bibliothèque de l'École des Chartes*, LIV (1893), 55–9, *Registrum Thome de Cantilupo*, ed. R. G. Griffiths and W. W. Capes (CYS, 1907), pp. lii–lviii, A. T. Bannister, *The Cathedral Church of Hereford* (London, 1924), pp. 167–75, *Reg. Swinfield*, pp. 234–5, 428, 430, *Reg. Gandavo*, pp. 247–53, *Reg. Woodlock*, pp. 179–80, Douie, *Pecham*, pp. 192–200 and D. Douie, 'The canonization of St Thomas of Hereford', *The Dublin Review*, ccxxix (1955), 275–87.
[204] Denton, *Royal Chapels*, pp. 146–7, Denton, 'Clement V's early career', p. 313, and, for further examples, Cuttino, *English Diplomatic Administration*, p. 38 n. 3 and *Reg.*, pp. 1192–3.

Canterbury.[205] So, with papal backing Edward was countering his archbishop's attack upon the privileges claimed for royal free chapels and royal clerks. More than this, the king was countering every major aspect of Winchelsey's policies towards the Crown, especially the archbishop's support for *Confirmatio Cartarum* and his resistance to the royal taxation of the clergy. Indeed, on 29 December 1305 Clement had released Edward from his sworn oath to observe *Confirmatio Cartarum*.[206] The terms of this papal declaration deserve careful study, not so much because this retreat, with papal support, from the grants and promises of 1297 can be shown to have been of great political moment in the relative calm of 1306–7, but rather because the bull reflects the king's attitude towards the political opposition which he had faced. Of the king's leading political opponents Winchelsey alone remained a snake in the grass.

For once the preamble in this bull addressed to Edward is no more extravagant in phraseology than the content deserves: 'It is a fitting and merited reward for the integrity of your majesty's devotion in the execution of the wishes of the apostolic see, that this see should remove what is obnoxious to you, abolish what is troublesome and procure what is profitable.' The bull relates the events of 1297 and shortly after, a story which must have been obtained from the royal envoys: the king in 1297 had gone to Flanders to defend his rights against many enemies; no small number of magnates, nobles and other men who opposed him took advantage of his absence, conspired against him, incited the people and spread many scandals, so that he had to make various unjust concessions – which they had sought from him with importunity before he left the kingdom – concerning the forests and other rights belonging to the Crown of old; he made these grants more under compulsion than willingly, and wisely circumvented the machinations of his opponents, wishing to avoid danger; when he returned, the same magnates and others obtained from him, by annoying and presumptuous insistence, a renewal of

---

[205] *Reg. Clement V*, no. 315, C. Burns, 'Sources of British and Irish History in the Instrumenta Miscellanea in the Vatican Archives', *Archivum Historiae Pontificiae*, ix (1971), p. 31, LRO Reg. iii (Dalderby), fo. 115r and Johnstone, *Edward of Carnarvon*, pp. 20–1, 75–6, 99–101.

[206] *Foedera*, i. ii. 978 and *Chartes des Libertés*, ed. Bémont, pp. 110–12.

the concessions, having produced royal letters ordering that a sentence of excommunication should be promulgated twice a year in all the cathedral churches of the realm against all those infringing the aforesaid concessions. The pope declared the concessions, and the sentences of excommunication promulgated for their observance, to be null and void. But it is not obvious what this papal annulment amounted to, for the story which it tells is not in fact a clear one. The concessions to which it refers appears to be no more and no less than *Confirmatio Cartarum*, though there is no record of its terms actually being renewed after 1297. Since the bull mentions only one set of concessions it does not seem to have included, unless by implication, the *Articuli super Cartas* of 1300 or the concessions of 1301 especially concerning the forests,[207] even though there are, as we shall see, sound reasons for believing that Edward was intent upon revoking all that he had conceded. The specific terms, if not the spirit and content, of *Confirmatio Cartarum* had been ignored after 1297–8 and were to some extent superseded by the grants of 1300–1. And the reference in the bull to the sentence of excommunication is curious, for, apart from a short-lived initial attempt by Winchelsey, *Confirmatio Cartarum* had *not* been protected by the promulgation of sentences. It was *Magna Carta* and the Charter of the Forest that had been so protected. All in all, it looks as though the king's envoys in 1305 had persuaded the pope that Edward had given way to the particular demands of his opponents in 1297, and honoured his acceptance of those demands, rather more than had actually been the case.

Even so, *Confirmatio Cartarum* with its emphasis upon consent to taxation had certainly had important and long-term political effects. While these could hardly be reversed by a papal bull, the difficulties which Edward had experienced after 1297, especially in attempting to avoid the need to tax both the clergy and the laity, were probably strongly in his mind in 1305–6. And we cannot help but link the annulment of *Confirmatio* with Clement's revocation on 1 February 1306 of that other major document concerned with consent to taxation, 'Clericis laicos',

[207] Cf. Denton, 'Clement V's early career', pp. 312–13.

which the pope declared had caused, and would continue to cause unless revoked, dangerous disruption and bitterness.[208] In order to obtain the annulment of *Confirmatio*, and also perhaps of 'Clericis laicos', the king's envoys had, of course, presented a one-sided view of the king's relations with and responsibilities towards his barons; for us to support Edward in thus defending his 'sovereign' rights would be equally one-sided.[209] Edward had a case to present and a cause to defend. So had Winchelsey.

Linked with the revocation of 'Clericis laicos' and *Confirmatio* was the suspension of the archbishop of Canterbury from office. Winchelsey, who was engaged in the visitation of the diocese of Winchester from 8 November to 25 February, had written on 2 January to the cardinals John Monachus and Richard Petroni, pleading for their assistance, since he had heard that the pope had recently made statements to the archbishop's proctors which threatened his position and which, he claimed, had no basis in truth, and he informed the cardinals that he was sending Walter of Thorpe and William of Dunbridge to the papal court.[210] Walter of Thorpe, dean of the Arches, apparently left London on 9 January.[211] But Winchelsey's pleading was all to no avail. The pope's letter of suspension, which cited the archbishop to appear before him, is dated 12 February 1306, and, as a letter of Clement's of 1313 reveals,[212] it granted exactly what Edward at this stage requested. It was addressed, in the surviving copies, not to the archbishop himself, but to those charged with informing him of his suspension and with citing him to appear personally before the pope within two months. The addressees in the two otherwise identical bulls were, on the one hand, the abbots of St Augustine's Canterbury and Westminster, and, on the other, Arnaud Lupi de Tilio, royal clerk, and Radulph Bria.[213] Clement

---

[208] Denton, 'Reynolds and ecclesiastical politics', pp. 250–1.

[209] Cf. Powicke, *Thirteenth Century*, pp. 703–4.

[210] *Reg.*, pp. 679–80, 1348 and see 1329.

[211] *Annales London.*, p. 144: and on 14 Jan. Bishop Salmon of Norwich left London to further his case at the papal court (with eventual success) against Winchelsey's attempts to prevent him from collecting first-fruits in his diocese (*Reg. Clement V*, no. 1288 and above, p. 48).

[212] Richardson, 'Clement V and Canterbury', p. 101 (from BL Add. 6159, fo. 150) and Denton, 'Canterbury archiepiscopal appointments', p. 325 n. 13 (from Paris, Bibliothèque Nationale, MS Nouv. Acq. Latin 321, fo. 8r).

[213] *Annales London.*, p. 145 and BL Add. 43972, fo. 76v; and Somner,

V's explanation of his actions, before the *mandamus* clause of the bull, is remarkable:

The higher the place attained in the Church of God by our venerable brother the archbishop of Canterbury, if he merits to be called venerable, the more he should walk in the paths of pontifical modesty by taking the greatest possible care that he does not commit those things which provoke against him divine majesty and the apostolic see. We observe indeed in him many perversities, and, though there are reasons for maintaining silence about them at the present, conscience presses upon us the need not to ignore them, but rather to show our concern by taking action to correct them, for while the excesses of prelates remain uncorrected so reprehensibly, the more easily do those under them take their actions as an example.

The new pope was preaching conciliation and compromise. Winchelsey was in effect accused of being a political extremist. Both now and later Clement's letters reflected the king's view of the archbishop. Winchelsey was seen as the perpetrator of vicious policies and perverse acts which brought great damage and increasing offence to the king and the kingdom. In view of the archbishop's intransigence the terms of this attack are perhaps not surprising. But, however we judge Clement, he was not simply acting as Edward's instrument. Because of his early career the pope probably had a firm understanding of the political position of the clergy in England. He was surely making a positive decision against strict sacerdotalism in England and against the fight for clerical liberty which Winchelsey had led. His main aim was to establish peace in, and between, England and France so that he would be able to fight, not the secular powers in the west, but rather the infidel in the east.

The news of his suspension was conveyed to Winchelsey on 25 March by Walter of Thorpe, now returned from the papal court.[214] He immediately appealed to the king for clemency (not it seems to the pope), but his appeal only occasioned from Edward, on 6 April, a very strongly worded protest against the archbishop

Antiquities, pt. II. app. p. 31 from Cant. D. & C., Reg. Q, fo. 43. For Arnaud see *Letters of Prince Edward*, ed. Johnstone, p. 3.
214 Somner, *Antiquities*, pt II, app. p. 31.

addressed to Clement and to four cardinals.[215] The king declared
that considering the ill-will of Winchelsey he knew of nothing
that would so much hinder his journey to the Holy Land as the
archbishop's stay within the realm. The flavour of this strident
letter can be quickly conveyed: 'We caused answer to be made to
the archbishop that he had borne himself to us in such wise in the
past and had without cause procured and committed against us
injuries and shameful and despicable acts, and through those
working for him and representing him our realm had been not
long ago so disturbed that it was not the archbishop's fault that we
were not wholly disinherited.' One of the cardinals to whom
Edward wrote in these terms was Thomas Jorz, the king's
Dominican chaplain. Jorz was a member of the king's embassy to
Clement and had been made a cardinal on 15 December 1305 in
succession to Walter Winterbourne, who had died on 26 August
1305.[216] The king's case against Winchelsey, that the archbishop's
plotting against him almost resulted in his downfall, came close to
a charge of treason. This is exactly how it was described ('proditio')
by William Thorne in his colourful account of Winchelsey's
disgrace, derived probably from the work of an earlier and contemporary author. But in his joy at the archbishop's undoing this
chronicler of St Augustine's abbey went too far in making his own
accusations. Winchelsey, he wrote, 'had plotted to expel the king
from the throne of his kingdom and put his son Edward on
the throne and deliver the father to lifelong imprisonment...
throughout the whole realm of England he had by the pride of his
lips, like a harlot, brought disgrace on the priesthood and the
clergy, exercised unheard of tyranny over the people, and refused
in his pride, when writing to the king, to name him in letters as
his lord....'.[217] There appears to have been some truth in this last
accusation, for in Winchelsey's less formal letters to Edward the
address omits the title of 'seignur' which Pecham had used in

[215] Prynne, III. 1092–3 (*CCR 1302–7*, pp. 430–1), *Foedera*, I. ii. 983 and *Liber de Bury*, p. 342.
[216] See *Vitae Paparum*, ed. Baluze, II. 43–4, 496–7, Ch. V. Langlois, 'Documents relatifs à l'histoire du xiii⁰ et du xiv⁰ siècle', *Revue Historique*, LXXXVII (1905), 68–71 (printing PRO SC1/15/182, /15/183, /16/117 and /21/149) and Hinnebush, *Early English Friars Preachers*, passim.
[217] Thorne, p. 387 (trans. of *Scriptores Decem*, p. 2004).

comparable letters.[218] There appears to have been some truth, too, in Thorne's report that the pope promised to 'everyone desiring to complain of the archbishop that he would do them justice'. While Thorne, of course, betrays a spirit of *parti pris*, the case he presented against Winchelsey was probably very similar to the one which the king's envoys had presented to the pope. Winchelsey's political opposition had been severe enough to be regarded by some as traitorous. By a papal alliance the king had found an extremely peaceful way of ridding himself of this particular 'turbulent priest'.

The king scarcely needed to reinforce, in his letter of 6 April, his case against Winchelsey, for the pope had already taken action; and the archbishop's pleas to cardinals for assistance in March and April were too late.[219] But the bull of suspension was not formally delivered to Winchelsey for several weeks, and he continued to act as archbishop.[220] A Canterbury chronicler tells us that the clerk entrusted to deliver the bull was overcome by the nature of his mission and 'at the request of friends' delayed presentation of the bull.[221] Nevertheless, the archbishop was planning to leave England, for, by early April at the latest, he paid the tribute of forty marks to the count of Boulogne to enable him to cross to Wissant.[222] On 11 April royal orders went out to prevent the arch-

218 Compare Winchelsey's letters in French (*Reg.*, pp. 810–11, 1336–7 and PRO SC1/21/84) with Pecham's (e.g. *Reg Epistolarum Peckham*, i. 72, 109, 111).
219 *Reg.*, pp. 1348–9.
220 There appears to be no letter extant from Winchelsey as Edward I's archbishop after one dated 2 May 1306: BL Harl. 1761, fo. 69r.
221 BL Harl. 636, fo. 230v: 'Si vint de ceo la bulle tost en Engletere, et la conisaunce privee de cele notefiee fust a celi erceveske. Mes le clerke ke la porta taunt de sueaute en la bosoigne [...] fist a la requeste de amys ke cele pronuncier ne voloit, tant ke a Dovre fust lerceveske venu en la priurie hostile sun chemyn devers la curt esploytaunt la xiiii kalende de Jun le iour seynt Donstan, ilukes en la chambre le priur cele bulle primes au dit erceveske pronuncia et cil tauntost le rochet et le anel de li hosta et puys en la vespree la mer passa.'
222 See *Literae Cantuar.*, iii. 387–8, Douie, *Pecham*, p. 53 and Somner, *Antiquities*, pt ii, app. p. 19 from Cant. D. & C., Reg. Q, fo. 31v (trans. by W. P. Blore, *Canterbury Cathedral Chronicle*, xxviii (1937), pp. 10–12). Both the archbishop and the bishop of Rochester were omitted from the enrolled list of those summoned by writs (issued on 5 April) for the parliament of 30 May; but both apparently sent proxies: see *Parl. Writs*, i. ii. 164 and D. Pasquet, *An Essay on the House of Commons* (Cambridge, 1925), p. 235, printing PRO E368/76 m. 50, and see E159/79 m. 40. *Annales London.*, p. 146, has the bishop of Rochester there in person.

bishop from taking money or treasure in mass out of the realm, and a week later the sheriffs of the south-eastern counties were instructed to seize all his goods.[223] Winchelsey travelled to Dover, where on 18 May in the priory of St Martin he was at last formally presented with the bull suspending him and summoning him before the pope.[224] Before dawn on 19 May he set sail. The man who less than twelve months before had been the archbishop of Bordeaux had brought about his downfall, but the achievement, if it should be so described, belonged to Edward. As if to demonstrate to all the difference between a prelate deeply in disgrace and a politically successful prelate, Winchelsey's friend Anthony Bek, bishop of Durham, crusader and royal clerk, who had been recently created patriarch of Jerusalem by Clement V, arrived in London from the papal court two days before Winchelsey set out from Dover. Bek was too independent to be always in royal favour, but, whether Winchelsey was in office or not, the bishop of Durham could now regard himself with some justification as the senior prelate in England.[225] Winchelsey had not been deprived of office because of a short-term jurisdictional conflict, easily resolved; rather, the issues were long-term and fundamental, and Edward was bent on never having him back.

Winchelsey left England very quietly indeed. He was powerless to act against his suspension. He had been upright, conscientious, consistent in his policies and always concerned about the welfare of the realm; but, though he had not been an underhand or malicious schemer, in his relations with the king he was not a man to compromise his conscience. He may have been too stern to be liked by many, and Anthony Bek was apparently the only man to plead for him against the king and the pope.[226] The issues for which Winchelsey had fought were very far from dead, but in 1306 they were not major issues of the moment, and the chroniclers have very little to say about his dismissal. Guisborough

---

[223] *CCR 1302–7*, p. 375 and *CFR*, I. 536. Three of the archbishop's household clerks, Simon de Greyelle, John Mansel and Robert Crul, were charged in the exchequer with holding on to goods of the archbishop worth 1,000 marks, but were acquitted: PRO E159/79 m. 43d and /80 m. 27d.

[224] Somner, *Antiquities*, pt. II, app. p. 31 from Cant. D. & C., Reg. Q, fo. 43r.

[225] See Fraser, *Bek*, pp. 165, 200–1.

[226] Richardson and Sayles, 'Parliament of Carlisle', p. 437.

tells us a good deal about trailbaston, and about Clement V, and also about Anthony Bek, but not a word at this juncture about Winchelsey.[227] Some chroniclers note his suspension briefly, but do not mourn his departure.[228] At Canterbury there was certainly the delight of the St Augustine's chronicler, but only a few signs of anger from the cathedral priory. The only reference to the suspension in a large letter-book belonging to the prior, Henry of Eastry, is a note in a later hand;[229] and all that apparently remains among the extant archives of the dean and chapter of Canterbury to relate the attack upon their archbishop in the spring of 1306 is a formal memorandum, with the statement that the suspension took place without any hearing of the case.[230] One surviving Canterbury chronicle did, however, see the suspension as an evil act and recalled the archbishop's protection of spiritualities in the face of the grievous exactions of the king.[231] In addition, Rishanger says that Winchelsey had in fact acted 'from a good and clear conscience'.[232] But the Canterbury biographer, probably writing in the third quarter of the fourteenth century, provides the most ardent defence of Winchelsey's innocence, accusing the king of malice and hatred and declaring his amazement that the archbishop should have been charged to answer for excesses against the holy see and the holy canons.[233] Indeed, despite the terms of Clement's bull, it would be very difficult to interpret Winchelsey's 'excesses' as directed against the Church or the papacy.

The parliament which met at Westminster very shortly after Winchelsey's departure was concerned with the granting of an aid, a thirtieth and twentieth, for the knighting of Prince Edward and for the Scottish war, now renewed because of the rebellion of Robert Bruce.[234] The prince was knighted, along with over a

227 Guisborough, pp. 359–66; and the annals of Worcester are also silent.
228 *Flores Hist.*, III. 130, *Annales London.*, p. 145, Trivet, p. 407, BL Arundel 56, fo. 75r and Cont. Gervase, p. 324.
229 CUL Ee. v. 31, fo. 104.
230 'absque aliqua cause cognitione prehabita': Somner, *Antiquities*, pt II, app. p. 31 from Cant. D. & C., Reg. Q, fo. 43r.
231 BL Harl. 636, fo. 230v.   232 Rishanger, p. 421.
233 *Anglia Sacra*, I. 16.
234 For this assembly see H. G. Richardson and G. O. Sayles, *Parliaments and Great Councils in Medieval England* (London, 1961), pp. 24–30, reprinted from *Law Quarterly Review*, LXXVII (1961), 401–7: they did not regard it as a 'parliament'.

hundred others.[235] The lower clergy were not represented in the parliament and the three bishops who attended in person,[236] Anthony Bek, Walter Langton, and Ralph Baldock, can all be described as *curiales*. There was no question of taxing the clergy directly on their spiritualities; they were in any case being taxed for the king by papal mandate. But it is essential to note that the new lay tax *was* a tax on all the temporalities of the clergy, not, it seems, just on those temporalities excluded from the 1291 assessment of clerical income.[237] The distinction between spiritualities and temporalities which the king had insisted on making between 1301 and 1303, but which Winchelsey had strongly opposed, apparently held firm for this occasion too, and once again the prelates and religious houses appear to have been taxed on their temporalities both for the papal tenth and for the tax on movable property. The king's message still was that the ecclesiastical wealth classed as 'temporal' was under royal control. With Winchelsey absent no one, it seems, complained.

It is certain from events at the time of this parliament that the papal annulment of the king's concessions in 1297 and after was being interpreted as the annulment of the perambulations of the forest conceded in 1301. The author of *Flores*, when describing the bull's publication in early April, referred to it as an absolution from the oath concerning disafforestation.[238] The executors of the bull, appointed by the pope, were the king's treasurer, Walter Langton, and the ex-royal chancellor, William Greenfield, archbishop of York (both of whom were appointed by the king to act as his regents while he was in Scotland),[239] and in May and June these two prelates were ordering publication of the bull annulling the king's concessions in the dioceses of the two ecclesiastical provinces, and their efforts were seen as the revocation of the conceded disafforestation.[240] Disafforestation had been forced upon the king as the implementation of the terms of the Charter of the Forest, and the king had agreed, too, to the promulgation

---

[235] *Flores Hist.*, III. 131–2 and *Annales London.*, p. 146.
[236] See above, p. 234 n. 222.   [237] Willard, *Parliamentary Taxes*, pp. 101–2.
[238] *Flores Hist.*, III. 130.   [239] PRO E159/79 m. 41d.
[240] *Foedera*, I. ii. 979, *Reg. Gandavo*, pp. 209–11, PRO E315/35/248, *Historical MSS Commission: The MSS of Lincoln etc.* (14th Rep., app. VIII, 1895), pp. 231–3, *Annales London.*, p. 146 and *Reg. Halton*, I. 264–7.

of sentences of excommunication against anyone infringing the Charter. In his Ordinance of 27 May 1306 concerning the forests specific reference is made by the king to the revocation of the disafforestation and to the revocation of the sentence of excommunication. In this new Ordinance, with its preamble as grandiloquent as a papal bull, the king declared his desire to follow the path of the Lord's commandments.[241] Whether or not the king had a 'duty' to maintain the charters is open to debate, but it is surely misleading to imply that Edward did not resent being forced to observe the charters: 'Edward had resented not his duty to observe the charters but the attempt to take advantage of his difficulties.'[242] Edward had only accepted the renewal of the charters in 1297–1301 with the greatest reluctance. And his difficulties and the fight for liberties had been part of the same story.

It is not clear from the terms of his bull that the pope understood which sentences of excommunication he had annulled. Edward knew that the only sentence of excommunication to which he had agreed had been against all infringers of the charters. And, whatever the ambiguities of the bull, we can be confident that the king now felt freed from his oath to observe the baronial demands of 1297–1301, as embodied especially in *Confirmatio Cartarum* and in the 'bill' presented to the Lincoln parliament. Winchelsey had been clearly associated with both. William Thorne made specific reference to the archbishop's opposition to Edward in the Lincoln parliament, and the archbishop's biographer noted that the king's enmity sprang from support which Winchelsey had given to the prelates and magnates who were petitioning for a perambulation of the forest and for other rights which the Crown had usurped.[243] The king's opponents had campaigned for perambulation and disafforestation in 1300–1 rather than in 1297–8. One other action in 1306, often noted, must be associated with the king's rejection of the concessions of January or February 1301:

---

[241] *Stat. Realm.* I. ii. 147–9, Prynne, III. 1141–2, and see Stubbs, *Constitutional Hist.*, II. 162, *Select Pleas of the Forest*, ed. G. J. Turner (Selden Soc., XIII, 1901), p. cv, Ch. Petit-Dutaillis and G. Levebvre, *Studies Supplementary to Stubbs* (Manchester, 1930), pp. 225–7 and *Eng. Hist. Documents*, III. 921.

[242] Powicke, *Thirteenth Century*, p. 703.

[243] Thorne, pp. 365, 388 and *Anglia Sacra*, I. 16.

Henry of Keighley, who had been the bearer of the 'bill' presented
by the prelates and barons, and for whom the king said that he
had searched a long time, spent a brief spell in the Tower during
the summer of 1306.[244]

The Anglo-papal alliance had brought considerable advantages
to Edward, but they must not be exaggerated. While the annulment of concessions was not a paper victory, it seems to have
amounted to little, in practical terms, beyond the reversal of the
policy of disafforestment. There was apparently no declared
intention of going back on the concessions, for example, concerning prises. Indeed, as a result of petitions at the parliament of
Carlisle early in 1307, the king agreed in principle to make full
amends for prises, during the period 1294–7, for which no payment had yet been made, and reimbursements were approved,
too, for money and treasure taken as a result of the scrutiny of
religious houses in 1294.[245] The departure of Winchelsey brought
the Crown and the papacy into much closer contact than was
usual, and the difficulties which this was to present to the king
were already becoming apparent quite early in 1306. Clement had
not made completely open-handed concessions, and agreement to
the papal tax of the first-fruits of all ecclesiastical benefices vacant
within the next three years had been part of the settlement with
the king.[246] It was a very unpopular tax. And the arrangements
for the administration of the see of Canterbury demonstrate the
inherent problems in the way of Crown and papacy working in
harmony.

Clement had suspended Winchelsey 'from the administration
of the church of Canterbury in spiritualities and temporalities'.

---

[244] Too much can be made of this, though we can hardly doubt the direction of
Keighley's sympathies: the evidence tells us only that this knight of the shire
had 'carried' the 'bill', which had been 'pressed outrageously' upon the king
in the parliament of Lincoln by Winchelsey (here named perhaps because of
seniority) and the other members of the baronial committee. See esp. Madox,
Hist. of Exchequer, II. 108, *Eng. Hist. Documents*, III. 510, 522, Stubbs,
Constitutional Hist., II. 158, Powicke, *Thirteenth Century*, p. 704 and above,
p. 187.
[245] See PRO E159/80 mm. 14d, 18, 49, 54. The Knights Hospitallers made
their claim for repayment of the prise, in 1294, of £2,664 11s 4d (see above,
p. 69); but, in fact, they were still seeking remedy in 1314 (*Rot. Parl.*, I.
298–9).
[246] Lunt, 'First levy of papal annates'.

Had he then the accepted right to suspend the 'temporal disposition' as well as the 'spiritual jurisdiction'? He certainly believed so, for in bulls of 20 April he appointed, to administer the spiritualities, William Testa and William Géraud de Sore (Peter Amauvin replaced William Géraud in 1307), and at the same time he appointed, to administer the temporalities, none other than the king's treasurer, Bishop Langton.[247] However appealing the appointment of Langton may have been to the king, he would not accept it. The bull appointing Testa and Géraud was published on 6 June in the church of the Arches, London; but, when the second bull was revealed in the presence of the king, he declared that he would allow no one deputed by the pope to administer any temporalities in his realm, just as the pope did not permit the king to interfere concerning spiritualities. So he appointed, on 8 June, Humphrey de Waleden as custodian of the temporalities of the archbishopric. But this did not solve the problem, for Clement argued that the temporalities had been taken into the king's hands against the pope's will and in contravention of the holy canons.[248] Certainly, if the pope had the authority to waive the administration of the temporalities (at which the king had not complained), he could surely also dispose of the administration of the temporalities; it was essentially the same point at issue here as in the dispute between the king and the papacy (which had begun in 1299) concerning the clauses in bulls of provision bestowing upon bishops temporalities as well as spiritualities.[249] Edward was not, at first, willing to concede on

---

[247] See *Reg. Gandavo*, pp. 212–19, Cant. D. & C., Reg. Q, fo. 44, old fo. 32 (not all of which is printed in Somner, *Antiquities*, pt II, app. pp. 31–2), *Reg.*, p. xxv and *Councils*, p. 1230. In addition to refs in the latter, for the work of the papal administrators of the spiritualities see *Chertsey Cartularies*, I (Surrey Record Soc., XII, 1933), 34–5, Norwich, Dean & Chapter Muniments, Reg. I, fos. 242r–243v and Cartae nos. 1110, 2421 (noted briefly in *Norwich Charters*, ed. Dodwell, p. 170), and Cant. D. & C., Sede Vacante Scrapbooks, I. 178, Cartae Antiquae R18, and Reg. I, fo. 280. The pope had appointed administrators of both spiritualities and temporalities when Walter Langton had been suspended from the bishopric of Coventry and Lichfield in March 1302: *Reg. Boniface VIII*, no. 4637 (*CPL* I. 601) and *Historical MSS Commission: Fourteenth Report Appendix VIII* (1895), pp. 214–15.

[248] Prynne, III. 1095–7. Humphrey de Waleden was made a baron of the exchequer on 7 Nov. 1306: PRO E159/80 m. 27.

[249] *Councils*, pp. 1226–7 and Cheney, *Notaries Public*, pp. 59–60. And see Prynne, III. 1132.

what he saw as a basic matter of principle and of custom, but he made a conciliatory move in September and agreed that the fruits and profits of the temporalities during the suspension should be given to the pope, and he also conceded to the pope the authority 'to ordain concerning ecclesiastical benefices appertaining to the collation of the archbishop'. This went a long way to meeting the pope's demands, but not far enough, and Clement's continuing support was of great importance to the king. At length, in March 1307, the custody of the temporalities was handed over *in toto* to the administrators of the spiritualities.[250] Thus, the papal deputies, whom Prynne centuries later called the 'two Roman Harpyes', secured full control of the archbishopric.

Yet the papal deputies, together or singly, could not quite act as though they were the archbishop of Canterbury. Their presence created difficulties. Although papal delegates could not normally signify the royal chancery of contumacious excommunicates for capture, Testa did so as keeper of spiritualities;[251] but, on the other hand, the king seems to have been eager to prevent Testa and Géraud from taking purgations from clerks convicted in the royal courts.[252] There was confusion about the place of consecration of the bishop-elect of Bangor, and Testa, who exercised his office in London, was perhaps himself eager to prevent the consecration from taking place at Canterbury.[253] And conflict arose concerning the valuable church of Reculver, vacant because of the death of Simon of Faversham on 20 July 1306. Since the king held the temporalities of the see at that time, he presented to the church Nicholas of Tingewick, royal physician, and pleaded with Testa to institute Nicholas and with the pope to grant a dispensation to Nicholas so that he could hold Reculver along with the church of Coleshill, in the diocese of Salisbury; but Clement claimed, it seems unsuccessfully, the right of provision, since Simon of Faversham had died at the papal court.[254]

---

[250] See Prynne, III. 1179–80 and *Foedera*, I. ii. 1012 (*CPR 1301–7*, p. 512), and Madox, *Hist. of Exchequer*, II. 224.
[251] Logan, *Excommunication*, pp. 26–33 and PRO C85/7/16 and /18.
[252] *CCR 1302–7*, p. 403.
[253] See above, p. 52, and see W. E. L. Smith, *Episcopal Appointments*, p. 12.
[254] *CPR 1301–7*, p. 461, *CCR 1302–7*, p. 419, Prynne, III. 1096–7, 1155–6, Cant. D. & C., Cartae Antiquae R18 and *Reg.*, pp. 1044–6.

While these were relatively minor problems and disputes, it is surprising that a king who had staunchly defended royal rights should so easily accept papal delegates in control of the arch-bishopric of Canterbury. But it is even more surprising that the king tolerated a situation in which these same administrators of the see were also the appointed papal tax collectors. Testa and Géraud had been commissioned on 1 February 1306 to collect the new papal tax of annates, and Testa became general papal collector in England on 23 March, with responsibility for the collection of arrears of papal tenths, census, Peter's pence, procurations, legacies, pecuniary penalties and obventions.[255] Edward and his advisers – especially perhaps Walter Langton – must have been fully convinced of the benefits to the Crown of the new close relationship with the papacy, which was now, after all, a Gascon rather than a Roman papacy. But could the alliance last? A strong, indeed furious, attack against papal taxes and against William Testa manifested itself in the fully representative parliament held at Carlisle from January to March 1307.[256]

The petitions presented to the king against papal provisions and papal financial exactions were a vigorous defence of the English Church and of the rights of English patrons and benefactors. The Anglo-papal alliance had stirred up an intense opposition. The king was presented with arguments which he might well in different circumstances have used himself, concerning, for example, the loss of patronage caused by provisions and the dubious right of the papacy to tax temporalities.[257] While these anti-papal petitions of 1307 must be seen in the context of the current com-pliant policies of the king, they were in no way critical of the king's position in relation to the English Church. Indeed, they were formulated with the 'state of the Crown' very firmly in mind. Although some of the complaints were similar to ones which the clergy under Winchelsey's guidance had addressed to Boniface VIII in 1297 (as concerning Peter's pence and the

255 Lunt, *Financial Relations*, p. 621.
256 See esp. *Councils*, pp. 1231–6, Lunt, 'Testa and parliament of Carlisle', Richardson and Sayles, 'Parliament of Carlisle', and Guisborough, pp. 370–7.
257 For earlier statements of a similar kind on these two issues see *Councils*, p. 814, *Parl. Writs*, I. ii. 20, *Foedera*, I. ii. 740 (*CCR 1288–96*, pp. 134–5) and above, pp. 201–2.

collection of goods of intestates),[258] it cannot easily be argued that these petitions were the kind which Winchelsey, had he been present, would have been likely to initiate.

We must not, however, forget that the absent archbishop, and other like-minded prelates, now had good reason for strong anti-papal feeling. It would be misleading to label Winchelsey's political outlook, at any stage of his career, as 'papalist', and we must resist the simple belief that the reason for his exile was his 'insistence on exact obedience to papal executive mandates'.[259] Nonetheless, he had been able to combine successfully his whole-hearted concentration upon the well-being, as he saw it, of the English Church with respect for the head of the Church and for the canons of the Church. Clement V made a good balance between these responsibilities much more difficult for him, and others, to achieve. It is quite clear that, although the prelates did not openly associate themselves with the anti-papal complaints at Carlisle, the outcry had come from churchmen as well as laymen. The version of the petitions which was addressed to the pope rather than the king came, so the document states, from 'the clergy and the people'.[260] There is a very strongly ecclesiastical flavour, too, in that lively piece of propaganda which appeared at the parliament under the pseudonym 'Peter son of Cassiodorus'.[261] It is strange that this letter addressed to the English Church should have been dismissed as unimportant. The suggestion has been made that Guisborough was perhaps wrong when he wrote that it was read before the king, the cardinal (Peter of Spain), and all the prelates, for 'important people do not waste their time with tedious and obscure arguments put forward by pseudonymous writers of open letters'.[262] The letter is rhetorical, but it is neither tedious nor obscure. It is linked in content with the petitions, mentioning as it does the papal tenth, the tax on first-fruits, and the claim upon the goods of intestates, and it achieved a wide circulation. It is a spirited piece of polemical writing against

[258] See *Councils*, pp. 1182–5 and Graham, 'A petition to Boniface VIII'.
[259] Fraser, *Bek*, p. 202.   [260] *Rot. Parl.*, I. 207.
[261] For MS copies see *Councils*, p. 1232 n. 7, BL Cotton Vesp. B xi, fos. 58r–59r and Cotton Galba E x, fo. 70r; and for comment see Cheney, 'Law and letters in Durham', pp. 68–9.
[262] Richardson and Sayles, 'Parliament of Carlisle', p. 431.

Clement V, deploring the removal of good pastors and appointment of unlettered relatives to high office, and declaring that the priesthood, divine service and the giving of alms were being overthrown. The beliefs that lie behind this attack cannot have been far removed from those of Winchelsey, the defender of the priesthood, of spiritualities and of cure of souls. But we can perhaps see in the outburst at Carlisle a reason for the lack of any notable support for the exiled Winchelsey in 1306–7. His opposition had been to the king and to the policies of royal government. But to the pseudonymous writer Edward was the most Christian king. In 1307 the threat to the English Church was seen to come, not in fact from Edward, but from the papacy and especially from the new French pope.

Winchelsey stayed near the papal court throughout his suspension, roughly ten months at Bordeaux and ten months at Poitiers.[263] According to the annals of London the pope professed himself willing to give a just hearing to the archbishop,[264] but, since there were no specific charges against him, there was no case to be heard. It was a long time before Clement even granted him an audience. Thorne wrote that he was spurned by Clement and for almost a year he could not get permission to speak with the pope,[265] and Winchelsey himself, writing in the autumn of 1306, asserted that even after a long wait the pope had failed to grant him audience of any kind.[266] Edward I pleaded with Clement to remove Winchelsey completely from office and appoint a Gascon in his stead, but the pope refused.[267] One letter from Winchelsey addressed to the prior of his cathedral church, Henry of Eastry, tells us of his predicament.[268] This letter serves, in the first place, to dispel any suggestion that Winchelsey was 'set upon following the example of Becket' or that he 'felt himself to be treading in the steps of St Thomas';[269] when he was described in *Flores* as the

---

263 For the itinerary of Clement see R. Fawtier, *Tables des Reg. de Clém. V*, I. 1–4; Winchelsey followed the pope to Poitiers in April 1307 (*Reg.*, p. 1331).
264 *Annales London.*, p. 150.
265 *Scriptores Decem*, p. 2005 (Thorne, p. 388).
266 *Reg.*, p. 1350.
267 Richardson, 'Clement V and Canterbury', p. 101.
268 *Reg.*, pp. 1349–51.
269 See K. Edwards, 'Political importance of bishops', p. 314, Richardson, 'Early coronation records', p. 5 and idem, 'English coronation oath', p. 137.

'new Thomas', this was no more than a rhetorical flourish, and his biographer simply wrote that the archbishop had commended his exiled state to Christ and St Thomas.[270] As always Winchelsey's attitude was calm and considered. His letter reveals an uncertainty concerning what action he should take to gain restoration to his see, and, in taking stock of all the advice given to him at the curia, he was eager that Prior Eastry should understand the details of the situation and should offer his advice also. Remarkable though it seems, Winchelsey had been advised by some that he had no hope of returning to Canterbury unless he made some payment to the pope. His answer to this suggestion had been that he was in no position to meet financial demands and that, in any case, he would thereby contravene canon law and suffer deprivation of his see for simony. But the mediators between himself and the pope had found a means whereby a promise of payment could be lawfully made to Clement V. The question was whether he should agree to this solution or whether he should continue to follow the advice of some of his cardinal friends and of members of his own household by rejecting this attempt on the part of the pope to trap him[271] and by suffering evil rather than consenting to it. There is a similarity in spirit between the advice which Winchelsey clearly favoured ('a good end is not to be achieved by evil means') and the saying which is quoted by Murimuth[272] as a favourite of the archbishop ('enmity brings no harm where evil holds no sway'). Winchelsey was choosing the course of patience.

A changed political situation in England was needed to bring about the recall of Winchelsey. The death of Edward I on 7 July 1307 was revealed, we are told, to the archbishop in a vision,[273] but it was five months before Edward II decided, suddenly it seems, upon a reconciliation with him. The arrest of Walter Langton within a few weeks of Edward I's death had probably facilitated the reconciliation with Winchelsey.[274] There is no

---

[270] *Flores Hist.*, III. 292–3 and *Anglia Sacra*, I. 17.
[271] 'Nec pater superior nobis laqueum mittere deberet.'
[272] Murimuth, p. 13.
[273] *Flores Hist.* III. 328. Exequies for Edward, the first, it seems, held in the papal curia for a king, were performed in the cathedral at Poitiers during the week ending 28 July: see Ullmann, 'Curial exequies'.
[274] See Beardwood, 'The trial of Langton', p. 11 and Davies, *Baronial Opposition*, pp. 55–6.

certainty in the idea that the campaign in the papal curia against the archbishop was continued at the beginning of the reign without the king's knowledge and against the king's will.[275] Clement V's account of the events, written over five years later, must be studied in conjunction with Edward II's own letter to the pope of 16 December 1307, in which the king referred to the messengers he had already sent to the pope to plead for the archbishop's complete removal from his see. Edward had thus, on the face of it, admitted that he had attempted to secure his father's original wish for Winchelsey's dismissal, but he now claimed not only that he himself could find no fault with Winchelsey, but also that at the time of sending his messengers he had been unaware that his father had renounced the 'rancour, ill-will and wrath' which he had conceived for the archbishop. It is impossible to substantiate this assertion that Edward I had in some way changed his policy towards Winchelsey; it was perhaps a face-saving claim designed to justify the archbishop's recall. The letter went on to say that the archbishop's suffragans and others of his clergy repeatedly asked for his return and that the king needed him to perform his traditional duty of celebrating the royal coronation. The clergy as a body, having perhaps presented their request at the Northampton parliament of 13–16 October, appear at last to have made some effort to aid the archbishop, an effort which may have been occasioned by the possibility that the archbishop of York would be commissioned to crown Edward.[276] The new king was amenable to their request, maybe because of the clergy's grant to him of a fifteenth of their income. In the event, Winchelsey's arrival was delayed because of illness and Edward II was crowned on 25 February by the bishop of Winchester, acting as Winchelsey's commissary. The bull, dated 22 January, revoking the suspension

[275] Richardson, 'Clement V and Canterbury', p. 100, idem, 'Early coronation records', p. 3, K. Edwards, 'Political importance of bishops', p. 315 n. 4, *Foedera*, II. i. 23 and *Concilia*, II. 290–1.
[276] Clement's revocation of any commission already made for the crowning of Edward II (*Reg. Clement V*, no. 2374, *CPL*, II. 33 and *Concilia*, II. 291–2) was accepted by the monks of Christ Church Canterbury as the revocation of a commission made to the archbishop of York (*Literae Cantuar.*, III. 386). The author of *Annales Paulini* (pp. 259–60) states that while the pope proposed to commission a cardinal, the king wished to be crowned by the archbishop of York and the bishops of Durham and London.

was published in London by Testa and Amauvin on 15 February
and Henry of Eastry was appointed to act, for a few weeks, as the
archbishop's vicar-general.[277] Winchelsey landed in England on
24 March 1308. The author of 'Polistoire' describes the monks of
Canterbury crying with joy as they escorted the archbishop in
procession to their cathedral church.[278] It was a triumphant return.
As in July 1297, this reconciliation with the Crown in no way
implied the archbishop's submission. He again resumed full
administration of his see without retracting any of his policies and
without buying favour or influence in any quarter. But much had
changed during his exile.

WINCHELSEY THE ORDAINER

When the archbishop returned to England in the spring of 1308,
baronial discontent with Edward II, because of his favours to
Gaveston and his retreat from Scotland, was already increasing.[279]
Winchelsey, now in his sixties, had to adjust to a changed situation, a pope who was always inclined to support the Crown and a
new king with an insecure hold upon his government. After
almost two years in exile, the victim of Edward I's wrath and of a
royal/papal compact, it would be surprising if he had not felt
dispirited and disillusioned. To a man so devoted to the defence of
the rights of the Church, the pope's behest[280] that he should refrain
as much as possible from offending Edward II must have seemed
both feeble and inappropriate. Also, Winchelsey was now a very
sick man. The exhaustion of following the papal court and the
intemperate climate of France caused, according to his biographer,
some form of paralysis: 'for a long time he completely lost the
strength and power of movement in his limbs'.[281] He was thwarted
by illness for the rest of his life. The bad state of his health

---

[277] See *Councils*, p. 1231 n. 1 (not restored on 15 Jan. as *Reg. Stapeldon*, p. 18),
Reg., pp. 1331–2 and Cant. D. & C., Cartae Antiquae A194 (see Cheney,
Notaries, p. 122).
[278] BL Harl. 636, fo. 231. See also *Annales Paulini*, p. 263 and Bridlington, p. 33.
For the restoration of his goods see *CCR 1307–13*, pp. 83–5.
[279] McKisack, *Fourteenth Century*, pp. 4–6, R. S. Hoyt, 'The coronation oath of
1308', *EHR*, LXXI (1956), 370–83 and Maddicott, *Lancaster*, pp. 70–4.
[280] *Reg.*, p. 1046.
[281] *Anglia Sacra*, I. 16.

prevented a speedy return to England in 1308 and made it necessary for the bishop of Winchester to deputise at the king's coronation; frustrated a punctual meeting with the king in June 1309; caused a break in the proceedings of the ecclesiastical council later in the year; prevented him from presiding over the council of December 1310 and from attending the parliament of December 1311; and necessitated the appointment in February 1313 of the bishop of Llandaff, John of Monmouth, as his vicar-general in spirituals.[282]

There was certainly now a change in the temper of the archbishop's relations with the Crown. While suspicions remained, for example of what might be ordained in ecclesiastical councils,[283] and while the political division between archbishop and king soon became very wide, yet Edward II was perhaps not so sharply and intensely distrustful of the archbishop as Edward I had been. With a king who was more changeable and erratic, Winchelsey was not in quite as exposed a position, and there were very few clashes now between the archbishop and royal clerks, largely no doubt because the archbishop during these last years of his career was too ill to undertake the travelling necessary for visitations. In 1326 Winchelsey's illness was cited in correspondence between Walter Reynolds and Pope John XXII as one of the reasons why the bishops of the province of Canterbury had not been visited for so long.[284]

During the whole period 1308–13 there was apparently only one noteworthy jurisdictional dispute between the king and the archbishop, concerning the church of Maidstone.[285] Winchelsey chose to ignore two papal reservations and in 1310 appointed to the church of Maidstone Stephen of Haslingfield, ex-chancellor of the university of Cambridge. But early in 1311 supporters of Guy de Val (a kinsman of Edward II), who as a result of one of the

---

[282] Richardson, 'Early coronation records', pp. 3–5, *Reg. Woodlock*, p. 371, *Councils*, pp. 1266–7, 1296, *Reg. Gandavo*, p. 417, *Reg.*, p. xxxi and *Concilia*, ii. 422.

[283] *Councils*, pp. 1265–6, 1367–8.   [284] *CPL*, ii. 254.

[285] *Reg. Kellawe*, i. 223–42, *Reg. Clement V*, nos. 5512, 5972 (*CPL*, ii. 70, 74–5), *Cal. Chanc. Warr.*, i. 347–8, 353, Emden, *Cambridge*, p. 292, *Reg. Gandavo*, pp. 395–7, *Reg. Woodlock*, pp. 552–3, 560, PRO C85/7/46, *CCR 1307–13*, pp. 317–18, *Foedera*, ii. i. 207, and *Jean XXII, Lettres Communes*, ed. G. Mollat, v (Paris, 1909), nos. 19650–1.

papal reservations had been nominated by Queen Isabella for the benefice, took the church by storm, forcibly ejecting Stephen of Haslingfield, who was, along with a number of Winchelsey's men, imprisoned by the sheriff of Kent. This resulted in denunciations and excommunications by the archbishop, who was able to take advantage of the king's weak position in 1311, for in June the keeper of the realm, the earl of Gloucester, ordered the release of all the archbishop's men who had been made captive by the sheriff of Kent. Soon Stephen of Haslingfield was back in possession of Maidstone. Although the royal candidate eventually became rector of Maidstone, this was after Winchelsey's death. In defending his right to collate Maidstone church, Winchelsey had stood against not only royal interference but also the bulls of provision. This defiance of papal provisions, evident too in 1308 after Clement had provided Bernard de Bovisvilla to the church of Reculver,[286] is reminiscent of the attitude of Grosseteste. Exile by papal mandate had not killed Winchelsey's determination to protect his interests as archbishop and may even have stimulated his spirit of independence.

The relative paucity of particular legal·disputes between archbishop and Crown in this period is not an indication that Winchelsey's outlook had changed. The essential elements in his fight for ecclesiastical freedom remained: notably, the protection of the English Church from direct royal taxation and the presentation of grievances against the encroachments of the king's courts. To begin with taxation, it must be stressed that despite the undoubted financial constraints upon Edward II this was not a period of especially critical need. The clergy, for a number of reasons, were to be put under much greater pressure to contribute to the royal treasury for the war in Scotland after Winchelsey's death in 1313 and, even more so, after Clement V's death in 1314. Two important factors in the period 1308–13 were, on the one hand, the successful resumption by Winchelsey of control over clerical taxation and, on the other hand, the continuing taxation of the clergy by the pope for the king. The strength of Winchelsey's leadership meant that Edward II made few efforts to persuade the

---

[286] *Reg. Clement V*, no. 2627 (*CPL*, II. 38), *Reg.*, pp. 1044–6, and see Graham, 'Sidelights on rectors of Reculver', pp. 9–10.

English clergy to grant direct taxes. In contrast to the recurring concern with royal taxation of virtually all the archbishop's councils during the previous reign, there is scarcely any indication that royal subsidies were seriously under discussion in any of the six councils of 1308–13. Even so, we cannot doubt that taxation was still the most important single issue affecting the constitutional relationship of the Crown and the clergy.

During Winchelsey's absence two taxes had been granted, to both of which he would probably have offered some opposition. The thirtieth and twentieth of 1306 had been assessed on all the temporalities of the clergy.[287] More important than this tax was the direct clerical grant made in Edward II's first parliament at Northampton in October 1307. The laity conceded a twentieth and fifteenth, and the clergy a fifteenth.[288] This fifteenth was on the spiritual and temporal income of the clergy as assessed in 1291. The tenths for seven years granted by Clement V in 1305 had come to an end with Edward I's death, and the instalment due on 1 December 1307 was the last to be collected.[289] The grant of a fifteenth ensured that the clergy continued to be taxed: it was to be paid at two terms, 26 March and 25 June 1308. As a grant to the king at the very beginning of his reign it is possible that Winchelsey did not disapprove. But it is unlikely that he would have accepted the concession without any discussion,[290] as the silence of the sources suggests may have been the case; and he would in all probability have been happier if the tax had been granted in an ecclesiastical council rather than in parliament. It was the first direct subsidy for the king on spiritual as well as temporal income since the tenth given for the Scottish war in the autumn of 1297, and no further direct subsidy was to be granted during Winchelsey's tenure of office. The method of taxing the

---

287 Above, pp. 236–7.
288 *Parl. Writs*, ii. ii. 15–16, and app. p. 5b (as *CCR 1307–13*, pp. 14–15), *Reg. Swinfield*, p. 441, *Reg. Kellawe*, ii. 960–3, 969–71, 975–8 and Lunt, 'Clerical tenths during the reign of Edward II', p. 181.
289 Lunt, *Financial Relations*, p. 384.
290 There was delay in the payment for the Canterbury diocese: in July 1310 the contribution to the fifteenth of £627 9s for the diocese, the collection of which was the responsibility of the archbishop, was set against money from the issues of the archbishopric paid into the exchequer during the suspension: *CCR 1307–13*, p. 273.

clergy was redefined following the practice during the last years of Edward I's reign of taxing *all* the temporalities of the clergy along with the temporal goods of the laity. Now, the temporalities of the clergy assessed in 1291 were taxed once again along with their spiritualities, and goods on any land acquired by the clergy since the assessment of 1291 (whether it was an inheritance, or a reward, or whether it was held at farm, either on account of a wardship or an escheat, or in any other way) were taxed along with the lay movables.

In 1309 taxation continued in the two ways which caused no opposition from the clergy: in the parliament of April 1309 a twenty-fifth on lay movables was granted (excluding the temporalities assessed in 1291);[291] and taxation for the king by papal mandate, on clerical income as assessed in 1291, was renewed with the order for the collection of a triennial tenth, which began in October 1309.[292] Three-quarters of this triennial tenth, collected between 1309 and 1312, was for the king, and these papal taxes were, in all but name, royal subsidies. The need for clerical consent was thus bypassed. That this was possible of course weakened the political position of the clergy; but, at the same time, the reaction of the clergy to the demands made upon them after Winchelsey's death shows beyond doubt that under Winchelsey's guidance they were holding firmly to the principle of consent to all taxes upon their income which were not ordered by papal mandate. A council was convoked in December 1310 especially to give consent to advancing payments of the triennial tenth.[293] Winchelsey clearly favoured this concession but insisted upon the need for consent in council since it concerned the whole clergy. Although Winchelsey was absent from the council, his influence was closely felt. The advancing of two of the terms of the papal tax was made after the archbishop, bishops and certain of the magnates had succeeded in obtaining the revocation of writs demanding prises to supply the king's Scottish expedition; here was a reassertion of the principle fought for in 1297–1301 that prises should not take place against

---

291 *Parl. Writs*, II. ii. 38–9 (and *Rot. Parl.*, I. 445–6).
292 Lunt, *Financial Relations*, pp. 384–6, and see Denton, 'Reynolds and ecclesiastical politics', p. 253.
293 *Councils*, pp. 1285, 1290–7 and Clarke, *Representation and Consent*, pp. 332–3.

the owner's will.[294] Also, the concession concerning the papal tenths was only made on the understanding that the date of the last term of the triennial tenth (24 June 1312) remained as in the original papal mandate. The king was allowed no long-term benefit because of the speedy collection of the tenth, and it is a mark of Winchelsey's control that the question of advanced payments to papal tenths was treated as a matter for the consent of the whole clerical body.

Between April 1311 and Winchelsey's death Edward made unsuccessful efforts to obtain a direct clerical subsidy. He pleaded with the council of 1311 to grant him a shilling in the mark of clerical income (approximately a thirteenth) or some comparable aid, for his war in Scotland.[295] But there is no record of any reply from this council or from the councils of 1312 and 1313, and no evidence that the clergy considered making him a grant. Even the northern province firmly refused the request for a subsidy.[296] Nor was the charitable subsidy of fourpence in the mark, which was granted to the archbishop by the clergy of the southern province in 1312, impeded by the royal protest against it.[297] Since the collection of the first charitable subsidy in 1300 Winchelsey's confidence had increased, for the collection of the subsidy of 1312 was ordered without delay, without any attempt to conceal the grant from the king and without any pretence that payment was not compulsory.[298] This tax of a fortieth was to be collected from all clerical income as assessed in 1291 and with full canonical censure.[299] For the first time, therefore, Winchelsey was in effect asserting that with the consent of an ecclesiastical council he had full authority to levy a tax for his own financial needs and the needs of the churches of his province on the income of all the clergy including the exempt religious houses. The king claimed that no religious house which was a royal foundation should make such a payment without *royal* consent,[300] and the abbey of Bury

---

294 *Councils*, p. 1291: 'prout in aliis brevibus regiis super hoc confectis quod nullius bona contra suum beneplacitum capiantur directis singulis vice-comitibus est contentum.' Also see *Liber Albus*, nos. 486–8, 497–8.
295 *Councils*, pp. 1305–6.
296 Ibid., pp. 1340–2.
297 Ibid., pp. 1367–8.
298 Du Boulay, 'Charitable subsidies', pp. 149–54.
299 See the mandate in *Councils*, pp. 1372–3.   300 Ibid., pp. 1367–8.

St Edmunds in an appeal to the pope claimed that the subsidy was being levied under the guise of apostolic authority.[301] It seems that royal writs of prohibition did enable some to escape payment,[302] but the general collection of the subsidy remained unchallenged. Instead of granting an aid to the king, the clergy had granted an aid to the archbishop.

Immediately after Winchelsey died in May 1313 the king made an unsuccessful attempt to lay his hands on what remained of the subsidy granted to the archbishop, falsely claiming that it had been given at the king's request and for the needs of the kingdom. He put the prelates and conventual churches under pressure to give him loans of money, and he obtained a large loan of over £33,000 from Clement V in exchange, remarkably, for the mortgaging to the pope of the revenues of Gascony.[303] The effects of Winchelsey's death were certainly felt immediately. The appointment of the royal chancellor, Walter Reynolds, as his successor was itself a reaction to Winchelsey's determined leadership, for it was soon abundantly clear that Reynolds had a quite different political outlook. Under Winchelsey's guidance the English Church, following the principle of consent embodied in Boniface VIII's bulls 'Clericis laicos' and 'Coram illo fatemur', had secured control of its own finances. It is true that by papal command the clergy had been frequently taxed for the benefit of the king; but the total tax upon clerical income and possessions received by Edward II between Winchelsey's return from suspension until his death fell far short of the total for 1295 alone.[304]

During this last period of Winchelsey's career there were no dramatic occasions, as during 1297 and 1298, when sentences of excommunication against invaders of ecclesiastical property and in defence of the charters were an open and direct challenge to the

---

[301] *Concilia*, ii. 422.

[302] *Reg. Woodlock*, p. 614; and it is hardly likely that St Augustine's Canterbury contributed to the subsidy, for they appear to have successfully resisted the smaller subsidy of the previous year to pay for representatives of the clergy to be sent to the council of Vienne (see *Reg. Roffense*, pp. 106–8 and *Councils*, p. 1298 and n. 4).

[303] Denton, 'Reynolds and ecclesiastical politics', pp. 250–6, idem, 'Canterbury archiepiscopal appointments', p. 321 and Renouard, 'Édouard II et Clément V', pp. 125–41.

[304] See Appendix.

actions of royal ministers and the policies of the king's government. But the archbishop continued, as in 1309–10 and 1312,[305] to defend clerical liberties by the use of sentences of excommunication and continued to fight for *Magna Carta* and to stress that those contravening *Magna Carta* were under sentence of major excommunication.[306] He deplored the innumerable and grave burdens and the intolerable injuries with which the clergy were oppressed and afflicted, and sought to defend the priesthood by the republication of canons and statutes and to enumerate the cases in which sentences of excommunication were incurred *ipso facto*. Far from retreating from an interest in political matters, he was drawn, as we shall see, by the crises of the new reign into a close involvement with the affairs of the realm. He excommunicated Gaveston should he return from exile, and he defended the Ordinances with sentences of excommunication; and in the midst of the political disorders of 1312 he stood as the guardian of the tranquillity of the realm, ordering denunciations and excommunications of all who broke the peace of the realm. In 1297 Edward I had sought to denounce his opponents as excommunicates since they were disturbers of the peace.[307] In 1312 the case was different. But Winchelsey's opposition to the Crown remained.

In the first of Winchelsey's councils of the new reign (held from 24 November to 9 December 1309 and much concerned with the process against the Templars), the work of 1300–1 was continued with the preparation of grievances which were presented to the king on 16 December.[308] There is interesting evidence about the way in which the complaints were drawn up: several days were given to the bishops so that they could confer with the representatives of the clergy of their dioceses, and the grievances were then assessed, sorted and redrafted in legal terms. Thus, the particular complaints came from the clergy as a whole but were deliberately reduced to general *gravamina* by clerks trained in both laws. On this occasion, seven clauses of the 1280 grievances and the whole of the 1300–1 set of grievances, exclud-

---

305 *Councils*, pp. 1267, 1274–5, 1373–5.
306 Ibid., p. 1270.   307 Above, pp. 147–8.
308 *Councils*, pp. 1266–7, 1269–74, and see Jones, 'Bishops, politics and the two laws', pp. 222–3. For a set of the *gravamina* of 1309 not noted in *Councils* see Cant. D. & C., Cartae Antiquae C256, described in Jones, p. 244.

ing only c. 34, were re-presented (now with added comments upon the royal responses to these earlier *gravamina*),[309] and they were supplemented by a relatively short new set of thirteen articles.[310] Altogether this comprised the longest and most comprehensive set of clerical *gravamina* ever presented to the Crown. The additional complaints served both to fill the gaps revealed by the selection of earlier articles and also to bring the grievances up to date by taking into account new examples of incursions upon ecclesiastical liberties. Clause 7, for instance, claimed that cases concerning whether or not chapels belonged to particular parish churches were being brought into the king's courts, which had no competence to deal with the issue of parochial status, and clause 8 complained of interference with a bishop's right, when there was reasonable cause, to refuse to institute clerks presented to benefices by the king. With clause 12 secular interference in cases of bigamy became a formal grievance for the first time. The clamouring for redress of grievances culminated in the *Articuli Cleri* of 1316, though these articles can hardly have given much satisfaction to the clergy.[311] Defending the Church against the encroachments of secular courts was a hard struggle; it is an impressive fact that the clergy vigorously continued the struggle in the years immediately following Winchelsey's death despite an almost complete lack of leadership in this direction from the episcopate.

At the same time as preparing articles to present to the king, the clergy prepared petitions to be sent to the pope and articles to be presented at the general council of Vienne.[312] And one of the important developments of 1309–10 was the support which Clement V was giving, even before the autumn council of 1309, to the clergy in their attempts to impress upon the Crown the need for the protection of their rights.[313] Firm support in what was a defence by the clergy of their interpretation of the 'freedom' granted in *Magna Carta* had been rarely given by the papacy.

---

[309] These comments, almost certainly of 1309, are printed with the earlier complaints to which they refer in *Councils*, pp. 872–8, 880–2, 1206–18, and see *Reg.*, pp. 1013–31.

[310] And, of these, c. 6 was apparently excluded for it echoes c. 20 of 1300–1: see *Councils*, pp. 1213–14, 1272 n. h.

[311] Denton, 'Reynolds and ecclesiastical politics', pp. 269–70.

[312] *Councils*, pp. 1266–7, 1353–6.

[313] For refs. see *Councils*, p. 1285 nn. 2, 3.

In 1308 Clement's exhortation to the king had concerned the imprisonments of the bishops of Coventry and Lichfield, St Andrews, and Glasgow and the treatment of papal agents; but in the bull 'Supra montem' of 28 October 1309, sent it seems to each of the bishops, and delivered to Winchelsey on 14 February 1310, the pope's complaints, which he required to be presented to the king, included in condensed form the most important grievances which the clergy had been presenting for decades. Although the papal letter pre-dates the clergy's new *gravamina*, it must have read like a précis of them. The pope complained that writs of caption following excommunication were ignored, that ecclesiastical jurisdiction was being impeded by royal writs of prohibition, that bishops were not being allowed to deal with criminous clerks, that the clergy were being compelled to appear in the royal courts to answer every kind of charge, and that royal officials were inflicting grave damage upon episcopal lands, monasteries, priories and churches. Winchelsey presented the papal petition to Edward, in the presence of ten of his suffragan bishops and Anthony Bek, on 28 February, at the time of the parliament in which, only a fortnight later, the king agreed to the appointment of ordainers. It was a critical time for Edward II but it is clear that the clergy were not in a strong position to take advantage of the crisis. Papal support at this juncture in fact did little to strengthen the hand of the clergy. For the king it was only a minor set-back to Clement's conciliatory policies. What the clergy needed, above all, was the active support of the magnates. The Ordinances, as we shall see, reveal some coalescence of the interests of prelates and magnates, but, with taxation no longer so pressing and crucial a matter, of equal importance to both clergy and laity, there was no issue among the clergy's grievances which was likely to elicit firm backing from secular leaders. The *gravamina* were, after all, solely concerned with clerical privilege.

Thus, Winchelsey in the different climate of a new reign had pushed forward with the policies in which he believed, protecting his Church from royal taxation, defending clerical interests by the use of excommunication and petitioning the king to give greater respect to ecclesiastical rights. All this was political action. But much more has been inferred from the evidence. Winchelsey has been seen by many as the leader of those opposing Edward II. He 'resumed the leadership of the opposition as soon as he returned from the exile into which Edward I had driven him'; 'contemporary opinion regarded him as the leader of the reforming movement'; 'he was able far more effectively than the earl of Lancaster to assume the leadership of both the baronial and episcopal opposition'.[314] These are large claims. Winchelsey may, indeed, have been the most distinguished, perhaps even the most resolute, of the king's opponents. But to what extent did he give leadership and direction to disaffected earls and magnates, and to all those intent upon reform?

Winchelsey had arrived in England just in time to take part in the proceedings of the Easter parliament of 1308, at which there was concerted opposition to the king, demanding that Gaveston should be exiled. In Winchelsey's declaration of the banishment of Gaveston and of his excommunication should he return we are told that all were agreed at the Easter parliament that Gaveston was at the root of the dissension in the realm.[315] Certainly, Edward was compelled to submit in the face of a large alliance: Philip IV of France backing the earls, with the earl of Lincoln at their head.[316] Winchelsey brought to the alliance the support of the English Church. The direction, and strength, of Winchelsey's sympathies are not in doubt. But he had acted with other prelates, and we do not know whether he was personally an active and influential protagonist in the attack upon Gaveston. Winchelsey led his Church, but he never led the magnates. Nor could he expect, any more than in Edward I's reign, the total allegiance of all his bishops: it is no surprise that Bishop Salmon of Norwich and Bishop Reynolds of Worcester took part in the successful mission to the pope in March 1309 to secure the revocation of the excommunication of Gaveston.[317]

Support for the king returned after Gaveston's departure for

---

[314] Tout, *Edward II*, p. 77, J. H. Trueman, 'The Lords Ordainers of 1310', *Medieval Studies*, XXI (1959), 251 and K. Edwards, 'Political importance of bishops', p. 315.

[315] *Reg. Gandavo*, p. 238.

[316] Maddicott, *Lancaster*, pp. 80–90, Phillips, *Pembroke*, pp. 25–8 and K. Edwards, 'Political importance of bishops', p. 315.

[317] The future bishop, Adam Orleton, king's clerk, was also on the embassy: Haines, *Church and Politics*, p. 9.

Ireland on 25 June 1308; but the events of 1309, with the emergence of Thomas of Lancaster in the front rank of the baronial opponents, mark the first stages leading to the Ordinances.[318] It was certainly a year of increasing tension between the archbishop and the Crown. The conflict between Winchelsey and the archbishop of York concerning the latter's practice of bearing his cross in the Canterbury province reached a critical point at the Westminster parliament of 27 April to 13 May 1309.[319] Winchelsey had given careful instructions to the bishops of Lincoln and London of the policy to be adopted if William Greenfield had his cross carried before him on his way to Westminster.[320] Greenfield defied the archbishop of Canterbury, who, ignoring the king's suggestion that the two archbishops should attend the proceedings on alternate days, refused to be present at the parliament, as also did his suffragan bishops, if Greenfield persisted in having his cross carried. Edward only succeeded in placating Winchelsey by sending the archbishop of the northern province back to York. The parliament could then proceed with the bishops of the southern province in attendance. So much we learn from the chronicles of Canterbury. And relations with the Crown had not at all improved by the time of the Stamford parliament, summoned to meet on 27 July. Winchelsey no doubt felt great resentment because Gaveston had returned, and the archbishop was very concerned about the implications of the bull, dated 25 April, which revoked the favourite's excommunication. By the king's orders the bull had been read to Winchelsey on 11 June 1309, but the archbishop was clearly unwilling to publish it.[321] Then, after receiving the summons to parliament, Winchelsey ordered the consecration of John Droxford (keeper of the king's wardrobe) as bishop of Bath and Wells to take place at Canterbury only a fortnight after the opening of parliament at Stamford. Although

318 See esp. Maddicott, *Lancaster*, pp. 90–106 and Harriss, *King, Parliament and Public Finance*, pp. 107–12, 160–5.
319 Cont. Gervase, pp. 322–3 (as also BL Harl. 636, fos. 231v–232r), identical with the passage in Cant. D. & C., Reg. Q, fo. 53r, printed in Somner, *Antiquities*, pt II. app. pp. 11–12.
320 Somner, *Antiquities*, pt II, app. p. 11, *Reg. Baldock*, pp. 100–3 and LRO Reg. III (Dalderby), fos. 154v–155r.
321 *Reg. Swinfield*, pp. 451–2, *Reg. Gandavo*, pp. 313–17, *Reg. Woodlock*, pp. 370–1 and K. Edwards, 'Political importance of bishops', pp. 317–18.

there were many precedents for arranging a consecration to take
place very shortly after a meeting of parliament,[322] the king interpreted Winchelsey's action as direct provocation and threatened
to issue a writ of prohibition unless he cancelled the consecration.[323] The archbishop took no account of the threat, but he was
prevented from carrying out the consecration because of the
presence of Droxford at the parliament. After examining the
excuses of the bishop-elect, he ordered the consecration to take
place on 9 November. As with the barons,[324] the Stamford parliament seems to reveal a breach in the ranks of the episcopate.
Some were willing to negotiate with the king, Gaveston at his
side; others were absent.[325] The evidence suggests that it may
have been to some extent a test of episcopal allegiance, whether to
the king on the one hand or to the archbishop on the other. At any
rate, the bishops who were present were all known to have, in
varying degrees, royalist sympathies: Bishops Bek of Durham,
Langton of Chichester, Baldock of London, Reynolds of Worcester, Woodlock of Winchester, Salmon of Norwich, as well as
Droxford bishop-elect of Bath and Wells. Winchelsey's poor state
of health would, in any case, almost certainly have prevented him
from undertaking the journey to Stamford. But there appears to
be some truth in Murimuth's assertion that Winchelsey, in
particular, was disturbed by Gaveston's return and that he did not
wish to treat with the king in parliament.[326] The archbishop was
certainly disturbed, too, by the succession of king's clerks elected
to the episcopal bench since the beginning of the reign: Reynolds
to Worcester, Stapledon to Exeter and now Droxford to Bath and
Wells. When he preached at the ecclesiastical council later in the
year, with these three new bishops present, he rebuked the bishops

---

[322] As in 1297, 1302 and 1305 (Cont. Gervase, p. 316, *Worcester*, p. 553, *Reg.*,
pp. 805–6 and *Parl. Writs*, I. ii. 56–61, 116–30, 159–60).
[323] *Cal. Chanc. Warr.*, p. 291, *Reg.*, pp. 1113–14, *Reg. Gandavo*, pp. 323–4, 344–6.
Concerning Droxford's earlier preferments see Prestwich, *War, Politics and
Finance*, pp. 167–8.
[324] Maddicott, *Lancaster*, pp. 104–5.
[325] See McKisack, *Fourteenth Century*, p. 9, K. Edwards, 'Political importance of
bishops', pp. 318–19, PRO C53/96 mm. 10–11, LRO Reg. III (Dalderby), fos.
162v, 164r and *Reg. Stapeldon*, p. 548: those known to be absent were Ghent
of Salisbury, Swinfield of Hereford, Dalderby of Lincoln, Martin of St David's,
Stapledon of Exeter and Orford of Ely.
[326] Murimuth, p. 14.

'badly elected through influence or ambition, and those who do not stand up for the law of the Church'.[327]

Without any question the archbishop brought his influence to bear upon the affairs of the realm. The council of 24 November to 17 December 1309 was held up three times when the prelates dealt with the 'business of the king and the kingdom' or were called before the king's council.[328] We may doubt, even so, Winchelsey's political effectiveness in 1309. It is difficult to think that he did not wholeheartedly favour the demands first made of the king at the April parliament, conceded along with the Statute of Stamford in late July or early August and insisted upon early in 1310.[329] It was very largely the complaints of 1300–1, notably concerning prises, that were being reiterated in 1309 by the magnates, knights and burgesses. Ecclesiastics, of course, stood to benefit from some of the renewed demands and renewed concessions. But the clergy were apparently isolated from the actions of the laity in 1309 even more than had been the case in 1300–1. There was now no reference at all to the possibility of the clergy granting a direct tax on their income. They had no bargaining counter, not even at this stage the request from the king of a grant which they could turn down. There is no mention in the magnates' petitions of ecclesiastical rights and no indication that clerical liberties were in the minds of those who drafted either the petitions or the concessions. The clerical grievances stood completely apart from the lay grievances. Whatever Winchelsey's influence in the background, and whatever his involvement in 1310 and after, the opposition which was building up in 1309 was essentially baronial.

Early in 1310 there was a new sense of urgency and new sense of unity among the earls and magnates, born of anger especially at the king's continued obduracy about Gaveston and about prises.[330] The political and constitutional struggle against Edward II

---

[327] *Councils*, p. 1264: 'reprehendit episcopos male per preces electos vel ambitionem, necnon et eos qui non stant pro iure ecclesie.' And see W. E. L. Smith, *Episcopal Appointments*, pp. 12–14, 47.   [328] *Councils*, pp. 1268–9.

[329] *Rot. Parl.*, I. 443–5 and *Stat. Realm*, I. ii. 154–6, and see Harriss, *King, Parliament and Public Finance*, esp. pp. 107–12 and Maddicott, *Lancaster*, pp. 97–8, 103–4.

[330] For accounts of the events of 1310–11, used in what follows, see Davies, *Baronial Opposition*, pp. 357–93 and Maddicott, *Lancaster*, pp. 106–20.

came to a head, and the earls and barons could have been in no doubt, from the first, of Winchelsey's complete support. The new movement for reform in 1310 must have appeared to Winchelsey as a continuation of the struggle with Edward I, and he joined the movement willingly. There was a large attendance of bishops at the parliament which was summoned to meet at Westminster on 8 February 1310 and which finally assembled on 27 February after Edward had sent Gaveston away: most of the bishops are known to have been present, the exceptions being Walter Langton, who was still in royal disfavour, Wouldham of Rochester and Swinfield of Hereford.[331] The influence of the prelates can be seen immediately, for the articles presented to the king requesting the appointment of ordainers were specifically 'articles of the prelates, earls and barons'; and the 'overturning of the liberties of the Holy Church' and the 'attacks which your ministers make upon the goods of the Holy Church' were among the major complaints.[332] Once again it was pleaded that 'the terms of the Great Charter should be fully maintained'. That the Church's grievances are so clearly represented at this stage is perhaps an indication that the magnates were playing for the archbishop's unqualified co-operation. On 16 March the king agreed that ordainers should be appointed, and a committee of prelates and magnates met to discuss the position on the following day.[333] At this meeting the bishops arrived at a firm statement of policy with regard to the ordaining movement: they agreed that they would not promise anything 'to the prejudice of the Church of Rome, or the liberty of the Church, or the good of their order'. The archbishop conveyed a policy statement of the bishops to the lay members of the committee in the form of a personal oath: 'I promise that, saving my estate and order and the liberty of the Church of Rome, I will keep and hold that which shall be ordained about the state of the household of our king and his realm by those commissioned

[331] See *Parl. Writs*, ii. ii. 41, *Reg.*, p. 1043 and *Annales London.*, p. 170 (the bishopric of Ely was vacant). Although the bishops of the northern province were summoned and apparently present (see *Reg. Greenfield*, v. 312, *Reg. Halton*, ii. 241 and Fraser, *Bek*, pp. 224, 249), they stood aloof from the opposition to the king.
[332] *Annales London.*, pp. 168–9.
[333] *Reg. Reynolds*, p. 16 (as also BL Cotton Charters xvi. 58), *Annales London.*, pp. 169–71 and *Reg.*, pp. 1065–6.

by him as ordainers, declaring that, if anything contrary to the aforesaid be ordained, it will not proceed from my intention and I will not hold it nor be bound by it in any wise.' Though he had certainly now formed a close pact with the magnates, Winchelsey's rôle was decisively and exclusively that of leader of the English Church. On 20 March, three days after the meeting of prelates and magnates, the ordainers were elected in parliament and there were seven bishops, forming a third of the chosen body: Winchelsey, along with Simon of Ghent (Salisbury), John of Monmouth (Llandaff), David Martin (St David's), John Langton (Chichester), Ralph Baldock (London) and John Salmon (Norwich).[334]

The archbishop's interest was centred upon the confirmation of *Magna Carta* and the consequent reassertion of the liberty of the Church; and he was concerned that the decisions of the ordainers should be sanctioned by the Church and should be published with full ecclesiastical support. The effect of clerical participation is evident again in the preliminary Ordinances drafted in March 1310, with their insistence upon the retention of all ecclesiastical liberties, as well as upon the observance of the Great Charter in every detail.[335] But, in addition, it has been said that Winchelsey provided the lords ordainers 'with brains and with a policy' and that he 'seems to have been regarded as leader of the ordaining movement'.[336] It is hard to find material support for these beliefs. None of the contemporary or near contemporary chroniclers in their descriptions of the work of the ordainers suggests that Winchelsey played so prominent a part. Apart from simple inclusion among the names of the ordainers,[337] he is mentioned only in relation to the publication of the Ordinances, and the excommunication of all infringers.[338] Two chronicles relate the events of

---

[334] See K. Edwards, 'Political importance of bishops', pp. 319–20. For the oath sworn by the ordainers on 20 March see *Parl. Writs*, II. ii. app. p. 27 and BL Cotton Cleo. C vii, fo. 36v. The king's chancellor, John Langton, received the oath from Winchelsey and each of the other ordainers, and Winchelsey received Langton's oath.

[335] *Annales London.*, pp. 172–3, *Foedera*, II. i. 113 and *Rot. Parl.*, I. 446–7.

[336] Tout, *Edward II*, p. 19 and K. Edwards, 'Political importance of bishops', p. 321.

[337] As in *Annales London.*, p. 172 and *Flores Hist.*, III. 333.

[338] *Annales Paulini*, p. 270, *Flores Hist.*, III. 147 and Guisborough, pp. 385–6; and see Clarke, *Representation and Consent*, p. 160.

1310–11 without even referring to him.[339] Trokelowe's statement that the archbishop encouraged the magnates in seeking fearlessly their liberties against the king adds nothing to our knowledge.[340] The picture has been obscured by the fact that Winchelsey was at the head of virtually all lists of the ordainers, with the result that in some formal references to the Ordinances his name was cited to the exclusion of others. This was the case in the preamble to the Ordinances themselves.[341] It was perhaps this practice which played some part in the association of the Ordinances with Winchelsey's name after his death. Another factor seems to have been the veneration which Thomas of Lancaster had for the archbishop's life and work. In a letter to the king in 1317, the earl of Lancaster, who was later to initiate the attempt to gain canonisation for Winchelsey, referred to the Ordinances made in the time of Archbishop Robert.[342] The tradition which linked the names of Lancaster and Winchelsey must not be used as direct evidence for their respective rôles in 1310–11. The nature of the tradition can be easily illustrated: when the Ordinances were made public Lancaster placed a commemoration tablet at St Paul's, and the author of the *Croniques de London* later noted that 'God performs many miracles in the church of St Paul at the tablet which was placed there by the said Thomas of Lancaster in remembrance that the king had granted and affirmed the Ordinances which were made by the holy Robert Winchelsey, archbishop of Canterbury, and by all the great and wise men of England, to the great profit of the whole kingdom.'[343] Miracles and sanctity were to surround the names of both Lancaster and Winchelsey, and there was an attempt to gain canonisation for both men. The archbishop had certainly given full support to the ordaining movement, but

---

[339] Bridlington, pp. 36–40 (and this account does include a list of the other episcopal ordainers) and *Vita Edwardi II*, pp. 9–21.

[340] Trokelowe, p. 81 (cf. K. Edwards, 'Political importance of bishops', p. 321).

[341] See *CFR*, II. 108, *Foedera*, II. i. 145, *Gascon Rolls 1307–17*, ed. Y. Renouard (HMSO, 1962), no. 566 and *Stat. Realm*, I. ii. 157–8.

[342] Murimuth, app. p. 273. In the Latin version in Bridlington, p. 51, the word 'tempore' has probably been lost before 'bone memorie domini Roberti'.

[343] Ed. G. J. Aungier (Camden Soc., old ser. XXVIII, 1844), p. 46. See also CUL Gg. i. 15 (The Brut Chronicle), fo. 186v, R. Higden, *Polychronicon*, ed. J. R. Lumby, VIII (RS, 1866), 302, Maddicott, *Lancaster*, pp. 329–30 and *Documents of St Paul's Cathedral*, ed. W. S. Simpson (Camden Soc., 2nd ser. XXVI, 1880), pp. 11–14

there is little to indicate what part he played in the actual formulation of the Ordinances and nothing to indicate the extent of his interest in the details of the proposed control of the king's government and reform of the royal household.

Winchelsey appears now to have united his bishops against the king more effectively than ever before, though Walter Reynolds, at least, probably remained loyal to Edward. Before the Ordinances were published in September 1311 three ecclesiastical councils of the province of Canterbury had met in London within twelve months, and although the concern of the clergy was very largely with the process against the Templars, there was a firm, if not an antagonistic, attitude towards royal requests for financial aid.[344] In the Ordinances there was a renewed emphasis upon the maintenance of *Magna Carta*, and also of the Charter of the Forest, and insistence upon the termination of extortions that had affected both laity and clergy, like prises and the *maltote*. Clause 12 is especially illustrative of the influence of the bishops, for here was an attempt to deal effectively with those who maliciously procured false writs of prohibition to halt cases being heard in the ecclesiastical courts.[345] The procurers of the writs should be punished by fines or by imprisonment, and the ecclesiastical ordinaries should obtain damages. This was a clerical grievance which the Ordinances sought to remedy. But the clause stands as the only direct link between the clergy's *gravamina* and the work of the ordainers. The backing of the Church was of particular importance in the publication of the Ordinances and in the denunciation of all infringers.[346] Yet, even though we can thus point to the significance of the work of the lords spiritual, it is difficult to avoid the conclusion that the new Ordinances of 1311, with the additional articles of October or November, represent in their detail and especially in what was novel a primarily baronial and lay plan of reform. The leaders of this movement of reform were probably the earl of Lancaster and the earl of Warwick.[347]

All the same, the Ordinances and the struggle to maintain them

344 Above, pp. 251–2.
345 *Stat. Realm*, I. ii. 158 and *Eng. Hist. Documents*, III. 530.
346 See K. Edwards, 'Political importance of bishops', p. 321 and n. 6, McKisack, *Fourteenth Century*, p. 12 and Davies, *Baronial Opposition*, pp. 366–7.
347 See McFarlane, *Nobility of Later Medieval England*, p. 234.

were the culmination of Winchelsey's career. His illness was becoming increasingly severe and he was, in all probability, approaching his seventieth year. His relations with the king were never to recover. There was added tension in the autumn of 1311 about the form in which Edward had summoned the archbishop and clergy to the prorogued parliament of November.[348] The 'premunientes' clause had been changed, and the archbishop was ordered to summon the proctors of the clergy only to affirm – not, as had become usual, to do and to affirm – what was to be ordained. After the king had assured the archbishop that nothing prejudicial to himself or to the Church was intended, Winchelsey ordered the clergy to attend the parliament, but he himself was prevented by illness from making the journey.

No doubt Winchelsey placed great hope in the terms of the Ordinances, but the king had no intention of adhering to them. Even before Christmas, it seems, Gaveston had returned from his third exile, having been out of England for little more than a month.[349] On 18 January 1312 Edward, declaring that Gaveston's exile had been against the laws and customs of the land, ordered all his sheriffs to accept the favourite as a good and loyal subject;[350] and on 23 January Walter Langton, who had suddenly been brought back into royal favour, was, against the terms of the Ordinances, appointed as treasurer.[351] On 26 January the king ordered the observance only of those Ordinances which were not prejudicial to himself and to the Crown.[352] The ordainers were not slow to take action against this defiance, and Winchelsey's alliance with the magnates was reinforced. At the end of February Winchelsey ordered his suffragan bishops to come to London for a meeting with the magnates on 13 March.[353] He had been driven

---

[348] See Clarke, *Representation and Consent*, pp. 130–1, J. Armitage Robinson, 'Convocation of Canterbury: its early history', *Church Quarterly Rev.*, LXXXI (1915), 112–13, *CCR 1307–13*, p. 439, *Reg. Gandavo*, pp. 410–11, 419, *Reg. Reynolds*, p. 28, *Liber Albus*, p. 35 and Wake, *State of the Church*, app. p. 34 (from LRO Reg. III (Dalderby), fo. 234r and Norwich Dean & Chapter Muniments, Reg. IX, fo. 13).

[349] McKisack, *Fourteenth Century*, p. 22 and Maddicott, *Lancaster*, pp. 121–2.

[350] *Foedera*, II. i. 153.

[351] See Davies, *Baronial Opposition*, pp. 389–92 and McKisack, *Fourteenth Century*, pp. 23–4.

[352] *Foedera*, II. i. 154.

[353] *Reg. Gandavo*, pp. 418–19, and see Phillips, *Pembroke*, p. 32.

into intervening very directly and positively in the affairs of the realm and we must assume from his later reference to it that he was himself well enough to attend the baronial and episcopal assembly.[354] The importance of the gathering was recognised by contemporary chroniclers: the author of the *Vita Edwardi* wrote that Winchelsey denounced Gaveston and that the earls made secret plans for military action, and the annalist of London noted that the ordainers, filled with anger, made careful plans for defence.[355] The king sent his representatives, including the bishop of Norwich,[356] but they did not succeed in tempering the wrath of his opponents, who had as one of their aims the prevention of Langton from taking up his responsibilities as treasurer. The extreme measures of the following three months, leading to the murder of Gaveston on 19 June, thus appear to have been initiated by the meeting of March in which Winchelsey had played a significant part.

Four days after the meeting the archbishop summoned a further provincial council to meet in London on 18 April; it seems that this did not give some of the prelates enough time in which to return to London, and absentees were later resummoned for 8 May.[357] According to the author of *Flores* it was before both clergy and magnates that Winchelsey excommunicated his suffragan bishop, Walter Langton, for infringing the Ordinances.[358] But Adam Murimuth's account may be more reliable, for he was to represent Winchelsey on this very issue at the papal curia: he states that Winchelsey excommunicated Langton because he did not agree to attend the provincial council to answer the challenge that he should adhere to the Ordinances.[359]

Given his own view of the boundaries of his ecclesiastical responsibilities, Winchelsey was supporting the Ordinances in every possible way. The important provincial council of the spring of 1312 was the last over which Winchelsey presided. Although the council was largely concerned with the process against the

---

[354] *Councils*, p. 1357. He was back in Teynham by 17 March: ibid., p. 1358.
[355] *Vita Edwardi II*, pp. 22–3 and *Annales London.*, p. 203.
[356] *Foedera*, II. i. 159 (*CCR 1307–13*, p. 451).
[357] *Councils*, pp. 1356–76.
[358] *Flores Hist.*, III. 148–9; and see Beardwood, 'The trial of Langton', p. 10.
[359] Murimuth, p. 18.

Templars, questions concerning the maintenance of the Ordinances were separate items on the agenda.[360] As far as the evidence has shown, it was unusual for Winchelsey to introduce for discussion in a council of his clergy a matter of such direct political concern, though *Confirmatio Cartarum* must have been discussed in council in late 1297 and certainly in 1298. The bishops agreed that they were bound by their oaths to keep the Ordinances and bound by the duties of their office to enforce, as far as possible, the observance of the Ordinances by others. They decided also that all infringers should be excommunicated and the sentences of excommunication should be published. The excommunication of Walter Langton may have resulted from this decision. The bishops also agreed that it was not a fitting time to inform the pope that adherence to the Ordinances was in the public good, but that the earls should be informed of the consequences of breaking their oaths. The clergy were asserting their right to act as guardians of the peace of the realm and to put forward a firm policy on a question which was of great secular, as well as ecclesiastical, consequence, and they saw no need to confer with the pope on the matter. The Ordinances were glorified as 'to the honour of God and the benefit of the Church, the expedient relief of the lord king and of the kingdom and the succour of the poor and the oppressed'.

In May 1312 the king was faced with a firmly united opposition group, but the murder of Gaveston in June soon broke up the opposition and diverted attention away from the Ordinances. What part Winchelsey played in the remaining events of the year is not clear.[361] He can only have been a disappointed man. He had worked earnestly for the Ordinances, but it was rapidly becoming obvious that they would not be maintained. Once again his attempt to gain a lasting commitment to the preservation of the liberties of the Church was ending in failure. His control of the English Church had been determined, just, and, all things considered, successful. Yet, after the major achievement concerning taxation in 1297, there was no other issue on which he had

---

[360] *Councils*, pp. 1369–71.
[361] K. Edwards, 'Political importance of bishops', pp. 324–5 and *Councils*, p. 1377.

obtained significant royal concessions. Clause 12 of the Ordinances, for example, granting relief on the thorny question of writs of prohibition, became a dead letter. A general failure to obtain satisfactory redress of grievances played into the hands of the royal clerks and the courtier bishops. Winchelsey was in a long tradition of conservative churchmen; his intense belief in the separate status of the priesthood and his conviction that the welfare of the realm was tied to, and dependent upon, the welfare of the Church prevented him from exercising any influence of a constructive sort over either Edward I or Edward II. He represented an entrenched point of view which still carried great force. But the fact that he stood so frequently as the opponent of secular authority must have lowered his standing in the eyes of many, for there was in England, as the parliament of Carlisle in 1307 had shown, a very strong allegiance to kingship and to the rights of the Crown. For him the traditional advisers of the Crown included the bishops *as bishops*; in reality, the king's episcopal advisers were government officials.

Winchelsey's dispute with Edward II had reached its crisis in 1312; but the king had called for papal assistance, and Clement intervened. The archbishop's last visit to London, in the autumn of 1312, was to treat with papal nuncios, the cardinal priest of St Prisca and the bishop of Poitiers. In December he travelled south to Otford, near Sevenoaks, where he remained until his death on 11 May 1313. The king and the pope schemed secretly to obtain a successor who was more amenable to the Crown, and the appointment of the king's chancellor and confidant, Walter Reynolds, was the outcome. Winchelsey's name in death was to be linked directly with the Ordinances, but the *Confirmatio Cartarum* of 1297 was undoubtedly a greater achievement. He had set himself against arbitrary exactions and arbitrary rule, and both Edward I and Edward II were weaker because of his leadership of the English Church.

Chapter 6

ROYAL CLERKS AND THE CURE OF SOULS

Winchelsey had been sufficiently influential and astute to achieve united clerical decisions in ecclesiastical council after ecclesiastical council; but not far beneath the surface, and especially among the higher ranks of churchmen, there was an unwillingness to accept sacerdotalist views. This dissent is seen particularly in the careers and actions of royal clerks. With some clerks, refusal to be occupied in the affairs of secular government was a matter of the highest principle; but the continuing dependence of royal government, at all levels, upon the clergy needs no stressing. The policies of royal government were often shaped, if not determined, by the king's ministers, many of whom were churchmen.

We have seen bishops and magnates with distinguishable aims, different policies promoted by the Church and the Crown (as in 1296–7) which were apparently designed to set clergy and laity apart, and distinct attempts to draw a line between spiritualities and temporalities, not only in a material sense, which was relatively simple, but also in terms of political control, which was far from simple. At different times and on different issues each of these distinctions had a reality of its own. Yet, the king could claim an overriding patronage of the English Church, Winchelsey *and* Lancaster were popular saints, laymen rarely revealed themselves as enemies of the clergy, and the clergy's spiritualities and temporalities were usually taxed, whether for pope or king, together. Surely there is some point at which the 'spiritual' could, in practice, be set quite apart from the 'temporal'? Was not the quintessential activity of the priesthood, the cure of souls, under the sole control of the Church and its courts? Not even at this point – as will be seen, notably from the disputes concerning royal free chapels – can a clear line be drawn. To many, sacerdotalism must have smacked of the idealism of the scholastic.

We cannot doubt that Winchelsey believed that the policies of the Crown presented a dire threat to the position and rights of the English Church. The central dilemma of his career was that, on the one hand, he was intent upon the preservation of the ideal that men of the cloth should not be enmeshed in secular affairs, and yet, on the other hand, he recognised that the only way in which progress could be made in the defence of ecclesiastical rights was by exerting political pressure upon the king at times of crisis and especially when the interests of the clergy coincided with the interests of the magnates. *Confirmatio Cartarum* demonstrated that involvement in politics at a high level could bring results. But if we survey the whole range of the clergy's grievances and the legal wrangles in which Winchelsey became involved, we might well conclude that the archbishop, for all his determination, achieved relatively little. Indeed, the attitude of the Crown towards the Church courts appears to become more rather than less aggressive. The re-establishment after 1301 of successful relations between Crown and papacy was one of the reasons for Winchelsey's political weakness. But another reason was the division of outlook within the clergy's own ranks. Complaints from ecclesiastical councils were often against the procedures of royal government and of royal courts. Were these not, in many cases, complaints of the non-royal clergy against the royal clergy? I have examined the gulf within the episcopate between the learned prelates and the curialist prelates, studied the rapidity of the submission of the royal clerks to Edward I early in 1297, and noted the significance of the archbishop's legal actions against royal clerks in the period preceding his suspension. Much more research is required in order to evaluate the ecclesiastical viewpoint of the influential churchmen who did not accept the teaching and policies of Winchelsey. Were the royal clerks, a large number of whom were university-trained and held high office in the Church, back-sliders and time-servers, as they have often been portrayed?[1] Here I must limit myself to a study of the issues and principles involved in some specific cases where Winchelsey opposed the clergy who were in royal service. For the archbishop the defence of the English Church's liberty was certainly an internal as well as an

---

[1] See, for example, *Flores Hist.*, III. 291 and Bury, p. 138.

external matter. He regarded some churchmen, as Pecham regarded Robert Burnell, as of the order of Aaron rather than of the
order of Melchizedek: Aaron had made the people 'naked unto
their shame among their enemies'.[2]

The claim by Anne Deeley that the Crown was intent upon a
'gradual but bold extension' of its patronage rights has been
confirmed and further substantiated in a recent valuable study of
royal ecclesiastical patronage by P. C. Saunders.[3] Indeed, the extension of royal rights and the increase in the number of benefices
in the gift of the Crown – beginning distinctly in the second half
of the reign of Edward I – were more marked and more rapid
than has been generally supposed. This growth, which, as Saunders
shows, was to change the composition of the beneficed clergy in
the dioceses, was caused in part by the Crown's appropriation of
some large comital baronies, and also by a rigorous defence of
established rights. There was, for example, a notable increase in
the number of royal presentations arising from vacancies in royal
monasteries. In addition, there was a clear policy of amplifying
where possible the Crown's legal claims. The king was eager to
exercise control over benefices which could on occasion come
under his patronage, so that he might act on this pretext to prevent
the division of prebends or the appropriation of churches to
monasteries.[4] Much more damaging to the Church was the
stronger assertion, late in Edward I's reign, of the claim that the
king could exercise at any time his right of patronage if it had
been neglected, regardless of the rules of lapse: 'no time runs
against the king'. The pope made a similar claim concerning his
right to make provisions. The strength of the Crown's position,
and of the position of the royal clerks, rested on the fact that the
cognisance of advowson cases belonged to the royal courts. Extending this cognisance, the king refused to accept the Church's
assertion that a vicarage was 'entirely spiritual'. Thus, disputes
concerning the patronage of vicarages were brought into the king's
courts, and the king appointed at times to vicarages during episcopal vacancies.[5] The cases which faced Winchelsey when he became

[2] *Reg. Epistolarum Peckham*, i. 47, and Exod. 32:25.
[3] Deeley, 'Papal provision and royal rights', p. 505, and Saunders, 'Royal Eccles.
Patronage', esp. pp. 251–328.   [4] See the Dodderhill case, above, pp. 215–17.
[5] Howell, *Regalian Right*, pp. 192–5, *Councils*, p. 1215 and *Stat. Realm*, i. ii. 77.

archbishop must be studied with these developments in mind. It is important to remember, too, that, although a dispute almost always turned on the nature and extent of the king's own rights, the king's clerks were often the moving agents, seeking out vacant churches and pursuing in the courts their own particular interests. It is well known that the Crown was aiming to counteract the expanding papal claims of provision; but the king and his clerks were also threatening the rights, which were certainly not expanding, of the English prelates.

The first disputes between Winchelsey and royal clerks arose because of royal presentations to vacant churches (or churches claimed as vacant) while the temporalities of the see of Canterbury were in the king's hands from 8 December 1292 to 4 February 1295. Although some direct patronage belonged to the Crown, especially in a few of the royal free chapels, most of the king's appointments to benefices derived from wardship of lay fees or from custody of vacant royal abbeys and custody of vacant bishoprics. By the second half of the thirteenth century the king's rights of patronage *sede vacante* were firmly established. Having taken possession of the temporalities of a bishopric, the Crown exercised those rights of advowson which pertained to the bishop *sede plena*. This meant that the king could fully grant, or 'collate', vacant prebends in cathedral churches, for these were regarded, in the main, as benefices without cure of souls; but in order to fill vacant churches with cure of souls he must 'present' his candidates to the custodian of the spiritualities, who possessed the right of 'institution' to the church. As with other issues in the working together of Crown and Church, this procedure can be represented as an example of mutual respect and co-operation. Yet many instances can be cited in which there was neither respect nor co-operation, and the disputes which arose concerning royal clerks immediately after Winchelsey became archbishop illustrate both the nature and the extent of the conflict. In case after case the archbishop strove to defend his rights. Despite many obstacles put in his way he vigorously pursued a royal servant, Brunus de Podio, who claimed to be rector of the church of Shepperton in the London diocese. When the archbishop instituted Walter Reynolds to the church of Wimbledon, at the presentation of the king, he specifically re-

served the right to ordain a vicarage in the church.[6] Three of the
cases arising from royal presentations *sede vacante* merit more
detailed discussion.

After the wealthy church of Pagham had become vacant,
Edward presented, in March 1294, Theobald of Bar, who was the
brother of the king's son-in-law, the count of Bar.[7] Theobald was
described as in royal service. He was in the process of accumulating
a large number of benefices, including canonries and prebends at
York, Lincoln, Paris, Rheims, Liège, Beauvais, Troyes, Verdun,
Toul, Metz and Le Mans. The prior and chapter of Christ Church
Canterbury, as keepers of the spiritualities, did not institute
Theobald to Pagham but rather, as in other cases, granted him
only the custody of the fruits of the church. This was described
later by Winchelsey as 'a kind of temporal custody' constituting
no entitlement to the church, a fact which Winchelsey discovered
when he visited the deanery of Pagham soon after he became archbishop. Theobald had not been instituted to the cure of souls, and
as an alien absentee who was not in priest's orders he can hardly
have endeared himself to Winchelsey. But it proved very difficult
to remove him from Pagham, and the archbishop's dispute with
him lasted until 1302. In May 1299 Winchelsey granted the
church to his own clerk Ralph of Malling to be held *in commendam*. In the meantime Theobald had taken the matter to
Rome; and he obtained there a papal provision to the church and,
later, a mandate for the removal of Malling and for the protection
of his own position. One of the executors of the papal mandate
was the abbot of St Michael's Verdun, whose excommunication of
Winchelsey in 1301 was announced in all the churches of the city
of London. The story, much abbreviated here, illustrates the kind
of scheming in which the influential could engage. Theobald had
gained both royal and papal support, and Winchelsey had to fight

---

[6] *Reg.*, pp. 81, 121–2, 131–4, 201, 265–6, 334–5.
[7] Pagham church had almost 1500 parishioners and was assessed at £110 for the
rector: *Reg.*, p. 540 and *Taxatio*, p. 138b. For this dispute see *CPR 1292–1301*,
pp. 66, 476, *CCR 1296–1302*, p. 285, *Reg. Boniface VIII*, nos. 1942–3, 3856
(*CPL*, 1. 572, 591), *Annales London.*, pp. 102–3, *Reg.*, pp. xvii, 346, 362–3,
416, 540–2, 602–12, 748–9, 754–5, 763–5, CUL Ee. v. 21, fo. 59v (noted in *Cal.
Institutions*, ed. Woodruff, p. 98), Cant. D. & C., Reg. I, fos. 225v–227v, 230
and *Worcester Sede Vacante Register*, pp. 60–1 (copies of the bulls calendared
here are also in Lichfield Joint Record Office, Reg. W. Langton, fos. 24v–25r).

the case with great vigour. He rightly claimed that the facts had been distorted in Theobald's favour at the papal court. He indicated, for example, that the bull of provision even stated that the king had the right to collate to parish churches *sede vacante*, which would have constituted a right of lay investiture. The legal wrangle had led, as was so often the case, to violence, and the 'displaying of banners', in the parish itself. Winchelsey's efforts were eventually rewarded. The papal auditor of causes heard the evidence and in 1302 ordered the absolution of the archbishop, and of Ralph of Malling, from the sentences of excommunication; and Theobald dropped his claims to English benefices the follow-year when he became bishop of Liège.

Another case concerned a man of much lower status, a chancery clerk Thomas de Capella, who procured his own presentation to the church of Sevenoaks in October 1294.[8] The prior and chapter of Canterbury had ordered the usual inquiry but had not instituted; and because Winchelsey did not institute in 1295 he was impleaded in the king's bench by the writ *quare impedit*. The ecclesiastical ordinary's right of institution was of little practical worth if it did not include the right to refuse institution when a presentee was deemed unsuitable. The unsuitability of Thomas de Capella was probably a major factor in this case for, quite apart from the fact that he was unlikely to be resident in his benefice, his sanity had been questioned in 1292 and his disappearance for a year had caused concern to the bishop of Lincoln, for he was already rector of Bletchingdon in the Lincoln diocese.[9] But the king's court treated the matter in terms of defending the king's right of advowson. The church of Sevenoaks had been regarded as vacant because the rector, Master Roger of Sevenoaks, had been made treasurer of Hereford cathedral, to which dignity cure of souls was attached, and presumably Roger had no dispensation for plurality. Winchelsey claimed in the king's court that Sevenoaks, while vacant *de iure*, was not vacant *de facto*, for Roger had held

---

[8] See *CPR 1292–1301*, p. 88, CUL Ee. v. 31, fo. 63v (noted in *Cal. Institutions*, ed. Woodruff, p. 113), PRO KB27/146 m. 31d, /149 m. 41, *Reg.* pp. 20–1, 54, 61–4, 148–9, 255–6, 272–3, 423, 426, *CCR 1296–1302*, p. 219 and *Reg. Sutton*, v. 206–7, vi. 30.

[9] *Reg. Sutton*, iii. 181, iv. 42, 70, 124 and *CPR 1292–1301*, p. 267.

on to the church. But this argument carried no weight and the writ *ut admittas* was awarded to the Crown. Because Winchelsey still took no action, he was impleaded, at Michaelmas 1296, to answer for his contumacy, and the sum of £7,000 was claimed as damages. He was summoned by the writ *quare non admisit*, which was a legal process regarded as in itself injurious to episcopal rights.[10] As viewed in the king's court Winchelsey's case was weak, for, although the former rector was still in possession, the inquisition held late in 1294 had certainly found the church to be vacant. The archbishop objected that the question of the vacancy or the plenarty of churches was a matter for court christian, but the objection fell on deaf ears. Winchelsey submitted. He instituted Thomas de Capella to Sevenoaks late in 1296, as a result of which Thomas resigned from the rectory of Bletchingdon. Thomas was again regarded as insane early in 1297, and he resigned the church of Sevenoaks in 1298 – though it was at least three more years before the resignation took effect. In the face of a lawful presentation, backed by the king's bench and the action *quare non admisit*, it had proved extremely difficult, if not impossible, for the archbishop to refuse to institute.

A third case involved, not a chancery clerk, but the king's chancellor himself.[11] John Langton, who followed Robert Burnell as royal chancellor and served the king in this capacity from 1292 to 1302, had been presented by the king in March 1293 to the rectory of Reculver, which was valued at £113 6s 8d and was the ancient church of one of the principal demesne manors of the see of Canterbury. He was granted custody of the church by the prior and chapter of Christ Church. During the first years of his primacy Winchelsey was concerned only, it seems, to settle a dispute between the vicar of Reculver and the parishioners and to impose penances upon certain parishioners. The bitter conflict with John

[10] *Councils*, pp. 687, 1270–1, and see Gray, 'The *ius praesentandi*', pp. 501–6, Jones, 'Relations of two jurisdictions', pp. 115–32 and Saunders, 'Royal Eccles. Patronage', pp. 172–91, 322–7.
[11] See Emden, *Oxford*, p. 1099, *CPR 1292–1301*, pp. 8, 542, CUL Ee. v. 31, fo. 40r (noted in *Cal. Institutions*, ed. Woodruff, p. 103), *Reg. Boniface VIII*, no. 3005, *CPL*, I. 526, 581, *Reg.*, pp. 87–9, 101–2, 350–8, 373–5, 377, 382, 388, 707, 891–5, *Reg. Gandavo*, p. 58 and Graham, 'Sidelights on rectors of Reculver', pp. 3–7.

Langton, the rector, began in 1299, after John had failed, despite the king's support and a visit to the papal curia, to gain confirmation of his election to the bishopric of Ely.[12] The pope, on 29 June 1299, had provided John instead to the archdeaconry of Canterbury, and for this reason, if for no other, it was important, one might think essential, that he establish good relations with his archbishop. But Winchelsey had taken decisive action about Reculver. This case was not brought into the king's court; and the reasons for Winchelsey's claim that Langton had no right to Reculver are not, in fact, stated in the surviving letters. The main reason was probably that, as in other cases, he had not been instituted to the cure of souls. There may have been another reason: by 1299 Langton had obtained a dispensation for his plurality, but he was still no more than a subdeacon and this could have provided legal grounds for Winchelsey's attack upon him. The archbishop had now collated Thomas of Chartham to Reculver, declaring that he could do so because the church was vacant, *de iure* and *de facto*. How he could justify this claim at the same time as maintaining that Langton had unlawfully taken possession of the fruits of the church for four years and more is not clear. Langton's men apparently seized the rectory and its houses by force; and Winchelsey ordered their removal and the publication of sentences of excommunication against the intruders. Seven years after the royal chancellor's presentation to Reculver the archbishop thus succeeded in installing his own nominee. Although Langton's appeal to the pope resulted in the case being delegated in 1301 to the bishops of Salisbury and Rochester and the dean of St Paul's, success already seems to have rested with Winchelsey. In November 1300 the benefice is attributed to Thomas of Chartham on the king's patent roll, and Thomas remained in possession. Peace of a sort had been made between Winchelsey and Langton, and the latter vacated the chancellorship of the realm in August 1302. He continued as archdeacon of Canterbury until he became bishop of Chichester in 1305. As archdeacon he associated himself with Winchelsey's opposition to the royal abbey of St Augustine's Canterbury; and though he was prosecuted for plurality as a result of Winchelsey's visitation of

12 Above, pp. 41–2.

the Norwich diocese, the case was discharged.[13] It looks very much as if Winchelsey, at the height of his political influence, had effectively obstructed John Langton's attempts to combine his ecclesiastical duties with his high office in royal government.

These three disputes concerning the churches of Pagham, Sevenoaks and Reculver arose because of the king's exercise of patronage *sede vacante*, but this right in itself was not in dispute between archbishop and king. One of the main causes of conflict was Winchelsey's defence, or attempted defence, of his own right to withhold institution, a right which could be undermined, for example, by the awarding of the writ *ut admittas* in the king's court following advowson disputes.[14] Whatever the legal arguments used in different courts, the fundamental question must have been the unsuitability, in Winchelsey's eyes, of the king's presentees. We can hardly be surprised that he did not want royal clerks as rectors of his own churches. Nothing would prevent them, however, from obtaining churches throughout the realm, for benefices were the main form of reward for the men who served the king.

To raise the issue of the suitability of clerks is, of course, to pose many questions. But there were some abuses of beneficed clerks which bishops and the Church courts could attempt to correct, in particular plurality, absenteeism and failure to take orders. These were notoriously the abuses of royal clerks, and it was often on the grounds of breach of canon law in these areas that Winchelsey launched his attacks upon the servants of the Crown. The evidence relating to the cases already examined provides indications of the importance of these issues: Theobald of Bar claimed to the pope that he had acted in the belief that the king of England had obtained a papal grant exempting royal clerks who possessed benefices with cure of souls from the requirement to take orders; Thomas de Capella had been excused by Edward I from appearing

---

[13] Graham, 'Winchelsey and St Augustine's', p. 46, *CCR 1302–7*, p. 254 and Lambeth Palace Lib., MS 244, fo. 24r.

[14] C. 13 of the *Articuli Cleri* of 1316 (*Stat. Realm*, I. ii. 173, and see Denton, 'Reynolds and ecclesiastical politics', pp. 269–70) allowed that the examination of the suitability of royal presentees belonged to the ecclesiastical judge. It is doubtful whether this concession proved to be of practical significance.

before the archbishop, since, engaged as he was in the king's chancery, he could not do so 'without inconvenience to the king and his people'; and for many years John Langton was a pluralist without dispensation and, for even longer, did not proceed beyond the subdiaconate. Plurality, absenteeism and failure to take orders were treated as separate issues, though in practice they were closely linked. The necessity of obtaining dispensations for pluralism and for non-residence and the necessity of ordination to the priesthood within a year of institution to a benefice with cure of souls were now established canons of the Church, set down at the council of Lyons in 1274, published in England in the council of Reading of 1279 and embodied in the Sext of 1298.[15] The efforts of Pecham to implement these decrees in 1279 had aroused antagonism from the royal clerks and from Edward I. The Crown, protecting its officials from hindrance by other courts,[16] had built up defences for royal clerks against ecclesiastical interference.

In the case of pluralism, the attitude of many churchmen, not excluding popes, in fact assisted the Crown. Dispensations were obtained from Rome, by royal supplication, in large numbers and with apparent ease, though the papacy was more amenable in the matter at some times than at others. Dispensations were often retrospective, listing as they usually did the churches held by the man dispensed. They were perhaps sought, as a rule, when a pluralist felt that his position might be challenged and often, it seems, when a pluralist had already gained as many churches as his influence over respective patrons allowed. It is clear that the acquiring and the holding of many churches, whether by royal clerks or others, was widely condoned. Taking comfort from the fact that parishes were being served by vicars and curates, there were bishops who accepted the pluralism of rectors as a fact of life.[17] Some bishops, and not only those who had once been

---

15 *Sacrorum Conciliorum...Collectio*, ed. J. D. Mansi, xxiv. 90–3 (cc. 13 and 18), *Councils*, pp. 840–2, 853–7 and Sext., I. 6. 14 and I. 16. 3. See Douie, *Pecham*, pp. 98–104, Churchill, *Canterbury Administration*, I. 115–16 and Thompson, 'Pluralism', pp. 35–73.

16 See refs in Jones, 'Relations of two jurisdictions', pp. 145–8.

17 See C. H. Lawrence, *St Edmund of Abingdon* (Oxford, 1960), p. 127, Douie, *Pecham*, p. 99, Powicke, *Thirteenth Century*, pp. 475, 487, Pantin, *English Church in Fourteenth Century*, pp. 35–41 and Gray, 'Canon law in England', pp. 53–60.

pluralists themselves, were not always willing or able to stand firm against royal clerks. Other churchmen, especially learned churchmen, disapproved strongly of pluralism. It was probably still a question for keen debate among theologians, though most of them, as apparently was the case earlier in the century, would surely have firmly opposed it. After all, was the spiritual income of parish churches being used for truly spiritual purposes? Pecham and Winchelsey, for example, often fought against pluralists when they encountered them on visitation. But they could do little in general to counteract the abuse. Pecham had felt himself to be mocked by the compromises he made for pluralist royal clerks.[18] It was even less in Winchelsey's nature to accept compromises. He must likewise have felt mocked.

As for non-residence and non-ordination, the king claimed time and again that clerks in his service should not be compelled either to reside in their churches or to proceed to the priesthood.[19] The privilege of non-residence, it was said, had been enjoyed from time immemorial; and the king declared, in 1283, that he was not obliged to obey the statutes of the council of Lyons about the priesting of rectors. It was stated in one version of the replies to the 1280 clerical grievances that the king had been given a papal privilege exempting his clerks from the requirement of residence, but the only known papal grants (of 1247, 1252, 1272, and also of 1289) concerned the non-residence either of royal clerks for a stated period or of a stated number of royal clerks.[20] While there was no general papal privilege, popes had thus often made concessions to the Crown. Bishops made concessions, too, for episcopal licences of non-residence were sometimes granted to royal clerks, even occasionally specifying that service of the king was the reason for absence from a rectory.[21] The procedure assisted bishops them-

---

[18] *Reg. Epistolarum Peckham*, I. 199. For a concession by Pecham concerning non-ordination see Cheney, *Notaries Public*, p. 146.

[19] See, for example, *Councils*, p. 857, *Reg. Orleton*, p. 196, W. E. L. Smith, *Episcopal Appointments*, p. 129, CCR 1302–7, pp. 88, 193, Robinson, *Beneficed Clergy in Cleveland and East Riding*, p. 26 n. 97 and Cheney, 'Law and letters in Durham', p. 65 n. 1.

[20] *Councils*, p. 879 n. 2 and *Foedera*, I. i. 285, 496. Also see F. Pegues, 'The *clericus* in the legal administration of thirteenth-century England', *EHR*, LXXI (1956), 558.

[21] *Reg. Corbridge*, I. 217–18, *Reg. Greenfield*, IV. 170, *Reg. Gandavo*, p. 836, *The Register of J. de Grandisson 1327–69*, ed. F. C. Hingeston-Randolph

selves, for they sought from each other licences for their own clerks: thus Walter Langton petitioned Winchelsey and Winchelsey himself petitioned John Dalderby.[22] Boniface VIII, however, issued a strongly worded declaration against non-residence in his bull 'Traxit hactenus' of 29 March 1296.[23] In this 'irrefragabilis constitutio', which has been overlooked by most historians, Boniface referred directly to those who absented themselves from their churches in order to serve emperors, kings, princes, barons and other magnates. The pope declared that all clergy having churches with cure of souls should reside personally and continually in their churches within a month of receiving notice of his decree, after which time the churches would otherwise be *ipso iure* vacant. This bull claimed for the papacy the sole right to grant dispensations for non-residence. The insistence upon the special licence of the apostolic see puts one in mind of 'Clericis laicos', dated the previous month. But 'Traxit hactenus' caused no crisis, presumably because it could not be put into effect. It attempted to counter an accepted and widespread practice, as well as to override an established episcopal right of granting dispensations. It was an extreme and impracticable measure which was quickly forgotten; but it carried a message which was certainly not only in the minds of the pope and of his advisers, for those who believed that the spiritual income of the Church should be free from the direct taxation of secular leaders also believed that the spiritual income of parish churches should be devoted entirely to the work of cure of souls. It appears that Winchelsey made no use of 'Traxit hactenus'. In practice it offered him no opportunity of success in opposing non-residence. Although 'Traxit hactenus' was not included in the Sext, Boniface did there revoke all papal indulgences which granted the fruits of churches to clerks who were absent from them.[24] The spirit of 'Traxit

(London, 1894–9), I. 579, *The Register of R. of Shrewsbury 1329–63*, ed. T. S. Holmes (Somerset Record Soc., IX and X, 1895–6), II. 528 and *Cal. Chanc. Warr.*, p. 248.

[22] *Liber de Bury*, pp. 290–1 and *Reg.*, pp. 719, 746–7.

[23] *Reg. Halton*, I. 94–5, *Historical MSS Commission: Various Collections*, I. 242 (from Cant. D. & C., Christ Church Letters II, no. 262), *Liber de Bury*, no. 420, BL Harl. 667, fo. 9, Durham Cathedral Lib., C. IV. 24, fo. 92 and Cambridge Corpus Christi Coll., MS 450, p. 150.

[24] Sext., I. 3. 15.

hactenus' was retained and is reflected in Winchelsey's belief that ecclesiastical ordinaries should not be prevented from compelling royal clerks to reside in their churches.[25]

Cases of delinquent royal clerks often came to Winchelsey's attention during visitations. Exercising metropolitical powers the archbishop demanded the inspection of the dispensations of the clergy, and no exceptions could be made for royal servants.[26] He might attempt to enforce the law by bringing charges against the bishop. A number of distinguished royal clerks held churches in plurality in the Worcester diocese, visited by Winchelsey in 1301, and the bishop, Godfrey Giffard, was accused of admitting some of them to benefices when they had no dispensations for their plurality.[27] The clerks in question were Ralph of Hengham, chief justice of the bench, John of Berwick, king's justice, Peter of Leicester, baron of the exchequer, and Master John of Caen, eminent notary public. Bishops, including Giffard, certainly on occasion refused to institute pluralists who had no dispensations,[28] but they could be faced with appeal cases in the court of the Arches and they were often under strong pressure to institute on the promise that papal dispensations were awaited and would be shown in due course. It was on just such a promise that Giffard, so he himself claimed, had instituted the four above-named royal clerks to the churches of Fairford, Severn Stoke, Budbrook and Stratford-on-Avon, and he pointed out to the archbishop that 'other bishops do likewise in similar cases'. The bishop's own council had already concluded in respect of Ralph of Hengham that 'he is of the king's council, wherefore it is not expedient to proceed against him'.[29] There is no evidence to suggest that the archbishop himself took action against either Ralph of Hengham or John of Berwick, whose many benefices included (for Ralph) a prebend in the royal free chapel of Penkridge and (for John)

[25] See the comment upon the reply to c. 10 of the 1280 grievances, added probably when they were re-presented in 1309: *Reg.*, p. 1017 and *Councils*, p. 880 n. a.
[26] See the notifications of visitation: *Reg.*, pp. 307–8, 496–7, 695–6, 788–9.
[27] Thomas, *Survey of Worcester*, app. p. 70 (*Reg. Giffard*, II. 550), and see Graham, 'Metropolitical visitation of Worcester', pp. 87–91.
[28] See Hereford and Worcester Record Office, Reg. Giffard, pp. 869–70, old foliation 422 (*Reg. Giffard*, II. 493), concerning Peter of Leicester and the church of Thornbury, and *Reg. Sutton*, IV. 88–91, 99, concerning John of Berwick and the church of Amersham. [29] *Reg. Giffard*, II. 516.

the deanship of the royal free chapel of Wimborne Minster.[30] Winchelsey did, however, take proceedings against Peter of Leicester in an attempt to deprive him of the church of Budbrook, which the archbishop declared to be vacant because Peter had not become a priest and had been admitted to other benefices having the cure of souls without a papal dispensation.[31] Peter seems to have gained the support of Bishop Giffard and only resigned Budbrook after he had obtained a dispensation from the pope to hold his other churches in plurality. It was not, even then, the candidate supported by Winchelsey who secured possession of Budbrook but rather a presentee of Ralph of Hengham. The capacity of the archbishop to enforce the law was weakened not only by the influence which royal officers could exert but also by the ready expectation of the pope's beneficence. The battle was, nevertheless, being fought, and, while compromise, intrigue and malpractice were common, there appear to be, during Winchelsey's period of office, few notorious delinquents to compare with Bogo de Clare of the previous generation.

The case of John of Caen, the fourth of the royal clerks named as pluralists by Winchelsey in 1301, deserves brief attention.[32] As an indication of his favour with the king, we find included among John's benefices the deanery of the royal free chapel of Stafford and prebends in the royal free chapels of St Martin-le-Grand, Wolverhampton and Penkridge, and also in St Mary's Hastings, claimed as a royal free chapel. At the end of a petition to the king, late in Edward I's reign, John informed the king that he had been 'hindered and vexed continually by the archbishop of Canterbury because of various pleas'. We know a little about these pleas, for John was certainly pursued by Winchelsey for more reasons than holding the church of Stratford-on-Avon in plurality. This notary public acted as the king's leading spokesman in the wrangle concerning the status of St Mary's Hastings, and the archbishop's objection to his possession of a prebend there

---

[30] See Powicke, *Thirteenth Century*, pp. 356n, 363n, *VCH Dorset*, i. 113 and *Foedera*, i. ii. 766.
[31] *Reg.*, pp. 450–1, 745–6 and Lambeth Palace Lib., MS 244, fos. 9r, 80r.
[32] See Cheney, *Notaries Public*, pp. 143–51 and *Edward I and the Throne of Scotland 1290–1296: an Edition of the Record Sources for the Great Cause*, ed. E. L. G. Stones and G. G. Simpson (Oxford, 1978), i. 50.

belongs, as we shall see, to the story of the conflict concerning this church. In addition, when visiting the London diocese in 1303 Winchelsey cited John to appear before him because he had not been ordained priest within a year of obtaining the church of Stanford Rivers in Essex.

Another prominent royal clerk who was obstructed by Winchelsey was Peter of Dene, master of arts and doctor of canon and civil law.[33] Peter was a man of intrigue, described by the annalist of St Mary's York as a 'dreadful serpent'. He served not only the king but also the royal abbey of St Augustine Canterbury, whose rights he agreed to defend in 1300 against the archbishop, prior and archdeacon of Canterbury in return for a yearly pension of ten pounds. At about the same time, Winchelsey's visitation of the Chichester diocese revealed that Peter's possession of the church of East Tangmere was irregular, and after investigation of the case stringent measures were taken against him: in February 1302 he was excommunicated, deprived of all his benefices – including the church of Lindsey in the Norwich diocese, as well as canonries and prebends – and ordered to restore the fruits of the church of East Tangmere held unlawfully by him for more than three years. The Crown's aid was enlisted by Peter and in July 1302 a commission of oyer and terminer followed his complaint that a gang of men (among whom was Richard of Ruxley, later recorded as steward of the lands of the see of Canterbury) had attacked his houses at Lindsey, stolen his goods and beaten his servants 'while he was on the king's service and under his protection'. Peter's bitterness against Winchelsey continued, for in 1304 we find him appealing to the papal curia in an unsuccessful bid to frustrate the archbishop's efforts to secure the election of Ralph Baldock as bishop of London. Peter suffered little in the long run from Winchelsey's opposition. He soon obtained further benefices, and, like many other royal clerks,[34] he found employment and preferment in the diocese of York.

[33] See *Reg.*, pp. xxi–xxii, Emden, *Oxford*, pp. 2168–9 and Robinson, *Beneficed Clergy in Cleveland and East Riding*, p. 47 and plate IV, and from the sources esp. *Reg. Gandavo*, I. 68–9, *Annales London.*, p. 104, *CPR 1301–7*, p. 86 and *Reg.*, pp. 671–3.
[34] J. L. Grassi, 'Royal clerks from the archdiocese of York in the fourteenth century', *Northern History*, V (1970), 12–33.

We know from surviving letters of Winchelsey's to the king that for more than two years before the archbishop's suspension there was correspondence between them about the position of royal clerks.[35] Edward pleaded with Winchelsey to be gracious towards clerks who were in his service. Protesting his loyal and sincere regard for the king's honour and profit the archbishop undertook to do as much as he was able 'without open offence to God and without offending our conscience'. In fact the most that he would apparently concede was an acceptance, in some instances, of delays in the proceedings initiated in his court, just as there were adjournments in many of the cases against Winchelsey in the king's court. In the register of the archbishop's court of audience some of the cases for the period 1304 to 1306 are against royal clerks, amongst them Hervey de Stanton, Brunus de Podio, William de Halstede, Arnaud Lupi de Tilio and Edmund of London.[36] In the case of Edmund of London it is specifically noted that royal letters in his support were produced in the archbishop's court. Proceedings had been initiated against Edmund as a result of the visitation of the London diocese in 1303. He was prosecuted for not being ordained priest and for holding the church of Shenfield in plurality with the churches of Whittlesford and Lympsham, along with prebends in the royal free chapel of Wolverhampton and the college of St Mary's Hastings. Despite the royal letters on his behalf he continued to be summoned by the archbishop until early 1306; soon afterwards he gained papal dispensations allowing him to continue to hold his churches.[37] Winchelsey's visitation of the Norwich diocese in 1304 added to the dissension concerning royal clerks. The king enjoined that there should be no proceedings during the visitation against a number of named clerks: William of Brickhill, Robert of Chishall, Peter of Dunwich, John of Sheffield and Walter Bacon. Suits were certainly heard in the archbishop's court against the last two, with successive adjournments, and in the case of another royal clerk,

---

[35] *Reg.*, pp. 811–12, 1337 and PRO SC1/21/84. See above, p. 211.
[36] Lambeth Palace Lib., MS 244, fos. 17r, 31r, 40r, 62v, and see *Reg.*, pp. 334–5, 713.
[37] See Lambeth Palace Lib., MS 244, fo. 5r, *CPL*, II. 39, 92 and *Reg. Baldock*, pp. 135–6.

Ralph of Dalton, the court passed sentence, depriving him of his Norfolk church of Barney.[38]

Although Winchelsey had been occasionally successful in challenging individual royal clerks, his authority had often been defied or circumvented. His actions might run counter to Edward's wishes, but, at the end of the day, his court was no match for the king's. After Winchelsey's return from suspension he did not go on visitation and the disputes with royal clerks died down. To attempt to compel royal clerks to reside in their benefices had been, in any case, to cry for the moon. The opposition to specific clerks had frequently been an opposition to royal patronage claims and to claims of royal prerogative rights. So it was, also, in the disputes concerning the royal secular colleges, known as royal free chapels. Here, too, the archbishop's achievements were limited. Royal rights over these churches were being protected and expanded, largely through the efforts of the king's clerks, many of whom derived a substantial portion of their income from the prebends of the colleges. The case for a growth of royal ecclesiastical patronage in Edward I's reign is confirmed and strengthened, as we shall see, from a study of the disputes concerning royal free chapels.

Of the royal secular colleges, ten possessing churches with cure of souls had survived the far-reaching reforms in ecclesiastical organisation of the twelfth and thirteenth centuries with their parishes or deaneries free from ordinary ecclesiastical jurisdiction: St Martin-le-Grand London, Wimborne Minster, Wolverhampton, Stafford, Tettenhall, St Mary's Shrewsbury, Bridgnorth, Penkridge, Derby and St Oswald's Gloucester. In addition, the freedom of Bosham was still being contested in the fourteenth century. The king appointed the deans in the first seven of these churches,[39] the patronage of Penkridge and Derby having passed to the archbishops of Dublin and the deans of Lincoln, and St Oswald's Gloucester having become an Augustinian priory in the patronage of the archbishops of York. The exclusive or almost exclusive control of the Crown, or of those who held rights by grant of the Crown, over these churches was altogether anomalous

---

[38] *CCR 1302–7*, p. 193, *Cal. Chanc. Warr.*, pp. 223–4, PRO SC1/14/95 and Lambeth Palace Lib., MS 244, fos. 16v, 32v, 33v, 34r, 47v–48r, 114v.
[39] For the deans see *VCH London*, I. 564, *Dorset*, II. 113, *Stafford*, III. 309, 320, 330 and *Shropshire*, II. 122, 128.

as far as the Church was concerned. The 'exemption' of these churches and deaneries was nonetheless customary and long-established, and Edward I continued his father's vigorous defence of the Crown's prerogative rights. They were rights which Winchelsey did not accept, since for him spiritual jurisdiction exercised directly by the Crown could only be usurped jurisdiction.

Seven of the 'exempt' deaneries were in the diocese of Coventry and Lichfield and an eighth, Wimborne Minster, was in the diocese of Salisbury. Winchelsey visited neither diocese, and thus made no direct challenge to the freedom from ordinary jurisdiction claimed by these royal chapels. St Martin-le-Grand London and St Oswald's Gloucester were not, however, left in peace. It was during his visitation of the diocese of London in 1303 that the archbishop defied the privileged status of St Martin-le-Grand, the most important of the royal colleges.[40] The king, defending the freedom of the college and its prebends, sued Winchelsey in the king's bench for exercising the office of visitation and other rights pertaining to ordinary jurisdiction in this church and its appurtenant chapels. Winchelsey could not condone what he regarded as a blatant affront to ecclesiastical authority, but there was not the remotest chance that he would be able to weaken the established rights of St Martin-le-Grand. The case was adjourned, term by term, until the end of the reign. The archbishop also attacked during his London visitation the freedom claimed for the royal hospital of St Giles-in-the-Fields and so caused a commission of oyer and terminer to be brought against those who had aided him in breaking open the hospital gates. St Giles-in-the-Fields was one of the few royal hospitals that had a parish attached to it, and this, we can be sure, was the primary reason for Winchelsey's entry by force to the church.[41] How could he connive at the existence of parish churches which stood outside the authority of the Church?

During his visitation of the Worcester diocese in 1301 Winchel-

---

[40] PRO KB27/176 m. 20, /178 m. 103, /179, m. 71, /182 m. 78d, /184 m. 63d and /186 m. 55d and Prynne, III. 1041. For St Martin-le-Grand see Denton, *Royal Chapels*, esp. pp. 28–40 and R. H. C. Davis, 'The college of St Martin-le-Grand and the Anarchy, 1135–54', *London Topographical Record*, XXIII (1972), 9–26.
[41] See *CPR 1301–7*, pp. 189, 357, PRO KB27/181 m. 11, R. Newcourt, *Repertorium Ecclesiasticum* (London, 1708–10), I. 611–12 and Denton, *Royal Chapels*, p. 8.

sey opposed the privileges of the priory of St Oswald's Gloucester and in doing so took up a cause already unsuccessfully promoted, in recent years, by Archbishop Pecham and Godfrey Giffard, bishop of Worcester.[42] The royal college of St Oswald had been given by William Rufus c. 1093 to the archbishop of York and his successors, who held the church and its deanery – the deanery of Churchdown – not, essentially, as a distant adjunct of the diocese of York but rather as a royal peculiar. Its rights as a royal free chapel were not impaired by the donation to the archbishops of York, nor by the conversion of the college into an Augustinian priory in 1152 or 1153. The exemption of the priory and the deanery from the diocesan bishop and the metropolitan was by royal and not by papal grant. The ancient rights of St Oswald's could not have been upheld in any ecclesiastical court; but it was in the king's court that the interesting and protracted dispute was to be fought out, even though the matter turned, it should be stressed, on the question of the exercise of spiritual jurisdiction.[43]

Having been refused entrance to St Oswald's in April 1301 Winchelsey excommunicated the prior and canons, and, despite their appeal to Rome, forbade anyone to communicate or trade with them. When Godfrey Giffard had done the same the previous year Edward had immediately revoked the order, declaring that he could not tolerate such an innovation. It was to prove more difficult for him to overrule the actions of the defiant archbishop. A few days after the attempted visitation Winchelsey was presented with the alleged proof of the priory's privileges, but on inspection of the transcripts that he had been given he could find no mention whatever of exemption. At this setback the prior claimed that the documents dealing with the exemption were in

---

[42] See Douie, *Pecham*, pp. 231–3, Thompson, 'Jurisdiction of archbishops of York in Gloucestershire', pp. 138–47 and PRO KB27/164 m. 66, and for the history of St Oswald's liberties see Denton, *Royal Chapels*, pp. 51–7.

[43] It was unwise to suggest that the judgment of the king's court could not itself 'constitute a decision against the extent of a bishop's jurisdiction': Denton, *Royal Chapels*, p. 113. For Winchelsey's dispute with St Oswald's see Thompson, 'Jurisdiction of archbishops of York in Gloucestershire', pp. 147–52, *Reg. Corbridge*, II. 38–40, 45–52, 65–9, 87–9, *Reg. Greenfield*, I. 215–18, *Reg. Geynesborough*, p. 204, *Reg.*, pp. 810–11, *CCR 1296–1302*, pp. 411, 526, *CCR 1302–7*, pp. 87–8, 191–2, 224–5, *Cal. Chanc. Warr.*, p. 157, *Select Cases King's Bench*, III. 138–44 and PRO KB27 esp. /175 m. 77, /178 mm. 1, 27d, /183 m. 15, /184 m. 60.

the treasury of the church of York, and Winchelsey granted him time to produce the evidence. When it failed to arrive the excommunication was duly published. In September Archbishop Corbridge assured the prior that the excommunication and the prohibition on all communications were null and void, and he notified him that he himself should excommunicate anyone who impeded the jurisdiction reserved to the archbishop of York in the deanery of Churchdown. As for royal writs of caption following excommunication the archbishop of York had no doubt that the king's support could be enlisted; and in February 1302 Edward did, on receipt of Corbridge's request, order his chancery not to accept any letters of signification from Winchelsey or Giffard concerning the priory of St Oswald. Documentary proof was being sought by the archbishop of York's legal advisers, but evidence of canonical exemption they would never find. Nor would they need that kind of evidence.

In May 1303 the king ordered Winchelsey to revoke the sentences pronounced against St Oswald's, but the archbishop declined to obey the order. Later in the year the archbishop was summoned to appear before the king, who also prohibited the new bishop of Worcester, William Gainsborough, from visiting the priory. From the beginning of 1304 three cases, all concerned with the same issue, opened in the king's bench: the king versus the archbishop, the king versus the commissaries of the archbishop and the prior versus the archbishop. Winchelsey and his agents had acted against the king's prohibition. The archbishop had to attempt to prove that St Oswald's was not of royal foundation and that ordinary ecclesiastical jurisdiction had in the past been exercised there. He was apparently justified in asserting that Bishop Walter Cantilupe had held ordinations in the priory and that the canons had been accustomed to go in procession to the abbey of Gloucester and pay their pentecostals there, and that they had received their oil and chrism from the archdeacon of Gloucester.[44] But this was insufficient evidence to overturn the ancient royal liberties of the church. Given the terms of reference of the royal court, the Crown's case was incontrovertible. In 1305 Winchelsey gave indications of his willingness to submit to the king's grace in

[44] *Reg. Giffard*, II. 532n and *Reg. Greenfield*, I. 32–3, 38–9, 181–5.

the matter. Judgment against him came in November. But his suspension from office preceded the exaction of any damages; and the revocation of his sentences of excommunication was made not in fact by himself but by the keeper of the spiritualities during his suspension.[45]

The king was not content with defending ancient rights which had survived largely unimpaired. He made attempts to increase the number of royal free chapels. This could only be achieved by encroachments upon episcopal jurisdiction. Two examples, concerning St Buryan's Cornwall and Tickhill *alias* Blyth Nottinghamshire, did not directly involve Winchelsey, but they illustrate royal policy. Edward I became patron of the collegiate church of St Buryan's when the earldom of Cornwall passed by inheritance to the Crown in 1300. Almost immediately, and for the first time, the Crown claimed this church and its deanery as a royal free chapel.[46] Occasionally, when the earldom of Cornwall had been in the Crown's hands, the Crown had possessed the temporary right to present to the church,[47] but there is no evidence to suggest that St Buryan's had previously been regarded as free from ordinary ecclesiastical jurisdiction. Edward first appointed as dean William Hamilton (who became royal chancellor in 1305) and then in 1301 the royal clerk Ralph of Manton. John Grandisson, bishop of Exeter, was to blame William Hamilton for the new policy towards St Buryan's, but his predecessor, Bishop Stapledon, blamed Ralph of Manton. The rights of the bishop of Exeter and the archdeacon of Cornwall in this church, its prebends and its deanery were being denied, and the case was first heard in the king's bench in 1304. Edward asserted that it had been the ancient free chapel of the king's ancestors and

[45] PRO KB27/187 m. 52d.

[46] For St Buryan's see esp. Denton, *Royal Chapels*, p. 116, *The Registers of W. Bronescombe and P. Quivil*, ed. F. C. Hingeston-Randolph (London, 1889), p. 167, *Reg. Roffense*, pp. 200–1, 503, *Cal. Inq. P.M.*, III. 476, *CPR 1292–1301*, pp. 617–18, *CPR 1301–7*, p. 122, Prynne, III. 933 (*CCR 1296–1302*, p. 587), *Cal. Chanc. Warr.*, I. 205, 402–3, 489, *Rot. Parl.*, I. 421, and notably the material in *Reg. Stapeldon* and in *Register of J. Grandisson*, ed. F. C. Hingeston-Randolph (3 vols., London, 1894–9), and PRO KB27 beginning in /175 m. 68 and /176 mm. 4d, 13d, 19d.

[47] *Rotuli Litterarum Patentium*, ed. T. D. Hardy (Rec. Commission, 1835), pp. 96b, 111, *Rot. Lit. Clausarum* (1833–4) I. 444b and *Rot. Chartarum* (1837) p. 196b.

progenitors and had reverted to the Crown as to its founder ('ut ad suam naturam'). There was no substance in the claim, and faced with the just opposition of Bishops Stapledon and Grandisson, Edward II and Edward III were to find the implementation of Edward I's policy at St Buryan's no easy task. The dispute was protracted, and at times violent, but eventually the Crown established its novel demands.

The conflict about the royal free chapel of Tickhill or Blyth was between the Crown and the archbishops of York.[48] The castle of Tickhill had been in the hands of the counts of Eu, and, having been given to Edward before 1272, became a royal castle at his accession to the throne. Although the castle itself did not remain continuously in the king's possession, the patronage of the castle chapel was retained and the king's clerk, John Clarel, was appointed as 'parson' of this chapel. Clarel already had in his hands most of the churches which had once formed the royal chapelry of Blyth. In brief, he now succeeded in combining these churches, which he alienated from the church of Rouen, with the castle chapel of Tickhill. In 1295 Boniface of Saluzzo, the king's kinsman and clerk, succeeded Clarel to the castle chapel and to the churches of East Bridgford, Lowdham, East Markham, Markham Clinton, Walesby, Wheatley and Harworth, and he claimed that as the king's nominee he was both rector and ecclesiastical ordinary in these churches. Despite the fact that the archbishops of York had fully established their ordinary jurisdiction over the churches, the royal free chapel of the twelfth century was, for a time, recreated. Archbishops Romeyn, Newark and Corbridge took up the struggle against the Crown, but it was

[48] I am grateful to Elizabeth M. Rushton for assistance with the unravelling of the complex history of this 'royal free chapel', which merits more detailed treatment than it has yet received. In the meantime, see esp. Denton, *Royal Chapels*, pp. 75-6, 115, *CPL*, I. 363, 488-9, *Les Registres d'Honorius IV*, ed. M. Prou (École française de Rome, 1888), no. 586, BL Lans. 402, fos. 10v-13r, BL Add. 35170, fos. 108v-118v, *CCR 1272-9*, p. 335, *CCR 1296-1302*, p. 344, *CCR 1313-18*, p. 215, *CPR 1281-92*, p. 470, *CPR 1292-1301*, pp. 120, 135, *CPR 1307-13*, p. 594, *CPR 1313-17*, pp. 259, 311-12, Prynne, III. 1189-90 (*CCR 1302-7*, p. 524 and *CPR 1301-7*, p. 549), *Cal. Chanc. Warr.*, pp. 9, 61, *Rot. Parl.*, I. 138, 329, *Reg. Romeyn*, I. 327, II. 239-40, *Reg. Corbridge*, II. 59-60, *Reg. Greenfield*, IV. no. 2045, Davies, *Baronial Opposition*, p. 593, PRO KB27 e.g. /22 m. 5d, /26 m. 44d, E175 file 1/13, /14, /22 m. 1, C85/176/47, /177/6 and E159/74 m. 35d.

Archbishop Greenfield who eventually succeeded in retrieving his episcopal rights.

A third case, that of St Mary's Hastings, was similar to St Buryan's and Tickhill and involved Winchelsey because of his visitation of the diocese of Chichester in 1299–1300. Hastings castle, like Tickhill castle, had been in the possession of the counts of Eu and had been granted to young Edward in 1254. When the honour of Hastings was given to John of Brittany in 1270 an exception was made of the castle and town of Hastings and the collegiate church of the castle.[49] Thus, the college came into royal patronage at Edward's accession. Already in 1272 it was referred to, for the first time, as the 'king's free chapel'. St Mary's Hastings was not a royal foundation,[50] could not claim to be of ancient demesne and had no history of freedom from episcopal jurisdiction. When the church had been temporarily in royal hands at earlier times the king had exercised the right of presentation, not institution, to the prebends.[51] It could be regarded now with justification as a free chapel in a royal castle, but as a church with cure of souls it had no claim to exemption. This important distinction the king and his clerks chose to ignore.

In May 1275 Edward ordered William of Faversham to visit the college both to select a dean from among the brethren of the chapel and also 'that there may be corrected and reformed in the same whatsoever you may find to need correction and reformation'. William of Faversham's visitation may have been the occasion for the setting-down of the customs of the college.[52] There is soon evidence of a clash between the canons of the college and the bishop of Chichester: two of the canons in a petition to the king sought a remedy, apparently in 1279, for the molestations of the bishop and his official who had summoned the canons

---

[49] Dawson, *Hastings Castle*, I. 21–4, 85, 93, 101–3 and *CPR 1266–72*, pp. 304, 313, 375.

[50] Just as a charter of King Athelstan was forged to give support to St Buryan's (*Reg. Grandisson*, I. 74, 84–6), so the canons of Hastings falsely associated the name of Edward the Confessor with the foundation of their church (see PRO SC8 E668, and Dawson, *Hastings Castle*, II. 571).

[51] *Rotuli Litterarum Patentium*, pp. 22b, 59, 87b, 93b, 106a, Dawson, *Hastings Castle*, I. 92–4, *CPR 1232–47*, pp. 496, 509 and *CPR 1247–58*, pp. 2, 5, 10, 361.

[52] Dawson, *Hastings Castle*, I. 111–12 (*CPR 1272–81*, p. 88 and PRO C270/18 m. 2).

to synods and placed an interdict upon the churches which belonged to the college, thus preventing the ministers of the churches from burying the dead, baptising children and celebrating mass.[53] The king took up the complaints of the canons. In 1286 the college was once again visited by royal deputy, this time by Ralph of Marlow 'proctor and warden' of the king's free chapels. The dean of the college was ordered to observe a number of articles, one of which enjoined that no canon or minister should be accountable to any ordinary making citations or any corrections, in prejudice of the liberty of the chapel.[54] The next crucial step was to achieve the right of collation to the prebends, that is, the right both to present and to institute. The king's chancery does not appear to have been following a set procedure in phrasing the letters of appointment to the prebends of Hastings, but it is clear that by 1291 collations had become the rule. An inquisition held in 1299 confirms that this method of appointment without regard for episcopal rights began with the preferment of Walter of Amersham to a prebend on 31 May 1291.[55] The college with its prebendal churches had been transformed into a royal spiritual peculiar, and this was the state of affairs when Winchelsey became archbishop.

The resistance of the bishops of Chichester, Gilbert of St Leofard and John Langton, led to petitions in parliament and a case in the king's bench which lasted from 1299 to 1307.[56] Throughout the proceedings the king's agents had very little success in producing any evidence to support the royal claim. Inquiries were held by Robert de Burghershe, keeper of the Cinque Ports, and by prebendaries of the church, Giles de Audenard and Walter of Amersham, but without satisfactory results. John of Caen, also a prebendary, took up the pleading for the Crown in the king's court, but neither he nor other prebendaries, John de Wichio, Edmund of London and Thomas of

---

[53] Prynne, III. 228–9 (Dawson, *Hastings Castle*, I. 110).

[54] Dawson, *Hastings Castle*, I. 114–15 (from PRO C270/18 mm. 2–3). For Ralph of Marlow see Denton, *Royal Chapels*, p. 103.

[55] See *CPR 1281–92*, pp. 131, 219, 263, 362, 429, 463, 505 and Dawson, *Hastings Castle*, I. 121 and 125 (from PRO C49 roll 17).

[56] See esp. refs in *Councils*, p. 1145 (see 1394), and *Cal. Chanc. Warr.*, p. 160, Prynne, III. 856–7, PRO E159/74 m. 36d, /75 mm. 15, 22 and SC8 E620.

Ripe, could produce the necessary evidence. For example, John of Caen put forward two letters of the countess of Eu as early letters of collation, but the bishop of Chichester, John Langton, explained that the word 'donatio' had formerly been used with the meaning of 'presentatio'.[57] When Winchelsey had attempted to visit the church in 1299–1300 he had been obstructed by the keeper of the castle, John de Wichio, whom he excommunicated as a result.[58] He then ordered a visitation by his commissaries, against the express command of the king, and succeeded in the institution of William of Lewes as dean of the college. Edward opposed this appointment by granting the deanery to Giles de Audenard, but for some years he was in fact unable to secure the installation of his own nominee; and Winchelsey annoyed the king further by opposing John of Caen's collation to a prebend. The archbishop was summoned before the king in 1305 to answer for his 'insolence' and his 'acts of outrageous defiance', and soon proceedings also began in the king's court against William of Lewes. Yet the Crown had no adequate defence for its assault upon the spiritual jurisdiction of the bishop of Chichester, as diocesan, and the archbishop of Canterbury, as metropolitan. In so far as the royal college possessed cure of souls, that is, parishes and parishioners, it had no right to exemption from episcopal control. This was eventually recognised, in June 1307, by the justices of the king's bench in the case against the bishop of Chichester. The admission of defeat for the king and his clerks, a month before Edward's death, had come only after a long and bitter struggle.

Individual royal clerks can be seen as the perpetrators of attacks upon episcopal rights of institution and visitation, for example William Hamilton and Ralph of Manton at St Buryan's, John Clarel and Boniface of Saluzzo at Tickhill, and John of Caen at Hastings. Some of the grievances which the clergy presented to the king were clearly directed against the actions of these clerks,[59]

[57] Bracton had made the same point: *Bracton On the Laws and Customs of England*, trans. S. E. Thorne (Cambridge Mass., 1968), II. 159–60. I am grateful to Dr P. C. Saunders for this reference.

[58] See *CCR 1296–1302*, pp. 375, 442, 600, *CCR 1302–7*, pp. 80–1, 326, *CPR 1301–7*, pp. 50, 397, *Reg.*, pp. 404–5, PRO C270/24/4, *Memo. de Parliamento*, p. 128, *Rot. Parl.*, I. 167 and PRO KB27/185 m. 51d.

[59] *Councils*, pp. 1144–5 c. 39, 1208 c. 4.

among whom there was little reverence for the attitude of a man like Winchelsey. The nature of the king's relations with his clerks is largely hidden from us, but it is clear that they were often working in concert, to their mutual benefit. Although each royal servant no doubt often pursued policies for his own individual gain, the royal clerks can be regarded as a group,[60] and their attitudes and activities, like those of the curialist bishops, ran counter to many of the decisions of the clergy and bishops who supported Winchelsey in ecclesiastical council after ecclesiastical council. Opposition to Winchelsey from these clerks, serving lay government, is more discernible than the opposition of any laymen as such. This must not, however, be regarded as a serious weakness in the case for the 'laicisation' or 'secularisation' of English society in the thirteenth century, as understood, for example, by Strayer.[61] Although the extent of the Church's influence and authority at the end of the thirteenth century has sometimes been under-estimated, it is undeniable that over ecclesiastical, even spiritual, affairs there was increasing control by royal government. Winchelsey's activities were a reaction to it.

The archbishop did not deny that the English Church had a part to play in serving the public weal ('utilitas rei publice').[62] For their part, the king and his clerks at times claimed to be defending the liberties of the Church. Thus, when the chapter of St Mary's Stafford and their dean, John of Caen, complained to the king in 1300 of an infringement of the right of sanctuary in this royal free chapel, they pleaded specifically that ecclesiastical liberty should be defended by the Crown; and when a former sheriff of London, Martin of Amesbury, was impleaded in the king's court in 1295 because a fugitive in St Paul's London had been chained and held in irons by the sheriff's ministers, the record in the memoranda roll notes that Martin was summoned to reply to the king 'since the laws and liberties of the Church should be maintained unimpaired in his kingdom by the lord king and his ministers'.[63] This was not simply paying lip-service to the first clause of *Magna Carta*, for the question was not *whether*

---

[60] Powicke, *Henry and Lord Edward*, pp. 713–16 and idem, *Thirteenth Century*, pp. 340–1.
[61] See esp. 'Laicization of French and English society'.
[62] *Reg.*, p. 233.   [63] PRO SC1/20/183 and E159/68 m. 32.

ecclesiastical liberty should be defended by the Crown, but rather in what respects and to what extent. The Church's liberty as seen by Winchelsey was capable of definition not only, at one level, by reference to canon law, but also, at another level, by reference to English custom. The king, however, was extending his control by ensuring where possible that custom changed and developed to the advantage of royal government. As we have seen time and again, one of the most crucial problems was where the line should be drawn between spiritualities and temporalities. The king was claiming the allegiance of the *communitas cleri* since it was he who protected both their temporalities and their spiritualities.[64] The prior of Ely stated the royal position in a case before the king's bench in 1295: the king has a duty to 'maintain and defend the rights and inheritances of Holy Church, which is always under age and, as it were, in his custody within his realm'.[65] In the face of undesirable papal interference, especially in relation to provisions and financial demands, it was often the position of the Crown and of the magnates as patrons of churches that was stressed. The king was seen as 'advowee paramount'.[66] But it is abundantly clear that an inescapable corollary of the anti-papalism indicated by these views was the disparagement of the liberty of the English Church. One of the reasons for the king's success was the acquiescence of many English churchmen in slights upon the *ius papale*. Added to this was the positive support felt for the rights of the Crown.

The archbishop of Canterbury and the English Church were sandwiched between royal and papal governments. It was no coincidence that Winchelsey's cause had flourished when Edward's relations with Boniface VIII were strained and had waned when the royal–papal alliance re-emerged. The archbishop had shown that sacerdotalism was not a spent force. There is no doubt that there was strong backing among large sections of the clergy for the fight for ecclesiastical freedom – strong backing, for example, for 'Clericis laicos'. But Winchelsey and his supporters could not fight alone. During his early years in office he had been politically most

[64] Wake, *State of the Church*, app. p. 14 and *Concilia*, II. 40–1.
[65] *Select Cases King's Bench*, III. xxvi and 203.
[66] For example, *Councils*, pp. 290, 814 and Howell, *Regalian Right*, pp. 186–7, 206–9.

successful. Like some of his notable predecessors he had 'erected barriers against the abuse of sovereign authority'.[67] Suspension undoubtedly caused him humiliation; but it had been the consequence of Edward I's own humiliation in the years 1297 to 1301. Although he continued the fight in Edward II's reign, it was not with the same vigour. The cordial relations of both Edward I and Edward II with Clement V weakened his position severely. With the elevation to Canterbury, soon after Winchelsey's death, of Walter Reynolds, the king's right-hand man, we have a glimpse of the future – to times when archbishops were 'more like permanent government officials and less like independent churchmen'.[68]

[67] J. Lingard, *The History of England* (London, 4th edn, 1837–9), III. 269, cited in G. Templeman, 'Edward I and the historians', *Cambridge Hist. Journ.*, x (1950), 21.
[68] Highfield, 'The English hierarchy', p. 138.

Appendix

TABLE OF ROYAL TAXATION OF THE CLERGY 1294–1313

The amounts given in the following table are an approximation (more accurate for the subsidies based on the 1291 *taxatio* than for the lay subsidies) of the sums demanded of the clergy and are not based on collection returns. Where returns survive they suggest that the proceeds rarely fell far short of the amounts granted. Also, the collection of arrears resulted in a degree of levelling-out. The clergy's contributions to prises and to customs dues are impossible to calculate, and both are therefore excluded from consideration here.

All the papal tenths, a large percentage of which were paid to the king, and the direct clerical grants (with the exception of the tenth collected in 1298) were based on the 1291 assessment of the clergy's spiritual and temporal income by the order of Pope Nicholas IV. This *taxatio* assessed the annual clerical income of the English clergy at about £210,000, £170,000 of which was for the Canterbury province.[1] These sums are the basis for the figures in the second and third columns of the table.

The taxes upon lay movables present a number of problems. Each tax was based upon a new assessment and thus requires a separate calculation.[2] The totals for each assessment can be easily obtained, but there is no way of accurately determining the percentage of the total paid by the clergy. Even so, an estimate must be made, since the contribution of the clergy to taxes on lay movables is an important feature of royal taxation. Local assessment rolls, where they survive, give a guide, but no more than a guide.[3] They suggest that perhaps in the region of a sixth of the

---

[1] See Stubbs, *Constitutional Hist.*, II, table facing p. 580.

[2] See above, p. 56 n. 2.

[3] For example, under the year of grants: 1294 (tenth and sixth), county of Hertford: PRO E179/120/3; 1295 (eleventh and seventh), borough of Colchester: *Rot. Parl.*, I. 228–38; 1296 (twelfth and eighth), Northumberland: *The Northumberland Lay Subsidy Roll of 1296*, ed. C. M. Fraser (Soc. of Antiquaries of Newcastle-upon-Tyne, 1968); 1297 (ninth), parts of Bedfordshire: *Taxation of 1297: Bedfordshire Rolls*, ed. Gaydon; and 1301 (fifteenth), see above, p. 203 n. 110.

Appendix

lay taxes was paid by the clergy. But it is often difficult, and was difficult at the time, to understand clearly the dividing line between the taxes upon temporal (along with spiritual) income and the taxes on lay movables. This was the general position: after 1291 the temporalities of prelates and religious houses not included in the assessment of that year were taxed with lay movables, as also was the property of the clergy which was personal and no part of the income of a church. In two of the taxes listed below (the fifteenth of 1301, collected from the clergy in 1303, and the thirtieth and twentieth of 1306, collected in 1307), the temporalities assessed with spiritualities in 1291 were included rather than excluded, and for these two taxes I have estimated the contribution of the clergy at a quarter rather than a sixth of the total. In the case of the tenth and sixth collected in 1295 there are particular reasons for thinking that the clergy contributed less than a sixth, possibly a tenth.

Since the following taxes have usually been described by reference to the year in which they were granted, it is important to note that they are included here under the year in which they were, for the most part, collected. Since precision is unattainable, all amounts are given in round numbers.

298

	Year	Lay Subsidies	Direct Clerical Subsidies	Papal Tenths	Total s
Before Winchelsey's return from Aquila as archbishop	1294		1st term of moiety £35,000 (above, pp. 74–7)	Seizure from collection of sexennial 10th £33,000 (above, pp. 63–7)	£68,000
	1295	10th and 6th £8,000 (of £82,000) (above, pp. 77–8)	2nd and 3rd terms of moiety[4] £70,000		£78,000
	1296	11th and 7th £9,000 (of £53,000) (above, p. 87)	10th £21,000[5] (above, pp. 86–8)		£30,000
	1297	12th and 8th £6,500 (of £38,500) (above, p. 94)	Fine of 5th £42,000 (above, pp. 104–34)		£51,500
		1st term of 9th £3,000 (of £34,500) (above, p. 169)			
	1298	2nd term of 9th £3,000	10th £20,000[6] (above, pp. 173–4)		£23,000

[4] Although the full amount due from the moiety was certainly not paid by the end of 1295, this is largely offset by the additional demands which had recently affected the clergy, as the seizure of private treasure (above, pp. 68–9).
[5] It is not clear that the two rolls of receipts (PRO E401/1643, /1647), giving a sum of £11,233, contain the total received by the autumn of 1296: cf. Prestwich, *War, Politics and Finance*, p. 187.
[6] A figure can only be arrived at by conjecture: this tax was a fifth in the York province and a tenth in the Canterbury province, but the yield was probably less, not more, than the usual tenth, since the spiritualities were taxed according to the less harsh Norwich *taxatio* and, in addition, not all of the proceeds of the tax were actually paid to the king. See above, pp. 189, 213.

Appendix

Year	Lay Subsidies	Direct Clerical Subsidies	Papal Tenths	Totals
1299				
1300				
1301				
1302			1st year of triennial 10th[7] £14,000	£14,000
1303	15th £12,500 (of £50,000) (above, pp. 201–4)		2nd year of triennial 10th £14,000	£26,500
1304			3rd year of triennial 10th £14,000	£14,000
1305				
1306			1st year of biennial 10th[8] £19,000 (above, p. 220)	£19,000
1307 *Granted during Winchelsey's suspension*	30th and 20th £8,500 (of £35,000) (above, pp. 236–7)		2nd year of biennial 10th £21,000	£29,500
1308	20th and 15th £6,500 (of £38,500) (above, pp. 250–1)	15th £14,000 (above, pp. 250–1)		£20,500
1309			1st year of triennial 10th[9] £15,500	£15,500

[7] Of which the king obtained two-thirds of the total: above, p. 200.
[8] Of which the king obtained all but £2,000 for the first year and the full collection of the second year: Lunt, *Financial Relations*, pp. 383–4.
[9] Of which the king obtained three-quarters: above, p. 251.

Year	Lay Subsidies	Direct Clerical Subsidies	Papal Tenths	Totals
1310	25th £5,500 (of £34,000) (above, p. 251)		2nd year of triennial 10th £15,500	£21,000
1311			5th term of triennial 10th £7,500	£7,500
1312			6th term of triennial 10th £7,500	£7,500
Collected after Winchelsey's death 1313			Annual 10th[10] £21,000 1st term of 1st year of new sexennial 10th[11] £10,500	£31,500

Total of taxation paid by clergy to the king: £457,000
(Excluding estimated clerical contributions to lay subsidies: £394,500)

Total of taxation paid by laity to the king: £303,000
(Including estimated clerical contributions to lay subsidies: £365,500)

[10] See Denton, 'Reynolds and ecclesiastical politics', p. 253.
[11] Ordered by the pope in 1311, and the proceeds seized by the king in 1314: ibid., pp. 253–4.

BIBLIOGRAPHY

As a rule all works referred to more than once have been included in this select bibliography. Primary material can be found in the first list through the abbreviated reference used in the footnotes; all secondary works appear, in the second list, under the author's name.

PRINTED SOURCES

Anglia Sacra: *Anglia Sacra*, ed. H. Wharton (2 vols., 1691)

Anglo-Scottish Relations, ed. Stones: *Anglo-Scottish Relations 1174–1328: Some Selected Documents*, ed. E. L. G. Stones (Oxford, 2nd edn, 1970)

Annales London.: *Annales Londonienses* in *Chronicles Edward I & II*, I. 1–251

Annales Monastici: *Annales Monastici*, ed. H. R. Luard (RS, 5 vols., 1864–9)

Annales Paulini: *Annales Paulini* in *Chronicles Edward I & II*, I. 253–370

Antient Kalendars: *The Antient Kalendars and Inventories*, ed. F. Palgrave (Record Commission, 3 vols., 1836)

Book of Prests: *Book of Prests of the King's Wardrobe for 1294–5: Presented to J. G. Edwards*, ed. E. B. Fryde (Oxford, 1962)

Bridlington: *Gesta Edwardi de Carnarvon Auctore Canonico Bridlingtoniensi* in *Chronicles Edward I & II*, II. 25–151

Bury: *The Chronicle of Bury St Edmunds 1212–1301*, ed. A. Gransden (London, 1964)

Cal. Chanc. Warr.: *Calendar of Chancery Warrants* (HMSO, 1 vol., 1927)

Cal. Inq. P.M.: *Calendar of Inquisitions Post Mortem 1292–1316* (HMSO, 3 vols., 1908–13)

Cal. Institutions, ed. Woodruff: *Calendar of Institutions by the Chapter of Canterbury Sede Vacante*, ed. C. E. Woodruff (Kent Archaeological Soc., Records Branch, VIII, 1923)

Bibliography

Cal. London Trailbaston Trials: *Calendar of London Trailbaston Trials Under Commissions of 1305 and 1306*, ed. R. B. Pugh (HMSO, 1975)

Cal. Var. Chanc. Rolls: *Calendar of Various Chancery Rolls 1277–1326* (HMSO, 1912)

Canterbury Professions, ed. Richter: *Canterbury Professions*, ed. M. Richter (CYS, 1973)

CCR: *Calendar of Close Rolls 1272–1313* (HMSO, 6 vols., 1892–1908)

CFR: *Calendar of Fine Rolls 1272–1319* (HMSO, 2 vols., 1911–12)

Chartes des Libertés, ed. Bémont: Ch. Bémont, *Chartes des Libertés Anglaises 1100–1305* (Paris, 1892)

Chartularium Univ. Paris.: *Chartularium Universitatis Parisiensis*, ed. H. Denifle and E. Chatelain (Paris, 4 vols., 1889–97)

Chronica de Melsa: *Chronica Monasterii de Melsa*, ed. E. A. Bond (RS, 3 vols., 1866–9)

Chronicles Edward I & II: *Chronicles of the Reigns of Edward I and Edward II*, ed. W. Stubbs (RS, 2 vols., 1882–3). Introduction reprinted in W. Stubbs, *Historical Introductions to the Rolls Series*, ed. A. Hassall (London, 1902), pp. 489–97

Concilia: *Concilia Magnae Britanniae et Hiberniae*, ed. D. Wilkins (4 vols., 1737)

Cont. Gervase: *The Continuation of the Minor Chronicle of Gervase of Canterbury* (*Gesta Regum Continuata*) in *The Historical Works of Gervase of Canterbury*, ed. W. Stubbs (RS, 2 vols., 1880), II. 106–324

Cotton: *Bartholomaei de Cotton Monachi Norwicensis Historia Anglicana*, ed. H. R. Luard (RS, 1859)

Councils: *Councils & Synods with Other Documents Relating to the English Church, II 1205–1313*, ed. F. M. Powicke and C. R. Cheney (Oxford, 2 pts, 1964)

Councils and Eccles. Documents, ed. Haddan and Stubbs: *Councils and Ecclesiastical Documents Relating to Great Britain and Ireland*, ed. A. W. Hadden and W. Stubbs (Oxford, 3 vols., 1869–78)

CPL: *Calendar of Papal Registers: Papal Letters 1198–1342*, ed. W. H. Bliss (HMSO, 2 vols., 1893–5)

CPR: *Calendar of Patent Rolls 1272–1313* (HMSO, 5 vols., 1893–1901)

Dunstable: *Annales de Dunstaplia* in *Annales Monastici*, III. 1–408

Eng. Hist. Documents, III: *English Historical Documents*: III, *1189–1327*, ed. H. Rothwell (London, 1975)

Bibliography

Evesham: J. H. Denton, 'The crisis of 1297 from the Evesham chronicle', *EHR*, XCIII (1978), 568–79

Flores Hist.: *Flores Historiarum*, ed. H. R. Luard (RS, 3 vols., 1890)

Flor. Wig.: *Florentii Wigorniensis Monachi Chronicon Ex Chronicis*, ed. B. Thorpe (English Hist. Soc., 2 vols., 1848–9)

Foedera: *Foedera, Conventiones, Litterae*, ed. T. Rymer (Record Commission, 3 vols. in 6, 1816–30)

Guisborough: *The Chronicle of Walter of Guisborough*, ed. H. Rothwell (Camden, 3rd ser. LXXXIX, 1957)

Hemingsby Register: *Hemingsby Register*, ed. H. M. Chew (Wiltshire Archaeological and Natural Hist. Soc. Records, XVIII, 1963)

Lancs. Lay Subsidies, ed. Vincent: *Lancashire Lay Subsidies*, I, ed. J. A. C. Vincent (Record Soc. Lancashire and Cheshire, XXVII, 1893)

Lanercost: *The Chronicle of Lanercost, 1272–1346*, trans. H. Maxwell (Glasgow, 1913)

Langtoft: *The Chronicle of Pierre de Langtoft*, ed. T. Wright (RS, 2 vols., 1866–8)

Letters of Prince Edward, ed. Johnstone: *Letters of Edward Prince of Wales, 1304–5*, ed. H. Johnstone (Roxburghe Club, 1931)

Liber Albus: *Liber Albus*, ed. J. M. Wilson (Worcestershire Hist. Soc., 1919)

Liber de Bernewelle: *Liber Memorandorum Ecclesie de Bernewelle*, ed. J. W. Clark (Cambridge, 1907)

Liber de Bury: *The Liber Epistolaris of Richard de Bury*, ed. N. Denholm-Young (Roxburghe Club, 1950)

Lincs. Assize Roll 1298, ed. Thomson: *A Lincolnshire Assize Roll for 1298*, ed. W. S. Thomson (Lincoln Record Soc., XXXVI, 1944)

Literae Cantuar.: *Literae Cantuarienses*, ed. J. B. Sheppard (RS, 3 vols., 1887–9)

Memo. de Parliamento: *Memoranda de Parliamento 1305*, ed. F. W. Maitland (RS, 1893). Part of intro. (pp. xxxiv–lxxxix) reprinted in *Maitland: Selected Essays*, ed. H. D. Hazeltine, G. Lapsley and P. H. Winfield (Cambridge, 1936), pp. 13–72

Murimuth: *Adae Murimuth Continuatio Chronicarum*, ed. E. M. Thompson (RS, 1889)

Norwich Charters, ed. Dodwell: *The Charters of Norwich Cathedral Priory, Part I*, ed. B. Dodwell (Pipe Roll Soc., new ser. XL, 1965–6)

Oxford Formularies: *Formularies Which Bear on the History of Oxford*, ed. H. E. Salter, W. A. Pantin and H. G. Richardson (Oxford Hist. Soc., new ser. IV and V, 1942)

Bibliography

Parl. Writs: *The Parliamentary Writs and Writs of Military Summons*, ed. F. Palgrave (Record Commission, 2 vols. in 4, 1827–34)

Potthast: *Regesta Pontificum Romanorum*, ed. A. Potthast (Berlin, 2 vols., 1874–5)

Prynne, III: W. Prynne, *The Third Tome of our Exact Chronological Vindication of the Supreme Ecclesiastical Jurisdiction of our... English Kings* (London, 1668, reissued 1670, 1672)

Records of the Trial of Langeton, ed. Beardwood: *Records of the Trial of Walter Langeton Bishop of Coventry and Lichfield 1307–12*, ed. A. Beardwood (Camden, 4th ser. VI, 1969)

Reg.: *Registrum Roberti Winchelsey*, ed. R. Graham (CYS, 2 vols., 1952–6)

Reg. Baldock: *Registrum Radulphi Baldock, Gilberti Segrave, Ricardi Newport, et Stephani Gravesend 1304–38*, ed. R. C. Fowler (CYS, 1911)

Reg. Benoît XI: *Le Registre de Benoît XI*, ed. Ch. Grandjean (École française de Rome, 1905)

Reg. Boniface VIII: *Les Registres de Boniface VIII*, ed. G. Digard, M. Faucon, A. Thomas and R. Fawtier (École française de Rome, 4 vols., 1907–39)

Reg. Clement V: *Registrum Clementis Papae V*, ed. monks, O. S. B. (index vol. R. Fawtier) (Rome, 9 vols., 1885–92, 1957)

Reg. Cobham: *The Register of Thomas de Cobham 1317–27*, ed. E. H. Pearce (Worcestershire Hist. Soc., 1930)

Reg. Corbridge: *The Register of Thomas Corbridge 1300–4*, ed. W. Brown and A. Hamilton Thompson (Surtees Soc., CXXXVIII and CXLI, 1925–8)

Reg. Drokensford: *Calendar of the Register of John de Drokensford 1309–29*, ed. E. Hobhouse (Somerset Record Soc., 1887)

Reg. Epistolarum Peckham: *Registrum Epistolarum Fratris Johannis Peckham, Archiepiscopi Cantuariensis*, ed. C. T. Martin (RS, 3 vols., 1882–5)

Reg. Gandavo: *Registrum Simonis de Gandavo 1297–1315*, ed. C. T. Flower and M. C. B. Dawes (CYS, 2 vols., 1934)

Reg. Geynesborough: *The Register of William de Geynesborough 1302–7*, ed. J. W. Willis Bund (Worcestershire Hist. Soc., 1907–29)

Reg. Giffard: *The Register of Godfrey Giffard 1268–1301*, ed. J. W. Willis Bund (Worcestershire Hist. Soc., 2 vols., 1902)

Reg. Greenfield: *The Register of William Greenfield 1306–15*, ed. A. Hamilton Thompson (Surtees Soc., CXLV, CIL, CLI–CLIII, 1931–40)

Bibliography

Reg. Halton: *The Register of John de Halton 1292–1324*, ed. W. N. Thompson (CYS, 2 vols., 1913)

Reg. Kellawe: *Registrum Palatinum Dunelmense: the Register of Richard de Kellawe 1314–16*, ed. T. D. Hardy (RS, 4 vols., 1873–8)

Reg. Martival: *The Registers of Roger Martival 1315–30*, ed. K. Edwards, C. R. Elrington, S. Reynolds and D. M. Owen (CYS, 4 vols., 1959–75)

Reg. Newark: see *Reg. Romeyn*

Reg. Orleton: *Registrum Ade de Orleton 1317–27*, ed. A. T. Bannister (CYS, 1908)

Reg. Pontissara: *Registrum Johannis de Pontissara 1282–1304*, ed. C. Deedes (CYS, 2 vols., 1915–24)

Reg. Reynolds: *The Register of Walter Reynolds 1308–13*, ed. R. A. Wilson (Worcestershire Hist. Soc., 1927 and Dugdale Soc., 1928)

Reg. Roffense: *Registrum Roffense*, ed. J. Thorpe (London, 1769)

Reg. Romeyn: *The Registers of John le Romeyn 1286–96 and of Henry of Newark 1296–9*, ed. W. Brown (Surtees Soc., cxxiii and cxxviii, 1913–17)

Reg. Stapeldon: *The Register of Walter de Stapeldon 1307–26*, ed. F. C. Hingeston-Randolph (London, 1892)

Reg. Sutton: *The Rolls and Register of Bishop Oliver Sutton 1280–99*, ed. R. M. T. Hill (Lincoln Record Soc., xxxix, xliii, xlviii, lii, lx, lxiv and lxix, 1948–75)

Reg. Swinfield: *Registrum Ricardi de Swinfield 1283–1317*, ed. W. W. Capes (CYS, 1909)

Reg. Woodlock: *Registrum Henrici Woodlock 1305–16*, ed. A. W. Goodman (CYS, 2 vols., 1940–1)

Rishanger: *Willelmi Rishanger, Chronica et Annales*, pp. 371–499 (*Annales Angliae et Scotiae, Gesta Edwardi Primi* and *Annales Regis Edwardi Primi*), ed. H. T. Riley (RS, 1865)

'Rishanger':[1] *Willelmi Rishanger, Chronica et Annales*, pp. 1–230 (*Chronica*), ed. H. T. Riley (RS, 1865)

Rôles Gascons: *Rôles Gascons*, ed. Ch. Bémont and Y. Renouard (Paris, 3 vols. in 4, 1885–1906)

Rot. Parl.: *Rotuli Parliamentorum* (Record Commission, 6 vols., 1783)

Rot. Parl. Hactenus Inediti: *Rotuli Parliamentorum Anglie Hactenus Inediti 1279–1373*, ed. H. G. Richardson and G. O. Sayles (Camden, 3rd ser. li, 1935)

Scriptores Decem: *Historiae Anglicanae Scriptores Decem*, ed. R. Twysden (London, 1652)

[1] See V. H. Galbraith, *The St Albans Chronicle* (Oxford, 1937), pp. xxxiii–xxxvi.

Select Cases Before King's Council: *Select Cases Before the King's Council 1243–1482*, ed. I. S. Leadam and J. F. Baldwin (Selden Soc., XXXV, 1918)

Select Cases King's Bench: *Select Cases in the Court of King's Bench Under Edward I/Edward II*, ed. G. O. Sayles (Selden Soc., LV, LVII, LVIII and LXXIV, 1936–55)

Select Charters, ed. Stubbs: W. Stubbs, *Select Charters* (Oxford, 9th edn, 1913)

Sext.: 'Liber Sextus Decretalium Bonifacii VIII' in *Corpus Iuris Canonici*, ed. E. Friedberg (Leipzig, 1879–81), II. 937–1124.

Snappe's Formulary: *Snappe's Formulary*, ed. H. E. Salter (Oxford Hist. Soc., LXXX, 1924)

Stat. Realm: *The Statutes of the Realm* (Record Commission, 11 vols. in 12, 1810–28)

Taxatio Nicholai IV: *Taxatio Ecclesisatica Angliae et Walliae Auctoritate P. Nicholai IV c. 1291*, ed. T. Astle, S. Ayscough and J. Caley (Record Commission, 1802)

Taxation of 1297: Bedfordshire Rolls, ed. Gaydon: A. T. Gaydon, *The Taxation of 1297: a Translation of the Local Rolls of Assessment for Barford*...(Bedfordshire Hist. Record Soc., XXXIX, 1959)

Thorne: *William Thorne's Chronicle of St Augustine's Abbey Canterbury*, ed. A. H. Davis (Oxford, 1934)

Trivet: *F. Nicholai Triveti...Annales Sex Regum Angliae*, ed. T. Hog (English Hist. Soc., 1845)

Trokelowe: *Johannis de Trokelowe et Henrici de Blaneforde... Chronica et Annales*, ed. H. T. Riley (RS, 1866)

Vita Edwardi II: *The Life of Edward II by the So-called Monk of Malmesbury: Vita Edwardi Secundi*, ed. N. Denholm-Young (London, 1957)

Vitae Paparum, ed. Baluze: *Vitae Paparum Avenionensium*, ed. É. Baluze (new edn by G. Mollat, Paris, 1916–28)

Worcester: *Annales Prioratus de Wigornia* in *Annales Monastici*, IV. 353–562

Worcester Sede Vacante Register: *The Register of the Diocese of Worcester During the Vacancy of the See, Usually Called Registrum Sede Vacante, 1301–1435*, ed. J. W. Willis Bund (Worcestershire Hist. Soc., 1 vol. in 2, 1897)

SECONDARY WORKS

Barraclough, G., 'Edward I and Adolf of Nassau: a chapter in medieval diplomatic history', *Cambridge Historical Journal*, VI (1940), 225–62

Beardwood, A., 'Bishop Langton's use of Statute Merchant recognizances', *Medievalia et Humanistica*, IX (1955), 54–70

'The trial of Walter Langton, bishop of Lichfield, 1307–12', *Transactions of the American Philosophical Soc.*, new ser. LIV. pt iii (1964), 1–45

Bellamy, J. G., *The Law of Treason in England in the Later Middle Ages* (Cambridge, 1970)

Black, J. G., 'Edward and Gascony in 1300', *EHR*, XVII (1902), 518–27

Blount, M. N., 'A Critical Edition of the Annals of Hailes (MS Cotton Cleopatra D iii, ff. 33–59v) with an Examination of Their Sources' (Manchester M.A. thesis, 1974)

Boase, T. S. R., *Boniface VIII* (London, 1933)

Boyle, L. E., 'The constitution "Cum ex eo" of Boniface VIII', *Medieval Studies*, XXIV (1962), 263–302

Brentano, R., *Two Churches: England and Italy in the Thirteenth Century* (Princeton, 1968)

Brown, E. A. R., '*Cessante causa* and the taxes of the last Capetians: the political application of a philosophical maxim', *Studia Gratiana*, XV (1972), 567–87

'Taxation and morality in the thirteenth and fourteenth centuries: conscience and political power and the kings of France', *French Historical Studies*, VIII (1973–4), 1–28

Callus, D. A. (ed.), *Robert Grosseteste, Scholar and Bishop* (Oxford, 1955)

Cheney, C. R., 'The punishment of felonous clerks', *EHR*, LI (1936), 215–36

'So-called statutes of Archbishops John Pecham and Robert Winchelsey', *JEH*, XII (1961), 14–34

Notaries Public in England in the Thirteenth and Fourteenth Centuries (Oxford, 1972)

'Law and letters in fourteenth-century Durham: a study of Corpus Christi College, Cambridge, MS 450', *Bulletin of the John Rylands University Library of Manchester*, LV (1972), 60–85

Pope Innocent III and England (Stuttgart, 1976)

Chew, H. M., *The English Ecclesiastical Tenants-in-Chief and Knight Service* (Oxford, 1932)

Churchill, I. J., *Canterbury Administration* (London, 2 vols., 1933)

Clarke, M. V., *Medieval Representation and Consent* (London, 1936)

Bibliography

Cokayne, G. E., *The Complete Peerage of England, Scotland, Ireland, Great Britain and the United Kingdom*, new edn by V. Gibbs, H. A. Doubleday and D. Warrand (13 vols., 1910–59)

Coote, H. C., *The Practice of the Ecclesiastical Courts* (London, 1847)

Cuttino, G. P., 'Bishop Langton's mission for Edward I, 1296–7', *University of Iowa Studies in the Social Sciences*, XI. no. 2, 1941 (Studies in British Hist.), 147–83

　English Diplomatic Administration, 1259–1339 (Oxford, 2nd edn, 1971)

Davies, J. Conway, *The Baronial Opposition to Edward II* (Cambridge, 1918)

Dawson, C., *The History of Hastings Castle* (London, 2 vols., 1909)

Deeley, A., 'Papal provision and royal rights of patronage in the fourteenth century', *EHR*, XLIII (1928), 497–527

Deighton, H. S., 'Clerical taxation by consent, 1279–1301', *EHR*, LXVIII (1953), 161–92

Denton, J. H., 'Pope Clement V's early career as a royal clerk', *EHR*, LXXXIII (1968), 303–14

　English Royal Free Chapels 1100–1300: A Constitutional Study (Manchester, 1970)

　'Royal supremacy in ancient demesne churches', *JEH*, XXII (1971), 289–302

　'Canterbury archiepiscopal appointments: the case of Walter Reynolds', *Journal of Medieval History*, 1 (1975), 317–27

　'Walter Reynolds and ecclesiastical politics 1313–16: a postscript to *Councils & Synods II*' in *Church and Government in the Middle Ages: Essays Presented to C. R. Cheney*, ed. C. N. L. Brooke, D. E. Luscombe, G. H. Martin and D. Owen (Cambridge, 1976), pp. 247–74

　'The *communitas cleri* in the early fourteenth century', *BIHR*, LI (1978), 72–8

　'The crisis of 1297 from the Evesham chronicle', *EHR*, XCIII (1978), 560–79

　'A Worcester text of the Remonstrances of 1297', *Speculum*, LIII (1978), 511–21

Digard, G., *Philippe le Bel et le Saint-Siège de 1285 à 1304* (Paris, 2 vols., 1936)

Douie, D. L., *Archbishop Pecham* (Oxford, 1952)

Du Boulay, F. R. H., 'Charitable subsidies granted to the archbishop of Canterbury 1300–1489', *BIHR*, XXIII (1950), 147–64

　The Lordship of Canterbury (London, 1966)

Bibliography

Edwards, J. G., '*Confirmatio Cartarum* and baronial grievances in
1297', *EHR*, LVIII (1943), 147–71, 273–300

Edwards, K., 'Bishops and learning in the reign of Edward II', *Church
Quarterly Rev.*, CXXXVIII (1944), 57–86

'The political importance of English bishops during the reign of
Edward II', *EHR*, LIX (1944), 311–47

'The social origins and provenance of the English bishops during the
reign of Edward II', *TRHS*, 5th ser. IX (1959), 51–79

Emden, A. B., *A Biographical Register of the University of Oxford to
1500* (Oxford, 3 vols., 1957–9)

A Biographical Register of the University of Cambridge to 1500
(Cambridge, 1963)

Flahiff, G. B., 'The use of prohibitions by clerics against ecclesiastical
courts in England', *Medieval Studies*, III (1941), 101–16

'The writ of prohibition to court christian in the thirteenth century',
Medieval Studies, VI (1944), 261–313 and VII (1945), 229–90

Fraser, C. M., *A History of Antony Bek 1283–1311* (Oxford, 1957)

Fryde, E. B., 'Financial resources of Edward I in the Netherlands
1294–8', *Revue Belge de Philologie et d'Histoire*, XL (1962),
1168–87

Galbraith, V. H., *Studies in the Public Records* (London, 1948)

Gibbs, M., and Lang, J., *Bishops and Reform 1215–72* (Oxford, 1934)

Godwin, F., *A Catalogue of the Bishops of England* (London, 1601)

Gough, H., *Itinerary of Edward I* (Paisley, 2 vols., 1900)

Graham, R., 'The taxation of Pope Nicholas IV', *EHR*, XXIII (1908),
434–54. Reprinted in Graham, *English Eccles. Studies*, pp. 271–
301

'An ecclesiastical tenth for national defence in 1298', *EHR*, XXXIV
(1919), 200–5. Reprinted in *Eng. Eccles. Stud.*, pp. 317–23

'Metropolitical visitation of the diocese of Worcester', *TRHS*, 4th
ser. II (1919), 59–93. Reprinted in *Eng. Eccles. Stud.*, pp. 330–59

'An interdict on Dover, 1298–9', *Archaeological Journal*, LXXVIII
(1921), 227–32. Reprinted in *Eng. Eccles. Stud.*, pp. 324–9

'A petition to Boniface VIII from the clergy of the province of
Canterbury in 1297', *EHR*, XXXVII (1922), 35–46. Reprinted in
Eng. Eccles. Stud., pp. 302–16

'The siege at Maidstone rectory in 1297', *Archaeologia Cantiana*,
XXXVIII (1926), 1–3

'The administration of the diocese of Ely during the vacancies of the
see 1298–9 and 1302–3', *TRHS*, 4th ser. XII (1929), 49–74

English Ecclesiastical Studies (London, 1929)

'Sidelights on the rectors and parishioners of Reculver from the register of Archbishop Winchelsey', *Archaeologia Cantiana*, LVII (1945), 1–12

'Archbishop Winchelsey: from his election to his enthronement', *Church Quarterly Rev.*, CXLVIII (1949), 161–75

'The conflict between Robert Winchelsey, archbishop of Canterbury, and the abbot and monks of St Augustine's, Canterbury', *JEH*, I (1950), 37–50

Gransden, A., *Historical Writing in England c. 550–c. 1307* (London, 1974)

Gray, J. W., 'The *ius praesentandi* in England from the Constitutions of Clarendon to Bracton', *EHR*, LXVII (1952), 481–509

'Archbishop Pecham and the decrees of Boniface', *Studies in Church History*, II, ed. G. J. Cuming (London, 1965), 215–19

'Canon law in England: some reflections on the Stubbs–Maitland controversy', *Studies in Church History*, III, ed. G. J. Cuming (Leiden, 1966), 48–68

'The Church and Magna Charta in the century after Runnymede', in *Historical Studies: Papers Read Before the Irish Conference of Historians*, VI (London, 1968), 23–38

Haines, R. M., *The Administration of the Diocese of Worcester in the First Half of the Fourteenth Century* (London, 1965)

'The education of the English clergy during the later middle ages: some observations on the operation of Pope Boniface VIII's constitution "Cum ex eo"', *Canadian Journal of History*, IV (1969), 1–22

The Church and Politics in Fourteenth-Century England: The Career of Adam Orleton c. 1275–1345 (Cambridge, 1978)

Harriss, G. L. 'Parliamentary taxation and the origins of appropriation of supply in England, 1207–1340', *Recueils de la Société Jean Bodin*, XXIV (1966), 167–79

King, Parliament and Public Finance in Medieval England to 1369 (Oxford, 1975)

Highfield, J. R. L., 'The English hierarchy in the reign of Edward III', *TRHS*, 5th ser. VI (1956), 115–38

Hill, R. M. T., *Ecclesiastical Letter-Books of the Thirteenth Century* (Oxford Bodl., MS B.Litt. e. 1; and privately printed)

Oliver Sutton, Dean of Lincoln, Later Bishop of Lincoln (1280–1299) (Lincoln Minster Pamphlets, no. 4, 1950)

Hinnebush, H. A., *The Early English Friars Preachers* (Rome, 1951)

Howell, M., *Regalian Right in Medieval England* (London, 1962)

Jacob, E. F., 'The archbishop's testamentary jurisdiction' in *Medieval Records of the Archbishops of Canterbury: Lambeth Lectures Dedicated to I. J. Churchill* (London, 1962)

Johnstone, H., *Edward of Carnarvon, 1284–1307* (Manchester, 1946)

Jones, W. R., 'Bishops, politics and the two laws: the *gravamina* of the English clergy, 1237–1399', *Speculum*, XLI (1966), 209–45

'Patronage and administration: the king's free chapels in medieval England', *Journal of British Studies*, IX (1969), 1–23

'Relations of the two jurisdictions: conflict and co-operation in England during the thirteenth and fourteenth centuries', *Studies in Medieval and Renaissance History*, VII (1970), 79–210

Kantorowicz, E., *The King's Two Bodies* (Princeton, 1957)

Kemp, E. W., *Canonization and Authority in the Western Church* (London, 1948)

Counsel and Consent (London, 1961)

Kimball, E. G., 'The judicial aspects of Frank Almoign tenure', *EHR*, XLVII (1932), 1–11

Lawrence, C. H., 'The Thirteenth Century' in *The English Church and the Papacy in the Middle Ages*, ed. C. H. Lawrence (London, 1965), pp. 119–56

Le Bras, G., 'Boniface VIII, symphoniste et modérateur' in *Mélanges d'Histoire du Moyen Âge Dédiés a la Mémoire de Louis Halphen* (Paris, 1951), pp. 383–94

Le Neve, J., *Fasti Ecclesiae Anglicanae 1300–1541*, revised edn by J. M. Horn, B. Jones and H. P. F. King (London, 12 vols., 1962–5, 1967)

Fasti Ecclesiae Anglicanae 1066–1300, revised edn by D. E. Greenway (London, 3 vols., 1968, 1971, 1977)

Little, A. G., and Pelster, F., *Oxford Theology and Theologians c. 1282–1302* (Oxford Hist. Soc., XCVI, 1934)

Lloyd, T. H., *The English Wool Trade in the Middle Ages* (Cambridge, 1977)

Logan, F. D., *Excommunication and the Secular Arm in Medieval England* (Toronto, 1968)

Lunt, W. E., 'First levy of papal annates', *American Hist. Rev.*, XVIII (1912–13), 48–64

'The account of a papal collector in England in 1304', *EHR*, XXVIII (1913), 313–21

'Collectors' accounts for the clerical tenth levied in England by order of Nicholas IV', *EHR*, XXXI (1916), 102–19

313

'William Testa and the parliament of Carlisle', *EHR*, XLI (1926), 332–57

The Valuation of Norwich (Oxford, 1926)

'Clerical tenths levied in England by papal authority during the reign of Edward II' in *Anniversary Essays Presented to C. H. Haskins* (Boston and New York, 1929), pp. 157–82

'The consent of the English lower clergy to taxation during the reign of Henry III', in *Persecution and Liberty: Essays in Honor of G. L. Burr* (New York, 1931), pp. 117–69

Papal Revenues in the Middle Ages (New York, 2 vols., 1934)

Financial Relations of the Papacy with England to 1327 (Cambridge Mass., 1939)

Maddicott, J. R., *Thomas of Lancaster, 1307–22: A Study in the Reign of Edward II* (Oxford, 1970)

The English Peasantry and the Demands of the Crown 1294–1341 (Past & Present Supplement 1, 1975)

Madox, T., *The History and Antiquities of the Exchequer* (London, 2nd edn, 2 vols., 1769)

Maitland, F. W., *Roman Canon Law in the Church of England* (London, 1898)

Marrone, J., and Zuckermann, C., 'Cardinal Simon de Beaulieu and relations between Philip the Fair and Boniface VIII', *Traditio*, XXXI (1975), 195–222

Matthew, D., *The Norman Monasteries and Their English Possessions* (Oxford, 1962)

McFarlane, K. B., 'Had Edward I a policy towards the earls?', *History*, L (1965), 145–59. Reprinted in next item, pp. 248–67

The Nobility of Later Medieval England (Oxford, 1973)

McKisack, M., *The Fourteenth Century* (Oxford, 1959)

Mitchell, S. K., *Taxation in Medieval England* (New Haven, 1951)

Moorman, J. R. H., *Church Life in England in the Thirteenth Century* (Cambridge, 1955)

Morris, J. E., *The Welsh Wars of Edward I* (Oxford, 1901)

Pantin, W. A., *The English Church in the Fourteenth Century* (Cambridge, 1955)

'Grosseteste's relations with the papacy and the crown' in Callus (ed.), *Grosseteste*, pp. 178–208

Parker, Matthew, *De Antiquitate Britannicae Ecclesiae* (London, 1572)

Phillips, J. R. S., *Aymer de Valence, Earl of Pembroke 1307–24* (Oxford, 1972)

Bibliography

Pollock, F., and Maitland, F. W., *The History of English Law* (Cambridge, 2 vols., 2nd edn reissued 1968)

Post, G., *Studies in Medieval Legal Thought: Public Law and the State 1100–1322* (Princeton, 1964)

Powicke, F. M., *King Henry III and the Lord Edward* (Oxford, 2 vols., 1947)

   The Thirteenth Century 1216–1307 (Oxford, 2nd edn, 1962)

Prestwich, M., *War, Politics and Finance Under Edward I* (London, 1972)

   'A new account of the Welsh campaign of 1294–5', *The Welsh History Review*, VI (1972–3), 89–94

Renouard, Y., 'Édouard II et Clément V d'après les rôles gascons', *Annales du Midi*, LXVII (1955), 119–41

Richardson, H. G., and Sayles, G. O., 'The parliament of Carlisle: some new documents', *EHR*, LIII (1938), 425–37

Richardson, H. G., 'Early coronation records', *BIHR*, XVI (1938), 1–11

   'The English coronation oath', *TRHS*, 4th ser. XXIII (1941), 129–58

   'Clement V and the see of Canterbury', *EHR*, LVI (1941), 97–103

Robinson, D., *Beneficed Clergy in Cleveland and the East Riding 1306–40* (York, Borthwick Papers XXXVII, 1969)

Roensch, F. J., *Early Thomist School* (Dubuque, 1964)

Rothwell, H., 'The disgrace of Richard of Louth, 1297', *EHR*, XLVIII (1933), 259–64

   'The confirmation of the charters, 1297', *EHR*, LX (1945), 16–35, 177–91, 300–15

   'Edward I and the struggle for the charters, 1297–1305' in *Studies in Medieval History Presented to F. M. Powicke* (Oxford, 1948), pp. 319–32

Russell, J. C., 'The canonization of opposition to the king in Angevin England' in *Anniversary Essays Presented to C. H. Haskins* (Boston and New York, 1929), pp. 279–90

Salt, M. C. L., 'List of English embassies to France, 1272–1307', *EHR*, XLIV (1929), 263–78

Santifaller, L., 'Zur Original-Überlieferung der Bulle Papst Bonifaz' VIII "Clericis laicos"', *Studia Gratiana*, XI (1967) (Collectanea Stephan Kuttner, I), 71–90

Saunders, P. C., 'Royal Ecclesiastical Patronage in England 1199–1351' (Oxford D.Phil., 1978)

Sayers, J., 'Monastic archdeacons' in *Church and Government in the Middle Ages: Essays Presented to C. R. Cheney*, ed. C. N. L.

Bibliography

Brooke, D. E. Luscombe, G. H. Martin and D. Owen (Cambridge, 1976), pp. 177–203

Smith, A. J. Cuthbert, 'Robert Winchelsey and his Place in the Intellectual Movement of Thirteenth-Century Oxford' (Oxford B.Litt., 1953)

 'Some aspects of the scholastic career of Archbishop Winchelsey', *Dominican Studies*, VI (1953), 101–26

Smith, W. E. L., *Episcopal Appointments and Patronage in the Reign of Edward II* (Chicago, 1938)

Somner, W., *The Antiquities of Canterbury* (2nd edn by N. Battely, London, 1703)

Strayer, J. R., 'Consent to taxation under Philip the Fair' in J. R. Strayer and C. H. Taylor, *Studies in Early French Taxation* (Cambridge Mass., 1939), pp. 3–105

 'Laicization of French and English society in the thirteenth century', *Speculum*, XV (1940), 76–86. Reprinted in *Medieval Statecraft and the Perspectives of History: Essays by J. R. Strayer* (Princeton, 1971), pp. 251–65

 'Defense of the realm and royal power in France' in *Studi in Onore di Gino Luzzato* (Milan, 4 vols., 1950), I. 289–96. Reprinted in *Medieval Statecraft: Essays by Strayer*, pp. 291–9

Stubbs, W., *The Constitutional History of England* (Oxford, 4th edn vol. II, 5th edn vols. I and III, 1891–8)

Thomas, W., *A Survey of the Cathedral Church of Worcester* (London, 1736)

Thompson, A. H., 'Pluralism in the medieval Church', *Associated Architectural Societies' Reports and Papers*, XXXIII (1915–16), 35–73

 'The jurisdiction of the archbishops of York in Gloucestershire', *Bristol and Gloucestershire Archaeological Society*, XLIII (1921), 85–180

Tout, T. F., *Chapters in the Administrative History of Medieval England* (Manchester, 6 vols., 1920–33)

 The Place of the Reign of Edward II in English History (Manchester, 2nd edn, 1936)

Trabut-Cussac, J. P., *L'Administration Anglaise en Gascogne sous Henry III et Edouard I de 1254 à 1307* (Geneva, 1972)

Ullmann, W., 'The curial exequies for Edward I and Edward III', *JEH*, VI (1955), 26–36

 Principles of Government and Politics in the Middle Ages (London, 4th edn 1978)

Wake, W., *The State of the Church and Clergy of England* (London, 1703)

Willard, J. F., 'The taxes upon movables of the reign of Edward I', *EHR*, xxviii (1913), 517–21

  'The taxes upon movables of the reign of Edward II', *EHR*, xxix (1914), 317–21

  Parliamentary Taxes on Personal Property, 1290–1334 (Cambridge Mass., 1934)

Wood, S., *English Monasteries and Their Patrons in the Thirteenth Century* (London, 1955)

Woodruff, C. E., 'The miracles of Archbishop Winchelsey', *Transactions of the St Paul's Ecclesiological Society*, x, pt iv (1938), 111–23

Wright, J. R., 'The Relations Between the Church and the English Crown During the Pontificates of Clement V and John XXII' (Oxford D.Phil., 1966)

INDEX OF MANUSCRIPTS

References to the pages of this book are in italic numerals.

LONDON, British Libr:
Add. 6159 (Register of Christ Church Cant.): *25–6, 231*
Add. 7965 (King's wardrobe book 1296–7): *118, 125, 131*
Add. 10374 (Letter-book of Whalley abbey): *134*
Add. 35170 (Register of Newstead priory): *290*
Add. 43972 (Cartulary of Little Wymondley priory): *231*
Arundel 56 (Trivet chronicle): *236*
Arundel 68 (Register of Christ Church Cant.): *19*
Cotton Charters xvi. 58: *261*
Cotton Cleo. C vii (Register of Christ Church Cant.): *262*
Cotton Cleo. D iii (Hailes chronicle): *73, 108, 111, 187, 193*
Cotton Dom. A xii (Anonymous chronicle): *171*
Cotton Galba E x (Register of Ramsey abbey): *243*
Cotton Jul. B iii (Abbreviated lives of archbishops): *28*
Cotton Vesp. B xi (Hagnaby chronicle): *7, 208, 243*
Cotton Vesp. E xxii (Register of Peterborough abbey): *88, 93*
Egerton 3663 (Register of Ramsey abbey): *187–8*
Harl. Charters 84 E31 and E32: *57*
Harl. 636 ('Polistoire' of Christ Church Cant.): *15, 180, 234, 236, 247, 258*
Harl. 667 (Book of statutes): *167, 280*
Harl. 1761 (Cartulary of Winchester abbey): *234*
Harl. 3860 (Chronicle related to Guisborough): *185*
Harl. 3911 (Cartulary of Holm Cultram abbey): *172, 186*
Harl. 3977 (Register of Bury St Edmunds abbey): *57*
Lansdowne 229 (Miscellaneous collection by Camden): *205*
Lansdowne 402 (Cartulary of see of York): *187, 290*
Royal 11 B v (Register of Merton priory): *172*
—— Corporation of London Records Office:
Liber Ordinationum: *189*
—— Lambeth Palace Libr.:
MS 99 (Lives of archbishops): *27*
MS 244: (Winchelsey's court of audience book): *42, 46, 48, 211, 214, 223, 277, 282, 284–5*
—— Lincoln's Inn Libr.:
MS Hale 185 (Register of Bath priory): *134*
—— Public Record Office:
C47 (Ecclesiastical documents) /22/11/75: *211, 223*
C49 (Parl. and council proceedings) roll 17: *292*
C53 (Charter rolls) /83: *104, 126, 137*; /84: *188*; /91: *214*; /96: *259*
C81 (Chancery warrants) /1660 B, C and D: *128*
C85 (Significations of excommunication) /5 and /6: *181*; /7: *211, 241, 248*; /176 and /177: *290*
C270 (Ecclesiastical misc.) /18: *291–2*; /24/4: *293*
E36 (Treasury of receipt books) /274: *148*
E101 (Various accounts) /308/16: *85*
E135 (Ecclesiastical documents) /10/7: *128*; /21/77: *117*
E159 (King's memoranda rolls) /67: *65, 68, 157*; /68: *49, 61, 65, 67, 76–8, 96, 294*; /69: *88–9*; /70: *89, 96, 104, 108, 114, 117, 119, 121, 125, 129, 131, 133, 143, 152, 154–5*; /71: *132*; /72: *42, 178, 185*; /73: *152, 185*; /74:

GENERAL INDEX

Aaron, 271
Abingdon (Berks.), abbey, 197
absenteeism, *see* non-residence
Adderbury, Thomas of, 46
Adolf, kg of Germany: Edward I's
    alliance, 83, 85, 99, 141
Albano, Berald cardinal bp of, *see* Got,
    Berald de
aliens: alien monasteries, 85, 128n,
    196, 218; lay aliens, 85
alms, free: *see* frankalmoign
Amauvin, Peter, administrator of see
    of Canterbury (1307–8), 48, 240,
    247
Amersham (Bucks.), church, 281n
Amersham, Walter of, canon of
    Hastings, 292
Amesbury, Martin of, sheriff of
    London, 294
amnesty: granted to kg's opponents
    (1297), 163, 165–6, 169–71
Angers (France), diocese of, 84n
Anian, bp of Bangor (1267/8–1305/6),
    128
Annales Londonienses, 206n, 213n,
    217–18, 244, 266
Annales Paulini, 246n
annates: *see* first-fruits; pope, papal
    taxation
Aquasparta, Matthew de, cardinal, 205
Aquila (Italy), 80
Aquinas, Thomas: *De Regno*, 13;
    doctrine on Trinity and on unity
    of form, 11–12, 14; works of,
    owned by Winchelsey, 13
Arches: church, and court, *see*
    London; dean, *see* Thorpe
Articuli Cleri (1316), 255, 277n
Articuli super Cartas (1300), 186, 191,
    194, 230

Arundel, earl of, *see* FitzAlan
Athelstan, kg, 291n
Audenarde, Giles de, canon of
    Hastings, 292–3
Aunsley, John of, 206
Avalon, Hugh of, bp of Lincoln
    (1186–1200), 20

Bacon, Walter, kg's clerk, 223, 284
Baldock, Ralph, kg's chancellor (1307),
    dean of St Paul's London (1294–
    1304), bp of London (1304/6–
    13), 38, 237, 258–9, 262, 276,
    283
Balliol, John, kg of Scotland (1292–6),
    85, 94
Bangor, bp of, *see* Anian (1267/8–
    1305/6), Iorwerth (1307–9)
bankers, Italian, 64–7, 81
Bar, Theobald of, bp of Liège (1303–
    12), 273–4, 277
Bardney (Lincs.), abbot of, 48
Bardolf, Hugh, tenant-in-chief, 46
Barney (Norf.), church, 285
Barnwell (Cambs.), priory, 65
Barraclough, G., 170
Basingwerk (Flint.), abbot of, 65
Bath, archdeacon of, *see* Bochard
Bath and Wells: bp of, *see* Burnell
    (1275–92), March (1293–1302),
    Droxford (1309–29); diocese, 25,
    clergy of, 115
Battle (Sussex), abbot of, 15
Beauchamp, Guy de, earl of Warwick
    (1298–1315), 205n, 207, 264
Beauchamp, William de, earl of
    Warwick (1268–98), 158
Beaulieu, Simon de, cardinal and bp
    of Palestrina, papal nuncio, 37n,
    51, 83–5, 88–9, 93–4, 98, 175

chronicle, *see Annales Paulini*;
churchyard, 42; deans, *see* Baldock, Legh, and Montfort,
William de; prebend of Oxgate,
10; teaching of theology at, 9–10;
and see councils

London, Edmund of, kg's clerk, canon
of Hastings, 284, 292

London, John of, kg's clerk, 224

Longespee, Nicholas, bp of Salisbury
(1291/2–7), 36, 115

Longespee, Roger, bp of Coventry and
Lichfield (1257/8–95), 36

Louth, Richard of, chamberlain of
exchequer, 162

Louth, William of, keeper of kg's
wardrobe (1280–90), bp of Ely
(1290–8), 38, 41, 89, 104, 114,
126, 132, 137, 151, 157–8

Lowdham (Notts.), church, 290

Lovetot, John, 53

Ludlow, Laurence of, merchant, 62

Lunt, W. E., 57, 202n

Lupi, Arnaud, de Tilio, kg's clerk,
231, 284

Lympsham (Som.), church, 284

Lyons, General Council of (1274), 197,
278–9

Madoc, Welsh rebel leader, 82

Magna Carta, 38, 103, 136, 138,
142–4, 153, 164–5, 167, 169,
172, 183–91, 194–5, 230, 238,
254–5, 261–2, 264, 294

Maidstone (Kent), 119, church, 248–
9

Maitland, F. W., 218

Malling, Ralph of, auditor in abp's
court of audience, 23, 273

maltote, 61–2, 78, 141–2, 164, 166,
172, 264

Manifesto (1297), 136n, 147–8, 225

Mansel, John, abp's clerk, 235

Manton, Ralph of, kg's clerk, dean of
St Buryan's, 289, 293

March, William of, kg's treasurer
(1290–5), bp of Bath and Wells
(1293–1302), 20, 21n, 38, 72–3,
104, 114, 125, 132, 137, 159

Margaret, sister of Philip IV, queen of
England, 193, 220

Markham Clinton (Notts.), church,
290

Marlow, Ralph of, kg's clerk, 292

Marston St Lawrence, prebend, *see*
Lincoln, cathedral church

Martin, David, bp of St David's (1296–
1328), 40n, 125, 259n, 262

Martival, Roger, bp of Salisbury
(1315–30), 14, 25

Mayfield (Sussex), 131, church, 23

McFarlane, K. B., 207

Meaux (Yorks.), abbey: abbot, 104n;
chronicle, 5, 19n

Meinill: custody of Meinilll lands, 44,
178; Nicholas de, 178

Melchizedek, 271

Melton, William, abp of York (1316/
17–40), 21n

Mepham, Simon, abp of Canterbury
(1328–33), 27

Merton (Surrey), priory, 197, prior,
130, chronicle, see *Flores Historiarum*

Mettingham, John of, kg's clerk,
justice of kg's bench, 51n, 108

Middleton (Hants.), church, 49

Middleton, Gilbert of, abp's clerk,
206n, 216

Middleton, John of, abp's clerk, 216–17

military service, 117–18, 140, 165,
and see servitium debitum

Minster (Kent), 180

moiety (1294), *see* taxation

Monachus, John, cardinal, 231

Monmouth, John of, bp of Llandaff
(1297–1323): 15–16, 39, 43, 46,
112, 137–8, 223, 262; early career
at Oxford, 9, 14, 34; appointment
to Llandaff, 34–5, 112; friendship with and support for
Winchelsey, *esp.* 34, 40, 43, 125,
130, 133, 159; Winchelsey's
vicar-general (1313), 43, 248

Montfort, Amauri de, son of Simon
de, 8

Montfort, Simon de, earl of Leicester
(1231–65), 20, 148, 226

General Index

St David's, bishop of, *see* Martin (1296–1328)

St Leofard, Gilbert of, bp of Chichester (1288–1305), 44, 69, 159, 197, 292

St Martin-le-Grand, *see* London

St Prisca, cardinal priest of, *see* Nouveau

St Radegund's (Kent), abbot of, 15

Salisbury (Wilts.): 7, 114–15, 119–20, *and see* parliaments; bp of, *see* Longespee, Nicholas (1291/2–7), Ghent, Simon of (1297–1315), Martival (1315–30); diocese of, report from concerning miracles of Winchelsey, 25, submission of clergy of (1297), 115, *sede vacante* (1297), 130; earls of, 36; 'edict' of (1297), 118, 128

Salmon, John, kg's chancellor (1320–3), bp of Norwich (1299–1325), 35–6, 39n, 47, 257, 259, 262, 266, dispute with Winchelsey concrning first-fruits, 47–8, 231n

Saluzzo, Boniface of, kg's clerk, 41, 290, 293

'Salvator mundi', *see* Boniface VIII

Sandwich (Kent), 22

Sardinia, William of, 179, 296n

Saunders, P. C., 271

Savoy, Boniface of, abp of Canterbury (1241/5–70), 45, 113

'Scimus fili', *see* Boniface VIII

Scotland: 160, 171–3, 184–5, 221; Scottish bps, 209n; Winchelsey's mission to (1300), 5, 44, 178–9. *And see* Balliol; Edward I; Wallace

scrutiny of stored money (1294), 67–9, 71–3, 77, 91, 164, 198, 239

Segrave, John de, knight, 137, 184

Segrave, Nicholas de, knight, 218n

Selling (Kent), 182

servitium debitum, 61–2, 131, 140

Sevenoaks (Kent), church, 274–5, 277

Sevenoaks, Roger of, 274

Sext, *see* Boniface VIII

Sheffield, John of, kg's clerk, 44, 223, 284

Shenfield (Essex), church, 284

Shepperton (Middlesex), church, 272

Shrewsbury, St Mary's, royal free chapel, 285

Smith, Cuthbert, 10, 12

South Malling (Sussex), 131

Southwark (Surrey), hospital of St Thomas, 49

Spain, Peter of, cardinal, 52, 243

Spicer, John, abp's chaplain, 22–3

spiritualities: 216, 269, 279–80, 295; of see of Canterbury, 239–41, 289, custodians of, 240, 272; taxation of, 38, 56–60, 114, 133, 151, 201, 237, 250–1, 269, 280, 298

Stafford, royal free chapel, 285, 294, dean, *see* Caen

Stamford: *see* parliaments: Statute of (1309), 260

Stanford Rivers (Essex), church, 283

Stanton, Hervey de, kg's clerk, 284

Stapledon, Walter, kg's treasurer (1320–5), bp of Exeter (1308–26), 6, 16, 38, 52, 148, 259, 289–90

Stirling, 210, 220, Stirling Bridge, battle of (1297), 160

Stratford-at-Bow (Middlesex), priory, nuns of, 76

Stratford-on-Avon (Warws.), church, 281–2

Strayer, J. R., 294

Striguil (Chepstow), castle of, 130

Stubbs, W., 31, 53, 57

study, licences for, *see* rectors

Sturry (Kent), 180

'Supra montem', *see* Clement V

Surrey: earl of, *see* Warenne; sheriff of, 213, 235

Sutton, Oliver, bp of Lincoln (1280–99): 46, 74, 132, 138; early career at Oxford, 13, 39; assessor/collector of papal tenth (1291), 65–6, 75–6, 81; supported Winchelsey (1297–8), 40, 100, 125, 130, 156–7, 159, 191

Sutton, Thomas of, 206n

Sutton, William of, knight, 188

Swinfield, Richard, bp of Hereford

General Index

Swinfield, Richard – *cont.*
(1282/3–1317), 13, 39, 46, 107,
125, 159, 227, 259n, 261

Tateshale, Robert de, kg's agent, 121
tallage, 17, 141–2, 152, 164
taxation:
general: amount of clerical contribution to taxation, 56, 78–9, 141,
and Appendix; consent to taxation, 59, 91, 95, 97, 103, 105, 122,
124, 127, 136, 142, 145, 149–51,
153, 159–60, 164–6, 168–9, 173,
189–91, 202–4, 226, 230, 251–3;
distinction between clerical and
lay taxation, *esp.* 55–60, 201–4.
And see charitable subsidies;
necessity; *maltote*; prises; tallage
clerical subsidies: twentieth (1283),
69; moiety (1294), 55, 71, 74–8,
86–7, 91, 100, 164, 299; tenth
(1295/6), 55, 86–8, 91, 100,
102–3, 299; fifth, from York
clergy (1296/7), 95, 104, 152n,
299; fifth, fine of (1297), 55,
108–9, 116–17, 121–30, 132–4,
141, 164, 299; attempt to impose
third or fifth (1297), 60, 149–52,
159, 165; fifth, from York clergy
(Nov. 1297), 152n, 299n; tenth
(1297–8), 55, 173–4, 188–9, 213,
299; fifteenth (1307/8), 55, 246,
250, 300
lay subsidies: tenth and sixth
(1294/5), 77–8, 297n, 298–9;
eleventh and seventh (1295/6),
87–8, 297n, 299; twelfth and
and eighth (1296/7), 94, 114,
297n, 299; attempt to impose
eighth and fifth (1297), 138, 143,
147, 152–3, 159–60, 165, 169;
ninth (1297/8), 169, 297n, 299;
twentieth discussed (1300), 186;
fifteenth (1301/3), 60, 187, 199,
201–4, 297n, 298, 300; thirtieth
and twentieth (1306/7), 204
236–7, 250, 298, 300; twentieth
and fifteenth (1307/8), 250, 300;
twenty-fifth (1309/10), 251, 301

papal tenths: sexennial (1274), 58,
64, 197; sexennial (1291), 49, 73,
75–6, 200, proceeds seized (1294),
56, 63–7, 81–2, 91, 200, 299; triennial (1301/4), 197, 200, 202–3,
300, proceeds seized (1303),
208–9; biennial (1306/7), 220,
250, 300; triennial (1309/12),
251–2, 300–1; annual (1313),
301; sexennial (1313/14), 301.
And see pope; Nicholas IV;
Norwich, valuation
Templars, *see* Knights Templars
temporalities: 56, 179, 202, 240, 295;
of bishoprics, 35n, 40, 44, 110,
120, 240; of see of Canterbury,
80–1, 112, 119, 127, 130–2,
188n, 218, 239–41, 250n, 272;
seizure and restitution of clergy's
(1297), 60, 107–33, 135, 150,
161; taxation of, 56–60, 78, 151,
201–4, 237, 242, 250–1, 269, 298
Testa, William, papal collector, and
administrator of see of Canterbury (1306–8), 48, 240, 241–2,
289
Tettenhall (Staffs.), royal free chapel,
285
Teynham (Kent), abp's manor, 52,
266n
Thetford, William of, 13
Thornbury (Gloucs.), church, 281n
Thorne, William, chronicler of St
Augustine's Canterbury, 5, 30,
49, 112, 180n, 233–4, 236, 238,
244
Thorney (Cambs.), abbey, 197
Thorntoft, William, kg's clerk, 216
Thorpe, Walter of, dean of the Arches,
217, 231–2
Tickhill (Yorks.), castle chapel, 290,
and see Blyth
Tingewick, kg's physician, 241
tithes, 30, 56–7
Tout, T. F., 32
trailbaston, inquiries and Ordinance of
(1305), 212, 236
'Traxit hactenus', *see* Boniface VIII
Trivet, Nicholas, chronicler, 149

338

Trokelowe, John de, chronicler, 19,
263
Twitham, Alan of, abp's chamberlain,
22–3
Tychfield, Henry de, notary public,
111

Udimore (Sussex), 147, 149, 153

vacancies: episcopal, *see* bishops;
monastic, 271–2
Val, Guy de, 248
Verdun (France), St Michael's abbey,
abbot of, 273
Vezzano, Geoffrey de, papal collector,
175
vicarages, 271
Vienne, General Council of (1311–12),
253n, 255
visitations, metropolitical, of Boniface
of Savoy and Pecham, 45, *and see*
Winchelsey
Vita Edwardi Secundi, 17, 266

Waleden, Humphrey de, 240
Wales: support for Winchelsey from
(1297), 130–1, 139; war (1283),
64; war (1294/5), 60, 63, 82;
Welsh language, 35
Walesby (Notts.), church, 290
Wallace, William, Scottish leader, 220
Walpole, Ralph, bp of Norwich
(1288/9–99), bp of Ely (1299–
1302), 14, 34, 39, 46, 48, 107,
125, 132, 138, 159, 203
Waltham (Essex), 137
Warenne, John de, earl of Surrey
(1240–1304), 184
Warwick, earl of, *see* Beauchamp
Warwick, Nicholas of, 213
Westminster: 220, *and see* parlia-
ments; abbey, 197, abbot, 48,
231; chronicler, *see* Flores His-
toriarum; Hall, 132; Statute of,
I (1275), 116n; Statute of, II
(1285), 195
Wharton, H., 27
Wheatley (Notts.), church, 290

Whittlesey, William, abp of Canterbury (1368–74), 27
Whittlesford (Cambs.), church, 284
Wich, Richard, bp of Chichester
(1245–53), 20
Wichio, John de, canon of Hastings,
292–3
William II, 287
Willoughby, Philip, chancellor of
exchequer, 108
wills: abp's prerogative jurisdiction for
probate of wills, 42, 46–7; Winchelsey's will, 7, 15n, 43
Wimbledon (Surrey), church, 272
Wimborne Minster, royal free chapel,
285–6, dean, *see* Berwick
Winchelsea (Kent), 144, 151, St Giles
church, 7
Winchelsey, Henry, brother of Robert,
7
Winchelsey, John, nephew of Robert,
7
Winchelsey, Robert, abp of Canterbury
(1293/4–1313):
general: appearance, 7; chancellor
of, *see* Berham; constitutions, 30;
court of audience, *esp.* 47, 181–2,
211, 223, 284, auditor, *see*
Malling; his 'familia', 22; as
'legatus natus', 45n; as mediator,
136–8, 143, 161, 192; prerogative rights for probate of wills,
42, 46–7; his proctor at Rome,
see Dunbridge, *and see* 155, 231;
relations with magnates, 19–20,
136–9, 170–1, 204–7, 260–8,
270; as temporal lord, 178;
visitations, 23, 43, 45–7, 50, 177,
211, 222, 231, 248, 276–7, 279,
281, 283–4, 286–7, 291, 293
early life: perhaps born mid-1240s,
8; rector of Wood Eaton, canon
of Lincoln, archdeacon of Essex,
8–10; master of arts, rector at
Paris, doctor of theology, chancellor of Oxford, and his
quaestiones and *quodlibeta*, 8–12
as Edward I's abp: election, 14;
confirmation and consecration,